POLITICAL VIOLENCE IN SRI LANKA: 1971-1987

POLITICAL VIOLENCE IN SRI LANKA 1971-1987

S.V.D. Gamini Samarnayake

GYAN

GYAN PUBLISHING HOUSE
NEW DELHI-110002

Political Violence in Sri Lanka: 1971-1987

Rs. 720

ISBN: 978-81-212-1003-4

Published in 2008 in India by
Gyan Publishing House,
4741/23, Main Ansari Road Darya Ganj
New Delhi-110002
Phones : 23282060, 23261060
Fax : (011) 23285914
E-mail: gyanbooks@vsnl.com
Website : http : // www.gyanbooks.com

Laser Typesetting by : Quick Media, Delhi
Printed at : Singhal Print Media, Delhi

DEDICATION

I would like to dedicate this book to my wife, Dharshini and daughter Madhri, for bearing with my obsession over many years and providing me with loving encouragement and valuable moral support

CONTENTS

List of Tables

Abbreviations

ADMK	Anna-Dravida Munnetra Kazhagam
CJC	Criminal Justice Commission
CNC	Ceylon National Congress
CP(M)	Communist Party (Moscow)
CP(P)	Communist Party (Peking)
CWC	Ceylon Workers Congress
DMK	Dravida Munnetra Kazhagam
ENDLF	Eelam National Democratic Liberation Front
EPRLF	Eelam People's Revolutionary Liberation Front
EROS	Eelam Revolutionary Organisation of Students
FP	Federal Party
IPKF	Indian Peace Keeping Force
JVP	Janatha Vimukthi Peramuna
LSSP	Lanka Sama Samaja Party – Ceylon Equal Society Party
LTTE	Liberation Tigers of Tamil Eelam
MEP	Mahajana Eksath Peramuna-People's United Front
SAARC	South Asian Association for Regional Cooperation
SLLF	Sri Lanka Freedom Party
TC	Tamil Congress
TELO	Tamil Eelam Liberation Organisation
TULF	Tamil United Liberation Front
UF	United Front
UNP	United National Party

Foreword

Political violence in Sri Lanka is only a tip of an iceberg. The mass of this iceberg, encompassing many socio-political contradictions of the modem age and modernism itself, undoubtedly spans beyond this island or South Asia. The major contradictions are on class/social and ethnic lines. One may even argue that political violence is not of modem origin but could be traced back, for example, to Rome during the Republic particularly in it's ascend and descend. The same thing could be said about ancient China. According to some, there is nothing new under the sun. Political violence has appeared and disappeared in a cyclical fashion from time to time in history. But the above fatalistic view does not supply a scientific understanding on political violence especially of modem times.

In modem times, what distinguishes one form of violence from the other is primarily the contextual character. This is true within and between countries, and also of international environments. Political violence arises out of particular socio-political conditions that needs to be studied systematically, as the author of this seminal book has done. Conflict over power perhaps is the only thread governing all political violence, if the term political could seriously be attributed, irrespective of time and space. This is apart from sporadic outbursts or spontaneous rebellions that may be rooted in actual grievances. It is not correct to say that ordinary people indulge in political violence, let alone terrorism, just because they have grievances or that they are poor. This is a myth. What cannot however be discounted or denied are the underlying socio-economic grievances or discontent over discrimination that creates breeding grounds for political violence or terrorism. Therefore it is within a complex and interconnected socio-political context on the one hand objective, and on the other hand subjective and ideological that political violence arises and even sustained by the parties that indulge in such practices. Sri Lanka is well known for those practices with two political insurrections in the South and a continuing separatist insurgency in the North.

This book by Professor Gamini Samaranayake on *Political Violence in Sri Lanka,* 1971-1987, based on his revised doctoral thesis submitted at the St. Andrews University (UK) in 1991, is an in-depth study of both sides of the coin - the socio-economic conditions on the one hand and political-ideological conditions on the other - from the perspective of a political scientist who have sought theoretical explanations for the genesis, evolution, methods and outcomes of political violence in Sri Lanka within its most formative period of 1971 and 1987. When that period is properly understood, there is no much difficulty for an intelligent reader to comprehend what happened thereafter, literally speaking until yesterday.

1971 was the first insurrection in Sri Lanka's predominantly Sinhala South led by the Janatha Vimukthi Peramuna (JVP - the People's Liberation Front) very much similar to the Naxalite movement in India or the Maoist movement in Nepal. 1987 was the second insurrection by the same outfit with similar objectives in mind, except that it was also a violent reaction to what was happening in Sri Lanka's predominantly Tamil North in between the two years. The interlude of overt political violence in the South between 1971 and 1987, except of course a spate of electoral violence, marked the emergence and spread of the separatist insurrectionary movement led by the Liberation Tigers of Tamil Eelam (LTTE) in the North, allegedly assisted by India. Then was the direct Indian intervention in 1987 with the Indian Peace Keeping Force (IPKF) and a devolutionary political package with the objective of bringing an end to the violent situation that was developing completely out of control in the island.

Although the story did not end there, the period that the author has chosen somewhat completed a formative cycle of political violence in Sri Lanka. In 1971, three countries became prominent for major episodes of internal political violence: Bangladesh, Uganda and Sri Lanka in that order of intensity. Violence in Uganda continued until 1978, while Bangladesh again erupting in 1975 to continue until 1992. Sri Lanka's story was somewhat different, but more complicated and complex. Erupting again through ethnic violence in 1983 and continuing through separatist war until today, Sri Lanka was complicated by a second social uprising in 1987. Sri Lanka has been the most protracted among the three cases mentioned and also intractable due to a combination of social/class and ethnic factors involved. Therefore, even for a non Sri Lankan, the case could have been insightful for a systematic political science study.

The present study by Samaranayake as an insider is a comprehensive analysis of events and theoretical interpretations thereof, useful for anyone Interested in studying political violence in general or violent politics in Sri Lanka. The coverage of over 16 years, with sequentially and causally interrelated events and processes, is a sufficient historical laboratory for the study that the author has undertaken for his Pill. Any attempt to artificially extend the period to superficially satisfy the general reader could have devalued the quality and rigor of the present publication. Therefore, as the Director of the National Centre for Advanced Studies in Humanities and Social Sciences (NCAS) in Sri Lanka, I do extent my special appreciation for the publisher for undertaking the present publication as a revised thesis and an academic work without requesting the author to substantially change the contents of the original thesis to make it a popular book. Nevertheless, with the lucidly written narratives and interesting episodes and events related, the general reader also would immensely benefit in understanding the tragic meaning of political violence in our countries through this publication, bearing in mind of course that repetitions do occur or necessary in thesis production.

There is much guidance that Professor Samaranayake has consequently offered for young political scientists or social scientists in general to know how to go about writing a good thesis. This is the primary value of the publication of Samaranayake thesis in book form, as I see it. At least three aspects of particular merit should be emphasized.

The first is undoubtedly the thorough study of the theoretical literature that underpins any study of political violence in any country in the contemporary period. There is no question that the author has been quite selective of theoretical literature, based on his own choice or on advice, but without neglecting any of the key theories on the subject of political violence. I leave it to the inquisitive reader to discover what the theories that the author has investigated, preferred or used were. The related value is the thorough investigation or critical analysis of these theories without merely browsing them through, as some thesis writers tend to do under the rubric of literature review.

The second is the sufficient corpus of research material both primary and secondary that he has scrutinized, investigated and analyzed to empirically narrate his story and also to verify, substantiate or dispute various arguments pertaining to that story of violence in Sri Lanka. Without that sufficiency of research material, an advanced study of the type that Samaranayake has produced could not have materialized. The author has also benefited from the experiential knowledge at least of the 1971 insurrection somewhat as a critical 'participant observer.'

The third or the most important of course is the thesis or the new knowledge that he has produced in understanding political violence in Sri Lanka whether in the South or in the North highlighting the primacy of political, organizational or ideological factors nevertheless revealing the subtle nexus between the socio-economic backgrounds of the insurrectionists and the psychological motives and patterns of political violence that they have indulged in. The author is of the view that political violence could not be interpreted or attributed to a single factor or causality. Multiple causes have affected, nevertheless within a specific context of country's painful or insufficient transition from a traditional society to a modern one.

As in any other thesis or study, there can be gaps, unanswered questions or even theoretical insufficiencies. No thesis is perfect or produces complete knowledge. As the author himself says, "the findings of this study clearly suggest that more extensive and additional research is necessary to fully understand the causes, nature and sequence of political violence." This is an open warrant to young researchers to follow suit and fill the gaps, answer the unanswered questions, and rectify the theoretical insufficiencies if there are any. Political violence is undoubtedly a troublesome area which requires greater attention of political scientists, sociologists and others through similar studies.

Professor Laksiri Fernando, B.A. (Ceylon), M.A. (New Brunswick), Ph.D. (Sydney) Professor of Political Science and Public Policy, University of Colombo and Director, National Centre for Advanced Studies in Humanities and Social Sciences.

Preface

This book is a revised version of my Ph.D. thesis submitted to the University of St. Andrews in 1991. The publication of this book was caught up in a certain controversy of perspectives and was therefore delayed in its publication. The subject of the book is obviously a topic which is of the greatest relevance currently to Sri Lanka. Sri Lanka has experienced political violence in the form of insurrection since 1971. Insurrection in Sri Lanka is significant due to its patterns and intensity akin to the Philippines. However, the Philippines is a country with more than 70 islands while Sri Lanka is just one island. As the Philippines, Sri Lanka has been beset with dual insurrections on the basis of the social classes and minority ethnicity. The political violence based on class is referred to as left-wing insurrection while the other strain of violence based on ethnicity is referred to as an ethnic insurrection. Although, academically and politically wide publicity has been granted to ethnic insurrection, left-wing insurrection continues to be a political phenomenon that needs to be reckoned with. .

However, insurrection in Sri Lanka is not a unique phenomenon. It is a prevalent tendency in many countries of the Third World. Sri Lanka since 1971 has experienced a sharp escalation of political violence which renders it suitable as a case study of insurrection in developing countries. The major focus of this study is a comparative analysis of the causes and patterns of the left-wing insurrection of 1971 and the ethnic insurrection up to the Indo-Sri Lanka Accord in June 1987. This book highlights the salient socio-economic and political factors that gave rise to ethnic insurrection countering the view that the majority vs. minority ethnic discrimination is the impetus behind the prevalence of political violence in Sri Lanka.

The main arguments of this book are that the left-wing as well as ethnic insurrections of Sri Lanka have been pre-planned and well organized and that the responsible violent movements in Sri Lanka have been mainly a result of the emergence of new social forces which came about due to socio-economic and political transformation. The analysis begins with a review of the theories of political violence. Of this review of theories, Huntington's theory of modernization relates more appropriately in analyzing the origin of the political violence movement in Sri Lanka. The origin and development of the Janatha Vimukthi Peramuna (JVP) and the Liberation Tigers of Tamil Eelam (LTTE) lay deeply rooted in socio-economic and political factors. The book shows that the socio-economic background of the leaders and members were diverse and often paradoxical, if not at odds to the groups' goals. The ethno-nationalist ideologies, and action-oriented strategies and tactics of the movements instilled group consciousness and goaded otherwise ordinary citizens to commit political violence. The pattern of political violence in Sri Lanka has been a highly emotive expression of anti-establishment and secessionist convictions on the part of the two movements. Finally the book proposes the necessity of politico-economic development to cope with the problem of dual insurrection in Sri Lanka.

I would like to acknowledge the support and advice given to me by many persons. The intervention of Professor Paul Wilkinson in the capacity of supervisor provided valuable guidance and criticisms which made the completion of this study possible. I have greatly benefited from his extensive knowledge of political violence movements and terrorism worldwide. The author also wishes to express his sincere appreciation to Prof. W.A. W. Warnapala, the Honorable Minister of Higher Education, Prof. Laksiri Fernando from the University of Colombo, Prof. Jerald Peiris and N.D. Samarawickrama from the University of Peradeniya for the pertinent suggestions they offered.

My period of study at the University of St. Andrews has been made possible by a generous scholarship from the Association of the Commonwealth Universities and by a leave of absence graciously granted by the University of Peradeniya. The assistance extended by the Queen Mother library at the University of Aberdeen and by the staff of the University of St. Andrew's Inter-Library Loans and Reference departments is also greatly appreciated. Last, but not least the assistance offered by staff at the Gyan Publishing House in New Delhi has sustained my determination to publish the book.

1

Introduction

Political violence is one of the oldest and most complex problems in modern politics and international relations. In a sense it reveals the more turbulent aspects of politics and thus has developed into a highly stimulating research area within the social sciences. The copious amount of contemporary literature on the subject of political violence indicates its dominant place in the modern discipline of political science. The contemporary field of political violence is a relatively recent outgrowth and expansion of the combined subject of political science and international relations. Until the 1960s, the study of political violence suffered relative obscurity within the social sciences. Harry Eckstein observes that this neglect was indicative of the lack of literature on the subject.[1] According to Ted Robert Gurr, of the 2,828 articles which appeared in the *American Political Science Review* from its inception in 1906 until 1968, it is apparent from their titles that only 29 articles addressed political disorder or violence. Furthermore, only 12 of these articles were concerned specifically with revolution, and 15 were published after 1961.[2] Social scientists have attributed this neglect to several circumstances.

The first of these claims that the methodological problems encountered in analysing the subject matter were a major constraint on the social sciences in producing studies of political violence. This argument maintains that the lack of theoretical processing and the limitations in applying analysis using the quantitative technique and controlled experiments, have contributed to the reluctance of social scientists to undertake studies of violent political behaviour.[3]

Secondly, a more widely accepted argument is that this neglect was related to the view that political violence was a disfigurement of political behaviour involving backward nations and demented individuals, or at best was a marginal phenomenon.[4] Finally, it has been suggested that the study of political violence was ignored because social scientists tend to be influenced in their choice of subject by excluding what is considered to be an illegitimate form of action.[5]

The gradual increase in attention devoted to the field of political violence since the early 1960s is largely attributed to the growing number of politically violent incidents at global level. The more salient incidents, which distinguish this period from any other previous era, are the Civil Rights Movement in America, the assassination of the Kennedy brothers and Martin Luther King Jr., and the Vietnam War.[6] In addition, the escalation of political violence in nations which have been identified as Third World countries has heightened the interest in this branch of scholarly research.[7] Furthermore, a majority of the social and political scientists have eventually accepted political violence as a legitimate field of study. This acceptance has proved to be an additional impetus to the further commitment of academic resources toward the timely study of the problem. Political violence is increasingly perceived as a representation of a form of struggle and expression.[8] Consequently, the subject of political violence has developed into an accepted sub-field in the discipline of political science and international relations.

Political Violence in the Third World

As mentioned above, political violence in the form of insurrection has been a significant factor in the political processes of the Third World since the World War II. A majority of Third World states have experienced military or civilian coups, insurrections, guerrilla war, ethnic riots, mutinies, political assassinations and political terrorism. The social and political evolution of the Third World countries has been wrought with violence in their historical development, has been conditioned by their colonial past, and is linked with the international environment. Since the World War II political violence in the

Third World has remained a crucial factor in national and international political changes. According to Gurr, between 1961 and 1968, some form of violent civil conflict reportedly occurred in 114 of the world's 121 larger nations and colonies.[9]

Moreover, William O. Staudenmaier finds that of the wars which have occurred since 1945, approximately 85 per cent have been intrastate or colonial wars and over 95 percent have been fought outside Europe—the traditional centre of the 'great power' system.[10] The forms of warfare have also changed overwhelmingly since the World War II and many can now be classified as guerrilla insurgencies. Furthermore, the *SIPRI Year-Book* (1987) listed 36 armed conflicts in 1986. Most of these insurgencies have been confined to the Third World countries. Only one conflict is recorded for Europe and that is the Northern Ireland (Ulster) conflict.[11]

The Third World has come to represent an arena of numerous insurrections which are rooted in diverse motivations and are of varying significance. The causes of the Third World insurrections have been attributed to cultural, social, economic and political factors. Udo Steinbach, however, has made a far-reaching study to group these factors into broad categories according to common denominators. He has defined four such broad categories as follows: national fragmentation, inequitable development, cultural clashes and liberation movements.[12]

The first, national fragmentation and its impact on conflict in the Third World is examined with reference to the emergence of nation-states. The emergence of nation states in Europe resulted from a long term historical process, characterized by internal conflicts and the driving forces of nationalism, which culminated in an inner unification of states. The national structures introduced to the Third World, however, were alien to the political or cultural traditions of these countries, especially in the Middle East and in Africa. The concept of nation-states was imposed upon the Third World by their colonial masters or was adapted by the elites of these subjugated countries to achieve their own political ambitions. Therefore, the development of these colonies into nation states often violated their "territorial, ethnic, religious, geographical, or cultural-historical traditions".[13] The ensuing consequences have been, the further fragmentation of these states and, more specifically, ethnic and sectarian divisions. Many internal conflicts, including demands for autonomy, have been attributed to the ethnic flavour of national fragmentation. The ethnic and tribal conflicts which had been dormant for some decades or centuries came to the fore after these countries gained independence, and are said to have contributed to the escalation of political violence in many of the countries in the Third World. Various national liberation movements based on the Muslims in the Philippines, the Tamils in Sri Lanka, the Karens in Myanmar (former Burma), and the Kurds in Iraq have been cited as examples of this pattern.

Secondly, insurrections in the Third World countries are identified with the violent attempts to achieve revolutionary changes in their socio-economic structures and political institutions. These violent attempts are attributed to several causes, the chief of which is that Third World countries are confronted with developmental problems of a socio-economic and political nature. The economic development of many Third World countries is so retarded that even the basic needs of the population cannot be fulfilled. Yet the governments of these countries are called upon to emulate the socio-economic and political objectives of industrialized countries. Third World governments must, therefore, improve their per capita income, provide for a more equitable distribution of resources, and attain a certain degree of independence from the industrialized nations. Thus the conflict between what these states can achieve and are expected to achieve causes unrest and turbulence, which subsequently leads to political struggles and ideological conflicts. This pattern is best exemplified by the struggles of the Hukbalahap movement and National Peoples Army (NPA) in the Philippines, the Naxalites movement in India, the J.V.P. in Sri Lanka, the Tupamaro in Uruguay and the Shining Path or Sendero Luminoso in Peru.

The economic aspect apart, the socio-political problems of these countries originates from their programmes for industrialization. The process of modernization in the Third World has not been accompanied by a reinforcement of the political institutions which provide greater participation for individuals, social groups, or religious and ethnic minorities.

Neither has there been an equitable distribution of social and economic resources in favour of the underprivileged sections of Third World societies.

Thirdly, Steinbach claims that the cultural front has become an area of conflict. Religious and cultural factors, he says, are intrinsically linked to the wider developmental problems. In spite of the overlapping of these factors, however, he contends that culture and religion form unique variables in mass mobilization. A rapid modernization process which depends on the endurance of cultural traditions and the manner of mass mobilization is not similar to a revolutionary process which depends exclusively on social or economic factors. Such a modernization process rejects western culture and civilization, and revives the indigenous culture by adapting it to meet the demands of the modern state. The internal expression of this conflict is the confrontation between "native chauvinism on the one hand and westernized elites on the other".[14] The international aspect of this internal conflict is the exclusion of external influence and power. Yet Steinbach goes on to observe that Iran is an example where even a chauvinist movement can be faced with new friction from foreign sources.

The liberation movements of the Third World are the fourth category, which is closely integrated with the other three factors mentioned above. Some Third World revolutions have been associated with or have resulted from the national independence movements against colonial rule. From a broad perspective, the objective of liberation movements in developing countries is to overthrow political institutions and socio-economic frameworks introduced by colonial powers. This objective includes diverse aims varying from gaining independence to secessionism. The main feature of these movements is that they have often been supported by other Third World countries rather than by the developed states, reflecting the unresolved political allegiances in many developing states. The Polisario in Western Sahara and PRETLIN in East Timor in Indonesia can be cited as examples of receiving inter-Third World assistance. Table 1.1 indicates some of the Third World countries which have faced political violence and the primary insurgent groups involved.

The political conflicts in the Third World can be attributed to a number of factors, which interact and reinforce each other and cannot be strictly compartmentalized at any given time. Nationalistic conflicts often concern the problems of integrating ethnic or religious groups. Many ethnic groups fail to identify with the state due to the lack of access in decision-making and the denial of equal rights and autonomy. National conflicts are intrinsically linked to the failure to integrate these groups in the developmental political process.

Table 1.1 Major Political Violence in the Third World

Country	*Year*	*Major Guerrilla Organizations*
Burma	1948	Karen National Union
Ethiopia	1962	Eritrean People's Liberation Front
Guatemala	1966	Guatemala National Revolutionary Unity
Colombia	1966	Armed Revolutionary Forces of Colombia
Philippines	1969	The New People's Army
	1970	Moro National Liberation Front
Sri Lanka	1971	People's Liberation Front
	1972	Liberation Tigers of Tamil Eelam
Angola	1975	National Union for the total independence of Angola
Indonesia	1975	Revolutionary front for the independence of Timor
Lebanon	1975	The Muslims and the Christians
Mozambique	1976	Mozambique Resistance Movement
W. Sahara	1975	Polisario Front
El Salvador	1979	Armed Forces of National Resistance
Kampuchea	1979	Khmer Rouge Forces
Peru	1980	Shining Path
India	1980	The Sikh
Sudan	1984	Sudan People's Liberation Army
Uganda	1986	Former government rebels

Source: The Economist, "The World's Wars", (March 1988), pp. 21-24.

Breakdowns in economic and political development in the Third World states lead to the presence of one or more of the following phenomena:

I. The weakness of the economy leads to discontent, provoking impatient groups in society to attempt seizure of power.

II. Weak political institutions are destroyed by rival forces within the state.

III. Existing socio-political and ideological concepts are called into question and new revolutionary ideas are introduced.

IV. Out-of-date traditional social structures are replaced by the forces of modernization.

V. The participation of the various ethnic or regional groups in the economic or political life of the state is neglected, leading to an intensification of tensions.[15]

Thus, the four categories of factors defined by Steinbach are often present simultaneously and interact to cause violence and conflict. The increasing trend toward political violence in the Third World, in the final analysis, is a reflection of the political and socio-economic transformations which have been occurring in these countries. The political violence further indicates several other factors which are not overtly visible but are none the less significant. Outbreaks of political violence underline the gravity of the political instability within these countries. The spread of political violence has curtailed freedom and thus has moved some states away from pluralism towards authoritarianism. In Third World states where there is less social and political cohesion the move towards authoritarianism has come more easily due to the weakness of institutional bases.[16] The Philippines and El Salvador can be cited as appropriate examples of Third World democracies which, when confronted with internal violence, moved rapidly towards an authoritarian state.

Finally, this instability is intrinsically linked to the international political processes and to the world economic system. The changes that are currently taking place in the Third World and the inevitable involvement of external powers are crucial for the maintenance of stability in the regional and global balance of power. Given these factors it becomes increasingly evident that the concentration of political violence in the Third World renders it an especially crucial area of study.

A Case Study Approach

Ted Robert Gurr has observed that there are relatively few case studies of political violence related to the non-Western World and even fewer systematic comparative studies or attempts at empirical theory.[17] This study is an examination of political violence in Sri Lanka[18] from 1971 to 1987 represented as a case study of political violence in the Third World. The reasons for selecting Sri Lanka as a case study rather than analyzing all possible cases in the Third World were substantive and practical. While case studies are rarely comparative in nature, they are often quite insightful. Furthermore, there is a tendency to focus on a particular type of violence rather than on the whole spectrum of political violence which diffuses the analyses.

Sri Lanka with its parliamentary-cum-presidential political system and socio-economic under-development provides a good case study of violent political processes in the Third World. It has been selected because the post-independence history of the country provides an appropriate framework for conceptualizing the main issues relating to the socio-political manifestations of political violence in the process of modernization, and for exploring the broad typology of political violence that would be observed in many Third World countries. Unlike most other Third World countries, Sri Lanka has developed a flexible and perhaps more viable parliamentary political system in which rival political parties have the opportunity to form alternate governments. This political structure has resulted from the gradual evolution of the constitutional system in Sri Lanka under the British Colonial Regime from 1798 to 1948. Sri Lanka's political history is manifest in the unlimited powers of the British governors in the early stages of the colonial period, in the limited responsibility accorded by constitutional changes with universal franchise in 1931, and in the complete independence in 1948. Since 1931 universal franchise has been used successfully and successively to elect representatives to the legislature.

In many newly freed countries violent political struggles were launched to gain independence whereas Sri Lanka achieved its independence without rancour or violence. Therefore, Sri Lanka has been considered as a non-violent and non-volatile nation compared to other developing nations in Asia and Africa.[19] In 1956 the dominant political regime was ousted from power by means of universal franchise. This change of regime was not a mere transfer of power but a silent revolution, which changed the country's political orientation from liberal laissez faire to socialistic nationalism. The main left-orientated political parties which preached revolution and socialism in confrontation with the existing capitalism and parliamentarianism were absorbed into the parliamentary system via the coalition governments formed with the moderate parties. This absorption of the revolutionary-motivated cadres stalled the possibilities of violent politics or revolution for the first 20 years of Sri Lankan independence. Consequently, by 1970 Sri Lanka was acclaimed as one of the few countries in the Third World which enjoyed a stable parliamentary democratic government.[20]

This political stability, however, suffered a sharp reversal when political violence broke out in Sri Lanka in April 1971. It was the beginning of a period characterized by youth-dominated political violence which was manifested on two fronts. The first was the political violence inspired by the revolutionary ideological motivations of the Sinhalese youth. The second strand of political violence was led by the Tamil youth who expressed national separatism.

The first significant incident of political violence in Sri Lanka was staged by the Janatha

Vimukthi Peramuna (Peoples Liberation Front) more popularly known as the JVP in April 1971. The origins of the JVP were secretive and its organizational and political activities were conducted undercover and in a clandestine manner. The potential cadres of this movement were Sinhalese-Buddhist youth who were disillusioned with the existing socio-economic and political framework, and the orthodox Marxists who formed the contemporary left-wing in Sri Lanka's parliamentary politics. The origin of the JVP dates back to 1964 although its existence and revolutionary activities came into the limelight much later. It was with the armed struggle to overthrow the government in April 1971 that the JVP gained recognition as a left-wing guerrilla organization which adhered to a revolutionary strategy.

The historical evolution of the JVP falls into four stages. The first stage covers the period from 1964-1971, during which it emerged as a left-wing guerrilla organization. The armed struggle which the JVP launched in 1971 was of a short duration and was quickly suppressed by the government in power with great force and intensity. Yet the brief conflict created turmoil in Sri Lankan national politics and international relations, unparalleled in its recent political history. As a result of the armed struggle, the JVP was proscribed in 1971 by the regime in power. By 1972 most of its members had either been imprisoned or killed, or had foresworn their allegiance to the cause. The JVP was permitted to resume its political activities in 1977 after the repeal of the Criminal Justice Commission Act by the United National Party Government.

The second stage covers the period from 1977-1983, which includes the post insurrectionary period during which the JVP felt compelled to revive itself as a political party willing to participate in a democratic framework. In fact during this period the JVP was called upon to transform itself from a covert threat into a political party which supported the process of parliamentary democracy. The JVP during its early stages rejected all forms of electoral politics and the parliamentary system. After 1977, however, they had to be content with participation in the existing electoral process beginning with the 1977 elections.[21] The JVP was formally recognized as a legitimate political party by the Election Commissioner in 1982. This new image of the JVP was reversed when ethnic violence broke out in July 1983. The JVP was proscribed once again and forced to revert to operation as an underground movement.

The third stage which deals with the post-1983 period contends with the JVP's renewed violent activities, particularly after the Indo-Sri Lanka Accord of July 1987 which they vehemently opposed. The ensuing presence of the Indian Peace Keeping Force (IPKF) gave the JVP sufficient cause to revive its guerrilla-cum-terrorist activities with greater intensity and scope. The JVP was crushed by the government by military means by the end of 1989. The fourth stage of the evolution of the JVP was initiated after the defeat of its second insurrection. Currently, the JVP is the third single powerful parliamentary party with 38 members in the National Legislature.

The failure of the left-wing insurrection in 1971 was followed by a new trend of political violence marked by guerrilla warfare and terrorism led by the Tamil youth. The motivation for this struggle was ethnic separatism. The first overt manifestations of this violence occurred in 1972. The first phase of Tamil political violence was initiated by a group of youth who called themselves the "Tigers". This is a blanket term applied to the many factions of the Tamil youth who have operated undercover and have been responsible for the terrorist and guerrilla activities since 1972. The proliferation of factions has led to the formation of more than 35 splinter groups.[22] Five Tamil guerrilla groups have achieved dominance over all the others. These five are the Liberation Tigers of Tamil Eelam (LTTE), the Tamil Eelam Liberation Organisation (TELO), the Peoples Liberation Organisation of Tamil Eeelam (PLOT), the Eelam People's Revolutionary Liberation Front (EPRLF) and the Eelam Revolutionary Organisation of Students (EROS).

Thus, since the early 1970's political violence has been a dominant feature in the politics of Sri Lanka. This growing trend of violence has not only impugned the national political authority but also has threatened Sri Lanka's territorial integrity and the established social order. Political violence in Sri Lanka cannot be considered an isolated phenomenon. It is only one of the many manifestations of the tendency for political violence in the Third World. Given this context the author has chosen to focus on the JVP and the LTTE as a comparative study for the following reasons.

Firstly, Sri Lanka illustrates the forms of political violence that takes place during the process of socio-economic and political modernization. From a broad perspective, politically motivated violence in Sri Lanka has manifest in several major manifestations including working-class turmoil in 1953, the general strike in 1981, a series of ethnic violence in 1956, 1958, 1977, 1981, and in 1983, political assassinations such as that of S.W.R. de Bandaranaike the then Prime Minister in 1959, and Alfred Doraiappa the Mayor of Jaffna in 1975, the coups d'etat in 1962, and in 1966, university student riots in 1965, 1968, and in 1976, post-election violence in 1970, and in 1977, revolutionary violence in 1971 and from 1987 to 1989 and separatist violence from the mid 1970s-upto date. Although youth violence is a recent phenomenon in Sri Lanka's contemporary politics, it has displayed a marked dissimilarity to the other dimensions of violence mentioned above. The differences are as follows:

(a) The motivations of this new trend of political violence have been either to overthrow the existing regime and capture political power, as in the insurrection of 1971, or to breakaway from the existing state and create a separate state based on ethnicity, as manifested in the political violence of the Tamil guerrilla groups from 1972 onward. The Insurrection of 1971 was the first organized armed struggle launched in Sri Lanka with an objective similar to the 'hartal' (turmoil) of 1953. What was experienced in 1956 and 1958 were racial riots. Although there may have been some political overtones in the violence before 1971, it was not until the 1971 insurrection that political motivations became the paramount force behind political violence in Sri Lanka.

(b) The political violence from April 1971 onward was also organized and pre-planned in contrast to the spontaneity of the prior incidents. The armed confrontations which come within the purview of this study were pre-planned and carried out by trained cadres of insurgent organizations.

(c) The youth domination of the 1971 and post-1971 political violence is another significant factor. In spite of the lack of systematic data and information on the social character of the participants of the pre-1971 violence, empirical observations have indicated that it was comprised of individuals of a mixed age range. This study is concerned with political violence which displays a marked youth participation and organization.

(d) The revolutionary-motivated insurrection of April 1971 and the ensuing agitation for a separate Tamil State through the use of terrorist and guerrilla strategies has molded the political and socio-economic pattern of Sri Lanka. Consequently, political violence has posed a serious challenge to the existing socio-economic system as well as to the political institutions of the country. No other politically motivated incident or organization has had such a profound impact within a short period at time in Sri Lanka's recent political history.

Secondly, these violent incidents and Sri Lanka's foreign relations have been closely linked. There is evidence to suggest that Sri Lanka's internal order and its place in the geo-political balance in South Asia are also significantly linked. In the recent past, Sri Lanka's political violence has tended to assume an international dimension, especially with the intervention of India which is a dominant country in the Third World, particularly in South Asia. Thus, since 1971 there has been a progressive internationalization of Sri Lanka's political violence, strongly enforcing its position as a good case study of political violence in the Third World context. Moreover, the insurgency of 1971 and the Tamil separatist guerrilla warfare provide a unique opportunity for comparative study.

Review of Literature

It has to be acknowledged that several scholars have studied political and ethnic violence in Sri Lanka, and have identified and discussed several factors as contributory to the political violence. They are: the socio-economic and political conditions of the postwar period, the shortcomings in the educational system, the unemployment crisis, the generation gap, the alienation of youth, the infiltration of radical political thought into Sri Lanka, and the systematic indoctrination of the youth.[23] In all these studies the main point of departure has been the violent incidents themselves; many causal factors have been analysed to justify the events. Most of the available studies are in the nature of event analysis, and thus they lack rigour and depth.

The focus of literature on Tamil violence has invariably been on the impact of the official language policy and the institutionalization of ethnic discrimination. As a result, the previous studies have relatively neglected the emergence of political violence as a paramount factor in Sri Lankan politics.[24]

It should be noted, however, that most of these studies were based purely on general assumptions. In none of these studies was there a systematic analysis of the causes which gave rise to these guerrilla organizations and their political objectives. The studies carried out so far have failed to analyse this important aspect which is essential for an in-depth study of a phenomenon of this nature. Consequently, this study is the first attempt to examine the deeper roots of Sri Lanka's political violence in a comparative context.

Hypothesis

This study focuses on the following hypotheses which emphasize the socio-economic and political factors contributing to political violence in Sri Lanka: (1) political violence in Sri Lanka has not occurred spontaneously and out of context but was pre-planned; (2) the political violence movements are mainly a result of the emergence of new social classes following recent socio-economic transformations; (3) political factors have been more contributive to the origin and development of politically violent organizations and to political violence itself than to psychological factors; and, (4) there is a strong correlation between the socio-economic background of the leaders and members of the political violence movements and the pattern of political violence.

The conventional Marxist explanation of political violence largely in terms of class conflict is no longer valid due to problems of its applicability to the countries of the Third World. Those countries are still in the process of evolving class boundaries and economic divisions which in turn are often camouflaged by other cleavages emanating out of ethnic, tribal, religious and cultural identities. Therefore, the author examines the above-mentioned hypothesis and its plausibility by using an analytical framework based on the following theories: Chalmers Johnson's theory of the Social System, James C. Davie's theory of the J-curve, Ted Robert Gurr's theory of Relative Deprivation, and Samuel P. Huntington's theory of Political Modernization. The author will conduct a broad study of the hypothesis mentioned above within the context of these theories and their applicability. Furthermore, these are some of the salient theories which represent the contemporary views of the phenomenon of political violence.

Study Procedure

In order to achieve a more systematic and analytical approach, this study is divided into seven major chapters. Following this introductory chapter, the second chapter of this book, is devoted to a review of relevant definitions, theories and typologies of political violence. The focal theories under discussion are that of Chalmers Johnson's Social-System theory, James C. Davies's J-curve theory, Ted Robert Gurr's Relative Deprivation theory and Samuel P. Huntington's Political Modernization theory.

In the third chapter, the scope of the study is narrowed to the long-term causes or preconditions which gave rise to the J.V.P. as an underground, politically violent organization. The socio-economic and political processes since the end of colonial period are examined in this context. The fourth chapter is a review and analysis of the preconditions which contributed to the origin of the Tamil guerrilla organizations. The impact of socio-economic and political changes on the ethnic relationships between the Sinhalese and the Tamils before and after independence are also evaluated.

The fifth chapter is devoted to the guerrilla organizations which have resorted to guerrilla warfare and political terrorism. They are examined from the following perspectives: origin and development of the organizations, infrastructure, the socio-economic background of their membership and leaders, methods of fund raising and their international links.

Inevitably the sixth chapter is concerned with the objectives, ideologies, programme and tactics of the guerrilla organizations which depend on violence as a stratagem. The seventh chapter deals with the mode and pattern of political violence from 1971 to 1987, the impact of violence, and the measures adopted by the state to counter and control political violence in Sri Lanka. The pattern of political violence is investigated focusing on the methods of armed attacks, participants, duration and intensity, the number of deaths and casualties, and the government response. Finally, an effort will be made in the concluding eighth chapter to establish which of the socio-economic and political factors identified in this study were most conducive to political violence in Sri Lanka during the period 1971-1987. This will consist of a comparison of the trends in contemporary Sri Lanka politics.

Limitations of the Study

As mentioned before, this study is concerned with political violence from 1971 to 1987, viewed as a comparative study between the JVP and the LTTE in Sri Lanka as a case study in the Third World. The author has not attempted, however, to present an in-depth or comparative study in relation to any other guerrilla or terrorist organization in the Third World. The present study is concerned with conflicts between the Sri Lankan Government and the people they govern. Therefore, another constraint of this study is that it does not focus on state-sponsored political violence and inter-group violence. In spite of these limitations, this study makes a serious attempt to examine the factors which impelled the youth of the Sinhalese and Tamil communities to play a decisive role in the guerrilla movements in Sri Lanka, and explores the context within which such organizations flourished and gained ground. As a result, this study may be particularly helpful to those researching similar guerrilla movements and activities in other Third World countries in the future.

References

1. Harry Eckstein, "Introduction Toward the Theoretical Study of Internal War", in H. Eckstein, ed. *Internal War: Problems and Approaches,* (New York: The Free Press, 1964), pp. 1-6.
2. Ted Robert Gurr, *Why Men Rebel,* (Princeton, N.J.: Princeton University Press, 1970), pp. 5-7.
3. Harry Eckstein, *op. cit.,* pp. 5-6.
4. Ted Robert Gurr, "Psychological Factors in Civil Violence", *World Politics,* No. 2, (1968), p. 245, and H.L. Nieburg, *Political Violence: The Behavioural Process,* (New York: St. Martins Press, 1969), p. 5.
5. Bienen Henry, *Violence and Social Change: A Review of Current Literature,* (Chicago: University of Chicago Press, 1970), pp. 6-9.
6. Von Der Mehden, Fred R. *Comparative Political Violence,* (New Jersy: Prentice Hall, 1973), p. 4.
7. The concept of the "Third World" was initially used following the first Afro-Asian Conference at Bandung in 1955. This concept emphasises the existence of a third force of states which differ from the western industrialised states and the socialist camp. It embraces all Africa except industrialised states and the socialist camp. It embraces all Africa except South Africa, all Asia except China and Japan, all Latin America, and all of the Middle East except Israel.
8. H.L. Neibuıg, James C. Davies and Ted Robert Gurr are a few among those of this view.
9. Ted Robert Gurr, *Why Men Rebel,* 1970, p. 1.
10. William O. Staudenmaier, "Conflict Termination in the Third World: Theory and Practice", in *The Lessons of Recent Wars in the Third World:* Vol. 2, Stephanie G. Neuman and Robert E. Harkavy, eds. (Lexington, Mass: D.C. Heath and Company, 1987), p. 228.
11. Stockholm International Peace Research Institute, *SIPRI Year Book 1988: World Armaments and Disarmament,* (Oxford University Press: 1988), pp. 285-286.
12. Steinbach, Udo, "Sources of Third World Conflict, in Third-World Conflict and International Security", Part 1, *Adelphi Papers,* No. 166, (1980), p. 21.
13. *Ibid.,* p. 21.
14. *Ibid.,* p. 22.

15. *Ibid.*, p. 23.
16. W. Scott Thompson, "Political Violence and the Correlation of Forces", *Orbis,* Vol. 19, No. 3-4, (1975-76), p. 1277.
17. Ted Robert Gurr, *op. cit.,* p. 6.
18. Until 1972 Sri Lanka was known as Ceylon. Although this present study is based largely on material before and after 1972, the author wishes to use the current name for convenience.
19. K.M. de Silva, "Sri Lanka in 1948: *The Journal of Historical and Social Studies,* Vol. 4, No. 1-2, (1974), p. 1.
20. James Jupp, *Sri Lanka-Third World Democracy,* (London: Frank Cass, 1978), p. 327.
21. Four members of the J.V.P. participated in the 1977 General Election. In 1978 they participated in the local government elections. In 1982 the J.V.P. participated in the District Development Council Elections, and the Presidential Election. It collected the highest number of votes polled by the leftist parties in the 1982 Presidential Election.
22. See, Appendix 1.
23. For a comprehensive bibliography of the 1971 Insurrection see. H.A.I. Goonetilake, *The Sri Lanka Insurrection of 1971: A Select Bibliographical Commentary,* (Leuven: Universite de Louvain, 1975).
24. For Tamil Violence see: H.A.I. Goonetilake, "July 1983 and the National Question of Sri Lanka – A Bibliography", in Committee For Rational Development, (eds), *Sri Lanka the Ethnic Conflict: Myths, Realities and Perspectives,* (New Delhi: Navrang, 1984) and Kumar Rupesinghe and Berth Verstappen, *Ethnic Conflict and Human Rights in Sri Lanka: An Annotated Bibliography,* (London: Hans Zell Publishers, 1989).

2

Theories of Political Violence: An Analytical Framework

Introduction

In this second chapter, the author focuses on a diverse and a wide ranging body of extant literature in order to build a theoretical framework for the study of political violence. The main objective of this theoretical analysis is threefold: firstly, to arrive at a working definition of political violence; secondly, to examine a theoretical framework which views political violence from an interdisciplinary approach; and finally, to examine the typologies of political violence and the variables which are used to measure it. For this purpose, the author undertakes an overview of definitions, theories and typologies of political violence on the basis of existing literature. Many different lines of argument and perspective are emphasized by researchers of this area. The author has been selective in his theoretical approach as a wide spectrum of theoretical techniques would cloud the analysis of the causes and patterns of political violence. Therefore, this chapter is divided under the following major headings: definitions of political violence, theories of political violence, Chalmers Johnson's Social-System theory, Davies's J-curve theory, Gurr's Relative Deprivation theory, Huntington's Modernization theory, and the analytical model.

Definitions of Political Violence

The concept of political violence is a broad area of study with significant variability in terms of its application and objectives. Its lack of independence as a specific field of study has rendered it a controversial and problematic concept. As P. Wilkinson observes, political violence is particularly difficult to clarify and analyse because it frequently involves the interaction and effects of the actions of many persons and collectives involving a multiplicity of motivations, psychological effects and subjective evaluations.[1] Harry Eckstein has observed that while earlier on the problem was the lack of a considered definition, the conceptualization now suffers from over-abundance and too much diversity.[2] Thus, the nature of the concept and the wide area it covers makes it almost impossible to arrive at a generally accepted single definition of political violence. Yet, there are certain important definitions which focus on some of the salient aspects of political violence and provide a working definition. The author will touch upon some of the important and explicit definitions of political violence.

Harry Eckstein in his definition of political violence chose to replace the term 'revolution' with that of 'internal war'. He defined political violence as "any resort to violence within a political order geared to change its constitution, rulers or policies".[3] Eckstein's replacement of the term 'revolution' with that of 'internal war' has raised much discussion and also criticism. One criticism is that some types of revolutions such as colonial revolts or military coups d'etat do not generally come within the purview of internal war. In addition, internal war is analogous to civil war, therefore rather than being unique, is best seen as one possible phase or stage in the development of a number of different types of revolution.[4] Considering the criticism of this definition it becomes evident that Eckstein's approach presents serious limitations as a working definition.

H.L. Nieburg has advanced the definition of political violence as "acts of disruption, destruction (and) injury whose purpose, choice of targets or victims, surrounding circumstances, implementation, and/or effects have political significance, that tend to modify the behaviour of others in a bargaining situation that has consequences for the social system".[5] Nieburg's definition, however, has been criticized on the grounds that it lacks precision and is too inclusive. Furthermore, the definition fails to distinguish violence perpetrated by the state or regime in power from the violence and related activities of the general populace.[6]

Samuel P. Huntington in his definition of political violence sought to limit the term revolution mainly to movements with objectives related to radical changes in the social structure, institutions and ideology. He defined a revolution as "a rapid, fundamental, and violent domestic change in the dominant values and myths of society, in its political institutions, social structure, leadership, government activity and policies".[7] Huntington's definition too has been subject to criticism mainly on the grounds that it disregards many significant types of political violence including peasant revolts, urban insurrections and provincial or national separatist rebellions.[8]

Moreover, political violence is not identical with or intrinsic to what has been studied under the concept of revolution. Adopting such a definition for the study of political violence would lead to the exclusion of many dimensions both in a theoretical and comparative context.

Chalmers Johnson defined revolution as a form of social change affected by the use of violence in government and/or regime and/or society.[9] Revolution in this sense means attempts made by non-governmental groups within a state to capture power and establish new political, social and economic structures. Lawrence Stone in analysing Johnson's definition has brought forward several serious limitations in its applicability. There are a wide range of governmental changes by means of violence which do not result in a mere replacement of personalities in positions of power, nor are they a pre-condition to the structuring of society. Furthermore, conservative counter-revolutions are excluded. Finally, the distinctions between colonial wars, civil wars and social revolutions are hard to define.[10]

For Ted Robert Gurr political violence means "all collective attacks within a political community against the political regime, its actors, including competing political groups as well as incumbents, or its policies".[11] According to Gurr's definition armed attacks are political violence against the state by non-governmental political actors. Gurr's definition of political violence too has raised questions, the most obvious of which is: if political violence is comprised of collective attacks against a political regime, how does he define the collective defense of non-state bodies against attacks by a regime. Thus his failure to define violence originating from the regime weakens his definition of political violence.

As shown above, there is no general agreement on the definition of the subject. This leads one to conclude that political violence is a very broad term that is applied to all kinds of violent acts with a political motive. Thus, political violence is used as a term for events variously labeled as riots, rebellion, internal wars, turmoil, revolution, insurrection and other forms of violence. It will not be the task of this study, however, to provide a generally agreed definition which covers all aspects of political violence. Therefore, the present study will examine political violence as pre-planned armed attacks by an organized group or groups to capture or change political power in a domestic political system.

Theories on Political Violence

The main purpose of this section is to give a general overview of the major theories pertaining to the study of political violence. Since the early 1960s, the growing interest in political violence has resulted in the formulation of numerous theories in this field. In a review of literature on political violence Jack Goldstone identified three generations of studies. The first generation, including works by Brinton and Edwards, was primarily descriptive in that it identified preconditions and stages in the process of revolution, but lacked a solid theoretical basis.[12] The second generation theorized about the determinants of revolutionary activity by focusing on the rebels' intentional actions, whether psychological in origin or rational but violent extensions of ordinary political conflict. The third generation, including Skocpol's study[13] has been more sensitive to the historical and social-structural context and thus is able to account for the diversity of outcomes.[14]

As mentioned above, this study does not attempt to survey literature on political violence as a whole but is an overview of the major theories belonging to the second generation from the following approaches: social-structural, social-psychological and politico-economic. The main reasons for emphasizing these three approaches are the following: First, they are basically concerned with internal or domestic forms of political violence. Secondly, the theoretical assumptions of the study are mainly derived from these approaches. Finally, these theories include the major theories in the field of political violence. As there are many arguments pertaining to these approaches the author will present each of the four theories in brief and go on to outline its major criticisms.

Chalmers Johnson's Social System Theory

This study will focus on Chalmers Johnson who is a major exponent of the social-system approach to political violence, having expostulated some of the salient points of the social structural argument. He made known his theory first in *Revolution and the Social System* (1964) and later in, *Revolutionary Change* (1966).

Johnson's simplest observation of violence is that it is a form of human behaviour. Having been influenced by Max Weber's analysis of social action, however, his final definition of violence is that it is action which deliberately or unintentionally disorients the behaviour of others.[15] It has to be noted that Johnson does not dwell on the concept of violence but chooses to focus on a universal model of revolution which, according to him, is a phenomenon of wide-ranging implications. By using Talcot Parsons' systems theory, Johnson views revolution as a means of social change which has to be studied within the social systems in which it occurs.[16] Revolution is the "purposive implementation of a strategy of violence in order to effect a change in the social structure."[17]

Johnson maintains that the key to both the study and the conceptualization of revolutionary violence lies in social system analysis. The main features of a social structure are defined as the roles, norms, status positions and the various functions of the components that make a structure. The emergence of pressures within a previously stable social system may present certain sources of change. The typology of social change is as follows:

(*i*) Exogenous (externally derived) value-changing sources such as: global communications; the rise of "external reference" groups, (e.g., the effects of the French and

Russian revolutions on neighbouring populations); the internal mobilizations and refugee migrations caused by wars; and the work of groups such as Christian missionaries, and Communist parties.

(*ii*) Endogenous (arising within the system) value-changing sources such as: the displacement of religious authorities; the corrosive effects on scholasticism of the theories of Bacon, Descartes and others; changes in values that are brought about as a result of intellectual developments; and the acceptance of creative innovations.

(*iii*) Exogenous environment-changing sources such as: the introduction of modern medical knowledge into underdeveloped countries, which often rapidly alters birth and mortality rates; market stimulation as a result of foreign trade; imported technological skills; military conquest; the migration of populations; and inter-systemic diplomatic relations.

(*iv*) Endogenous environment-changing sources refer to the internal technological innovations such as the invention of the wheel or the railroad.[18]

Once the pressures of these changes are exerted on a social system, the system could either adapt to these changes or fail to do so. What is important to this theory is the inability of a system to cope with such pressures as it creates a condition of "multiple dysfunctions". In a condition of multiple dysfunctions the role of the political elite is significant. Within the context of such a society "two clusters of mutually influencing necessary or remote causes of revolution should be operational for a revolution to occur".[19] First, there are the pressures created by a disequilibrated social system – a society which is changing and which is in need of further change if it is to continue to exist. One such variable is power deflation where the integration of a society subject to change depends largely on the "maintenance and deployment of force" by those who hold positions of authority. Afghanistan after the invasion by the Soviet in 1979 is put forward as an example of a social system characterized by power deflation.

The second variable occurs when "the use of force by the elite is no longer considered legitimate". When the use of force is thus considered there is a "loss of authority".[20] The existence of these two variables, however, does not indicate that a revolution is inevitable. Instead, the effective use of force may lead to a police state. South Africa and Iran in the year preceding the fall of the Shah are cited as examples of a police state. According to Johnson, the conditions generated by a disequlibrated social system can never themselves be sufficient causes of a revolution. The ultimate cause of revolution depends on some "ingredient", usually contributed by "fortune".[21] This ingredient either deprives the elite of its primary means of maintaining social behaviour (e.g. an army mutiny) or makes the revolutionaries perceive that they hold a position by which the elite could be deprived of their "weapons of coercion".[22] In this study, such final or immediate causes of revolution are referred to as 'accelerators'.

Thus the elite in a disequilibrated society is faced with the task of understanding that the society is disequilibrated and taking the necessary measures to restore equilibrium or resist pressures for change. Johnson argues that there are five alternate courses of action for an elite to adapt. They are: "conservative change", "barely adequate change", "abdication of authority", "an incompetent response", and finally "elite intransigence".[23] It is elite intransigence which always "serves as a remote cause of revolution".[24] For Johnson, elite intransigence means:

> The frank, willful pursuit of reactionary policies by an elite – that is, policies which exacerbate rather than rectify a desynchronized social structure, or policies that violate the formal, envalued norms of the system which the elite is charged with preserving.[25]

In a society with multiple dysfunctions and elite intransigence it is an accelerator or a "trigger" which finally brings about a revolution. An accelerator is a single event which bears two main implications. First, it indicates that the elite is no longer in a position to monopolize force. Secondly. it generates an understanding among the revolutionaries that any resort to violence against the system is likely to be successful.

This theory defines three broad types of such accelerators. The first type is the subversion of the armed forces as manifested in defeats in war and army mutinies. These accelerators are so forceful that they could bring about a revolution despite the absence of a revolutionary party. The second class of accelerator is based on a belief shared by the revolutionaries that they could overcome the forces of the authorities. Belief in divine intervention and the expectation that a single attack would lead to mass mobilization are among this type of accelerator. The third type relates to the strategy adopted by the revolutionaries, an example of which is guerrilla warfare.[26] Thus Johnson suggests an apparently simple causal model of revolution which has been represented as follows:

Changes + Multiple dysfunctions + Elite intransigence + Accelerator = Revolution.[27]

In the model of revolution thus demonstrated, Johnson goes on to discuss a typology of revolution which shall be addressed below when discussing the typologies of political violence in general. Chalmers Johnson identifies six types of political violence by adopting the following criteria, which have been discerned at an abstract level:

(*a*) Targets or aims of revolutionary activity: the revolution is aimed at substituting personnel in the government, replacing the entire political regime or forcing the resettlement of the community.

(*b*) Identity of the revolutionaries: they represent or originate from the elite or the masses.

(*c*) Revolutionary goals or ideology: eschatological, nostalgic, nation-forming elite or nationalist.

(*d*) Whether the revolution is spontaneous or pre-planned.[28]

Johnson finds it necessary, however, to further explain his criteria. In this context, the targets raise the first question as to whether a revolution results in the replacement of only a portion of the government, the entire regime or even the community.[29] Community is viewed as a dynamic concept, characterized by a division of labour, which unifies and is a means by which people perceive their social life. The criterion of mass or elite-led revolution, refer to those who perceive the dysfunctional conditions within the society. The criterion of ideology deals with the proposed methods of easing social dysfunction and the alternate regimes suggested by the revolutionaries. Johnson's six types of political violence are as follows:

1. *The Jacquer:* The target of a Jacquerie rebellion is the government. The rebellion has limited goals, and is characterized by a mass uprising of peasants who act spontaneously. The accelerators of this type of rebellion have immediate effects such as famines and wars. The conditions conducive for a Jacquerie may exist for some time but a particular occurrence such as a defeat in war may indicate that the elites are incapable of performing their role. A characteristic response would be a purge of local elites by the masses.
2. *The Millenarian Rebellion:* Millenarian rebellions are defined as those which are caused by unidentified sources of dysfunctions. The alternate way of recognizing the changes that are necessary to elevate the dysfunctions is to rely on the belief that supernatural forces would cause such changes. These rebellions have taken place in traditional societies which have been forced to change by external forces such as industrialism, imperialism and secularism.
3. *The Anarchistic Rebellion:* This category of rebellion occurs as a result of changes made in response to the dysfunctions perceived by the majority of the population. The motivation behind an anarchistic rebellion is the dissatisfaction with the previous changes and the perception of dysfunctions after such changes have occurred. Hence, these rebellions are made by members with a bleak future, and are aimed at the government or regime. Their ideology is based on an ideal, which means making additional but much more radical social changes.
4. *The Jacobin Communist Revolution:* This type of revolution attempts to transform almost every substructure in a society. The social system is characterized by multiple systemic dysfunctions. An

accelerator causes revolution within one group and this revolution in turn acts as an accelerator towards revolutions amongst other groups. The French Revolution and the Russian Revolution are two examples.

5. *The Conspiratorial Coup d'etat:* This pattern of revolution narrows Johnson's typology to a micro level. The conspiratorial coup d'etat is an attempt by a limited and select group, who share a common grievance, to bring about revolutionary change. Such revolutions are pre-planned and are void of mass support. The ideology of these revolutions is elitist or tutelary, e.g. the Egyptian coup of 1952, and the Ghana coup of 1966.

6. *The Militarized Mass Insurrection:* The distinguishing character of this form of revolution is that it is a pre-planned revolution with a revolutionary strategy and mass support. Although this type of revolution is launched by a mass segment of the population, it is engineered by a "conspirational revolutionary general staff", and is nationalist oriented. The more widely known revolutions which come within the purview of this typology are the Chinese Revolution (1937-49), and the Algerian Revolution (1945-62).[30]

It is noteworthy that Johnson continuously juggles the terms revolution and rebellion as if he refers to the same type of political violence. Johnson does not seem to recognize political terrorism as part of the pattern of political violence in this typology. Johnson himself admits, however, that the major weakness in his criteria of differentiation lies in his failure to consider the "type of system and the sources of dysfunction".[31]

Johnson's theory appears to be a carefully organized model of revolution, which discusses some of the important aspects of political violence. Unfortunately, in-depth studies of Johnson's approach and model have revealed several shortcomings which have important implications for the application of his theory. The first criticism is related to Johnson's definition of revolution, which is found to be inconsistent with his conception of violence and typology of revolution. Johnson's definition of revolution indicates that it involves violent social change, which means that revolutionary change is violent. Of the six types of revolution defined by Johnson, the Jacquerie, the Millenarian Rebellion, and the Anarchistic Rebellion do not result in a change of the existing regime. Once the uprisings have been defeated, the former regimes are restored to power, thereby avoiding any form of social change as perceived in Johnson's definition. The inconsistency in definition and typology is a weakness of Johnson's theory which restricts its definitional value and applicability to the study of political violence.

Johnson has further failed to predict the occurrence of events or a series of events prior to their occurrence as in any given causal model. His model states that multiple dysfunctions and elite intransigence are pre-conditions for a revolution, which is triggered by an accelerator. Finally, what activates a revolution is the understanding among a significant number of the populace that the elite no longer control the forces of authority. Johnson seems to have achieved a sequential model which merely examines a revolution "post facto", but fails to formulate a causal model predicting the occurrence of a revolution prior to its actual manifestation. In addition, the sequence given by Johnson is questionable as all revolutions do not follow the same sequential pattern.

The concept of accelerators is crucial to Johnson's model. He defines three types of accelerators which mark the starting point of a revolution. Johnson contends that the "final cause of revolution is some ingredient usually contributed by fortune". The use of the concept of fortune or fate is hardly acceptable for the analysis of such a complex phenomenon as political violence. Perhaps the most significant limitation of Johnson's theory lies in its inability to deal with the socio-economic and political processes of a given society. Societies which have been subject to colonialism are particularly relevant in considering the forms of socio-economic and political changes which take place. Johnson's apparent neglect of politico-economic changes poses a serious limitation. A theory based on a mono-causal explanation thus cannot be applied to analyse political violence which has been subject to distinct socio-economic and political processes. Furthermore, according to Johnson the following indices are symptoms of social dysfunction: suicide rates, heightened ideological activity, the proportion of uniformed armed police forces to the total population, and the ratio of political to general crimes. Johnson's attempts to measure the disequilibrated social system can hardly be termed as even suggestive and Johnson as much as admits its primitive quality.[32] As has been seen, Johnson's theory is characterized by definitional inconsistency, weakness in the application of the causal model, and inability to comprehend the significance of the concept of disequilibrium within the frame work of certain Third World societies.

James C. Davies' J-Curve Theory

The J-curve theory of revolution, as presented by James C. Davies, has been reformulated and adapted to the study of other indicators of political violence. In this discussion the author examines the J-curve theory, including one of its adaptations, and then focuses on its applicability to the study of political violence in Sri Lanka.

The most systematic attempt to relate the dynamics of frustration-aggression to political violence is Davies's theory of the J-curve. He has been influenced in its formulation by the Marxist theory that revolutions occur when there is socio-economic degradation, and by de Tocqueville's theory that revolutions occur when economic conditions improve. Consequently, revolution is seen by Davies as the effect of neither poverty nor economic improvement alone but of a certain sequence of the two. Thus influenced, Davies maintains that revolutions are most inevitable in societies, which first have experienced economic and social growth, and are subsequently faced with a period of "sharp reversal during which the gap between expectations and gratifications quickly widens and becomes intolerable".[33] The period of socio-economic improvement is marked by expectations to satisfy needs. What is significant is that when this period of growth and heightened expectation is followed by a period of decline, a mental or psychological condition of anxiety and frustration is generated. The relevance of this mental state of mind or social mood is emphasized in relation to its impact on the political instability of a society.[34]

Davies observes that people who are at a marginal state or level of existence and are deprived of resources, remain politically passive and inactive. This passivity is explained by the fact that within the framework of an impoverished society, people tend to endure hardships and detach themselves from any activity other than mere survival. The family remains the basic unit of interaction, and social contact is restricted to the limits of survival. Such levels of low social interaction do not permit a high level of political awareness and participation. Davies' conclusions are based mainly on studies and reports of the Minnesota starvation experiment conducted during World War II, and the reported behaviour of victims/inmates in Nazi concentration camps.[35] The studies indicated a constant preoccupation with food on the part of people who are on the verge of starvation. Davies admits though that these conditions would not prove to be of such extremes in normal circumstances. Nevertheless, the high degree of passivity and concern for mere existence dominates life and erases the scope for community action. It is only when the influence of these bonds are reduced that people find themselves in a position of "proto-rebelliousness" – that is, the frustration built up in these circumstances could be thwarted by natural causes or minor social reforms.

According to Davies, it is the dissatisfied state of mind, rather than the tangible provision of 'adequate' or 'inadequate' supplies of food, equality or liberty which produces the revolution. Thereby, he argues that conditions conducive for a revolution necessitate a period of sharp reversal after a long period of socio-economic development and a continued expectation of heightened opportunities to attain basic needs. These needs are divided into four broad categories:

(*i*) physical needs (food, clothing, shelter, health and safety from bodily harm);

(*ii*) social affectional needs (ties of family and friends);

(*iii*) needs for self-esteem or dignity; and

(*iv*) self-actualization.[35]

Each category of the "proto-revolutionary" society is affected by the deprivation of any of these diverse needs, and the gap differs from category to category. What is intrinsically important in this argument is that the basic needs of the would be revolutionaries are threatened or are perceived of as being threatened. This threat does not imply that people would be reduced to impoverished conditions, but does create a state of mind or mood that basic needs are threatened or will not be fulfilled. It is a mental condition rather than an absolute threat which is operational within the society. Davies argues that "political stability and instability are ultimately, dependent on a state of mind, a mood, in a society".[37] If the frustration which emerges from this mental condition "is sufficiently widespread, intense and focused on government, the violence will become a revolution that displaces irrevocably the ruling government and changes markedly the power structure of society or a rebellion modifying but not displacing the system within which it is contained".[38] In the broadest sense, he sees revolution as a series of violent civil disturbances which cause the displacement of one ruling group with another and which has a broader popular basis of support.

The options of averting a revolution are two-fold. Rising expectations could be controlled by the use of force. The forced reduction of expectations, however, could serve as an effective means of overcoming revolutionary conditions only in limited circumstances. The most effective means, according to Davies, depends on the government's response to newly emerging needs. The gratification of dynamic needs by the ruling group eliminates the possibility of widespread and intense frustration building up in a society, thereby greatly reducing the likelihood of a revolution occurring.

In a further development of the J-curve theory, Davies found it necessary to discuss the forms of violence, which occur in conditions of regression and frustration. The J-curve argument maintains that the ensuing frustration from socio-economic regression gains direction and meaning only when it is focused against the government. The violence, which results from such frustration, could finally emerge as a revolution or a rebellion. Davies states that "revolution and rebellion differ in result but have like origins".[39] In a revolution the government is overthrown and far-reaching changes are made in the social and power structure. In a rebellion, however, the system is subject to modification rather than displacement. A revolution involves wider participation, greater depth and intensity of feeling, all of which have been developing for years, and which will result in intense political violence and thus in lasting bitterness. Rebellions, on the other hand, are unsuccessful revolutions because the anger is not sufficiently developed, intense and widespread to withstand the pressure imposed by the government. The economic conditions in a rebellion are not grave enough to produce a revolutionary mental condition amongst a wider population. Davies makes a further distinction between revolution, rebellion and civil war by observing that "revolution succeeds, rebellion fails and civil wars leave the question open".[40] In addition, Davies cites riots and demonstrations as examples of violent outbreaks falling into the pattern of the J-curve. The widening of the applicability of the theory of revolution to other indicators of violence, however, does not imply that it is a universal model which covers all revolutions. Nevertheless, to substantiate his argument Davies discusses the French Revolution of 1789, the Dorrs Rebellion of 1842 (Rhode Island), the American Civil War of 1861, the Russian Revolution of 1917, the Nazi revolution of 1933, the Egyptian Revolution of 1952, and the Black rebellion of the 1960s in greater detail.

The J-curve theory as discussed above has been the basic source for Raymond Tanter and Manus Midlarsky's adaptation of a theory of revolution. Instead of the concept of economic growth and regression this theory applies the concept of "achievement". Achievement is perceived of as a concept with many aspects varying from socio-economic development to cultural and political development. A high rate of achievement increases aspirations which are defined as optimism arising from the past. Achievement and aspirations are interdependent variables, which rise together and increase the need to acquire social commodities. When conditions are on the reverse, however, and achievement decreases, the variable of expectations is introduced to approximate with the decrease in achievement. The gap between expectations and achievement is potentially revolutionary, and the widening of the gap signifies a more profound and intense revolution spanning a longer period of time.[41] In their approach Raymond Tanter and Manus Midlarsky test the relationship between particular indicators of achievement and revolution.[42]

At a superficial level the J-curve theory and its adaptation give useful insights to the study of revolution, and together serve as a useful model. In applying the theoretical framework of the J-curve, however, it becomes evident that there are significant constraints on its wider applicability especially in Third World societies. According to the J-curve argument, the means of predicting a revolution depend on assessing the mood of the people. Their mental condition is an indicator of the level of frustration which subsequently leads to a revolution. Davies suggests investigative techniques which have been applied by other social scientists to assess the mood of the people during political instability. One such technique is that of systematic public opinion analysis.[43] Davies further cites strikes, employment level, exports and cost of living as data from which the mood of the people could be inferred. Although indices such as strikes and cost of living are more relevant in assessing the mood of the people, cruder indicators such as value of exports may prove useful. This technique involves the application of data collected over an extended period.

What is significant in discussing the possible means of inferring the people's state of mind is the following question: How does one apply these methods within the socio-economic and political framework of Third World countries. The interview method involves assessing some overt expression of the people's political ideas and feelings. Many Third World countries are characterized by political instability, weak opposition and the use of government force. In light of such conditions the interview method has been questioned as a valid method of investigation, and an effective means of inferring the people's state of mind. For example, Sri Lanka has experienced a curtailment of political freedom and violence at the electoral level since the 1960s.[44] A repressive government has sought to weaken the political opposition and to impose tight control of all means of expressing effective political protest by the people such as strikes, demonstrations and elections. Any attempt to derive an assessment of the people's mood in this political climate should be based on other indicators than those derived from the interview method or those suggested by Davies. Davies himself admits that where there are seeds of revolution, established governments are not likely to welcome social scientists in search of data or allow them to conduct public opinion surveys inquiring about attitudes toward the government.[45] Political indicators would be most useful within such a context. Nevertheless, the J-curve theory is more concerned with the psychology of potential rebels than with their social or political situation, or the different kinds of responses they meet from other groups and above all from governments.

The techniques of analysis referred to by Davies were conceived and have been perfected in societies which are characterized by a high degree of industrialization, a distinct division of labour, urbanization, and a highly advanced and sophisticated system of communication. Given the features of these societies, the population is characterized by socio-economic and political individuation. Third World countries, however, are characterized by a flexible division of labour, predominantly a rural sector, a less complex differentiation of social and economic roles and, more significantly, by a less social and political individuation. Consequently, it is hardly possible to observe a sudden decline of output of goods and services after a period of prolonged and more or less steady economic growth in Third World countries such as Sri Lanka. Furthermore, evidence pertaining to Sri Lanka in the subsequent chapters challenges the theoretical weakness of the "revolution of rising expectations" where socio-economic and political factors are more important than a 'state of mind' in explaining political violence. Evidently these techniques of analysis and Davies' theoretical formulation were expounded in totally different societies which have already undergone diverse modernizing social, economic and political processes. The disparity extant in the socio-economic and political context, however, is not the only reason for the limitations in applying the J-curve hypothesis to Third World societies.

There are significant limitations in Davies' theoretical formulation as empirical applications reveal that it is impossible to define the extent and duration of frustration on the basis of survey data. In some instances Davies' analysis spans a period of about fifty years during which the "state of mind", is supposedly transmitted. The problem in this context is not only the prohibitive time frame but also the form in which this state of mind is transmitted and how it is measured.[46] Thus, the predictive power of the J-curve is almost non-existent, quite contrary to the expectations of an analysis of revolutionary situations. What Davies achieves is an analysis or explanation of revolutionary actions only after they have occurred. He cannot predict, however, when a revolutionary outbreak is to take place, as he acknowledges.[47]

Furthermore, Davies is unable to suggest a means by which one could define when the gap between expectations and gratifications becomes intolerable. He merely suggests that at some stage a mental mood develops where the gap is no longer bearable. The next criticism of the J-curve theory is that he fails to explain how the revolutionary mood or state of mind is changed into revolutionary action, which is sufficiently intense to overthrow the regime in power.

Another limitation in the empirical analysis of this theory is that it does not classify the groups which experience this frustration within a society and subsequently resort to political violence. Nor does it disclose whether these frustrated clusters are the same clusters which resort to violence. In societies with class and caste stratifications such definitions become important in analysing political violence. The evidence of discontent prevails among various segments of society prior to revolution as well as in social and political continuity. Hence what Davies fails to achieve is a distinction between pre-revolutionary frustrations and the frustrations that contribute to political continuity.[48]

Davies cites examples from the pre-revolutionary situation in Russia to support his argument that conditions conducive for a revolution exist when socio-economic growth is arrested and heightened expectations are frustrated. The Mexican experience, however, indicates that these are not essential pre-conditions for a revolution.[49] Unlike the Russian situation, the conditions of the Mexican peasantry were ignored by the regime in power and any changes led to the further deprivation of the peasantry. The mass support for the revolutionary violence of 1915 in Mexico was more the result of deteriorating conditions than of frustrated expectations of improvement. Hence, Davies' argument that revolutions do not occur in conditions of impoverishment is strongly negated. Eckstein observes that the chief problem with the J-curve theory is the abundance of counter examples. Consider for instance the many countries in which the Great Depression of the 1930s did not increase political violence.[50]

Tanter and Midlarsky's study of seventeen revolutions from 1955 to 1960 was based on the concepts of achievement and aspiration. Regrettably, however, they have not circumvented the basic weaknesses of the J-curve argument but have merely widened the indicators of violence. It has to be noted that Davies does not lay claim to the formulation of a complete and all-embracing theory of revolution. It is evident, however, that in Davies' theoretical and practical application, his emphasis on social and economic conditions seriously limits the theoretical understanding of revolution. Political factors and certain historical processes are some of the salient factors, which enter into the explanation of revolution. Thus, it is a combination of factors rather than one factor alone which provides an adequate understanding of revolution.

Gurr's Theory of Relative Deprivation

The social-psychological theories purport to explain the occurrence of political violence. They draw heavily on the frustration-aggression model to formulate a casual model of violence. In contrast to the J-curve theory which is concerned with defining the conditions in which a revolution may occur, the proponents of relative deprivation trace the origins of revolutionary motivation to the minds of the masses. Theorists such as Gurr, Feierabend and Nesvold have constructed models on the basis of this theory. Since Gurr's model of political violence is the most sophisticated of these, the author concentrates on Gurr's model of civil strife. Gurr's theory is an attempt to analyse the following three aspects of political violence: its sources, magnitude, and forms.

In tracing a causal link in political violence, Gurr finds that the development of discontent is followed by politicization of that discontent and finally, by its realization in "violent acts against political objects and actors".[51] The fundamental variable, which is the psychological variable, is relative deprivation. Within the context of this theory relative deprivation is defined as:

Actors' perception of the discrepancy between their value expectations and their value capabilities. Value expectations are the goods and conditions of life to which people believe they are rightfully entitled. Value capabilities are the goods and conditions of life they think they are capable of getting and keeping.[52]

Values are defined by Gurr as "the desired events, objects, and conditions for which men strive".[53] They are divided into three general sets: welfare values, power values and interpersonal values. Welfare values are those that contribute directly to physical well-being and self-realization. Power values are those that determine the extent to which men can influence the actions of others yet avoid unwanted interference in their own actions. Interpersonal values are the psychological satisfactions sought in non-authoritative interaction with other individuals and groups.[54] Therefore, relative deprivation is not a discrepancy between an ideal position and reality. Rather, it is a discrepancy between what is perceived as being possible to achieve, and what one is legitimately entitled to but does not receive or attain. The stronger the goals that people aspire to, the higher the relative deprivation if they do not succeed. Deriving a causal link from the psychological theory, Gurr sees anger as a response to deprivation, and aggression as a response to anger. One of the facets determining the intensity and duration of this anger is defined as a perception of a wide discrepancy between expectations and capabilities, which results in a higher level of discontent. Furthermore, as greater importance is attached to the effected values, fewer alternatives are available and there is less time to make a decision.[55] In Gurr's analysis of relative deprivation he finds it as a dynamic concept where the patterns of change are operational in value expectations and value capabilities. More formally Gurr's central proposition is :

$$RD=\frac{Ve-Vc}{Ve}$$

Where, RD stands for "relative deprivaton" , Ve stands for "value expectation" , and Vc stands for "value capabilities".[56]

As a means of evaluating the intensity and the scope of the relative deprivation within such a context, three patterns of disequilibrium are defined. The first is decremental deprivation where a group's value expectations remain relatively constant but their value capabilities are perceived to decline. In such circumstances people lose what they once had or expected to obtain, and instead experience relative deprivation in relation to their past condition. Such events as decreases in the production of material goods, decline in the political elite's capacities to maintain order or resolve crises, the imposition of foreign rule, and the loss of faith in societal integration, beliefs and norms of action, are cited as instances of decremental deprivation. This form of relative deprivation is also considered possible among one or more segments of society as members of a particular group may experience loss in relation to other groups. Instances of such loss are: the imposition of progressive taxation on the wealthy and of regressive taxation on the poor; the loss of political influence by the elites; the barring of the opposition from political activity; and the loss of middle-class influence and status vis-à-vis the working class.[57]

In aspirational deprivation, value capabilities remain relatively static while expectations increase or intensify. The experience of anger is generated by the following: lack of means for attaining expectations; increases in demands for greater amounts of value held in various ways such as material goods, or more political order and justice; increases in demands for previously weakly-demanded values; or demands for new values such as the participation of colonial groups in politics.[58]

Finally, in progressive deprivation there is a substantial and simultaneous increase in expectations but a decrease in capabilities. Gurr refers to progressive deprivation as a "generalized version" of the Davies model. It is said to occur when value capabilities, which

> have stabilized or declined following a long-term period of steady improvement in people's value positions, have led to expectations of continued improvement. According to Gurr, progressive deprivation is most common in societies in which ideological and systemic change is occurring simultaneously. The situations Gurr cites as being potentially conducive to progressive deprivation are economic depression in a growing economy and the articulation of the ideology of modernization in societies unable to live up to this promise of progress.[59] All three patterns have been found to be causal for political violence.

For measuring deprivation, Gurr compiles two general types of measures to ascertain (1) persistent (long-term) deprivation and (2) short-term deprivation. These measures are constructed from aggregate indicators and some of which that are relevant for long-term deprivation are: (*i*) economic discrimination (exclusion of some groups from the economic arena); (*ii*) political discrimination (exclusion of groups from the political arena); (*iii*) political separation which include separatist, regional or ethnic groups; (*iv*) the dependence upon foreign capital by the country in question; (*v*) religious cleavages; and (*vi*) lack of educational opportunity.[60] The indicators that he has used measure short-term deprivations are: (*i*) short-term trends in trade values, 1957-60 compared with 1950-7; (*ii*) the same in 1960-3 compared with 1950-60; (*iii*) inflation in 1960-63 compared with 1958-61; (*iv*) the GNP growth rates in 1960-63 compared with the 1950's; and (*v*) the index of 'adverse' economic conditions during 1960-63 which includes factors such as crop failures, unemployment, and new restrictions on political participation and representation by the regime.[61]

According to him the causal links between discontent and participation in strife by the population is mediated by intervening variables within society. The main societal variables discussed by Gurr are coercive potential, institutionalization, social facilitation and the legitimacy of the political regime in which strife occurs.[62] Priority is given to the deterrent effect of punishment by the state. Gurr fails, however, to discern a linear relationship between increasing levels of coercion and declining levels of violence. Instead, he perceives force as a variable which intensifies resistance and invokes greater force from the dissidents.[63] High levels of coercion appear to limit the extent of strife but comparative studies have failed to establish a relationship. These studies have indicated, however, the importance of "loyalty of coercive forces to the regime" as a deterring factor.[64] In his model of measuring the 'composite coercive potential' Gurr applies the following formula:

$$\text{Coercive Potential} = 10\text{ L } \{2\,(\text{HiR}) + 1(1\text{OR})\ 1 + \text{P}$$

where L = "Loyalty score"; HiR = the higher of the "scaled military and security forces participation ratios"; lOR = the low of the "participation ratios"; and P = "coercive forces strife participation" score.

The mediation of institutionalization is found to be a variable which directly affects the level of violence. Societal structures increase value opportunities and provide the discontented with a non-violent means of expression. Hence, an increase of institutionalization denotes a lower level of violence.

The third variable deals with the social and environmental conditions that facilitate violence within a society. The two main facets that are subject to special consideration are the levels of previous civil strife, and the social and structural facilitation. The working hypothesis in this context is that the higher the levels of civil violence in the past and the higher the levels of social and structural facilitation, the higher the levels of violence.[65]

The fourth variable was arrived at by Gurr after operationalizing the above variables in relation to strife. Legitimacy of the regime means that people become less aggressive when the frustration they experience is perceived to be justifiable. These variables discussed above determine the magnitude of civil strife.[66]

In order to measure the magnitude of civil strife Gurr utilizes three composite variables: pervasiveness, duration, and intensity. Pervasiveness is the degree or extent of participation of the affected population, duration is the length of time the violence lasts, and intensity is the extent of human casualties.[67]

Pervasiveness is measured in terms of participants per 100,000 population, duration in days and casualties in terms of human deaths and wounded.[68] In "A Causal Model of Civil Strife", Gurr coded data on 1000 odd strife events occurring in 114 polities between 1961 and 1965 to measure causality by means of mathematical analysis of event data. His main sources were *The New York Times, The Newsyear, and The Africa Digest.*

By applying correlation, regression analysis and complex mathematical calculations Gurr arrives at a "hypothetical curvilinear relationship between coercive force size and total magnitude of strife (T.M.C.S.)". T.M.C.S. can be examined graphically: when it goes up the level of coercive force present increases.[69] Within this context, Gurr tests his premise that violence varies in magnitude with the level of intensity in relative deprivation. Within the course of his T.M.C.S. analysis Gurr concludes that in his multivariate analysis several important changes occur:

None of the mediating variables appear to effect the relationship between persisting deprivation and strife, i.e., there is a certain inevitability about the association between such deprivation and strife. Persisting deprivation is moreover equally potent as a source of conspiracy, internal war, and turmoil. With the partial and weak exception of institutionalization, no patterns of societal arrangements nor coercive potential that are included in the model have any consistent effect on its impact.[70]

Thus the conclusion of Gurr's analysis is that there is a persistent relationship between deprivation and levels of strife, and that mediating variables are not operational in such a context. In addition, the magnitude of coercive force and the magnitude of violence have a curvilinear relationship. This means that an enlargement of military and internal security forces causes a substantial increase in the magnitude of violence to a point but then there is a marked decrease. The countries with a higher coercive force tend to have more strife. Gurr concludes with the premise that force increases violence.[71]

Ted Gurr formulated a three-fold typology of political violence based on the following aspects: who participates, whether it is the elite or the masses, and whether or not the violence is highly organized.[72] Gurr goes on to define three forms of political violence. They are as follows:

Turmoil: Correspondingly unplanned and unorganized mass conflict. It is usually found occurring in the form of political strikes, riots, political clashes and localized rebellions.

According to Gurr, the difference between turmoil and the other two forms of civil strife can be reduced to differences in the degree of organizational clarity of goals and extent of citizen participation.

Conspiracy: Planned political violence involving a few participants as in political assassinations, small scale terrorism, small-scale guerrilla warfare, coups and mutinies.

Internal War: Large-scale, organized, widespread and mass civil strife involving extensive violence as in widespread terrorism, guerrilla war, civil war and revolution.[73]

Gurr has utilized a variety of techniques and aggregate indicators in an attempt to prove his theory. Paradoxically, due to the complexity of his techniques and their proliferation, the weaknesses of the theory have increased. It becomes increasingly evident from the data which Gurr has utilized that the validity of Gurr's theory is questionable. In measuring the magnitude of violence Gurr relies heavily on event data derived from secondary sources. For instance, data on the number of participants and casualties is determinative of the intensity and pervasiveness of the violence. Information obtained in conditions of political violence regarding the number of participants and casualties could hardly be accurate because most of the data would be inaccessible and some participants would operate undercover. The data pertaining to these aspects of the insurrection of 1971 in Sri Lanka has been contradicted by scholars and remains a matter of conjecture. Hence, the magnitude of the civil strife measured on the basis of inaccurate data could be misrepresented. Furthermore, the priorities and interests of the sources reporting the incidence of violence could vary, and such a variance affects the validity of the data.

Charles Tilly finds that Gurr depends on quantitative analysis to substantiate his argument that socio-economic and political deprivation, collective discontent and political violence form a likely pattern and a tentative base for his theory. Some of the salient reasons given by Tilly for his doubts are that Gurr's data came from sources rather distant from the events under study, deal with the short term, and relate to the states as a whole rather than to the differences between them. The data further includes cross-sectional data which could vary in effect from country to country.[74]

Tilly further contends that Gurr's variables were reformulated and adjusted to be compatible with the data to which Gurr had access. According to Tilly, the application of the determinate models to fresh situations would be a more apt test to discern the validity of the theory.[75] Furthermore, on the basis of his won studies, Tilly finds that the less the model of political violence applies, as a result of the discontent of a total population, the less the frustration-aggression argument yields. Tilly in his studies finds that an important part of collective violence is the violence carried out by representatives of the state. In Gurr's analysis this form of violence is subsumed as the action of dissidents, whereas Tilly contends that a majority of the violence is initiated and carried out by "troops, police and other specialized repressive forces".[76]

Once again Gurr's failure to concentrate on the interactions among those who participate in political violence within a state has been highlighted by Tilly as a result of his own work. Tilly maintains that such an analysis could be attained by focusing on structural analysis which deals with aspects such as class conflict and class structure.[77]

Another limitation of Gurr's theory lies in his generalization of the "intensity of anger [and] motivation of the resentment" where he fails to provide scientific means of measurement.[78]

Gurr's assertion that the magnitude of violence varies according to the available institutional means of expressing non-violent anger, is also found to be limiting, considering the practical experiences of the American Civil War, the endemic civil violence in post-colonial India, and the intensity of civil violence in Northern Ireland. In addition, Gurr does not explain how or why some aggression is mediated into actual violence. P. Wilkinson asserts that "*Why Men Rebel* can be more accurately described as the presentation of a model than a theory".[79]

In his book *Why Men Rebel* and in his article, "The Causal Model of Civil strife", Gurr sets out to define the causes of civil strife. Within the framework of his theory, however, priority is given to the magnitude of civil strife and the measures of assessing that magnitude. Thus, the conceptual question which was raised in his theory is subsumed in his operational effort.[80]

The models utilized by Gurr are also questionable. For instance, in measuring the coercive potential score, Gurr uses a model which fails to account for data error, and relies on a model of accuracy which is open to manipulation. The models utilized to measure the other mediating variables experience similar shortcomings.

Moreover, Gurr's theory does not offer any hypothetical propositions about what variables determine the kind of political violence that ensues. His concern is with psychological determinants of the likelihood and magnitude of violence, not with what determines the quality of resultant strife, whether it is, for example, assassination, mutiny, coupd' et. at., civil war, terrorism, strikes or revolution. What is missing is a discussion of how and why such anger turns in some cases toward the governing regime and produces political violence.

Furthermore, Gurr perceives political violence as a behavioural phenomenon rather than as a structural phenomenon which is inherent in the social structure of a society.[81] Consequently, in Gurr's theory there is no room for discussion of the socio-economic structures and political processes which are essential to any theory of the development of political violence. Another definitional weakness which Gurr fails to circumvent is the distinction between violent and non-violent protests. All forms of protest, which reach beyond the institutional limits are covered by the term civil strife.[82]

Gurr's classification of political violence comes under three main types: revolutions, guerrilla wars and civil wars. What Gurr fails to discern is that within the context of such violence, the regime as well as its adversaries would be involved in violent interaction. Thus, throughout his theory Gurr perceives political violence as being derived from the relative deprivation experienced by the masses and not from the violence exerted by the regime. In applying Gurr's theory to the Third World, where regimes also have to be studied within the context of political violence, the author finds theoretical and conceptual weaknesses which reduce its applicability.

Samuel P. Huntington's Theory of Modernization

Huntington, who is one of the major exponents of the modernization thesis, seeks to explain the process of violence and revolution in terms of social changes and political development. He draws a distinction between countries, which are governed effectively and those which are devoid of effective government. The countries which are governed effectively are characterized by a stable political system, by a mutually shared vision of the people and their leaders of what comprises public interest and other fundamentals of a public community, and finally by the government's ability to command the loyalty and obedience of the citizenry. The countries which are not governed effectively depict contrary characteristics and are potentially revolutionary.

Huntington, in widening the scope of the modernization theory, perceives that the characteristics of countries, which are not effectively governed, are most evident in the modernizing countries of Asia, Africa, and Latin America. He observes that the predominant trends in most of these countries since the Second World War have been the following: conflict based on ethnicity and class; recurring incidents of rioting and mob violence; unstable political leadership committed to disastrous economic and political policies; the spread of corruption among those in authority and power; the violation of the basic rights of citizenship; the curtailment of the powers of the legislature and courts; and the fragmentation or disintegration of mass-based political parties. The possible impacts of these trends on the political sphere include: coups, revolutionary violence, insurrection, guerrilla warfare, tribal or communal tension, and dictaatorship.[83]

According to Huntington, these conditions of violence and instability are largely attributed to the "rapid social change and the rapid mobilization of new groups into politics coupled with the slow development of political institutions".[84] This process of social change or modernization is defined as a "multifaceted process involving changes in all areas of human thought and activity".[85] In spite of the multifaceted nature of the process of modernization, Huntington emphasizes the relevance of social mobilization and economic development to violence and revolution.

Social mobilization in its broadest sense, results in some of the basic changes in social development. Literacy, education, increased communication, mass media exposure and urbanization, are the main features of social mobilization that change the values, attitudes and expectations of a traditional society to those of a modern society.[86] Such changes give rise to new aspirations and hopes, and widen the sphere of political activity. The un-fulfillment of these hopes and aspirations widens and strengthens political participation and consciousness. Since social change undermines the traditional political authority, it becomes necessary for political development to accompany the degree of social change. When political organization and institutionalization are low, however, the potential for political disorder and instability are high.[87] Accordingly, "in the absence of strong and adaptable political institutions, such increases in participation mean instability and violence".[88] In substantiating his argument Huntington cites the rapid expansion of education in Sri Lanka from 1948 to 1956 as the cause of the ensuing political instability and radical changes in electoral politics. He states that the expansion in education was not aimed at creating a work force equipped with the skills relevant to the country's needs. The long-term result was unemployment of educated persons. Huntington summarizes the dilemma of the unemployed arguing that "the higher the level of education of the unemployed alienated, or otherwise dissatisfied persons, the more extreme the destabilizing behaviour which resullts".[89] Thus, social mobilization is a vital aspect of modernization when combined with economic development has its implications regarding political development. Huntington perceives that economic development is a channel, which satisfies the aspirations generated by social mobilization and reduces the frustration in society. Rapid economic growth, however, could also operate as a destabilizing force as follows:

1. The economic changes undermine traditional social structures and create a social group who are classless and prone to revolutionary protest.
2. The emergence of a "new rich" class who are not adjusted to the existing order, and who desire political power and social status compatible with their economic status, threatens the fulfillment of the government's compromises with the lower classes.
3. The escalation of migration especially from the rural areas to the cities generates alienation and political extremism.
4. An increase in the population concurrent with a declining standard of living leads to a wider gap between the rich and the poor.
5. An absolute but less than proportional increase in the incomes of some groups heightens their dissatisfaction with the existing order.
6. A curtailment of consumption in order to promote investment generates mass discontent.
7. Increased literacy, education and access to the mass media may heighten aspirations beyond the possible levels of fulfillment.
8. Ethnic and regional conflicts are heightened over the distribution of investment and consumption.
9. Finally, the scope for group organizations is enhanced, but the strength of group pressure generates greater demand which the government is unable to meet.[90]

The operation of these variables increases the rate of frustration beyond the level of demand which the rate of economic development can achieve. Although the scope of political participation is widened, it leads only to further frustration because the political system is overloaded with demand. Greater social mobilization, economic development and political participation thus undermine the traditional institutions and attitudes of society by creating heightened aspirations and hopes, which the system is unable to fulfill in the short-term. Therefore, what creates political instability is the lack of political institutionalization, which can accommodate such an expansion. In this context, revolution is the extreme case of the expansion of political participation.

Huntington views a revolution as a phenomenon confined to the modern context as it is dissimilar to other forms of political violence. His pattern of revolution is based on two variables: the nature of pre-revolutionary society; and the nature of pre-revolutionary regimes. Within the modern context, however, revolutions are once again limited to the modernizing societies within which political development has not accompanied the level of social and economic development.[91] Furthermore, the "great revolutions" have occurred either in centralized traditional monarchies, or in narrowly based military dictatorships or in colonial regimes.[92]

Huntington proposes a two-fold typology of revolution as the western and the eastern. Some of the salient differences between the two types of revolution are as follows:

(*a*) In the western version of revolution the existing political institutions collapse, and the participation of new groups in politics creates new political institutions; whereas, in the eastern version, a revolution starts with the participation of new groups in politics and the establishment of new political institutions, and then is followed by the destruction of traditional political institutions.

(*b*) Another distinction is that in the western context there is a period of anarchy following a revolution marked by a struggle for power. The eastern revolution, on the other hand, is characterized by a period of "dual power" during which the revolutionaries expand their power and authority while the government continues to exercise its authority in some parts.

(*c*) In the western pattern the struggle is concentrated among several revolutionary groups, whereas in the eastern revolution the struggle is polarized between one revolutionary group and the government.

(*d*) The western revolution gains ground in the urban centres and then exerts its power in the countryside. In the eastern revolution control of the countryside occurs before the revolutionary movement seizes the centres of power.

(*e*) The western revolution overthrows a weak, traditional regime. The eastern revolution, on the contrary, is directed against a regime which has been exposed to modernization but is only partially modernized, yet is strong enough that it can only be overthrown by a prolonged rural insurrectionary process.[93]

The pattern of revolution having been discussed, it is relevant to identify the social forces participating in a revolution. A revolution not only requires political institutions which are incapable of accommodating the expansion of political participation, and which thus provide the additional impetus for social forces seeking such an expansion. Huntington identifies two such forces: the peasantry and the urban middle class.[94] A revolutionary peasantry is a necessary precondition for a revolutionary overthrow. Huntington notes that: "each of the major revolutions in western as well as non-western societies was in large part a peasant revolution". This was as true in France and Russia as it was in China.[95] It is the urban middle class, however, which provides the leadership and is the "true revolutionary class in most modernizing societies".[96] The alienation of the urban middle-class intelligentsia is not a product of physical suffering. Rather it is an opposition which stems from purely psychological factors such as insecurity, personal alienation and guilt, and an overriding need for a secure sense of identity.[97]

Thus, revolutions are won by a coalition of social forces in which the peasants and the middle class are significant players.

Charles Tilly, in analysing the theory of social change, mobilization and political institutionalization, finds that the theory offers a "plausible" explanation of revolution, government instability and collective violence in the poorer countries. The explanation is found to be plausible in the sense that it ignores the fact that relatively peaceful countries are also subject to more rapid changes. Modernization can cause disintegration but there is no assured evidence that political violence and revolution are an integral part of social change.[98] Tilly, who criticizes Huntington's theory, nevertheless finds that the theory sums up most of the relevant aspects relating to revolution and large-scale structural change. As Huntington draws from a wide range of contemporary and historical material, the variables are apt to suggest why the theory of modernization is considered important to the study of political violence.

According to Tilly, there are several factors which distinguish Huntington's theory. First, Huntington's combined application of three factors namely, rapid social change, mobilization and political institutionalization explains stability and instability, whereas other theorists have applied these factors separately. As a result Huntington's theory provides an acceptable explanation for the concentration of violence in the poorer countries of the world.[99] Finally, Tilly finds that Huntington's departure from psychological variables and the pursuit of explaining "why, when and how" men become discontented is his most valuable contribution to the study of revolution.

Tilly finds Huntington's contention, that the degree of instability is linked to the degree of modernization, an invalid or arguable observation as the suggested evidence is questionable. Huntington's examples of modernizing states are either based on the short-term experiences of the existing governments or deal with their support to destructive political movements. What is necessary to validate such an argument is information on the experiences and degree of "social and economic modernization" in the same states over the long term. Tilly points out, that similar studies have sometimes revealed contrary experiences.[100] The nexus between political instability and modernization becomes vague as the theory develops. The political impact of modernization thus remains ambiguous due to the theoretical weaknesses inherent in the models of social mobilization, political participation and levels of institutionalization.[101]

Huntington contends that modernization generates corruption because traditional norms and values are undermined by rapid social and economic change. Huntington concludes: "hence, the society which has a high capacity for corruption also has a high capacity for violence".[102] This argument, however, has been refuted by Claude Ake, who maintains that modernization cannot be said to increase corruption merely by altering the criterion of what constitutes corruption. The alteration of the criterion could conceivably decrease corruption.[103]

Having discussed some of these theoretical weaknesses, it becomes necessary to focus on Huntington's conceptualization of revolution. His concept of revolution is limited to a great extent to those revolutions which brought about rapid societal transformations. By virtue of his definition, he stresses the importance of fundamental changes in society. In this context, struggles for independence is excluded from his definition, because they are focused on a struggle between different ethnic groups and do not always result in a "rapid" and violent" change in the social structure.

Another aspect of this theory, which highlights its weakness, is the identification of social forces participating in a revolution and the unification of forces. The social forces are clearly defined as the urban middle class and the peasantry. Huntington fails, however, to provide data on the process of social mobilization and the time frame for forming a coalition, which could also vary by type.[104]

Furthermore, his assumption of a clear cut urban-rural dichotomy seems unrealistically simple given the complex nature of the political, social and economic relations between the two sectors. The weakness in this broad urban-rural dichotomy lies in the limited focus on political relations between the urban and the rural sectors, while completely ignoring the economic and social relations which, the author contends, are equally important in determining the level of political participation. The relationship between the urban and the rural sectors in some Third World countries, such as Sri Lanka, is much more complex than is suggested in Huntington's analysis. This is due to other cleavages such as class and other stratifications based on economic relations.[105] For instance, in Sri Lanka, the armed uprising of 1971 was launched mainly by the rural youth who were frustrated over the lack of socio-economic and political opportunities available to them. Their degree of frustration, however, was not shared by the peasantry in general or by the urban middle class. Hence, the generalization of a broad urban-rural dichotomy seems unrealistic considering the disparities between and within the two sectors.

As an overall theory, Huntington fails to predict the development of a revolution prior to its occurrence. Huntington's theory of political modernization, like other theories, has been adjudged as weak in many respects as a theoretical approach to the study of political violence in the Third World countries.

The Analytical Model

The study of political violence in Sri Lanka requires an interdisciplinary approach if a deeper understanding is to be attained. Of the theories already discussed in this chapter, Huntington's theory of modernization is more relevant to the examination of the socio-economic and political changes which have contributed to the origin of political violence movements in Sri Lanka. Huntington's "supposed macro" politico-economic approach, however, is subject to modification because he fails to address all pertinent aspects of the problem of political violence. Therefore, for the subsequent discussion of political violence in Sri Lanka the author proposes the following aspects as an analytical framework:

(1) the preconditions of political violence, namely the long-term socio-economic and political factors which gave birth to the political violence movements;

(2) the origin and nature of political violence movements, and the socio-economic background of the members and leaders;

(3) the ideologies and strategies of the guerrilla groups;

(4) the precipitants or short-term causes of political violence; and

(5) the response of the successive Sri Lankan governments and the extent of international involvement.

Summary

The above discussion indicates three main factors regarding the literature on political violence. The first is that there is no general agreement on the definition of the subject. This leads one to conclude that political violence is a very broad phenomenon that is applied to all kinds of politically-motivated violent acts. Thus, political violence is used as a term for events variously labeled as riots, rebellion, internal wars, turmoil, revolution, insurrection and political terrorism. It will not be the task of this study, however, to provide a generally agreed definition which covers all aspects of political violence. Therefore, the study will examine political violence as pre-planned armed attacks by organized groups to capture or change political power in a domestic political context.

Likewise, the above discussion indicates two main factors regarding the literature on typologies of political violence. The first is that there is no definite criterion for the classification of typologies of political violence. Therefore, each author has his own classificatory scheme and set of terminology to explain the same process or processes. The second factor is that most typologies are developed on the basis of one or more of the following attributes: objectives, type of society, type of regime, participants, geographical distribution, intensity and forms of organization. Among these factors, a predominant amount of emphasis is based on the variables of "objective" and "class". Although, a number of important aspects have been introduced, a precise typology is yet to come.

Finally, there is no comprehensive and generally agreed theory of political violence.

Nevertheless, the theories which are discussed in this study are the important and leading theories in this area of study, and provide valuable insights towards the understanding of political violence. Several empirical, methodological, and conceptual problems, however, were noted. Hence, the author focuses on the following aspects in order to examine the political violence in Sri Lanka: the preconditions of political violence, forms of organizations, socio-economic backgrounds of guerrillas, ideologies and strategies of guerrilla groups, government response and international involvement.

This chapter concludes the review of the major theories on political violence, and proposes an analytical framework, which will be utilized in the subsequent chapters of this study. The following third and fourth chapters examine the preconditions of political violence in Sri Lanka which is a case study in this context.

References

1. P. Wilkinson, *Terrorism and Liberal State,* (London: Macmillan, 1986), p. 31.
2. Harry Eckstein, "Theoretical Apyproaaches to Explaining Collective Political Violence", in Ted Robert Gurr, ed. *Hand Book of Political Conflict: Theory and Research,* (New York: The Free Press, 1980), pp. 136-137.
3. Harry Eckstein, "On the Etiology of Internal Wars", *History and Theory,* Vol. 4, No. 2, (1965), p. 133.
4. Perez Zagorin, "Theories of Revolution in Contemporary Historigraphy", *Political Science Quarterly,* Vol. 88, (1973), p. 27.
5. H.L. Nieburg, *Political Violence: The Behavioural Process,* (New York: St. Martin's Press, 1969), p. 13.
6. Perry Mars, "The Nature of Political Violence", *Social and Economic Studies,* Vol. 24, (1975), p. 228.
7. S.P. Huntington, *Political Order in Changing Societies,* (New Heaven: Yale University Press, 1968), p. 264.
8. Perez Zagorin, *op. cit.,* p. 28.
9. Chalmers Johnson, *Revolution and the Social System,* (Standford: The Hoover Institution on War, Revolution and Peace 1964), pp. 4-6.
10. Lawrence Stone, "Theories of Revolution", *World Politics,* Vol. 18, 1966, p. 160.
11. Ted Robert Gurr, *Why Men Rebel,* (Princeton: Princeton University Press, 1970), pp. 3-4.
12. Crane Brinton, *The Anatomy of Revolution,* (Englewood Cliffs N.J.: Prentice Hall, 1938); Lyford P. Edwards, The Natural History of Revolution, (Chicago: University of Chicago Press, 1927).
13. Theda Skocpol, *States and Social Revolutions,* (Cambridge: Cambridge University Press, 1979).
14. Jack A. Goldstone, "Theories of Revolution: The Third Generation", *World Politics,* Vol. 32, No. 2, (April 1980), pp. 425-453.
15. Chalmers Johnson, *Revolutionary Change,* (Boston: Little Brown, 1966), p. 8.

16 *Ibid.,* p. 3.

17. *Ibid.,* p. 57.

18. *Ibid.*, pp. 67-72.
19. *Ibid.*, p. 91.
20. *Ibid.*, p. 91.
21. *Ibid.*,
22. *Ibid.*
23. *Ibid.*, pp. 96-97.
24. *Ibid.*, p. 94.
25. *Ibid.*
26. *Ibid.*, p. 99.
27. A.C. Cohan, *Theories of Revolution: An Introduction,* (London: Nelson, 1975), p. 128.
28. Chalmers Johnson, *Revolution and Social System,* Hoover Institute Studies, 3, (Stanford University, 1964), pp. 27-28.
29. *Ibid.*, p. 28.
30. *Ibid.*, pp. 34-57.
31. *Ibid.*, p. 30.
32. Chalmers Johnson, *Revolutionary Change, op. cit.,* (1966), p. 132.
33. James C. Davies, "Toward a Theory of Revolution", in James C. Davies, (ed), *When Men Revolt and Why: A Reader in Political Violence and Revolutions,* (New York: The Free Press, 1972), p. 136.
34. See, Appendix 2.
35. James C. Davies, *op. cit.,* p. 136.
36. James C. Davies, "Circumstances and Causes of Revolution: A Review", *Journal of Conflict Resolution,* Vol. 11, (1967), p. 255.
37. James C. Davies, "Toward a Theory of Revolution", *op. cit.,* p. 136.
38. James C. Davies, "The J-curve of Rising and Declining Satisfactions as a Cause of Revolutions and Rebellion", in Hugh Davies Graham and Ted Robert Gurr, (eds), *Violence in America: Historical and Comparative Perspectives,* (Beverly Hills: Sage Publications, 1979), p. 415.
39. *Ibid.*, p. 416.
40. *Ibid.*, p. 418
41. See, Appendix 3.

42. Raymond Tanter and Manus Midlarsky, "A theory of Revolution", *Journal of Conflict Resolution,* Vol. 11, (1967), pp. 263-280.

43. According to Davies the same technique had been applied in Germany during and after the blockade of 1948. The results had indicated a sense of security which was lacking earlier. James C. Davies, "Toward a Theory of Revolution", 1971, p. 146.

44. Elections have always been marred by a few acts of violence since Sri Lnkan independence in 1948. From 1965 the pattern of electoral violence changed and assumed a form of systematic organized political revenge. Since 1970 the violence had spread to most parts of the country and had escalated in intensity. The violence often led to grave crimes, including looting, arson, destruction of property and even rape and murder.

45. James C. Davies, "The J-curve of Rising and Declining Satisfaction as a Cause of Some Great Revolutions and a Contained Rebellion", in Graham and Gurr, (eds), *Violence in America,* 1979, p. 418.

46. Ekkart Zimmermann, *Political Violence, Crises, and Revolutions: Theories and Research,* (Cambridge: Schenkman, 1983), p. 362.

47. James C. Davies, "Comments: The J-curve and Power Struggle Theories of Collective Violence", *American Sociological Review,* Vol. 39, (1974), p. 609.

48. Rod Aya, "Theories of Revolution Considered", *Theory and Society,* Vol. 7, (1979), pp. 53-54.

49. For Mexican Revolution see: Eric R. Wolf, *Peasant Wars of the Twentieth Century,* (London: Faber and Faber, 1971), pp. 3-50.

50. Harry Eckstein, "Theoretical Approaches to Explaining Collective Political Violence" in T.R. Gurr, (ed), *Handbook of Political Conflict,* 1980, p. 158.

51. Ted Robert Gurr, *Why Men Rebel, op. cit.,* (1970), p. 48.

52. *Ibid.,* p. 24.

53. *Ibid.,* p. 25.

54. *Ibid.,* pp. 25-26.

55. *Ibid.,* p. 59.

56. Faye Crosby, "Relative Deprivation Revisited: A Response to Miller, Bolce, and Halligam", *American Political Science Review,* Vol. 73, (1979), p. 107.
57. *Ibid.,* pp. 46-47.
58. *Ibid.,* pp. 50-52.
59. *Ibid.,* pp. 52-56.
60. Ted Robert Gurr, "A Causal Model of Civil Strife: A Comparative Analysis Using New Indices", *American Political Science Review,* Vol. 62, (1968), p. 1110,
61. *Ibid.,* p. 1111.
62. *Ibid.,* p. 1105.
63. Ted Robert Gurr, *Why Men Rebel, op. cit.,* (1970), p. 232.
64. Ted Robert Gurr, "A Causal Model of Civil Strife: A Comparative Analysis Using New Indices", *The American Political Science Review* Vol. 62, (1968), p. 1105.
65. *Ibid.,* p. 1106.
66. *Ibid.*
67. *Ibid.,* p. 1107.
68. *Ibid.,* p. 1108.
69. *Ibid.,* pp. 1116-1117.
70. *Ibid.,* p. 1120.
71. *Ibid.,* p. 1124.
72. Ted Robert Gurr, *Why Men Rebel, op. cit.,* (1970), p. 11.
73. *Ibid.,* p. 11.
74. Charles Tilly, "Review of Why Men Rebel by Ted Robert Gurr", *Journal of Social History,* Vol. 4, (1971), p. 418.
75. *Ibid.,* p. 418.
76. *Ibid.,* p. 419.
77. *Ibid.,* p. 420.
78. Paul Wilkinson, "Social Scientific Theory and Civil Violence", in Y. Alexander, D. Carlton, and P. Wilkinson, (eds), *Terrorism: Theory and Practice,* (Colorado: Westview Press, 1979), p. 59.
79. *Ibid.,* p. 59.
80. A.C. Cohan, *op. cit.,* p. 231.
81. Peter Abell, and Robin Jenkins, "Why do Men Rebel? A Discussion of Ted Robert Gurr's 'Why Men Rebel'", *Race,* Vol. 13, (1971), pp. 89-92.

82. Terry Nadin, "Violence and the State : A Critique of Empirical Political Theory", *Sage Professional Papers in Comparative Politics,* (Beverly Hills: Sage, 1971, pp. 20-25.
83. Samuel P. Huntington, *Political Order in Changing Societies, op. cit.,* (1968), p. 3.
84. *Ibid.,* p. 4.
85. *Ibid.,* p. 32.
86. *Ibid.,* p. 33.
87. *Ibid.,* p. 5.
88. *Ibid.,* p. 47.
89. *Ibid.,* p. 49.
90. *Ibid.,* pp. 49-50.
91. *Ibid.,* p. 265.
92. *Ibid.,* p. 275.
93. *Ibid.,* pp. 266-273.
94. *Ibid.,* p. 276.
95. *Ibid.,* p. 293.
96. *Ibid.,* p. 289.
97. *Ibid.,* p. 371.
98. Charles Tilly, "Does Modernisation Breed Revolution?", *Comparative Politics,* Vol. 5, (1973), p. 431.
99. *Ibid.,* p. 431.
100. *Ibid.,* p. 432.
101. *Ibid.,* p. 434.
102. Samuel P. Huntington, *Political Order In Changing Societies, op. cit.,* (1968), p. 63.
103. Claude Ake, "Modernisation and Political Instability: A theoretical Exploration", *World Politics,* Vol. 26, (1974), pp. 580-581.
104. Ekkart Zimmermann, *Political Violence, Crises and Revolutions: Theories and Research, op. cit.,* (1983), p. 323.
105. *Ibid.,* p. 324.

3

Preconditions of Political Violence in Sri Lanka: The 1971 Insurrection

Introduction

The conditions of political violence are multiple and complex. Harry Eckstein makes a distinction between preconditions and precipitants.[1] Preconditions of political violence are long-term socio-economic and political factors that generate discontent and pave the way to the creation of violent organizations. Precipitants are short-term factors that ignite political violence. The main objective of this chapter is to examine the long-term socio-economic and political factors, which serve as preconditions for the origin of political violence movements (P.V.M.) in Sri Lanka. S.P. Huntington claims that by the 1960s every Third World nation was subject to the process of modernization and that the causes of political violence in these states lay within this process.[2] Therefore, of the theories discussed in Chapter 2, Huntington's theory of modernization is particularly relevant to the preconditions of the political violence movements in Sri Lanka.

Chapter 3 is an examination of the factors which led to the political violence movements involved in the insurrection of 1971, while Chapter 4 will be devoted to the factors which caused the political violence movements in the Sri Lankan Tamil community. In order to examine the preconditions of political violence in 1971, this chapter is separated into the following sections: colonial impact, economic change, industrialization and employment, peasant agriculture, internal migration, social mobilization, growth of population and urbanization, educational expansion, literacy and the mass media, expectations and aspirations, economic development, unemployment and underemployment, political modernization, ruralisation of elections, political participation and development, the political party system, and left-wing parties. The socio-economic and political changes are not of recent origin but have had a long gestation period dating back to colonialism. Therefore, this study is prefaced by a brief historical introduction to the colonial period.

The Impact of the Colonial Period

Sri Lanka has a long history of colonialism under three major European powers: the Portuguese, the Dutch, and finally the British. The Portuguese annexed parts of the maritime region to their colonial empire since their arrival in 1505. However, the annexure of the maritime regions was in phases as there was strong resistance from the successive kings of Sri Lanka. The Portuguese ruled the Maritime Provinces until the Dutch took control of those provinces in 1654. The Portuguese and the Dutch ruled the same territories for nearly three hundred years with only minor disruptions to the traditional native system. It was the British who brought about major changes in the socio-economic and political structure of the country when they captured first the maritime areas in 1796, and then the entire country in 1815. The British during the 150 years of their rule succeeded in gradually changing the traditional native system and introducing modern socio-economic and a political system.

During the 19th Century, however, the British were also primarily intent on accumulating wealth and collecting revenue as their predecessors had done. Since the changes did not come into effect until 1833, the pre-colonial, socio-economic structure was retained until then.[3] It was not until the 1830s that the need arose to abolish the prevailing feudal structure in order to pave the way for a capitalist mode of production, which entails a modernization of the economy. The development of a capitalist system within the framework of a feudal system, and the subsequent destruction of the feudal system, necessitated the creation of a process of basic capital accumulation, the formation of a labour class from the peasantry, and avenues for money and means of production to be concentrated among a limited number of people in the society. With these aims in view, measures were taken to create certain changes and reforms.

The Colebrooke-Cameron Commission of 1829 was appointed by the British Government to investigate the prevailing socio-economic and political system in Sri Lanka and to recommend appropriate reforms accordingly. After thorough investigation, the Commission submitted recommendations, which extended to all aspects of the Sri Lankan socio-economic and political system. Some of the salient recommendations which were implemented included: the formal abolition of the system of "rajakariya" or service tenure, the placement of the whole country under a unified administrative and political system, the setting up of Executive and Legislative Councils, the unification of the judicial system under the control of the Supreme Court, and the introduction of English as the medium of education.[4]

The Colebrooke-Cameron Reforms marked the beginning of a process of socio-economic and political modernization in Sri Lanka. It was the first well-integrated attempt to develop an infra-structure for capitalist economic development and was perceived as the "dividing line between the past and present".[5] The economy was thereby restructured to create the necessary framework for the introduction of the plantation economy.

The Economic Change

The introduction of the export-import oriented economy was based at first on the coffee plantations. The eventual failure of the coffee plantations, however, rendered it necessary to concentrate on tea, rubber and coconut, which were potentially more profitable. The cultivation of such large-scale plantation crops necessitated the extensive availability of land. It was for this specific purpose the colonial government introduced the Crown Lands Encroachment Ordinance No. 12 in 1840. This law declared "all forest, chena, unoccupied or uncultivated lands to be Crown lands until the contrary was proved".[6] Thus, the purpose of enacting the Crown Lands Ordinance was to evict the peasants from their hereditary land and turn them into wage labourers. This measure facilitated the annexing of the peasant lands to the plantation economy. The onus of proving ownership of the lands was placed on the peasantry, the majority of whom could hardly do so. Thus the "chena" (shifting cultivation) lands on which "slash and burn" cultivation had been practiced for centuries became the property of the Crown. These Crown lands were subsequently sold to the coffee planters at nominal rates. It is estimated that between 1833 and 1843 approximately 258,042 acres of Crown land were sold.[7] In the period 1833-1939 two and half million acres of Crown land were sold to private individuals.[8] The land which was vital to the plantation economy was made available by the British colonial government while the necessary capital was provided by private companies.

The success of the plantation economy depended to a great extent on the availability of wage labour. The Colbrooke Reforms of 1833 formally abolished the system of "rajakariya" or service tenure in anticipation of the creation of a new wage labour force from among the Sinhala peasantry.[9] The wide sweeping measures to evict the peasants from their lands succeeded, but the intention of converting them to a wage labour force was far from fulfilled. This failure is largely attributed to the fact that the indigenous peasantry was averse to wage employment.[10] S.B. de Silva highlights the operation of other extraneous factors which deterred the peasantry from responding positively to wage labour. Low wages, accompanied by the infrequency of wage payments, was further aggravated by the exploitation of the peasantry by "kanganies" (foremen) and traders. In other words, the plantation system was not attractive as an alternative livelihood for the peasants.[11]

There is no common consensus among scholars regarding the factors which prevented the peasants from being absorbed into the labour force. It is evident, however, that the British Raj was unsuccessful in creating a wage labour force from among the peasantry. This trend left the British colonial government with one other alternative and that was to import labour from Southern India. Beginning with about 3,000 workers in 1839, the process of importing labour grew steadily and in 1844 there were about 77,000 immigrant labourers in Sri Lanka. During the two decades thereafter, the average rate of net importation of immigrant labour rose to over 5,000 per year. In 1891, the total immigrant labour force had reached 235,000, which increased to 500,000 by 1921. By the pre-independence year of 1931 there were 700,000 immigrant plantation workers in Sri Lanka.[12] According to W.H. Wriggins, the immigrant labour force and their families comprised 10 per cent of Sri Lankas' total population in 1953.[13]

The colonial government evidently took every possible measure to provide incentives for the growth and expansion of the plantation sector. From about 1835, large scale coffee plantations were cultivated in the hinterland of Sri Lanka. The coffee plantations flourished for about 40 years until about 1870, when a leaf disease began to destroy the crops and coffee declined in importance as a plantation crop. The colonial planters, however, were dauntless. They soon replaced coffee with tea, rubber and coconut, which in that order of importance, continued to dominate the plantation economy far into the future. By the latter half of the 19th century, plantation agriculture was firmly rooted as the backbone of the country's economy and of the capitalist mode of production.

Industrialization and Employment

Although industrialization is usually an important variable in the process of economic modernization, it has little or no bearing on the modernization process in Sri Lanka. Prior to independence there was no industrial sector beyond those activities related to the plantation economy. A few important factories were established in the private sector before 1939, which consisted of a cotton mill, a tile works, two match factories, two distilleries and a few engineering work shops. Until 1959, however, there was no concerted drive towards industrialization.[14]

Plantation agriculture was accompanied by the development of transport and communication networks. Over and above this, the introduction of the English educational system saw the emergence of an English-educated middle class which was comprised mainly of lawyers, doctors, merchants, contractors, and transport agents. Although Sri Lanka remained basically an agricultural country, Table 3.1 indicates that approximately half of the gainfully employed population composed of the non-agricultural labour force.

As Table 3.1 shows between 1921 and 1971, the percentage of the gainfully employed people engaged in agriculture, forestry, fishing and similar pursuits declined from 62.4 to 49.4 percent. In the same period, non-agricultural employment rose from 37.7 to 50.4 percent. Furthermore, about two-thirds of all gainfully employed persons, including more than 80 per cent of those engaged in agriculture and related pursuits, were paid workers.[15] The proportion of the workforce engaged mainly in agriculture has declined slowly: 53 per cent in 1953, 50 per cent in 1971 and 46 per cent in 1980-81.[16]

Table 3.1: Gainfully Employed Population by Major Occupational Groups (%)

Occupation	*1921*	*1946*	*1968*	*1971*
Agricultural, forestry, fishermen, hunters, etc.	62.4	52.9	51.6	49.6
Craftsmen, production process, transport and communications workers	15.1	13.5	23.0	24.4
Sales and clerical workers	6.8	7.9	10.4	12.9
Service and recreation workers	6.5	9.0	8.2	5.4
Professional, technical, managerial and related workers	2.1	2.9	5.5	5.2
Others and unspecified	7.2	13.6	1.3	2.5

Source: Department of Census and Statistics, *Ceylon Year Book 1950*, (Colombo: Government Press, 1951), p. 221; Department of Census and Statistics, *Statistical Pocket Book of Ceylon 1970*, (Colombo: Department of Government Printing, 1971), p. 38; and Department of Census and Statistics, *Statistical Pocket Book of the Republic of Sri Lanka, 1973*, (Colombo: Department of Government Printing, 1974), p. 26.

It is obvious that economic development in Sri Lanka occurred at the expense of the agrarian society. This economic process not only integrated Sri Lanka into the complex network of the global economy but also exposed its economy to the vagaries of the international market.

Peasant Agriculture

The profound economic changes in Sri Lanka, as described above, had adverse effects on the agrarian sector especially on the independent peasant farmer. Traditional agriculture was neglected as the plantations received widespread attention. The technical modernization of the 19th century was confined to the plantations, whereas the technology of production in paddy cultivation remained backward and stagnant. The existence of two systems of agriculture within the agrarian sector marked the transformation of a feudal agricultural economy to a dual economy. S. Ponnambalam observes this situation as follows:

> By the time coffee collapsed in the 1880s, there had emerged in the country a dual economy. One was a highly developed, organized, foreign-owned, capitalistic plantation economy producing for export in the central Highlands. The other was a tradition-bound, primitive, self sufficing, subsistence peasant economy producing for domestic consumption in the remainder of the wet and dry zone areas of the country.[17]

Under the colonial regime of the 19th century, it was also evident that different policies were being applied both to the foreign-owned export-oriented plantation sector and to the peasant sector which concentrated on production for domestic consumption. As K.M. de Silva concludes:

> The attitude to many problems of peasant agriculture can only be described as unimaginative, and misguided when not hard-hearted.[18]

When considered in retrospect, the economic modernization policies applied by the British in Sri Lanka during the colonial period had long-lasting effects on the country's peasant, economy which was gradually reduced to a state of underdevelopment and impoverishment. As S.B. de Silva sees it, the peasant economy settled at a lower equilibrium with a more impoverished peasantry.[19] The eviction of the peasantry from their lands generated the problems of landlessness and land fragmentation. Landlessness was a problem with many facets, of which the most important was the inability of many peasant families to get access to irrigated paddy land and the highlands for shifting cultivation.[20] The land cultivated by the peasants was limited in extent, the soil was infertile, and the technology of production was primitive. By the end of the British colonial period, the phenomenon of landlessness had become the main feature of the agrarian question. These conditions further deteriorated with the free importation of rice from abroad to serve plantation interests, thus reducing the number of profitable crops within Sri Lanka.

The peasants in turn had to depend almost entirely on the self-sufficient economy prevailing in the lands held by the landowners. This system reduced the peasant to the status of a sharecropper. Table 3.2, which compares the cultivated acreage with the peasant population per acre, indicates the limited extent of land available to the peasantry in Sri Lanka between 1871and1959.

Table 3.2. Estimated Cultivated Land and Population in the Peasant Agricultural Sector, 1871-1959

Year	*Cultivated Peasant Land*	*Annual growth rate since previous year*	*Peasant population (000s)*	*Annual growth rate since previous year*	*Peasant population per acre*
1871	954	—	1,831	—	1.9
1881	1,092	1.4	1,996	0.9	1.8
1891	1,243	1.3	2,219	1.9	1.8
1901	1,370	1.0	2,541	1.1	1.9
1911	1,544	1.2	2,818	1.0	1.8
1921	1,676	0.8	3,051	0.8	1.8
1931	1,809	0.8	3,941	2.5	2.2
1946	2,076	0.9	4,941	1.6	2.4
1953	2,206	0.9	6,044	2.9	2.7
1959	2,351	1.1	7,297	3.2	3.1

Source: Donald Snodgrass, *Ceylon: An Export Economy in Transition,* (Illinois: Richard D. Irwin, 1966), p. 48.

Surveys conducted on land distribution found that a high percentage of the peasantry were landless or owned marginal plots. A survey of eight districts during 1936-1938 found that landlessness among rural families was about 44 per cent.[21] In four districts, landlessness ranged from 50 to 56 per cent of all families. Surveys on landlessness carried out in 1950-51 found that 38 per cent of all families in the rural sector were landless.[22] Table 3.3 indicates the ownership of land by the size of holdings in Sri Lanka in the 1950s.

Table 3.3. Ownership of Land by Size of Holding (percentages)

Extent of Land (acres)	*Agricultural Families*	*Non-agricultural Families*	*Total*
No. land	26.3	45.1	37.7
Less than ½	16.0	25.3	21.6
½ 1	11.8	11.0	11.3
1 - 2	15.0	9.0	11.0
2 - 3	9.1	3.9	5.9
3 - 4	6.0	2.0	3.5
4 - 5	4.2	1.3	2.5
5 - 10	7.4	1.6	4.4
10 - 15	2.4	0.4	1.2
15 - 20	0.7	0.1	0.3
20 and over	1.1	0.3	0.6

Source: Department of Census and Statistics, Census of Ceylon, 1952, quoted from P. Wickramasekara, *op. cit.*, p. 9.

Agricultural land was further encumbered by a high incidence of onerous forms of tenancy and joint-ownership systems such as "thattumaru" (rotation of ownership) and "kattimaru" (rotation of plots). The prevailing share-cropping (ande-tenure) arrangement for paddy lands was quite oppressive as it entailed insecurity due to high rentals. This system of tenure on paddy parcels is displayed in Table 3.4. In the case of Sri Lanka, it is important to weigh land inequality by size of agricultural labour force and type of ownership because, as Huntington observes, in countries which have reached a high level of economic development, agriculture has a relatively minor role, and consequently even highly inequitable patterns of land ownership do not pose substantial problems of social equality and political stability.[23]

Table 3.4. The System of Tenure on Paddy Cultivation

System of Cultivation	*Per Cent of all Parcels*	
	1946	*1955*
Owner Cultivated	60.8	55.0
Share-cropped	25.9	28.7
Leased	3.6	13.7
Tattumaru	6.8	2.6
Others	2.9	-

Source: Department of Census and Statistics, *Census of Ceylon,* 1946, 1955.

It may be inferred then from Huntington's statement that an examination of land ownership in Sri Lanka is pertinent if not vital to a thorough review of the agrarian issues.

This process of paddy agriculture, set in motion by the British during the 19th Century, continued to make an impact on Sri Lanka's agriculture well into the 20th Century. Thus, on the eve of political independence in 1948, Sri Lanka was in a state of underdevelopment, characterized by a highly dependent economy with a narrow range of primary commodities. The primary products were tea, rubber and coconut, to which a major portion of the previous agrarian land was devoted. The ownership of these plantations was mainly monopolized by foreign-based sterling companies and British-owned rupee companies until the plantations were nationalized in 1972.[24] Indigenous agriculture was dominated by paddy cultivation and, therefore, was the most neglected aspect of the economy as it was limited to the growth of low profit secondary agricultural products. The acute land shortage aggravated the agrarian crisis in Sri Lanka.

The misery of the majority of the peasants was further aggravated by their large debts. According to a study conducted by the Ceylon Department of Census and Statistics in 1957, 54.3 per cent of the rural families and 60 per cent of the peasant families were in debt. The survey estimated the total indebtedness in the rural areas at Rs. 516 million or about Rs. 424 per rural family, a figure which at the time constituted about 34 per cent of annual income or 9 per cent of the value of property owned by each family.[25] Thus, a combination of factors reduced the peasantry to a marginal level of existence. Fragmented land holdings, primitive modes of production, high land rentals and low prices for products were some of the salient factors. Ivor Jennings summarises the situation as follows:

> In almost all the villages surveyed agriculture and its related industries provide a very low standard of living... The standard of living thus disclosed is so low that it is evident that a large majority of the people in the wet zone and the dry zone were permanently on the verge of starvation.[26]

The traditional forms of livelihood based on agriculture were thus no longer profitable and the rapid growth of the population limited the scope of expandable agricultural land.

Internal Migration

As a result of the country's well-developed transport network, internal migration was considerable. The only available data, however, concerns the state-sponsored resettlement movement. The problems of landlessness and land fragmentation were mainly concentrated in the wet zone. This rendered it necessary to draw up a programme of resettlement in the dry zone where land was available. The criterion adopted in selecting settlers gave preference to landless peasants in the congested wet zone. The programme of resettlement was initiated in 1928 with the Tabbowa Resettlement Scheme. The objective of peasant resettlement was to ease the pressure on land in the wet zone. By 1948, twelve schemes with 3,342 allottees and 26,737 acres had been colonized.[27] W.H. Wriggins claims that between 1945 and 1955 nearly 20,000 acres of dry zone land had been made available for cultivation and nearly 100,000 peasants had found new homes.[28] Peasant resettlement was stepped up after independence. The number of allottees increased to 16,532 with an acreage of 118,438 being assimilated by 1953.[29]

The rapid growth and expansion of the peasant resettlement schemes has been largely attributed to the virtual eradication of malaria which had been widespread, the rapid infrastructural development and deeper government commitment to the policy of resettlement. Village expansion schemes within the dry zone further contributed to easing the pressure on land in the wet zone.[30] The extensive resettlement schemes, however, were not a panacea for the agrarian problem within Sri Lanka. The tenurial problems, primitive technology and the inequalities of land distribution were not addressed by the resettlement programmes. It is indisputable that the settlement schemes succeeded in reducing the landless problem in the wet zone and to some extent prevented the generation of a landless peasantry. Yet within the resettlement schemes themselves, the availability of land did not coincide with population growth, and the problems of landlessness which were acute in the wet zone were reproduced in the dry zone settlements. Therefore, regardless of the intent behind the policies, the fact remains that there was little structural change in the Sri Lankan economy. S.P. Huntington observes that the inequality in the distribution of land ownership is among the more fundamental economic pre-conditions of insurgency and revolution:

> Where the conditions of land-ownership are equitable and provide a viable living for the peasant, revolution is unlikely. Where they are inequitable and where the peasant lives in poverty and suffering, revolution is likely, if not inevitable, unless the government takes prompt measures to remedy these conditions.[31]

In the 1950s, successive governments introduced tenancy reform laws. The first of these was the Paddy Lands Act of 1953 and later the Paddy Lands Act of 1958. Of the two acts the latter was a crucial piece of legislation as it concentrated on the insecurity of tenure and high rentals. The 1958 Act also made sharecropping (ande-tenure) permanent and inheritable. Furthermore, it made provision for the rents on land to be fixed at a maximum level of 25 per cent of the crop or at 12 bushels per acre. An island-wide network of village institutions called Cultivation Committees was created under the 1958 Act to function at village level and maintain the standards of cultivation. Prior to passage, however, the bill had been further amended in order to satisfy the more conservative groups within Parliament, thereby reducing the extent and depth of societal change which the 1958 Act, as proposed, had been intended to achieve.[32] These economic and technological changes led to social mobilization which is an aspect of the broader processes of modernization.

Social Mobilization

According to Karl W. Deutsch, 'social mobilization' is a name given to an overall process of change, within a substantial part of the population in countries which are moving from traditional to modern ways of life.[33] Social mobilization as it occurred in Sri Lanka will be examined under the following headings: growth of population and urbanization, educational expansion, and literacy, and the mass media.

Growth of Population and Urbanization

The rapid growth of population in Sri Lanka was the most significant development following the Second World War. This was attributed to the high fertility rate and the declining death rate brought about mainly by the expansion of health and welfare facilities. The following Table 3.5 indicates the historical changes in social statistics in Sri Lanka.

Table 3.5. Changing Social Statistics between 1946 and 1971

Social Statistics	*1946*	*1956*	*1960*	*1971*
Life expectancy in years	48	48	62	66
Infant mortality per 1000 live births	141	101	71	45
Maternal -do-	16	9	3	2
Birth rate per 1000 population	37	40	37	30
Death rate per 1000 population	20	14	9	8

Source: James Warner Bjorkman, "Health Policy and Politics in Sri Lanka: Development in the South Asian Welfare State", *Asian Survey,* Vol. 25, No. 5, (1985), p. 538.

The death rate per 1000 people dropped from 20 in 1946 to 14 in 1956. From then on the death rate gradually declined to 8 per 1,000 in 1971. On the other hand, the life expectancy at birth rose from 43 years in 1946 to 66 years in 1971. Consequently, as the following Table 3.6 indicates, the population growth within Sri Lanka increased rapidly from 1901 to 1971.

Table 3.6. Population Growth in Sri Lanka: 1901-1971 (in thousands)

Year	*Population*	*Year*	*Population*
1901	4,031	1946	7,122
1911	4,702	1953	8,290
1921	5,304	1963	10,641
1931	6,053	1971	12,748

Source: Gavin W. Jones and S. Selvarathnam, *Population Growth and Economic Development,* (Colombo: Hansa Fublishers Limited, 1971) p. 19.

What is evident from Table 3.6 is that the average annual rate of population growth for the period 1901 to 1946 was 1.3 per cent compared with the period 1946 to 1971 when it was 2.3 per cent. A noteworthy feature of this demographic expansion is the distribution of the population. Statistics on population growth reveal that a large proportion of the population was concentrated in the rural sector whereas the population growth in the urban sector was relatively slow. The following Table 3.7 is an illustration of the gap in urban and rural population distribution from 1946 to 1963.

Table 3.7. Population by Urban and Rural Sectors (in thousands)

Year	*Urban*	*Percent*	*Rural*	*Percent*
1946	1971	21.3	5244	78.7
1953	1751	21.6	6345	78.4
1963	2310	21.8	8276	78.2

Source: Department of Census and Statistics, Census of Ceylon, 1946, 1956 and 1963.

Table 3.7 shows a remarkably stable balance of population between the urban and rural sectors, with the rural sector retaining its substantial predominance over the urban sector in the period 1946-63. The limited growth in the urban population that took place is to be attributed mainly to natural increase within that sector rather than to migration from rural areas. Migration in Sri Lanka during this period was within the sector confined to migration from one rural area to another.

The slow expansion of urbanization is indicated in Table 3.8 given below which depicts the growth of towns in Sri Lanka by the size of population between 1946 and 1963. It is estimated that the number of towns with a population between 5,000 and 9,999 rose from 17 in 1946 to 23 in 1963, while the towns with a population of 20,000-49,000 increased from five in 1946 to 18 in 1963. It is obvious that Sri Lanka has experienced a slow rate of urbanization throughout the 20th century. This slow trend of population growth in the urban sector has been largely attributed to several factors.

Table 3.8. Growth of Towns in Sri Lanka by size of Population, 1946, 1953 and 1963 (in percentages)

Population	*1946*	*1953*	*1963*
2,000-5,000	24	20	21
5,000-9,999	17	13	23
10,000-19,000	12	21	21
20,000-49,000	5	6	18
50,000-99,000	4	6	5
1000,000 and over	1	1	2

Source: Gavin W. Jones and S. Selvarathnam, "Urbanisation in Ceylon: 1946-1963", *Modern Ceylon Studies,* Vol. 1, (1970), p. 201.

One of the main reasons cited is the lack of significant change in the economic structure which would otherwise have attracted a large segment of the rural population to the urban centres. Furthermore, the socio-economic policies adopted by successive governments accompanied by a concerted effort at social welfare prevented the rural population from moving to the urban sector.[34] Among these the state-sponsored peasant resettlement schemes and land settlement schemes which were concentrated in the dry zone resulted in a movement of the rural population.

Another significant phenomenon of the demographic scene was the high percentage of youth in Sri Lanka's population after the Second World War. Table 3.9 depicts the youth component of Sri Lanka's total population, and establishes that the total youth population aged 15 to 24 years increased rapidly from 1946 to 1971. In 1946, the number for those aged between 15 and 24 stood at 1.3 million but by 1971 it had doubled to 2.6 million. Hubert Muller views such a rapid escalation in the youth population as providing potential cadres for youth movements and revolts.[35]

Such a high proportion of youth in the demography of a country means that a large segment of the population requires access to education and employment. The provision of these is a burden which developing countries like Sri Lanka find it hard to bear.

Table 3.9. Age Distribution of Sri Lanka's Population (in thousands)

Years of Age	*1947*	*Per Cent*	*1971*	*Per Cent*
0-14	2478	32.2	4998	39.3
15-24	1322	19.8	2608	20.3
25-34	1027	15.5	1653	13.0
35-44	791	11.8	1304	10.3
45-54	516	7.7	970	7.8
55 and over	523	7.9	1181	9.3
Total	6657	100.0	12712	100.0

Source: Kearney, R.N., "Youth and Generational Cleavage in the Politics of Sri Lanka: Some Preliminary Observations". Unpublished typescript.

Educational Expansion

The rapid expansion of education within a framework of free education from primary school to university is another device for social modernization which has had a visible impact on political instability in Sri Lanka. The introduction of the Colebrooke reforms marked the beginning of a period of secularization of education and a process of gradual expansion. The formal educational system in pre-independence Sri Lanka was a two-tiered system based mainly on the English medium of instruction. The missionary-sponsored schools provided instruction in English for a fee, and were a way of gaining access to higher education and the professions. The non-fee levying schools, on the other hand, conducted education in local languages of Sinhala or Tamil and thus catered to a wider population. For a majority of youth this system offered a limited scope for upward mobility. The educational reforms of 1945 brought about revolutionary changes in the educational system and they had far-reaching results thereafter.[36]

The introduction of free education in 1945, with the setting up of a series of Central Schools on a regionally based electoral system, and the subsequent change over of the medium of instruction to the local languages in all schools, brought about a rapid expansion in opportunities for higher education.[37] From the perspective of the peasant population, the widening of avenues of education was welcome at a time when pressure on land was becoming more and more acute. The introduction of free education and the use of the vernacular or 'swabasha' languages were partly responsible for the expansion of enrolments in schools.

The period between 1945 and 1970 saw an escalation of primary and secondary school enrolments from about 867,000 to 2,716,000.[38] The expansion of primary and secondary education was followed by a rise in the number of university entrants. Until 1959 the medium of instruction of university education was English, so that the university education was confined to those who had attended the exclusive and expensive schools which concentrated on English education. These students were mainly of urban background. This trend was arrested by 1959, when universities were opened to students who needed instruction in the Sinhala and Tamil languages. In addition, the number of universities increased from one to four. Two of these universities were Buddhist seminaries ('pirivenas') which were elevated to the status of universities. The University College of Colombo was established as a separate university. The number of students seeking admission thus increased from 1,612 in 1948 to about 14,000 in 1970.[39] The lack of opportunity in the agrarian sector and greater scope of employment available to those with an education meant that the desire for education was the most important factor which influenced the thoughts, expectations and aspirations of the rural youth after independence in 1948. The educational reforms created a large student population from rural areas often with a continued marginal level of existence.

G.H. Peiris observes that due to the close links which existed between educational achievement at secondary and tertiary levels on the one hand and employment opportunities on the other, education functioned as a medium of social mobility.[40] The expansion of education, however, was not sufficiently organized and pre-planned to avoid major imbalances in intake and distribution. Instead of devising a system through which students could be evenly drawn from all fields of study, what was actually practiced was a lop-sided system of selection. In 1969, for example, 2,662 Social Science graduates graduated from the universities, while the output from the Science, Medicine, Engineering and Veterinary Sciences faculties were only 230, 205, 90 and 18 respectively. Ironically in a country with nearly 80 per cent of the population concentrated in the rural sector, there was only one agriculture graduate for every 100 liberal arts graduates.[41] The majority of the university students following the Social Sciences were young Sinhala-Buddhists from the rural areas. A survey conducted in 1967 indicates that 93 per cent of the students following courses in the Social Sciences and Humanities were Sinhala, compared to 47 per cent, 37 per cent, and 44 per cent of admissions in the faculties of Medicine and Dentistry, Agriculture and Veterinary Science, and Engineering, respectively.[42]

In addition, other studies have revealed that a majority of those who entered university to pursue studies in the Social Sciences and Humanities had received their primary and secondary education from Maha Vidyalayas (Government Colleges) and Madya Maha Vidyalayas (Central Colleges) which are based in the rural areas. Facilities to pursue studies in the Natural Sciences were not available in most rural-based schools. Hence, secondary education in these schools emphasized the Social Sciences which were taught in the vernacular or Swabasha (Mother-tongue Sinhala or Tamil). The failure of the government's attempts to develop science education in the rural areas was largely due to the lack of qualified teachers and laboratory facilities. There was no shortage of employment for those who were educated in the science-oriented courses.

Education and literacy kept expanding steadily after 1945. The generation which was reaching adulthood around 1970 had achieved significantly higher levels of educational attainment than the generations before them.[43] The differentials in educational levels between age groups in 1969/70 are indicated in the following Table 3.10.

According to the above Table, one-third of the population aged 45 and over had no schooling compared to over one-fourth who had completed middle school (tenth grade) or higher education. In contrast, less than one-twelfth of those aged 15-19 years and a similar fraction of those aged 20-24 years had no schooling. Within the 20-24 years age group, nearly 60 percent had attained a middle school or higher education.

Table 3.10. Educational Levels by Age Groups (1969/70) by Percentages

Educational Levels	*15-19 Years*	*20-24 Years*	*25-34 Years*	*35-44 Years*	*45 and over Years*
No schooling	6.8	8.2	12.8	21.5	33.3
Primary school	28.4	30.6	36.1	43.0	40.7
Middle school	56.5	40.8	34.9	26.9	21.2
Passed G.C.E.(O/L)	7.7	17.6	14.1	7.6	4.2
Passed G.C.E. (A/L) and Higher	0.6	2.8	2.1	1.0	0.6

Source: Department of Census and Statistics, Preliminary Report On the Socio-Economic Survey of Ceylon, 1969/70, (Colombo: Department of Census and Statistics, 1971), p. 10.

Literacy and the Mass Media

The statistics in the following Table 3.11 illustrate the expansion of literacy from 1881 to 1971. In 1901, 8.5 per cent of the female population aged 5 years and over were literate as compared to the male population of which 42 per cent were literate.[44] The figures for 1971, on the other hand, depict the growth of literacy to 70.7 per cent of females and 85.2 per cent of males aged 10 years and over.[45]

Table 3.11. Growth in Literacy Rate 1881-1971

Census Year	*All Persons*	*Males*	*Females*
1881	17.4	29.8	3.1
1891	21.7	36.1	5.3
1901	26.4	42.0	8.5
1911	31.0	47.2	12.5
1921	39.9	56.3	21.2
1946	57.8	70.1	43.8
1953	65.4	75.9	53.6
1963	71.9	79.4	63.8
1971	78.1	85.2	70.7

Source: Department of Census and Statistics, Statistical Abstract of Ceylon, 1967-1968, (Colombo: Department of Government Printing, 1970), p. 35; Department of Census and Statistics, Statistical Pocket Book of the Republic of Sri Lanka, 1973, (Colombo: Department of Government Printing, 1974), p. 15.

Furthermore, advancing social mobilization is obvious in the spread and coverage of the mass media. The number of licensed radio sets in Sri Lanka expanded from 10,000 in 1941 to 90,000 in 1954 and 405,000 in 1965.[46] By 1971 the number had surpassed 467,000.[47] Gurr perceives that expansion in literacy and education heightened expectations.[48] Moreover, Huntington argues, literates have higher aspirations and make more demands on government.[49]

3.11 Expectations and Aspirations

A similar tendency seems to be evident among the students from traditional peasant families who received a secondary education or higher and aspired to "White Collar" jobs which paid better salaries and were urban based. This development was identified by Denham as early as 1911 when he observed that:

> The younger generation seek escape from rural life, from manual toil, from work which they begin to regard as degrading, in an education which will enable them to pass examinations which will lead to posts in offices in the towns and so to appointments which entitle the holders to the respect of the class from which they believe they have emancipated themselves.[50]

The above observations sum up some of the aspirations of the educated rural youth. Furthermore, surveys conducted in this sphere revealed that youth who had completed secondary and higher education aspired for administrative, clerical or teaching jobs.[51] Table 3.12 further clarifies this point on the basis of job expectations of university students.

A survey among university students revealed that 87 percent desired public sector employment, 10 per cent private sector employment and 3 per cent self-employment.[52] Heightened expectations and aspirations seemed inevitable during the first decade of independence as education meant access to white collar employment. This tendency, however, was not to last long. Due to the limited availability of employment opportunities, the government's policy of expanding educational facilities generated a decline in the market value of education. Therefore, as Lloyd Fallers observes, in many of the newly independent states the educated underemployed or unemployed are more seriously alienated and politically disaffected than industrial workers.[53] By the mid 1960s, high expectations based on education began to decline and graduates qualifying in the Social Sciences especially in the Swabasha medium were disillusioned by the scarcity of suitable employment and low salaries. R.N. Kearney, explains the situation as follows:

> The broadening of opportunities for university education for the Sinhalese-Buddhist rural youth educated in the Sinhala language led to their crowding into the social studies and humanities curriculum, the graduates of which were in slight demand in the employment market.[54]

Education had previously proved to be a stepping stone to white-collar employment. Therefore, the young people who completed their education even after job opportunities had been narrowed continued to harbour the high expectations based on the previous experiences. A survey in 1968 found that 76 per cent of all those between the ages of 15 and 24 years who had completed the G.C.E. (O/L) and had not previously been employed sought white-collar jobs.[55] Moreover, a high demand for clerical employment among young people with secondary education was found in three separate surveys conducted between, 1968 to 1971.[56] Considering the nature and scope of the problems faced by the young people who were mainly from the agrarian rural sector, it becomes evident that a deep frustration seems to have been building up over a long period of time. R.N. Kearney points out that by the 1970s this frustration was far more intense among the Sinhala youth than it was among those belonging to the other ethnic groups in Sri Lanka.[57]

In broad terms educational expansion becomes dysfunctional only when the economy remains static and underdeveloped. As a result of high social mobilization, aspirations increased rapidly. Therefore, a high level of economic development is necessary to meet these high aspirations. According to Huntington, economic developments presumably increase the capacity of a society to satisfy those aspirations and, therefore, should tend to reduce social frustrations and the consequent political instability.[58] In order to understand this correlation it is necessary to examine economic development in Sri Lanka.

3.12 Economic Development

Sri Lanka's economy could be cited as being a classic example of an undeveloped dependant economy. The basis of the economy since the colonial period has been import-export oriented, first on coffee then on tea, rubber and coconut. During 1948-49, tea, rubber, and coconut contributed 90 per cent of the merchandise export earnings (63% from tea, 17% from rubber, and 10% from coconut). During 1971-72, the proportions were almost the same.[59] An economy so heavily dependent on export crops was also exposed to the instability and vagaries of the world market. As a result, during the Second World War and the Korean War, Sri Lanka accumulated large sterling balances. Between 1960 and 1970, however, the prices of tea and rubber, which were approximately 80 per cent of the export earnings, declined by 30 per cent and 40 per cent respectively. As a result after 1960, the decline in demand for raw materials produced in Sri Lanka lead to general economic deterioration.[60]

Both the prices of exports and imports were determined by external conditions and were subject to wide and unpredictable fluctuations. While Sri Lanka exported raw materials, it imported essential foodstuffs, consumer goods and capital items. While the income from exports declined, after 1960, import prices rose considerably. Consequently, after 1960 there was a growing balance of trade deficit. This deficit rose steadily from Rs. 95 million in 1965 to Rs. 328 million in 1966, and to Rs.627 million in 1969.[61] The immediate outcome of this trend was the expanding budget deficits. This fact was clearly indicated in the following Table 3.12.

Table 3.12. Sri Lanka's Budget Deficits From 1960 to 1970

Year	*Amount Rs / Ms*	*Year*	*Amount Rs / Ms*
1960-61	500	1965-66	682
1961-62	501	1966-67	723
1962-63	439	1967-68	850
1963-64	510	1968-69	947
1964-65	520	1969-70	1150

Source: Budget Speeches, 1960-1970.

The net result of this deteriorating economic trend was that the successive governments came to rely on more foreign loans and aid to finance the deficits. The dependency on foreign loans increased to such an extent that there was a crisis in the repayment of debts. Debt servicing began to become an intolerable burden, with 14 per cent of the total earnings for 1969 being utilized for this purpose.[62] According to statistics revealed by the Minister of Finance at his Budget Speech in 1970, Sri Lanka had obtained a total credit of Rs. 723.4 million from the International Monetary Fund (I.M.F.) between 1965 and 1970.[63] The direct results of a growing burden of debt were the devaluation of the local currency, the rupee, and the rise in the prices of most essential consumer goods, thereby increasing the cost of living. The cost of living index, which stood at 103.5 in 1960 and 121.5 in 1965 rose to 130.5 in 1970.[64] In addition, the growing tendency towards obtaining loans and aid from foreign countries and international financial institutions resulted in the increasing dependency of the country on external forces.

The declining economic conditions compelled the Sri Lankan Government to curtail expenditure on welfare services and subsidies. Among these subsidies the most politically significant was the rice subsidy which was cut back in November 1968. Furthermore, the worsening economic situation in the 1960s indicated the disparities of income distribution and the widespread poverty levels. A survey in 1963 indicated that 84.14 per cent of the workers received salaries between Rs. 25 and 200 a month, and that 45.9 per cent of the workers received incomes between Rs. 25 and Rs. 75 a month.[65] According to the socio-economic survey of 1969-70, about four-fifths of the population earned less than Rs. 200 and over a half received incomes of less than Rs. 100 per month.[66] A Central Bank survey in April 1972 revealed that over 9 million of the 12.8 million population received no income, and of the 3.5 million who had incomes, about half received monthly incomes ranging from Rs. 100 to 400, while the other half were paid less than Rs. 100[67] Only 175,000 of the population earned Rs. 400 a month. According to the World Bank report at the end of the 1970s, per capita incomes were still in the region of U.S. $230, and Sri Lanka remained among the poorest thirty-six low-income countries in the world.[68] Given these circumstances, Snodgrass concluded that opportunities for improvement were less favourable in the early 1970s than they had been 25 years before at independence.[69] The inability of economic innovation to meet the challenges posed by Sri Lanka's problems generated and fostered a sense of frustration particularly among the educated rural youth. The deteriorating and sometimes stagnant economy deprived the new generations the means of achieving their aspirations in keeping with their educational backgrounds. There was a rapid growth of the labour force without a correspondingly rapid expansion of employment opportunities. As a result, what emerged was unemployment and underemployment especially among the rural-based Sinhalese-Buddhist youth.

3.13 Unemployment and Underemployment

As in many Third World countries, accurate unemployment statistics are not available for Sri Lanka. Nevertheless, a number of surveys have revealed the magnitude of the problem. Unemployment is undoubtedly not a phenomenon of recent origin but its impact was not felt in the political arena of the country until about the mid 1960s. A significant characteristic of the unemployment trend was that it was predominantly concentrated among rural youth and young adults. During 1959-1960 the officially estimated total unemployed people stood at 340,000, of whom 80 per cent were in rural areas and 20 per cent in urban areas, and 250,000 were males and 90,000 females.[70] During, 1969-1970 the total figure climbed to 546,000.

The mid-1960s were crucial years for the unemployment crisis faced by the rural youth. A socio-economic survey conducted during 1969-1970 highlighted that there were some 550,000 unemployed comprising 13 per cent of Sri Lanka's total labour force in the age group of 15 and 59 year or approximately 43 per cent of the total population.[71] The following Table 3.13 indicates a comparative picture of unemployment as disclosed by a number of surveys.

Table 3.13. Available Estimates of Unemployment in Sri Lanka

Source	*Total Unemployment*	*% of Labour Force*
ILO Survey 1959-60 (Low Estimate)	340,000	10.5%
(High Estimate)	450,000	12.8%
Consumer Finance Survey 1963	457,000	13.8%
Population Census (Low Estimate)	265,000	8.0%
(High Estimate)	390,000	10.8%
Rural Employment Survey 1964	450,000	12.5%
Labour Force Survey 1968	450,000	11.0%
Labour Force Survey (Second Round) 1969	500,000	11.8%
Socio-Economic Survey, (First Round) 1969	552,000	13.1%

Source: Ministry of Finance, *The Economy of Ceylon, Trends and Prospects,* (Colombo: Department of Government Printing, 1971), p. 31.

The above estimated unemployed rate was high by any international standard. The unemployment problem had been and continued to be acute among the educated youth over a long period of time. By 1969 there were some 14,000 university graduates and 112,000 young persons with the General Certificate Examination (Ordinary Level) qualifications who were unemployed.[72] Around 14,000 graduates were accommodated in the workforce after 1970; however, 80 per cent of them received salaries between 200-300 rupees per month, which placed them below the poverty line.[73] The Dudley Seers Report, further notes that the rural-based graduates who had pursued studies in the Social Sciences and the Humanities were frustrated by the lack of employment opportunities.[74] The following Table 3.15 of unemployment by education shows the rate of unemployment among the G.C.E. (O/L) qualified and above. Moreover, it reveals that the level of unemployment among the under-25 age group is higher than the other groups.

These statistics show that the educated youth constituted the largest volume of the unemployed. Those with tenth or twelfth grade education in rural areas found it more difficult to secure employment than those in the urban areas. Thus, it was evident that a sense of frustration was fermenting among the educated rural youth over a period of time.

Table 3.14. The Level of Unemployment by Age, Sex and Education

Educational Level	*Age 12-24*			*25-34*			*35-39*		
	M	*F*	*Total*	*M*	*F*	*Total*	*M*	*F*	*Total*
No Schooling	25.2	10.6	17.0	-	2.3	1.4	0.2	3.8	2.1
Primary	23.5	17.2	21.7	2.8	8.2	3.9	1.1	3.1	1.4
Middle School	39.0	53.2	42.6	7.5	23.3	9.5	0.7	2.0	0.8
G.C.E. (O/L)	50.8	79.2	63.6	6.7	3.8	13.0	1.5	7.6	2.9
G.C.E. (O/L) and above	40.0	90.0	60.0	11.1	38.2	23.3	-	-	-
All Levels	33.4	40.3	35.6	5.2	14.4	7.9	0.9	3.6	1.5

Source: Department of Census and Statistics, *Preliminary Report on the Socio-Economic Survey of Ceylon, 1969-1970* (Colombo: Department of Census and Statistics, 1971), pp. 28 and 47.

In this context, unemployment was not the sole problem, the means of securing employment was another source of frustration for the educated youth. From the colonial period onward there had been a trend towards obtaining white collar employment on the basis of one's family or personal contacts. This system of obtaining employment facilitated the youth belonging to families of influence to secure stable jobs, while the youth in the rural sector who invariably belonged to peasant families were at a grave disadvantage. The government in 1970 found it necessary to address this problem and as a result introduced the system of appointing a political authority for each district. The political authority was a Member of Parliament belonging to the political party in office. The system further stipulated that a person seeking a job had to obtain a letter of recommendation from the political authority. This represented a form of patron-client relationship and proved to be a barrier hampering those supporting any opposition political party from securing employment. This system also created ways and means of perpetuating corrupt practices such as bribery and nepotism. Gananatha Obeysekara describes the nature of corruption and its relationship to the Insurrection of 1971 in the following manner:

> Since the jobs are scarce all competitive or open methods of recruitment have been abandoned, and the Government M.P. of the area is given tremendous power in their appointments. In the appointment of teachers for example each M.P. is given a fixed quota to fill. But very often the persons who get the jobs are kinsmen of the M.P. or those who have access to the patronage network through their elite connections. In some instances the wealthy of the area who are politically opposed to the M.P. in fact get the job owing to bribery or the capacity to manipulate the patronage system. Naturally the young men I interviewed harboured a felt sense of injustice a feeling which is extraordinarily widespread among the unemployed youth. This I think was an extremely important motive for young persons to join the insurgent movement.[75]

For S.P. Huntington, however, corruption is, of course, one measure of the absence of effective political institutionalization.[76]

Underemployment was another facet of the youth-related problems predominantly affecting the rural sector. Unlike unemployment, underemployment eludes definition and assessment. The underemployed can be described generally as a person being forced to accept employment below his or her educational level. Definite statistics on underemployment are not available, but are identified on the basis of low earnings. There is one definite factor, however, common to both unemployment and underemployment, and that is a sharp escalation since the 1960s. Government policies and the ensuing social and economic processes over a period of time created a considerable number of rural youth who were deprived of land and jobs. Moreover, these frustrated youth were further disillusioned by the static economic situation in the country during the 1960s and early 1970s.

Thus, the inadequacy of economic innovation to meet the challenges posed by the country's problems, generated and fostered a sense of frustration mainly among the educated rural youth. The deteriorating and sometimes stagnant economy deprived the new generations the means of fulfilling their aspirations in keeping with their educational backgrounds. S.P. Huntington argues that the higher the level of education of the unemployed, alienated, or otherwise dissatisfied person, the more extreme the destabilizing behaviour which results. Alienated university graduates prepare revolutions; alienated technical or secondary school graduates plan coups; alienated primary school leavers engage in more frequent but less significant forms of political unrest.[77] In broad terms, the expansion of social mobilization becomes social frustration when the economy remains static and underdeveloped. In this light, the economic development of Sri Lanka could not meet the aspirations generated by social mobilization. The, urbanization, the growth of literacy and educational expansion were not accompanied by the economic growth that was needed to facilitate greater scope and opportunity to fulfill the expectations and aspirations of the youth. As a result, what emerged was frustration and politicization among the rural Sinhalese-Buddhist youth. Hereinafter the author wishes to examine aspects of political modernization and its nexus with political violence movements in Sri Lanka.

3.14 Political Modernization

For S.P. Huntington, political modernization involves the rationalization of authority, the differentiation of structures and the expansion of political participation.[78] In order to examine this process, the following aspects will be covered: the nationalist movement, universal franchise, realization of politics, the political party system and the left-wing movement. All these aspects have a bearing on the growing trends of mass political participation and political mobilization in the country.

One of the principal effects of modernization on politics is increased participation in politics by social groups throughout society. S.P. Huntington views the early phases of modernization as being marked by the emergence of fundamentalist religious movements as in Sri Lanka.[79] A more tangible challenge to the British Raj was exerted indirectly by the Buddhist and Hindu revivalist movements of the 1880s led by the Sinhala-Buddhist and Tamil-Hindu intelligentsia. This religious-cultural assertion of the indigenous religions against the religions of the foreign rulers and their agents, the Christian missionaries, was a form of incipient nationalism. In many respects, opposition to the foreign occupation and to Western influences originated in, and was spearheaded by, the ethnocentric Sinhala-Buddhist nationalism. Their objective was to revive the glorious past of the ancient Sinhala civilization.[80]

In more political terms, however, the formation and founding of the Ceylon National Congress (C.N.C.) in 1919 marked the origin of the nationalist movement in Sri Lanka. As in other colonies in Asia, the nationalist movement in Sri Lanka was led by the English-educated, urban-based, westernized middle class.[81] As a result, the Sri Lankan nationalist movement was confined to this elite group and did not exert much influence outside its confines.[82] Their political agitation was confined to a series of petitions addressed to express grievances. Evidence was given to the constitutional Commissions, urging greater representation in the Legislative Council. They could not mobilize the masses into politics. There were no challenges to the authority of the British Raj because the nationalist movement was passive and subdued compared to neighbouring India. In this sense, Sri Lanka was the ideal colony in that it saw a peaceful transition from dependence to independence. The Declaration of Independence in 1948 was not achieved by means of a politically motivated independence struggle but was bestowed more as an award from His Majesty's Government.

Four and a half centuries of western colonialism had disrupted traditional political institutions. The creation of coherent and durable political institutions was among the most vital and difficult of the challenges confronting Sri Lanka and other developing nations of the Third World. The post-independece government structure, however, was based on the Soulbury Constitution of 1947 which introduced the Westminster-model of Parliament. The legislature consisted of a Senate and a House of Representatives, while the executive consisted of a Cabinet headed by the Prime Minister and the Governor General.

Sri Lanka also happened to be the first British colony in Asia to receive universal franchise. Nevertheless, it was not until after independence that political awareness and an active interest in politics spread widely and rapidly through the rural sector. This political passivity meant that independence certainly did not mark a breakthrough in the political structure, nor did it provide a new beginning and higher aspirations. It was in fact a transfer of power from the British to a pro-British Sri Lankan elite. The masses were cut off from active politics and remained as isolated from their new rulers as they had been under the British.

After independence the new government was dominated by a small upper class, thoroughly Anglicised, urban elite whose political vehicle was the United National Party (U.N.P.) established in 1947 bases on the National Congress. Its members were, as D.K. Rangnekar remarked, like the former colonial rulers in everything but the colour of their skins.[83] S.P. Huntington describes the nature of these elite as follows:

> This group was overwhelmingly urban, although Ceylon was 70 per cent rural. It was largely Christian, although 91 per cent of the Ceylonese were not and 64 per cent were Buddhist. Its language was English, which 92 per cent of the population could neither read nor write. In short, it was drawn from and represented a minority of less than 10 per cent of the population.[84]

Consequently the rural-urban gap widened and failed to assimilate the rural masses into the national political system. According to Huntington, national leaders who fail to mobilize popular support prior to independence do not rule for long after independence.[85] He identifies this process as the ruralisation of elections.

3.15 Ruralisation of Elections

In his study of ruralisation of elections, Huntington finds that the clearest cases displayed several common major characteristics. Some of these characteristics are as follows:

(*a*) The modernizing elite, who come from the urban-based middle classes, are driven out of office.

(*b*) The result is not one that has been anticipated or predicted by most political observers.

(*c*) The victorious party is able to secure its victory mainly because it mobilizes new rural voters to participate in politics.

(*d*) The leader of this party is invariably a former member of the modernizing elite who brakes away from the elite and assumes a popular and traditional charisma.

(*e*) In spite of the leader being a member of the elite, the other key members in his party come from the national rural elites.

(*f*) The issues which appeals to the rural voters are ethnic and religious issues and other marginal issues, which the victorious party is able to exploit.

(*g*) In most instances this new party secures the support of key religious figures in the rural sector whose work make a significant contribution to its victory.

(*h*) This victory of the opposition is viewed by its supporters and its opponents as a significant change in the political processes of the country.

(*i*) When this party assumes political power its policies are aimed at the rural sector, where a large part of its supporters are concentrated.

(*j*) These policies, however, antagonize the modernizing elite who resort to a military coup d' etat.

(*k*) In most instances the party which suffers defeat adapts itself to the new patterns of political participation and attempts its own efforts to mobilize the masses.

(*l*) In a few instances these parties are elected to power once again.[86]

These characteristics of ruralisation of elections are visible in the political processes of Sri Lanka since the 1950s, which was the beginning of a period of rapid politicization of the majority of the population. In fact this process was initiated by the national resurgence, along with the granting of universal suffrage in 1931. Consequently, issues related to religion and language became sensitive during this first post-independence decade and also stimulated mass awareness in politics, mainly in electoral politics.

The sensitivity of these issues and the rather emotional approach adopted by the post-independence politicians paved the way for a polarization based on religion and ethnicity between Sinhalese-Buddhist and Tamil-Hindu nationalism. The Sinhala language and the Buddhist religion were the pivots of Sinhala nationalism which were based on the support of the rural masses. The discontent and nationalist fervour of these rural masses were generated and fostered by a conviction that the Sinhalese-Buddhists were discriminated against during the colonial rule. The granting of independence did not change the colonial economic and political structure. The English language continued to be the language of administration. The medium of instruction in higher education was also confined to English which facilitated the monopolization of public service employment by those with an English education. By 1953 a mere 9.4 per cent of the population aged 5-years and over were literate in English. The exclusivity of English education was largely due to the fact that such education was in the hands of private, mostly Christian schools which were concentrated in the South-West and the North, and were expensive.[87] The limited access to English thus convinced the rural masses that the English language was a major barrier to their upward mobility. The continued use of the English language, both in administration and education after independence, was perceived as an instrument for the continuation of the privileged position of the urbanized elite.[88]

Language and religion were the issues which mobilized the rural masses in the 1950s. Their convictions and feelings of being discriminated against culminated in their making several demands. The first of these was that Sinhala should replace English as the official language. The other significant demands were the designation of Buddhism as a state religion, the state takeover of all privately assisted schools, and the declaration of Sri Lanka as a republic. The political leadership for this mass wave of Sinhala-Buddhist nationalism was given by the Sri Lanka Freedom Party (S.F.P.), founded in 1951, and by its electoral ally the Mahajana Eksath Peramuna (M.E.P.) or People's United Front.[89] The M.E.P. whose electoral programme responded to the national and cultural aspirations of the dissatisfied rural Sinhalese-Buddhist masses was elected to power in 1956. The M.E.P.'s electoral victory over the ruling U.N.P. marked a turning point in the post-independence political process of Sri Lanka. The deciding factor in the M.E.P. victory was its ability to mobilize the rural masses against the incumbent elite-based U.N.P. Government.[90] A number of political forces which had hitherto been excluded from politics gained entry to the political arena. A.J. Wilson observes that the most significant outcome of the M.E.P. victory was that the rural masses and the national-minded Sinhala intelligentsia had, for the first time, gained access to political power.[91] Michel A. Ames sums up the M.E.P. victory of 1956 more explicitly:

> For the first time since colonial rule was imposed on Sri Lanka (Ceylon) over 400 years ago Sinhalese villagers felt able to declare as some did when Bandaranaiaka's coalition succeeded to office, that it was now "Ape Anduwa" our government as opposed to rule by foreigners and alienated, westernized and christianised elites.[92]

For Calvin Woodward, what was most important was that the whole electoral episode made voters aware of the extent to which they could, through the vehicle of the political party, influence the course of affairs and effect the readjustment of policies vital to their own well-being.[93] After coming to power, the M.E.P. implemented the main Sinhalese-Buddhist demands, the primary one being that "Sinhala" be established as the official language. As a means of further expanding education, two leading Buddhist monastic educational institutions known as "pirivenas" were elevated to the status of universities and came to be known as the Vidyalankara and Vidyudaya universities. The Katunayake Airport and the natural harbour at Trincomalee, which were controlled by the British, were taken over by the State. For the first time, a Ministry of Cultural Affairs was established to promote and propagate the indigenous cultures. Furthermore, a Buddhist Sasana Commission was appointed to make recommendations and to uphold the "sangha" (Buddhist clergy) organization.

Economic reforms were rather limited in scope and consisted of the nationalization of the Port of Colombo and the private transport services.[94] The foreign policy of Sri Lanka moved away from the pro-western foreign policy of the U.N.P. Government to a more moderate and middle path orientation which initiated diplomatic ties with the Socialist bloc. The voting age was lowered from 21 to 18 years in 1959. In the meantime, the V.L.S.S.P. led by Philip Gunawardena, broke away from the M.E.P. government and Prime Minister S.W.R. de Bandaranayike was assassinated. The other aspirations and demands of the Sinhalese-Buddhist majority, however, such as the state takeover of assisted schools, employment in the state sector, and the armed forces being based on proportional religious representation, were realized during the S.L.F.P. regime of 1960-1965. In 1965, the U.N.P. was able to secure power only by adapting its appeal in such a manner as to compete with the S.L.F.P. Consequently, the Sinhalese-Buddhist rural masses had been mobilized into the electoral politics. On the other hand, their entry into politics also changed the dominant style, semantics, policies and the leadership within that system.[95]

Thus, post-independent Sri Lanka did witness some significant changes though these changes were not sufficiently profound to alter the basic power structure inherited from the British.[96] The U.N.P. and the S.L.F.P. were not successful in breaking the bonds of a dependent economy and their policies proved futile in the face of increasing unemployment, inflation and deteriorating standards of living. Thus, the changes and reforms were minor compared to the deeper problems of society and failed to address the problems of a declining economy. In spite of the fact that the official language, employment and education were subject to change, the socio-economic and political supremacy of English education prevailed. Tissa Fernando describes the situation as follows:

> Sinhala may be the official language but those who know English in addition to the local languages are at a distinct advantage in obtaining superior employment. English is used less widely today than it was three decades ago. But the attitudes, values and life style of

the English-speaking society are still widely accepted by the Ceylonese elite.[97]

With the granting of independence, however, wider social strata became involved in the political process as it was perceived that politics provided an avenue for reaching solutions to the acute problems within the context of Sri Lanka's underdeveloped economy and multi-group society.[98] Since the 1950s electoral politics in Sri Lanka have permeated the thinking, expectations and aspirations of the rural population. The following Table 3.15 depicts the voter turn-out in Sri Lanka in Parliamentary Elections between 1947 and 1970.

Table 3.15 Voter Participation in Parliamentary Elections 1947-70

Year of Election	*Number of Voters*	*Percentage*
1947	1,701,150	55.9
1952	2,114,615	70.7
1956	2,391,538	69.0
1960 March	2,889,282	7706
1960 July	2,827,075	75.9
1965	3,821,918	82.1
1970	4,672,656	85.2

Source: Department of Elections, ***Results of Parliamentary General Elections in Ceylon, 1947-1970,*** (Colombo: Department of Government Printing, 1971), p.6.

According to the above Table 3.15, in 1947, 55.9 per cent of the eligible voters cast their votes. In 1960, it increased to 75.9, and rose to 85.2 per cent in 1970—a clear indication of the increasing participation in electoral politics in Sri Lanka. The level of politicization is indicated by the voter turn-out since independence. It is the highest in Asia.

Before universal franchise was accorded to those over 18 years, the youth were mobilized mainly towards securing votes for the opposition and promoting its campaign against the incumbent party. After 1959, however, they were involved directly in political parties which encouraged young people to believe in the inevitability of progress and the fulfillment of their hopes. All the major parties founded and encouraged youth leagues, some of which had a wide membership. As they are dynamic, the youth leagues have made overt efforts to attract an ever wider membership. The competition for power motivated the parties to make rather exaggerated promises to the youth leagues; the party that made the greatest number of promises was likely to win the elections. Thus, the young people were motivated to participate more actively in electoral politics, especially in the elections of 1965 and 1970.

The signs of political participation of youth appeared in the mid 1960s in the form of student demonstrations, student strikes and the youth league activities of the left-wing parties. As an additional impetus, the revolutionary and radical political approaches at the global level also had its impact on the Sri Lankan youth. They were inspired by the romanticized exploits and the revolutionary valour of Che Guevara and Fidel Castro, the liberation struggle in Indo-China, and the growing student militancy in the Western countries.[99] These young people, who were the children of the nationalist forces which had supported the S.L.F.P. in 1956 against the pro-Western elites, were now attracted to the revolutionary forces operational in Sri Lanka.[100] As Huntington observes, the social and economic changes encouraged by the policy innovation lead new groups to demand entry into the political system and required the expansion of the system.[101] The potential of the political system in Sri Lanka to meet the increased participation and growing demands will be examined through the political development there.

3.16 Political Participation and Development

Political development has been viewed in terms of the capacity of the political system to implement collective goals, resolve the issues by which it is confronted, and adapt to challenges involved in the emergence of a modern polity. S.P. Huntington states that in modernizing societies, building the state means enlarging the bureaucracy, but more importantly also means establishing an effective party system capable of structuring the participation of new groups in politics.[102] The precondition of political stability is a party system capable of assimilating the new social forces produced by modernization.[103] Thus, Huntington defines political development in terms of the institutionalization of political organizations and procedures—that is, the processes by which they acquire stability. According to Huntington the level of institutionalization of a political system could be measured by the adaptability, complexity, autonomy and coherence of its organization and procedures.[104] For a nation seeking political order through democratic processes and broad popular participation, the evolution of an institutionalized political party system is of crucial importance. The following statement by Huntington, indicates the importance of political parties in Sri Lanka in terms of their relevance to political stability:

> Where new states emerge from colonialism with little or no inheritance of political institutions the stability of the polity depends directly on the strength of the party.[105]

Although there is difficulty in operationalising all these criteria, the author wishes to examine some of them by means of focusing upon the political parties in the country with special attention being given to the left-wing parties.

3.17 The Political Party System

The introduction of universal franchise in 1931, independence from the British Raj in 1948, and the adoption of a British-style parliamentary system of government, influenced the political parties which were playing decisive roles in Sri Lankan politics since independence. At independence in 1948, there were only a few political parties such as the Lanka Sama Samaja Party (Lanka Equal Society Party) which was founded in 1935, the Communist Party (C.P.) founded in 1943, the Tamil Congress (T.C.) and the United National Party, (U.N.P.) founded in 1947. Other parties were formed later as follows: the Sri Lanka Freedom Party in 1951; the Federal Party in 1949; and the Viplavakari (Revolutionary) Lanka Sama Samaja Party in 1951.[106] Consequently, by the mid-1950s a competitive party system had evolved in Sri Lanka. The growth of the party system was evident in the decline of independent candidates in parliamentary elections between 1947 and 1970. The number of elected independent candidates declined sharply between 1947 and 1970. In the election of 1947, 21 independent candidates were elected while in 1970 only two such candidates were successful.[107] The growth and development of competitive party politics encouraged the widening of political involvement and the proliferation of channels for political activity. Wider political participation generated a popular belief that the government was responsible for the welfare and progress of the people.

Once the parties were elected to power, however, these heightened expectations were barely realized due to inadequate material resources and administrative incapability. The recurrence of such unfulfilled promises made the rural youth aware of the fact that their ambitions and aspirations could not be achieved within the limitations of the existing system. Moreover, the significant political parties were dominated by older statesmen from elite backgrounds, leaving little or no opportunity for the rural youth to have an impact on their policies.[108] Nor did the parties provide opportunities for younger members to participate in responsible positions. Although youth were given chores at election time, after elections the permanent structure of the principal parties remained impermeable to the more enthusiastic or dedicated young people.[109] The decision-making positions in the political parties as well as in Parliament remained impenetrable to the younger age groups and this generation gap was reflected in the main spheres of politics. Table 3.17 below gives an insight into the age distribution of members of parliament and the general populace in 1971.

Table 3.16 reveals that 95 per cent of the Members of parliament were 35 years or older. Politics in Sri Lanka is the main avenue of upward mobility. Yet few political parties, if any, in Sri Lanka is capable of absorbing the large number of politically ambitious young individuals who emerged with the broadening of political participation. In this respect all the major political parties seemed equally unpromising for the career prospects and political aspirations of youth.

Table 3.16. Age Distribution of Members of Parliament, and Total Population 15 Years of Age and Over (1971, Percentages)

Age Group Years	*Members of Parliament*	*Total Population*
15-19	-	17.6
20-24	-	16.4
25-29	1.4	12.3
30-34	3.4	9.4
35-39	8.8	9.4
40-44	15.1	7.6
45-49	23.2	7.0
50-54	18.5	5.4
55-59	13.7	4.5
60-64	8.9	3.5
65 and over	6.8	7.0

Source: R.N. Kearney, *Politics and Modernisation in Modern Sri Lanka: A Society in Transition,* South Asian Series, No. 4, (1979), p. 77.

Furthermore, developments within the left-wing movement during the decade prior to 1971 played a significant role in the creation and character of the J.V.P. and other underground organizations. Hence it is important to trace the development and nature of the left-wing parties in Sri Lanka in order to understand their failure to absorbing the rural youth and the emergence of politically motivated violent movements in general.

3.18 Left-Wing Parties

Prior to 1960, the L.S.S.P., C.P. and the M.E.P. were the three main left-oriented political parties in Sri Lanka. The crisis in the Left from 1960 onward, however, proved to be an obstacle to attracting and absorbing the emerging youth population. This crisis (which shall be dealt with later in more detail) was caused mainly by fragmentation and disunity among the left-wing parties.

The history of the left-wing movement in Sri Lanka is characterized by fragmentation and disunity regarding their guiding ideologies. The first such ideological dispute materialized in 1939 on the question of Trotskyism versus Stalinism within the L.S.S.P. While the majority of the Central Committee members supported Trotskyism, the minority supported Stalinism. The outcome of this dispute was that both the pro-Soviet group and the Stalinists were expelled from the L.S.S.P. As a result, a new party emerged, the United Socialist Party, which in 1943 became the Communist Party of Ceylon.[110] The original L.S.S.P. had pledged support to the Fourth International and Trotskyism. The C.P. remained loyal to the Soviet Union and Stalinism. At the end of the Second World War, the L.S.S.P. faced yet another crisis when another group of Trotskyists broke away and organized the Bolshevik Leninist Party. By 1951, the L.S.S.P. and this breakaway group, known as the B.L.P., decided to reunite. This decision, however, caused yet another dispute and break-up in the L.S.S.P. The new group was led by Philip Gunawardana, and came to be known as the Viplawakari (Revolutionary) L.S.S.P. As Calvin Woodward observes much of the disunity might have been prevented if the movement had developed a centralized organization relatively soon after its formation.[111]

By 1960, the fragmentation of the left-wing parties was not yet at an end. Between 1960 and 1966, the process was repeated several times. Firstly, the decision taken by the L.S.S.P. to form a coalition with the S.L.F.P. Government in 1964 had grave repercussions for the party, and caused a further rift in the L.S.S.P. The anti-coalition faction formed the L.S.S.P. (R). This rift had serious implications for the L.S.S.P. as it was expelled from the Fourth International and was replaced by the breakaway L.S.S.P. (R).

Moreover, the ideological dispute between the Communist Party of the Soviet Union (C.P.S.U.) and the Chinese Communist Party (C.C.P.) in the context of the international communist movement was the next cause of a rift in the Sri Lankan C.P. in 1963-64. The Sri Lankan C.P. came to be divided into the pro-Moscow C.P. and the pro-Peking C.P. The C.P. (M) which was in the majority was committed to the pro-Moscow line internationally and advocated a parliamentary strategy in order to gain power. The C.P. (P), on the other hand, rejected the parliamentary strategy and upheld the revolutionary strategy adopted in the Maoist Chinese Revolution. By 1970 the ideological disputes had led to an increase in the number of left-wing parties in Sri Lanka to six. A left-wing movement in Sri Lankan politics had been needed since 1960 in order to absorb the radical forces, which had been increasing due to the unfavourable socio-economic changes that had taken place. What emerged, however, was not a strong unitary radical force capable of giving leadership to the politicized rural youth of the country, but rather a fragmented movement which was united only briefly, from 1963 to 1964, as a left-wing front. Obviously, a movement so lacking in unity and strength failed to assimilate the rural youth.

The generation gap and the wider socio-economic and educational disparities of the left-wing leadership and the radical youth further alienated the latter from the established left-wing political parties. The leaders of the left-wing parties were from the wealthy upper stratum of Sri Lankan society who had been educated at British universities. Of the 25 Marxist M.P.'s elected in 1970, seven were graduates of overseas universities' and another five had attended the University of Ceylon or the Colombo Law College. At least 12 had been educated at leading Colombo schools, such as St. Thomases, Royal and Ananda Colleges.[112] Without exception, they were all over 50-years of age, and were engaged in the elite professions as doctors or lawyers. By 1971, the left-wing movement had been active for 35 years, yet to a great extent its leadership was still confined to the first generation of founders. S.P. Huntington explains this situation as follows:

> So long as an organization still has its first set of leaders, so long as a procedure is still performed by those who first performed it, its adaptability is still in doubt.[113]

According to J. Jupp, the Marxist parliamentarians were no more representative of the people than anyone else. Because of their derivation from the English-speaking professional classes, they were even less representative than the S.L.F.P. They were a world away from the village-educated youth of the 1970s.[114]

From their very inception, the left-wing parties had focused on the urban working class and the minority castes in the urban coastal areas. At an electoral level their main power bases were concentrated in the low country Sinhalese areas of Southern Sri Lanka. Their preoccupation with the urban working class made them ignore the rural masses, especially the peasantry, thereby isolating a vital part of the population from left-wing politics. S.P. Huntington, relates the significance of the rural sector as follows:

> The source of political modernity is the city, the source of political stability is the country-side. The task of the Party is to combine the two. One major test of the institutionalization of a party and the adaptability of its leadership is the willingness of the latter to make the concessions necessary to win the support of the countryside. The strong parties and the stable party system are those which meet this test.[115]

The Sri Lankan left-wing parties, however, tended to ignore the radical potential of the rural masses and the gradual but steady radicalization of the unemployed rural youth.

The political image of the left-wing parties was a barrier to the assimilation of the rural youth. In their early years, the left-wing parties identified themselves with orthodox Marxist parties which were dedicated to the cause of independence. A governing factor was the objective of the left-wing parties to defeat Colonialism and Capitalism and to install an independent Socialist regime.[116] According to W.H. Wiggins, in the beginning the platform of the L.S.S.P. had independence as its first plank, and socialism as its second.[117] During the pre-independence period the left-wing parties were theoretically committed to the Marxist concept of revolution but had no practical strategy to capture power. The dedication of the left-wing parties to a peaceful path precluded their active participation in the agitation for independence from the British Raj. After independence, the left-wing parties continued to be devoted to parliamentary politics while preaching socialism. Sri Lanka's first general election in 1947 indicated the extent of support secured by the parties of the left-wing. They were elected as the main opposition party, thereby maintaining their stability within the framework of parliamentary politics. In spite of the fact that the left-wing parties had contested general elections since 1947, they did not make a clear-cut attempt to gain political power until March 1960.

The election victory of the M.E.P. in 1956 was an event of tremendous impact on the left-wing movement in Sri Lanka. After the victory of the M.E.P. the approach of the left-wing parties to the parliamentary system changed. It is clear that the main left-wing parties were mostly inclined towards parliamentary politics as the means for achieving a socialist state. Therefore, for the first time in 1960, the left-wing parties attempted to obtain a mandate to form a government. The General Election of March 1960 was thus a highlight in the history of the left-wing parties because the L.S.S.P. and the M.E.P. managed to get only 10 seats each, and the C.P. only four seats. It is also significant to note that, as shown in Table 3.17 below, the percentage of votes secured by the left-wing parties declined from 20.5 percent in 1947 to 13 per cent at the General Election of 1970.

Table 3.17. Performance of Marxist Parties of Sri Lanka in Parliamentary Elections

Election	*Parties*	*Votes*	*Percentage*	*Seats Won*
1947	3	387,544	20.5	18
1952	3	439,661	18.9	13
1956	2*	393,929	14.7	17
1960 March	3	790,041	25.7	23
1960 July	3	417,045	13.8	19
1965	6	528,663	13.1	15
1970	3	648,994	13.0	25

* The VLSSP, which contested as a part of the MEP, is not included.

Source: R.N. Kearney, "The Marxist Parties of Ceylon" in Paul R. Brass And Marcus F. Fernando, (eds), Radical Politics in South Asia, (Cambridge, Mass: Massachusetts Institute of Technology, 1973), p. 405.

Defeat at the general elections did not result in a reformulation of party strategy or a withdrawal from electoral politics. What emerged was an intermediate path in parliamentary politics in which the left-wing parties either arrived at a 'no contest' pact with the moderate political parties or formed coalition governments with them. From 1960 onward, the L.S.S.P. and the C.P. fought all the consecutive general elections in alliance with the S.L.F.P. The L.S.S.P. joined the S.L.F.P. Government in 1964, and the C.P. supported this coalition government. On the other hand, in 1965, the M.E.P. chose to join the U.N.P. Government. The continuous trend of forming alliances with the moderate political parties had grave repercussions not only for the parties of the left but on the left-wing movement in general. The entire scenario had a demoralizing effect on the emerging radical youth who had cause to believe that the principles of radical politics had been betrayed by forming governments, alliances and coalitions with the moderate parties. S.P. Huntington vividly explains a similar situation as follows:

> When it first appears each new party seems like a harbinger of progress and reform because it embodies the interests of a newly emerging social force. Once it has achieved a position within the political system, however, it changes as its constituency changes, and it eventually becomes the spokesman for vested interests.[118]

The lack of an adequate strategy through which political power could be captured, in addition to the fact that they entered into a coalition government with the moderate political parties, disillusioned the younger generation. The image projected by the left leaders was not an image which would appeal to the Swabasha-educated rural youth.

In the initial stages, two splinter groups from the orthodox left parties, the R.L.S.S.P. and the C.P. (P), attracted the young. These two parties posed a challenge to the theory of peaceful transformation in achieving socialism by advocating the concept of revolution based on an armed struggle. Of the two parties, the C.P. (P) became a rallying point for the radical element of the rural youth. It absorbed a layer of ambitious rural radical youth into the politics of the left. These young people were in search of a political organization through which they could express their grievances and also implement immediate social changes.

Subsequently, the ideology and programme of action adopted by these two parties failed to retain its appeal for the youth of the rural areas. Ideologically, the C.P. (P) expounded the blueprint of Mao's thought, while the R.L.S.S.P. was committed to pure Trotskyism. Their limitations were mainly in the sphere of mobilization as these two parties confined their activities mainly to trade unionism and failed to arrive at a viable mechanism through which the disillusioned rural youth could be mobilized. Though these political groupings were called parties, they lacked the continuing organization and social support which, according to Huntington, are the essence of the party.[119]

Given these circumstances, those who joined either the C.P.(P) or the R.L.S.S.P. with aspirations of attaining revolutionary change were soon to be disappointed and broke away from the parties. The further fragmentation of the left-wing parties created more than half a dozen left-wing groups which were eager to mobilize the rural youth for an armed uprising. S.P. Huntington observes this situation as follows:

> In every society affected by social change new groups arise to participate in politics. Where the political system lacks autonomy, these groups gain entry into politics without becoming identified with the established political organizations or acquiescing in the established political procedures.[120]

The political hierarchy consisted of an older generation that not only failed to come to grips with the socio-economic crisis encountered by the rural youth, but also failed to assimilate them into the existing political system. With the onset of economic deterioration there had been signs of political decay. This situation further led the youth to seek other means of creating an impact in the political arena. It is evident that the radical youth seemed to have arrived at the following conclusions: The U.N.P., the S.L.F.P. and the United Front were incapable of solving Sri Lanka's politico-economic problems within the framework of a parliamentary system. The left-wing parties too had degenerated to make a significant contribution to the revolutionary cause and, therefore, a revolutionary party had to be mobilized and formed to achieve a socialist society by means of politically motivated violence. The above mentioned preconditions, spanning several decades of Sri Lanka's socio-economic and political development, led to the origin of the J.V.P. and similar political violence movements.

3.19 Summary

The socio-economic and political factors provide the preconditions for the origin of political violence movements in Sri Lanka. It is argued that the Colebrooke Reforms marked the beginning of a process of socio-economic and political modernization in Sri Lanka. In their wake came the plantation economy which made systematic inroads into the traditional socio-economic fabric consequently leading to its disintegration. The traditional agricultural system was neglected and issues of land shortages and rural indebtedness loomed large in the ensuing agrarian crisis. This agrarian crisis, however, was accompanied by social mobilization which was characterized by a rapid growth of population, slow urbanization, a significant expansion of education especially with the advent of free education, a high rate of literacy and the spread of mass communication. As a result, expectations rose particularly in the crisis-effected rural sector.

The economic conditions which were imperative in meeting these high aspirations, however, were lacking because of the stagnation of the economy from the 1960s onward. The symptoms of economic decline since the 1960s were the rising budget deficits, rising inflation, unemployment and underemployment. Consequently, the semi-urban and rural youth found their aspirations falling far short of fulfillment and so were subject to a process of disillusionment and politicization by the mid-1960s.

Political modernization was overtly manifest in the nationalist movement, universal franchise, and the growth and expansion of political parties. The nationalist movement which was ethnic and elite-base was incapable of mobilizing the masses. Therefore, it was not until the 1950s that ruralisation of elections and mass political participation in Sri Lanka was realized. The victory of the M.E.P. in 1956 broadened political awareness and participation within the rural sector. The measures taken by the M.E.P. or the successive U.N.P. and

S.L.F.P. governments, however, failed to fulfill the aspirations of the semi-urban and rural youth and absorb them into the political system.

Given this political vacuum, the rural youth were politicized and radicalized by and attracted to the left-oriented political parties within Sri Lanka. However, because these parties lacked proper organization, unity and coherent programmes, the youth were not assimilated into the political party system. These were the preconditions which proved to be conducive to the origin and fostering of clandestine organizations which aimed at political violence within Sri Lanka. In the following Chapter 4 the author wishes to examine the preconditions which paved the way for the origin and development of political violence movements within the confines of Sri Lankan Tamil ethnicity.

References

1. Harry Ecktein, "On the Etiology of Internal Wars", *History and Theory,* Vol. 4, (1965), p. 140.
2. S.P. Huntington, *Political Order in Changing Societies,* (New Haven: Yale University Press, 1968), p. 41.
3. I.H. Vanden Driesen, *Economic History in Ceylon,* (Maharagama: Saman Printers, 1963), p.2.
4. G.C. Mendis, *Ceylon Under the British,* (Colombo: The Colombo Apothecaries Co. Ltd., 1946), pp. 35-42.
5. G.C. Mendis, *Ceylon Today and Yesterday: Main Currents of Ceylon History,* (Colombo: Associated Newspapers of Ceylon, 1963), p. 63.
6. S. Ponnambalam, *Dependence Economy in Crisis: The Sri Lankan Economy in Crisis, 1948-1980,* (London: Zed Press, 1981), p. 7.
7. I.H. Vanden Driesen, *op. cit.,* 1963, p. 43.
8. G.H. Peiris, "Agrarian Transformations in British Sri Lanka" *Sri Lanka Journal of Agrarian Studies,* Vol. 2, No. 2, (1981), p. 16.
9. Ashoka Bandarage, *Colonialism in Sri Lanka: The Political Economy of the Kandyan Highlands, 1883-1886,* (New York: Mouton Publishers, 1983), p. 249.
10. Donald Snodgrass, *Ceylon: An Export Economy in Transition,* (Homewood, Illinois: Richard D. Irwin, 1966), p. 24.

11. S.B. de Silva, *Political Economy of Underdevelopment* (London: Routledge and Kegan Paul, 1982), p. 210.
12. Kumari Jayawardene, *The Rise of the Labour Movement in Ceylon,* (Durham, N.C.: Duke University Press, 1972), p. 16.
13. W.H. Wriggins, *Ceylon: Dilemmas of a New Nation,* (Princeton: Princeton University Press 1960), p. 213.
14. N.H.S. Karunatilake, *Economic Development in Ceylon,* (New York: Praeger Publishers, 1971), pp. 176-177.
15. Department of Census and Statistics, *Census of Population, Ceylon, 1963,* Vol. 1, Part 11, (Colombo: Government Press, 1967), pp. 3-4.
16. B. Moore, *The State and Peasant Politics in Sri Lanka,* (London: Cambridge University Press, 1985), p. 22.
17. S. Ponnambalam, *op. cit.,* p. 22.
18. K.M. de Silva, *Sri Lanka: A Survey,* (London: Hurst and Company, 1977), p. 69
19. S.B. de Silva, *op. cit.,* p. 233.
20. P. Wickramasekera, Development and Peasantry: The Sri Lankan Experience, Unpublished *Paper Presented to the U.N. Centre for Regional Development,* Nagoya, Japan, (1983), p. 7.
21. *Ibid.,* p. 11.
22. *Ibid.,* p. 15.
23. S.P. Huntington, *op. cit.,* p. 381.
24. See, Appendix 4.
25. See, Department of Census and Statistics, *Survey of Rural Indebtedness in Ceylon 1957,* (Colombo: Government Press, 1959).
26. Sir Ivor Jennings, *The Economy of Ceylon,* (London: Oxford University Press, 1952), p. 59
27. Vijaya Samaraweera, "Land Policy and Peasant Colonization, 1914-1948", in K.M. de Silva, (ed), *History of Ceylon: From the Beginning of the Nineteenth Century to 1948,* (Peradeniya: University of Ceylon, 1973), p. 460.
28. W.H. Wriggins, *op. cit.,* pp. 292-293.
29. B.H. Farmer, *Pioneer Peasant Colonization in Ceylon: A Study in Asian Agrarian Problems,* (London: Oxford University Press, 1957), p. 165.
30. P. Wickramasekara, *op. cit.,* p. 6.

31. S.P. Huntington, *op. cit.*, p. 375.
32. M. More, *op. cit.*, pp. 54-65.
33. Karl W. Deutsch, "Social Mobilisation and Political Development", *American Political Science Review,* Vol. 55, (1961), p. 493.
34. Gavin W. Jones and S. Selvarathnam, "Urbanization in Ceylon, 1945-63", *Modern Ceylon Studies,* Vol. 1, (1970), pp. 199-212.
35. Hubert Muller, "Youth as a Force in the Modern World", *Comparative Studies in Society and History,* Vol. 10, (1968), pp. 237-260.
36. D.D. Saram, "Education: An Era of Reform", *Asian Survey,* 13, (1973), p. 1169.
37. *Ibid.,* p. 1169.
38. Robert Kearney, "Democracy and the Stresses of Modernisation in Sri Lanka", *Journal of South Asian and Middle Eastern Studies,* Vol. 1, No. 3, (1978), p. 89.
39. G. Uswatta Arachchi, "University Admission in Ceylon: Their Economic and Social Background and Employment Expectqations", *Modern Asian Studies,* Vol. 8, (1974), p. 290.
40. Gerald H. Peiris, "Basic Needs and the Provisions of Government Services in Sri Lanka: A Case study of Kandy District", *International Labour Office Report,* (Geneva: International Labour Office, 1982), p. 58.
41. Data from National Council of Higher Education, "The Framework of Plan for the Development of Universities in Ceylon: 1969-1978", cited in International Labour Office, *Matching Employment Opportunities and Expectations: A Programme of Action for Ceylon,* Vol. 11. p. 164.
42. G. Uswatta Arachi, "From Highway to Blind Alley, A Note on Youth and Higher Education", *Marga,* Colombo, Vol. 1 No. 3, (1973), pp. 75-85.
43. R.N. Kearney, "Politics and Modernisation", in Tissa Fernando and R.N. Kearney, (eds), *Modern Sri Lanka: A Society in Transition,* South Asian Series, (Syracuse N.Y.: Maxwell School of Citizenship and Public Affairs, 1979), p. 72.
44. Department of Census and Statistics, *Statistical Abstract of Ceylon, 1967-1969,* (Colombo: Department of Government Printing, 1970), p.35.
45. Department of Census and Statistics, *Statistical Pocket Book of Sri Lanka,* (Colombo: Department of Government Printing, 1973), p. 15.

46. N.D. Jayaweera, "Mass Media 1, The Radio" in *Education in Ceylon: A Century Volume.* Part 3, (Colombo: Ministry of Education and Cultural Affairs, 1969), p. 1217.
47. Department of Census and Statistics, *Statistical Pocket Book of Sri Lanka,* (Colombo: Government Printing, 1972), p. 92.
48. Ted Robert Gurr, *Why Men Rebel,* (Princeton: Princeton University Press, 1970), p. 96.
49. S.P. Huntington, *op. cit.,* p. 49.
50. E.B. Denham, *Ceylon at the Census of 1911: Being a Review of the Results of the Census of 1911,* (Colombo: Government Printers, 1912), p. 399.
51. G. Uswatte Aratchchi, "From Highway to Blind Alley, A Note on Youth and Higher Education", *Marga,* Vol. 1, No. 3, (1973), p. 84.
52. International Labour Office, *op. cit.,* p. 148.
53. Lloyd Fallers, "Equality, Modernity, and Democracy in the New States", in Clifford Geertz, (ed), *Old Societies and New States: The Quest For Modernity in Asia and Africa,* (New York: The Free Press, 1963). pp. 192-193.
54. R.N. Kearney, "Education Expansion and Political Volatility in Sri Lanka: The 1971 Insurrection", *Asian Survey,* Vol. 15, No. 9, (1975), p. 735.
55. International Labour Office, *Matching Employment, Opportunities and Expectation: A Programme of Action for Ceylon,* 1971, p. 33.
56. R.K. Srivatava, and S. Selvarathnam, "Youth Employment in Ceylon: Problems and Prospects", *Marga,* Vol. 1, No. 4, (1972), pp. 43-44.
57. R.N. Kearney, *op. cit.,* p. 742.
58. S.P. Huntington, *op. cit.,* p. 49.
59. H.M. Gunasekara, "The Economy of Sri Lanka, 1948-73", *The Journal of History and Social Studies,* Vol. 4, (1977), p. 787.
60. D.R. Snodgrass, "Sri Lanka Economic Development During 25 Yars of Independence", *The Journal of History and Social Studies,* Vol. 4, 1975, pp. 119-125.

61. Central Bank Annual Reports, cited from A.J. Wilson, *Politics in Sri Lanka,* (London: Macmillan, 1979), p. 39.

62. Central Bank of Ceylon, *Annual Report of the Monetary Board to the Minister of Finance for the Year 1969,* p. 13.

63. Of this sum, Rs.301.7 million had been paid back, leaving a balance of 421.7 million as of 20th May 1970. See, N.M. Perera, *Budget Speech, 1970-71,* p. 11., cited in A.J. Wilson, *op. cit.,* p. 109.

64. A.J. Wilson, *op. cit.,* p. 112.

65. Central Bank of Ceylon, *Survey of Ceylon's Consumer Finance 1963,* (Colombo: Central Bank, 1964), p. 61.

66. L.P. Fernando, *Political Violence in Sri Lanka: The April 1971 Insurrection,* (Unpublished M.A. Thesis: University of New Brunswick, 1976), p. 43.

67. A.J. Wilson, "Socialism in Sri Lanka", in Helen Deffosses and Jacques Levesque, (eds), *Socialism in the Third World,* (New York: Pargue Publishers, 1975), p. 258.

68. World Bank, *World Development Report,* (New York: Oxford University Press, 1981), p. 134.

69. Donald Snodgrass, "Sri Lanka's Economic Development During Twenty-five Years of Independence", *The Ceylon Journal of Historical and Social Studies,* Vol. 5, (1975), pp. 119-125.

70. "A Survey of Employment, Unemployment and Underemployment in Ceylon", *International Labour Review,* Vol. 87, (1963), p. 2510.

71. Central Bank Ceylon, *Socio-Economic Survey of 1969-1970,* First Round, Colombo, 1970, cited in A.J. Wilson, *Electoral Politics in an Emergent State,* (Cambridge: University Press, 1975), p. 13.

72. A.J. Wilson, *Politics in Sri Lanka, 1947-1979,* (London: The Macmillan Press, 1979), p. 53.

73. P.V.J. Jayasekara, "Sri Lanka in 1976: Changing Strategies and Confrontation", *Asian Survey,* Vol. 17, No. 2, (1977), p. 209.

74. International Labour Office, *op. cit.,* (1971), p. 20.

75. Gananatha Obeysekara, "Some Comments on the Social Background of the 1971 Insurgency in Sri Lanka", *Journal of Asian Studies,* Vol. 33, (1974), p. 382.
76. S.P. Huntington, *op. cit.,* p. 59.
77. *Ibid.,* p. 48.
78. *Ibid.,* p. 93.
79. *Ibid.,* p. 38.
80. A.J. Wilson, "Race, Religion, Language and Caste in the Sub-nationalisms of Sri Lanka", in Michel Robert, (ed), *Collective Identities, Nationalism and Protest in Modern Sri Lanka,* (Colombo: Marga Institute, 1981), p. 464.
81. B.H. Farmer, "Social Basis of Nationalism in Ceylon", *Asian Studies,* Vol. 24, No. 3, pp. 431-439.
82. Ivor Jennings, "Nationalism and Political Development in Ceylon", (New York: Institute of Pacific Relations, 1950), pp. 8-18.
83. D.K. Rangnekar, "The Nationalist Revolution in Ceylon", *Pacific Affairs,* Vol. 33, (1960), p. 363.
84. S.P. Huntington, *op. cit.,* p. 449.
85. *Ibid.,* p. 441.
86. *Ibid.,* p. 460.
87. R.N. Kearney, "Sinhalese Nationalism and Social Conflict in Ceylon", *Pacific Affairs,* (1964), p. 127.
88. S.U. Kodikara, "Communalism and Political Modernisation in Ceylon", *Modern Ceylon Studies,* Vol. 1, (1970), p. 99.
89. The Mahajana Eksath Peramuna (M.E.P.) or People's United Front was formed as a coalition of the Sri Lanka Freedom Party, (S.L.F.P.), the Viplavakari Lanka Sama Samaja Party, (V.L.S.S.P.), the Language Front and some independent members in the Parliament.
90. S.P. Huntington, *op. cit.,* p. 451.
91. A.J. Wilson, *Electoral Politics in the Emergent State: The Ceylon General Election of May, 1970.*
92. M.A. Ames, "Westernisation or Modernisation, The Core of the Sinhalese Buddhism", *Social Compass,* Vol. 20, (1973), p. 144.

93. Calvin A. Woodward, "Sri Lanka's Electoral Experience", *Pacific Affairs,* Vol. 47, (1974), p. 469.

94. E.F.C. Ludowyk, *The Modern History of Ceylon,* (London: Weidenfeld and Nicolson, 1966), p. 248.

95. S.P. Huntington, *op. cit.,* p. 452.

96. Tissa Ferna19561952ndo, "Elite Politics in the New States: The Case of Post-independence Sri Lanka", *Pacific Affairs,* Vol. 46, N1960 March1956o. 3, (1973), p. 377.

97. Ibid., p. 378.

98. A.J. Wilson, "Politics and Political Development Since 1948", in K.M. de Silva, (ed), *Sri Lanka-A Survey, op. cit.,* p. 283.

99. *Srilaka,* a L.S.S.P. oriented daily, translated Che Guevara's Diaries between August 25th and November 15th 1968. Sidney Wanasinghe, of Young Socialist translated and published Guevara's *Guerrilla Warfare,* in three parts in 1968 and 1969.

100. Mervin De Silva, "Sri Lanka: The End of Welfare Politics", *South Asian Review,* Vol. 6, No. 2, (1973), pp. 91-109.

101. S.P. Huntington, *Political Order in Changing Societies,* op. cit., p. 145.

102. Ibid., pp. 12-24, and "Political Development or Political Decay", *World Politics,* Vol. 17, (1965), p. 401.

103. S.P. Huntington, *Political Order in Changing Societies, op. cit.,* pp. 420-421.

104. *Ibid.,* pp. 12-24.

105. *Ibid.,* p. 91.

106. The Party was called the V.L.S.S.P. from its founding in 1950 to 1959. Since then it has been renamed the M.E.P.

107. Calvin A. Woodward, "Sri Lanka's Electoral Experience", *Pacific Affairs,* Vol. 47, (1974), p. 456.

108. Power in two major parties in Sri Lanka has always been highly centralized, partly because of the personalized rule which two families have exercised. The U.N.P. is dominated by the two related Senanayake and Jayawardena families. The S.L.F.P. is dominated by Bandaranaike family.

109. W.H. Wriggins, *op. cit.,* p. 30.

110. W. Howard Wriggins, *Ceylon: Dilemmas of a New Nation,* (Princeton: Princeton University Press, 1960), p. 127.

111. C.A. Woodward, "The Trotskite Movement in Ceylon", *World Politics,* Vol. 14, (1961-62), p. 315.

112. J. Jupp, *Ceylon: Third World Democracy,* (London: Frank Cass, 1978), pp. 295-296.

113. S.P. Huntington, *op. cit.,* p. 14.

114. J. Jupp, *op. cit.,* p. 296.

115. *Ibid.,* p. 434.

116. G.L. Lerski, *Origin of Trotskyism in Ceylon: A Documentary History of the Lanka Sama Samajaya Party, 1935-1942,* (Stanford, California: Hoover Institution For War, Revolution, and Peace, 1968), p. 27.

117. W.H. Wriggins, *op. cit.,* p. 125.

118. S.P. Huntington, *op. cit.,* p. 429.

119. *Ibid.,* p. 413.

120. *Ibid.,* p. 21.

4

Preconditions of Tamil Guerrilla Warfare

4.1 Introduction

In this fourth chapter, the author concentrates on the preconditions which gave rise to guerrilla organizations among the Tamil community of Sri Lanka. Several observations have been made regarding political violence based on ethnicity. According to Martin O. Heisler, ethnic divergences have been the single most important source of long-term conflict leading to civil war and insurgencies and even to the disintegration of states.[1]

Viewed in this context, political violence among the Tamils makes it imperative, firstly, to examine the factors which caused ethnic conflict primarily between the Sinhalese majority and the major minority, the Sri Lankan Tamils. K.M. de Silva observes that the ethnic conflict in Sri Lanka is not a simple and straightforward confrontation between a "callous majority" and an "oppressed minority".[2] It is traceable directly to the widespread social changes and the processes of modernization at work within the country. The thesis presented in this chapter is that the socio-economic and political changes contributed to the ethnic conflict, separatism and the origin of the Tamil guerrilla organizations which waged political violence. In order to examine the preconditions behind the political violence among the Tamil community, this chapter is separated into the following sections: ethnic pluralism, impact of the colonial period, internal migration, the policy of official language, state employment and unemployment, the policy of university admission, origin and development of ethno-political organizations, the role of the Federal Party, government response, the 1972 Constitution, separate state and the Tamil youth radicalization.

4.2 Ethnic Pluralism

According to Huntington, colonialism and ethnic heterogeneity would seem to be much better predicators of insurgency than poverty.[3] Furthermore, according to T.R. Gurr, theories of revolution and state violence tend to agree with the postulate that sharp internal cleavages along the lines of class, ethnicity and/or religion contribute to violent conflict.[4] Thus, the ethnic factor is one of the many impulses leading to political violence in the Third World. Therefore, the pluralistic nature of the Sri Lankan society necessitates an examination of the ethnic composition of the country before embarking on a study of the preconditions of its political violence.

Sri Lanka is a multi-racial and multi-religious society of which 74 per cent of the total population is Sinhalese, while the main ethnic minority, the Sri Lankan Tamils, represent 12.6 per cent of the total population. The representation of the other minorities is shown in Table 4.1. The size and rate of increase of a minority group is an important factor in ethnic conflict.[5] As shown in Table 4.1 the outstanding characteristic of the ethnic structure is the numerical preponderance of the Sinhalese majority.

Table 4.1 Ethnic Composition of the Population of Sri Lanka

Nationalities	*Number*	*Percentage*
Sinhalese	10,985,666	74.0
Sri Lankan Tamils	1,871,535	12.6
Sri Lankan Moors	1,056,972	7.1
Indian Tamils	885,233	5.6
Malays	43,378	0.3
Burghers	38,236	0.3
Others	28,981	0.2

Source: Department of Census and Statistics, Census of Populations and Housing in Sri Lanka, Preliminary Release, No. 1, (Colombo: Department of Census and Statics, 1981), p. 3.

The ethnic communities in Sri Lanka are divided by differences in race, language, religion and territorial concentration. The Sinhalese majority, who are said to be descendants of the Aryans of Northern India, speak Sinhala, an Indo-European language related to the language of Northern India.[6] Ninety per cent of the Sinhalese are Buddhists. Despite the fact that there is a pattern of regional concentration on an ethnic basis, this has been somewhat flexible. The Sinhalese are concentrated mostly in the southern, the western and the highland regions of Sri Lanka. The dry zone, which lies between the highland and the northern areas of the country, and which was once sparsely populated, has subsequently absorbed the surplus population from the western and highland regions.

The Tamils said to have originated from the Dravidian stock of Southern India, speak Tamil, a Dravidian language which is also spoken in Southern India.[7] Most Tamils are Hindus. Both the Sinhalese and the Tamil communities, however, have been exposed to the influence of Christianity. Most Sri Lankan Christians are Catholic Sinhalese living along the western coast. Table 4.2 shows the religious composition of Sri Lanka.

Table 4.2 Population by Religion in Sri Lanka 1981

Population	*Number*	*Percentage*
Buddhists	10,291,000	69.3
Hindus	2,302,000	15.5
Muslims	1,128,000	7.6
Christians	1;114,000	7.5
Others	15,000	0.1

Source: Department of Census and Statistics, Census of Populations and Housing in Sri Lanka, Preliminary Release, No. 1, (Colombo: Department of Census and Statics, 1981).

The Tamils are concentrated mainly in the Northern and Eastern provinces with only about one-third of them found to be in the other seven provinces.[8] Thus, the Tamils have a relatively well-defined territorial base. Arend Lijphart observes that clear boundaries between the segments of a plural society have the advantage of limiting mutual contacts and consequently of reducing the chances of ever present potential antagonisms erupting into actual hostility.[9]

However, the past relations between the two ethnic groups have had a profound influence in shaping their present relationships. Historically, the Sinhalese and the Tamils were involved in power struggles; for either the seizure of the Sinhalese throne by Tamil Adventurers or the contest for parts of the Sinhalese kingdom, or they participated in the wars between the Sinhalese kings and Southern Indian armies. Those historical battles between the Sinhalese and the Tamil kings were probably motivated more by feudal and territorial considerations than by ethnic factors.[10] Nevertheless, centuries of mutual separation accentuated their differences.

On the other hand, both communities developed clearly defined ideas and attitudes about the other. A few studies have been made of these attitudes. Howard Wriggins examined this aspect by using a study based on a sample of Sinhalese and Tamil students. According to this study the Sinhalese students characterized the Tamils as follows: cruel, clever, poor, thrifty, diligent, arrogant, clannish, mathematically-minded, self-centred, simple-living and loquacious. The Tamil students considered the Sinhalese to be lazy, proud, bold and selfish.[11] Consequently, there is no doubt that the two major ethnic communities displayed distinct ethnic dissimilarities. In fact, the existence of ethnic differences, often conceived of as primordial, can be viewed as problematic social constructions, not irreducible social components. Therefore, the fact that ethnic differences exist is not sufficient for ethnic conflict to occur. Clifford Geertz observes that Sri Lanka's aggravated primordial problem is not a mere legacy, an inherited impediment to her political, social and economic modernization; rather it is a direct and immediate reflex of her first serious—if still rather ineffective—attempt to achieve such modernization.[12]

Given Huntington's belief that communal ties are ascriptive, scholars often think of them as traditional in character. Communal conflict, consequently, is thought of as a more traditional form of conflict than say, conflict among social classes. Although, communal characteristics may be ascriptive, communal consciousness is creative and malleable. It is indeed often intensified, and in some cases initiated by the process of modernization.[13]

Parallel to Huntington's argument is the observation that the origins of the ethnic conflict in Sri Lanka are deeply rooted in the process of modernization initiated during the occupation of the British Raj. The process of modernization has stimulated communal conflict between the two communities by means of a variety of factors. The author, however, wishes to focus primarily on the factors which developed after the granting of independence in 1948. Nevertheless, it is not possible to make an in-depth study of the post-independence period in isolation. Such a study has to be viewed in the context of the impact of the colonial period.

4.3 Impact of the Colonial Period

When the Portuguese arrived in Sri Lanka in 1505, the island was divided into three separate kingdoms. There were two Sinhalese kingdoms: Kotte was based in the south-west maritime regions; Kandy was located in the Central Highlands. There was also a Tamil kingdom, centred around Jaffna in Northern Sri Lanka.[14] By 1594, the Portuguese had secured possession of the southwestern districts and in 1619, they annexed the Jaffna kingdom. Those areas were later conquered first by the Dutch in 1658 and then by the British in 1796. The Kandyan kingdom, on the other hand, remained unconquered until the British finally succeeded in annexing it to their empire in 1815. From the very beginning, the European powers administratively divided the Sinhala and Tamil areas into separate territories, leading to distinct and separate social formations characterized by different socio-economic and political structures. This administrative division was operational until 1833.

The impact of both the Portuguese and the Dutch periods on the ethnic conflict was minimal. The ethnic divisions between the two communities originated with the socio-economic and political developments of the country particularly during British colonial rule. Certain socio-political recommendations of the Colebrook-Cameron Commission in 1833 marked the beginning of a differential social mobilization between the Sinhala and Tamil peoples of Sri Lanka. The Commission's recommendations incorporated far-reaching changes in the form of a uniform and centralized system of governmental administration, English education and the Legislative Council.

For the purposes of administration, the island was divided into five administrative provinces: The Western, Northern, Eastern, Southern and Central, all of which came under the purview of a government agent.[15] In 1873, some provinces were further subdivided. The North Central Province was formed from the Northern Province. Two additional provinces were demarcated in the Central Province and were named as the Uva and Sabaramuwa provinces in 1886 and 1889, respectively. The centralization of government and administration, combined with the development of transport, brought the Sinhala and Tamil communities into closer contact.

The plantation economy opened the scope of economic advancement and offered employment in the governmental and private professional fields. The introduction of English education created direct competition for limited resources, e.g., for government employment and for the professions based on English education which became the primary means of economic advancement, social mobility and elite status. From the inception of the plantation economy, the benefits of English education were reaped by the Burghers,[16] the Tamils and the low-country Sinhalese.[17] For the Tamils, the geo-economic conditions during the colonial rule, especially in the Northern Province, limited their options for social mobility to education. Missionaries too concentrated on improving English education in this region. For example, in 1911, 4.9 per cent of Sri Lankan Tamil males were literate in English, as opposed to 3.5 per cent of the low-country Sinhalese males and 0.7 per cent of the up-country Sinhalese males. Those factors facilitated the Tamils in securing more professional jobs both in the public and the private sectors which resulted in a disproportionately higher representation of Tamils in employment than in the total population. This observation is supported by S.J. Tambiah's examination of the ethnic representation in Sri Lanka's public administrative services from 1870 to 1946.[18] Furthermore, Tambiah sees the following as the reasons for the Tamils' preponderance in English literacy and high economic standing:

The Ceylon Tamils also found attractive avenues of employment in the administrative services and the professions. Coming from the Northern region of Ceylon where land was both scarce and infertile, they had no scope for large scale agricultural activity which was possible in the case of the Sinhalese especially those in the low country.[19]

The low-country Sinhalese, however, who also had the advantage of an English education, entered the higher governmental services and private professions in direct competition with the Tamil community. According to Howard Wriggins there have always been more low-country Sinhalese than Tamils in the Sri Lankan civil service in terms of numbers. In relation to the total of each community in the population, there have been proportionately more Tamils and many more Burghers than Sinhalese in the public services. A service-wide census taken in 1951 showed that out of a total of 123,194 reported employees of the central government, those with Sinhalese background represented 81,374 and those with Tamil background represented 21,768. Of the remaining 20,000 who had an exclusively English educational background it would be plausible to assume that 10,000 were Sinhalese, 5,000 were Burghers and 5,000 were Tamils. This would yield a total of 27,000 Tamils out of the total public service force of about 123,000, or roughly 22 per cent.[20] Differential social mobilization widened the socio-economic cleavages and generated a new kind of ethnic competition between the two communities, particularly after independence. Huntington aptly observes a similar situation as follows:

> Ethnic or religious groups which had lived peacefully side by side in traditional society became aroused to violent conflict as a result of the interaction, the tensions, and the inequalities generated by social and economic modernization. Modernization thus increases conflict among traditional groups, between traditional groups and modern ones, and among modern groups.[21]

Moreover, Joseph Rothschild claims that for the consolidation of ethnic groups two main factors are essential. The first is the competition over relatively limited and valued resources and goals within the wider society, a competition which may lead to the mobilization of the main ethnic group who feel challenged and minorities who feel disadvantaged. The second is an elite with an ability and desire to mobilize those with a common objective into a self-conscious group.[22] In order to understand how the already existing competition between the two communities developed into conflict and then into a full-blown political violence movement, the socio-economic and political development of post-independent Sri Lanka will be examined. The most important factors for the study are the policies of: internal migration through state sponsored land settlement schemes, official language, public sector employment, and university admission.

4.4 Internal Migration

The main pattern of migration within the island was discussed in Chapter 3 of this study which involved the movement of persons, mainly Sinhalese, from the densely populated Southwestern wet zone to districts in the Northern and Eastern provinces. The impetus given to peasant resettlement schemes especially after independence was met by stiff opposition from the Tamil community. Their objections to the government sponsored "Colonies", sometimes situated within or at least in the peripheral regions of the Northern and Eastern provinces, were expressed as a serious threat to the regional demarcation of the "traditional Tamil areas".

When land resettlements were stepped up in the 1930s, landlessness and land fragmentation were acute problems for the Sinhalese as well as a substantial number of Tamils. Those problems were of particular concern to the Tamils because of their relegation to the non-arable lands and the lack of irrigable land for the expansion of agriculture. The opposition posed by the Federal Party (F.P.) to the resettlement programme was attributed to their claims that preference was given to Sinhala settlers over Tamils in the selection of allottees for the said schemes which were located predominantly in districts with a preponderance of Tamils. Table 4.3 illustrates the ethnic composition of the peasant colonies in the Northern and Eastern provinces at the end of 1953. It is evident that in areas where the Tamil population predominated, resettlement was much less than in the Sinhalese-dominated areas. In the Eastern Province, a total of 479,312 hectares of land were alienated to 16,532 allottees between 1931 and 1953. Of the land allotted, only 17.4 per cent was allocated to Tamils.[23]

Table 4.3 Sinhalese and Tamils in the Colonies of the Northern and Eastern Provincey

	Eastern Provinces			
Provinces	*Total*	*Sinhalese*	*Tamil*	*Tamil as a % of Sinhalese*
Northern	656	0	656	100
Eastern	5,199	2,979	2,223	75
Whole	16,532	2,976	2,879	17

Source: B.H. Farmer, Pioneer Peasant Colonization in Ceylon, (London: Oxford University Press, 1957), pp. 208-209, quoted from C. Manogaran, *op. cit.,* 1987, p. 91.

Consequently, as Table 4.4 indicates, the demographic distribution of the Sinhalese population in these areas changed between 1911 and 1981.

Table 4.4 Sinhalese in the Northern and Eastern Provinces (Percentage)

Districts	*Sinhalese*			
	1911	*1946*	*1971*	*1981*
Jaffna	0.1	1.1	0.9	0.6
Mannar	2.7	3.8	4.1	8.1
Vavuniya/Mullaitivu	10.7	16.6	16.8	11.4
Trincomalee	3.8	20.7	29.0	33.6
Batticaloa/Amparai	3.7	5.8	17.7	21.8
Total, North and East	1.8	4.9	11.0	13.2

Source: R.N. Kearney and Barbara Diane Miller, Internal Migration in Sri Lanka and Its Social Consequences, (London: Westviews Press, 1987), p. 97.

C. Monogaram estimates that more than 165,000 Sinhalese were added to the population in the Eastern and Northern provinces. This development dates from the advent of the peasant resettlement programme especially between 1953 and 1981.[24] Wriggins elaborates on the impact of colonization and on the suspicions and discord between the Sinhalese and the Tamils:

> Clearing and irrigating jungle land to be settled by peasants from the overcrowded Sinhalese and Tamil areas became a bitter apple of discord between the two communities. The land had lain under the rule of malaria, empty, and desolate until D.D.T. made its reconquest possible. Tamils consider these new lands to be areas they have traditionally inhabited. The Sinhalese see much historical evidence to prove that Buddhist civilization once flourished before the jungle and malaria made their conquest. Both argue that the settlement of peasants from other communities represent encroachment. And since political representation goes according to territorial constituencies, a significant change in the population structure of such areas would alter the balance of communal representation in the House of Representatives. Hence even land development has sharpened group conflict.[25]

Thus, internal migration through the land settlement schemes has sharpened ethnic conflict. It was the issue of official language, however, which brought the ethnic conflict to the forefront of Sri Lankan politics. Until then the Tamil politicians had not been very successful in mobilizing the Tamil people to support their political objectives.

4.5 Policy of Official Language

The policy of official language has been the major factor behind the ethnic conflict between the two communities since independence. The British Raj established the English language as the language of the government, the professions and higher education. Therefore, those receiving an English education were at a tremendous occupational advantage and could expect a higher social mobility than those who had been taught in the indigenous languages. The importance of this trend in language is indicated in Table 4.5.

According to Table 4.5, 80 per cent of the population did not have access to an English education and therefore, were illiterate in English.[26] It was to address this injustice that in 1944 the Sri Lankan Legislature agreed that both Sinhala and Tamil should replace English as the official language. The theme of the political slogan was "Swabasha", the vernacular languages, that should be given their rightful place. Until 1954, the main political parties were committed to the policy of Swabasha. The Tamils, however, were not enthusiastic about Swabasha because the British policies put the Tamils at an advantage and they were thus in a better position to gain access to an English education.

Table 4.5 Languages Spoken by Persons of 3 Years of Age and Over by 1953

Languages Spoken	*Numbers*	*Percentage*
Sinhala Only	4,289,957	58.9
Tamil Only	1,570,084	21.6
English Only	14,066	0.2
Sinhala and English	719,194	9.9
Sinhala and Tamil	307,570	4.2
Tamil and English	146,549	2.0
Sinhala, Tamil and English	233,567	3.2
Total	7,280,987	100

Source: Department of Census and Statistics, Census of Ceylon, 1953, Vol. 3, part 1, (Colombo: Government Press, 1960), p. 604.

The vernacular movement gained momentum after independence. The national resurgence, which extended as far back as the 19th century, was merged with the vernacular movement and had a significant impact in the political arena. The introduction of universal franchise and the need for a literate population, who are able to participate actively on a mass basis, was increasingly important for the English-educated Sri Lankans.[27] The vernacular movement, however, gained more momentum when the Sinhala Language was proposed as the official language instead of swabasha.

The introduction of mass politics led to the mobilization of forces which had hitherto been excluded from active politics. This and the pressure exerted by the Sinhala Buddhist nationalist forces compelled the Sri Lanka Freedom Party (S.L.F.P) to change its policy of Swabasha to Sinhala only, with the provision of reasonable use of the Tamil language in 1955. At the level of mass politics, the United National Party (U.N.P) was also compelled tactically to change its Swabasha policy to one of Sinhala only.[28] This change in language policy went hand in hand with popular slogans such as "Sri Lanka for the Sinhalese".[29] Once the Swabasha policy was changed, the United National Party (U.N.P.) was unable to mobilize the support of the Tamil community. The policy of "responsive co-operation" that they talked about and the United National Party's (U.N.P.'s) ally the Tamil Congress (T.C.) too lost their validity and viability among the Tamil community.

The General Election of 1956 was to be one of the most significant elections in the electoral history of Sri Lanka and its impact was to have lasting effects on Sri Lanka's ethnic relations and trends. The official language issue was foremost in the election campaign. The election manifesto put forward by the Mahajana Eksath Peramuna (M.E.P) a coalition led by the S.LF.P. in 1956 stated that Sinhala would be Sri Lanka's only official language but that the Tamil language would receive due recognition through its "reasonable use".[30] The Language debate transformed a relationship based on competitive coexistence into a phase of overt ethnic conflict between the Sinhalese and the Tamils. M.R.Singer sees the election of 1956 as the official beginning of the Sinhalese-Tamil conflict in Sri Lanka.[31]

The issue of language reached its climax in June 1956 when Sinhala was declared the official Sri Lankan language by the M.E.P. Government.[32] It also marked the beginning of a new phase in the Sinhala-Tamil ethnic relationship. As the Tamils saw it, to make Sinhalese the sole official language put Tamils in an inferior position and would no doubt give the Sinhalese-speaking people a competitive advantage in the entrance to public service, teaching, education and other desirable careers.[33] Consequently, in the Tamils view, Sinhala as a sole national language was a threat not only to their culture and identity but also to their monopoly over public sector employment and education. Bandaranaiake's original intention to write into the act certain statutory safeguards pertaining to the reasonable use of Tamil was abandoned when he succumbed to the pressure from the Sinhalese nationalists.[34] The generally peaceful climate within which the Sinhalese and Tamils had competed for resources since 1948 was abruptly changed into a phase of ethnic conflict after June 1956. The prime motive of the Sinhala only policy was initially as a protest against the privileged position of the English-educated elite. In the long term, however, the policy was instrumental in triggering an ethnic conflict between the Sinhala majority and the main Sri Lankan ethnic minority, the Tamils.

The impact of the Sinhala-only policy on the ethnic conflict will be examined further under the role of the Federal Party. It may be asserted at this point, however, that the official language issue has been the main bone of contention in the country since the 1950's because of its relevance to public sector employment and to education as a medium of instruction.

4.6 Public Sector Employment and Unemployment

In Sri Lanka, the state has been the largest employer partly due to a rapid expansion of state administrative services and of governmental involvement in the economy. The middle classes of the Sinhalese and the Tamil communities were the main competitors for public sector employment. It was this competition which gave the language issue a communal dimension. The geo-economic conditions in the predominantly Tamil areas were not conducive to any other source of employment and so the public service remained the main employer. Post-independent economic stagnation, especially in the 1950s, limited the scope for employment within the public sector. While employment dwindled, education expanded and modernization increased. This stimulated the number of people seeking employment in the public sector, predominantly among the low-country Sinhalese. As Sinhala was Sri Lanka's official language, the Sinhalese sought to correct the obvious imbalance of representation in the public sector employment. The enactment of Sinhala as the official language in 1956 offered better prospects for the Sinhala-educated to secure employment in the government sector. The Tamils perceived the Sinhala-only policy as a countermeasure aimed at ousting or excluding them from state employment and the private sector professions. Their fears were further reinforced by an additional requirement that those seeking state employment to have a working knowledge of Sinhala. From a Tamil perspective these measures seemed to have been designed to exclude large proportions of otherwise eligible Tamils from gaining access to state employment and thereby from attaining social mobility.

Unemployment and lack of opportunities for employment were phenomena faced by both the Tamil and Sinhalese youth from the 1960s onward. The Sri Lankan Tamil community still claims that Tamils have been denied fair access to employment and have been severely discriminated against in other ways. According to the data on the ethnic composition of unemployment, however, the Tamils have a low rate of unemployment compared with the Sinhalese community. Table 4.6 depicts the ethnic composition of unemployment in the country.

Table 4.6 Unemployment by Ethnicity (Percentages)

Community	*As a % of Population in the Community Group*		*As a % of Work Force in the Community Group*	
	1963	*1973*	*1963*	*1973*
Sinhalese	9.0	17.6	30.2	53.0
Tamil	3.5	5.3	11.6	17.7
Indian Tamil	3.7	6.3	6.7	12.3
Moors	4.0	5.4	14.9	21.3
Malays	0.7	11.7	2.8	13.5
Burghers	5.9	6.3	21.9	21.2
Others	-	9.1	-	28.6
All Ethnics	4.4	8.1	13.8	24.0

Source: Central Bank of Ceylon, Survey of Sri Lanka's Consumer Finances, 1973, (Colombo: Central Bank, 1974), p. 49.

Nevertheless, R.N. Kearney notes that:

A rapidly worsening employment situation was felt with particular severity by Tamil youth as they suffered not only from the general dearth of employment opportunities but from disadvantages and discrimination in obtaining the few existing jobs.[35]

Channels of employment and recruitment in the state sector were gradually politicized and became increasingly so after 1960. Competition increased among the Sinhalese for limited career prospects including state employment especially after Sinhala became the medium of education and was declared the official language. Thus, demands for access to limited state employment – even though the state was the largest employer – led to a system of political patronage in which the ruling parties made a habit of recruiting from party cadres. The absence of Tamil politicians in the governments after 1956 placed the Tamil youth in a most disadvantageous position. Newton Gunasinghe states thus:

> Irrespective of the regime being U.N.P. or S.L.F.P., opportunities existed for Sinhala youth to build up patron-client linkages with local politicians and press themselves forward. The Tamil Youth, especially those of the north and the east, did not enjoy this advantage, as their local politicians represented regional ethnic parties, enjoying no power at the centre.[36]

Table 4.7 depicts the decline of Tamil recruitment to the state sector between 1956 and 1970.

Table 4.7 Percentage of Tamils Employed in the State Sector

Services	*1956*	*1965*	*1970*
Sri Lanka Administrative Services	30	20	5
Clerical	50	30	5
Professions	60	30	10
Armed Forces	40	20	1
Labour	40	20	5

Source: U. Phadnis, "Ethnicity and Nation Building in South Asia", India Quarterly, Vol., 35, Part 3, (1979), p. 348.

The ratio of Tamil representation in the state sector is significantly lower than the ratio they enjoyed three decades ago. Prior to independence, 30 per cent of those employed in the government services in Sri Lanka were Tamils, but by 1975 the figure dropped to nearly 6 per cent.[37] A publication of the Ministry of Foreign Affairs entitled "Tamils in Sri Lanka" explains the situation of the state employment as follows:

> Prior to the granting of independence in 1948, the Tamils had an advantage over the Sinhalese in securing admission to the state services because educational facilities were readily available to them, as a result of a number of mission schools being set up in the Northern Province. With the granting of independence and the development of educational facilities in the non-Tamil areas it was to be expected that this advantageous position that they occupied would be steadily excluded. Over the years the intake of Sinhalese into the state sector had been comparatively increasing.[38]

The loss of the Tamils' long-standing dominance in government services, however, created frustration and disappointment among the Tamil youth. This situation was further aggravated by the new university admission policies introduced by the United Front (U.F.) Government.[39] The Sinhalese and Tamil conflict in the 1950s and 1960s over land settlement, language, and employment in the public sector was followed in the 1970s by the disagreement over the policy of university admission.

4.7 The Policy of University Admission

University education in Sri Lanka represented an opportunity for social and economic mobility. The rapid growth of university education is evident from the increase of the student population from 904 in 1942 to 19,723 in 1965.[40] Consequently, a significant feature of this growth was the changing ethnic composition of the university student population. Table 4.8 which indicate the percentage of university students by ethnic origin, reveals that in the mid 1960s the Sinhalese emerged as a privileged group, while at the same time, the Sri Lankan Tamils and Burghers lost their educational privileges. The reason was the introduction of Sinhala and Tamil languages as the medium of instruction at secondary schools and universities and an increase in the number of universities.

4.8 Distribution of University Students by Ethnic Origin (Percentage)

Ethnic Group	*1947*	*1953*	*1965*
Sinhalese	61.7	60.2	78.1
Tamils	29.4	33.7	19.1
Moors and Malays	2.8	1.7	2.0
Burghers	4.9	3.2	0.4
Indian Tamils	-	-	-
Others	1.2	1.2	0.8

Source: D.L. Jayasuriya, "Development of University Education: The Growth of the University of Ceylon, 1942-1965", University of Ceylon Review, Vol. 23, Nos. 1-2, (1965), p. 89.

There were discrepancies, however, in the distribution of facilities between the Sinhalese and the Tamil communities for scientific education and liberal studies. The rapid development of secondary education in the natural sciences dating from the 1950s, was given an added impetus when social science graduates found it increasingly difficult to secure employment during the 1960s. It became evident that the only assurance of employment lay in studying the natural sciences. Consequently, pressure and competition for admission to science-based courses at university level had increased by the 1960s. Tamil students who had been groomed for professional courses since the 1950s were better equipped to gain admission to science-related faculties than in the past. In addition, Tamil representation in these courses in the 1960s was fairly high compared to their lower ethnic representation in the wider population. The attraction of guaranteed employment was irresistible to the Tamil community which otherwise faced only limited opportunities in state employment. Table 4.9 indicates percentage of university students by faculty and ethnicity in 1964.

Table 4.9 University Students by Faculty and Ethnicity in 1964 (Percentage)

Ethnic Group	*Arts Law*	*Science Engineering*	*Medicine Dentistry*	*Agriculture Veterinary*	*All Faculties*
Sinhalese	85.0	59.0	54.5	54.7	73.1
Tamils	12.0	37.2	40.5	40.5	23.4
Moors/Malay	2.0	2.5	2.5	2.5	2.1
Burgher	0.5	1.1	1.1	1.1	0.7
Others	0.5	0.2	1.5	1.5	0.7
Total	4,183	1,279	1,601	177	7,180

Source: D.L. Jayasuriya, *op. cit.,* p. 91

According to Table 4.9, by 1964, 85 per cent of the university students studying social sciences, law and the humanities in Sri Lankan universities were Sinhalese. The percentage in the science-based faculties, however, was much lower: 59 per cent in science and engineering, 54.5 per cent in medicine and dentistry, and 54.7 per cent in agriculture and veterinary sciences. On the other hand, Sri Lankan Tamils, though representing only 12 per cent of the students in the social sciences, held 37.2 per cent of the places in the science and engineering courses, 40.5 per cent in medicine and dentistry, and 41.9 per cent in the veterinary and agricultural sciences at the University of Sri Lanka.[41] By 1970, Tamils had secured 35.3 per cent of the total admissions to science courses at the university, of which 10.8 per cent of the places were in medicine.[42] It was in the 1970s that the ethnic imbalance in the admission to the science, engineering and medical faculties of the universities surfaced as a major issue between the two communities.

The Sinhalese community, on the other hand, viewed this situation as a denial of equal opportunities. Those sentiments were further aggravated by allegations brought forward by some sections of the community regarding the honesty of Tamil examiners. The marks for examinations given in the Tamil medium recorded a much higher average than for those given in the Sinhala medium. As a result, there were suspicions that Tamil examiners leniently marked the answer scripts of Tamil students. The allegations of favouritism became more intense as the number of Sinhala students applying for entry to the science and engineering faculties increased dramatically in the 1970s. The allegations were investigated but were never substantiated.[43]

Sinhalese pressure led to a change in the system for admission to the Sri Lankan universities for education in the natural sciences. Thus, in the early 1970s, the U.F. Government took measures to reform the system of university admissions in order to take into consideration the previous extremely limited facilities available to some students in the rural sector. Once again the changes impacted primarily the Tamil youth. The system of university admission up to 1972 was based on the results of the final examination at the G.C.E. Advanced Level. Under the new admissions system which was the method of standardization was readjusted based on the media of study and a district quota system. In 1974 the government found it necessary to again readjust the admissions system adopted the previous year. There were four such readjustment schemes: Standardization of admissions in 1973; standardization and district quotas in 1974; standardization and 100 per cent district quotas in 1975; and standardization based on 70 per cent on marks and 30 per cent on district quotas in 1976.[44] The government introduced a standardization procedure based on marks necessary for university admissions according to which "persons taking the examination in the Tamil language were required to achieve a higher score than those taking the examination in Sinhala in order to gain admission to the university".[45]

The introduction of the standardization and district quota system reduced the number of Tamil students entering the university education.[46] Table 4.10 indicates the decline in the intake of Tamil students to science-based faculties in universities between 1969 and 1974. This shortfall is most evident for the period 1973 to 1976. For instance, the percentage of Tamil students entering engineering courses fell from 40.8 per cent in 1970 to 24.4 per cent in 1973, and 13.2 per cent in 1976. The percentage of Tamil students enrolled in science courses fell from 35 per cent in 1970 to 15 per cent in 1978. The number of Tamil medical students declined from 50 per cent in 1970 to 30 per cent in 1973, 26 per cent in 1974 and 20 per cent in 1975.

Table 4.10 University Admission by Ethnicity From 1970 to 1975 (Percentage)

Year	*Science*			*Arts*		
	Sinhalese	*Tamils*	*Others*	*Sinhalese*	*Tamils*	*Others*
1969/70	57.7	39.8	2.5	88.4	7.5	4.1
1970/71	60.6	35.3	4.1	88.9	7.6	3.5
1971/72	63.6	33.6	1.8	92.6	4.8	2.6
1973	67.4	29.5	3.1	91.5	6.1	2.6
1974	75.4	20.9	3.7	86.0	10.0	4.0

Source: C.R. de Silva, "Weightage in University Admissions: Standardisation and District Quotas in Sri Lanka, 1970-75", Modern Ceylon Studies, Vol. 5, No. 2, (1974), pp. 172-173.

C.R. de Silva assessed the impact of the standardization and district quota system on the ethnic conflict, and states that there is little doubt that it represented a major blow to the Sri Lankan Tamils.[47] Overall, the admission of Tamil students to science-oriented courses dropped from 35.5 per cent in 1970 to less than 21 per cent in 1973.[48] At the opposite end of the scale, the Sinhalese emerged as the main beneficiaries of the new system. The representation of the Sinhalese in science-based courses rose from 75.4 per cent in 1974 to over 80 per cent in universities.[49]

The systematic but drastic cutback in university admissions compelled the frustrated Tamil youth, who found themselves confronted with the limited access to higher education and the grim problem of unemployment, to seek a way out by fighting for a separate state. The sentiments of Tamil youth are expressed in the following quotation, said to have been made in 1976:

> If we are not wanted and are discriminated against, then what future do we have? Government jobs are closing down on us. We do have enough lands to survive, but one does not want to live on bread alone. Some of us would like to go for Medicine, Engineering and government services, but even if we make the grade initially, we will

> not reach the de facto decision-making centres. It is a question of our own honour and dignity as a community, to get what is our due on merit basis, without discrimination and patronage. If this is not possible why not have the parting of ways.[50]

Thus, political rivalries between communal groups intensified with the removal of the colonial rule and the socio-economic changes that strengthened the desire for educational opportunities, non-agricultural employment and governmental services. The government policy of reducing the imbalance in land, state employment and education in favour of the Sinhalese community served to intensify the Tamils' communal consciousness and political mobilization. Huntington observes a similar situation as follows:

> The efforts to create a nation state, where one did not exist before, also raise new issues to inflame group conflict. So long as the state did not penetrate the society and the people did not participate in the state, many of these problems could be avoided. Once the state begins to play a more important role in society, questions concerning national symbols, language, education policy become of critical importance.[51]

Consequently, the above-mentioned socio-economic changes since independence have broadened political participation in keeping with the formation of political parties along ethnic lines. This has served to reinforce and politicize ethnic competition. Nevertheless, the author wishes to examine the development of ethno-political organizations and parties within the context of the constitutional reforms during the British period.

4.8 Origin and Development of Ethno-Political Organizations

The origin and development of ethno-political organizations and their policies played an important role in the development of ethnic consciousness and competition after the introduction of ethnic representation in the Sri Lankan Legislature by the British in 1833. The Legislative Council from 1833 to 1920, however, was not constituted on the basis of racial proportion.

There were about the same number of unofficial members of the Sinhalese and the Tamils in the Council despite the clear majority of the Sinhalese in the Sri Lankan population. Despite this discrepancy, the English-educated middle-class leaders of both communities did not display any animosity against each other. The unity of the Tamil and the Sinhalese leadership was clear in the election of Sir Ponnambalam Ramanathan, a Tamil to the Legislative Council in 1912 by limited franchise; and by the formation of the Ceylon National Congress (C.N.C.) in 1919 as a united organization.[52] This political solidarity was also exhibited by the Tamil leadership in 1915, when they supported the victimized Sinhalese leaders aftermath of the Sinhalese-Muslim riots.

The political homogeneity and integration of leadership, however, was not to last long due largely to changes in the representation introduced by the Constitutional Reforms of 1920. The 1920 reforms combined the communal and the territorial representation, causing an imbalance in the ratio of legislative representation in favour of the Sinhalese majority. The disequilibrium resulted in a confrontation between the elite politicians of the two communities. While the Tamils wished to maintain the system of communal or ethnic representation, the Sinhalese upheld the territorial principle.[53] As a result, the Tamil leaders in 1921 broke away from the National Congress and formed a separate ethno-political organization known as the "Tamil Mahajana Sabha" (the Great Council of the Tamils). The Mahjajana Sabha provided the means by which the Tamils could articulate their demands as a minority community. The breakaway also marked the beginning of a trend of forming political organizations based on mono-ethnic rather than national motivations. The visible manifestations of the trend were the formation of the "Sinhala Maha Sabah" (the Great Council of the Sinhalese) in 1936, the Ceylon Indian Congress in 1939, and the Tamil Congress in 1944. The competition among these ethnic groups for a share of colonial political power by means of constitutional reforms, increased with the formation of the Tamil Congress. Consequently, the subsequent years were marked by communal conflict over reforms on representation leading towards independence.

Furthermore, the introduction of universal franchise in 1931 widened the scope of Sri Lanka's process of political development based on greater participation. Although universal franchise broadened the constituency of the political elite of all ethnic groups, it thereby aggravated the existing inter-group tensions. In its wake, therefore, it left a further strain on the already deteriorating relationship between the Tamil and the Sinhalese political elites. The positive effects of universal franchise benefited the Sinhala majority who already held about two-thirds of the seats in the State Council, which had been introduced by the Donoughmore Constitution.[54] In 1931, of the 50 elective seats out of a total of 61 seats in the House, 38 seats had been secured by the Sinhalese majority.[55] As a result of universal franchise, the Sinhalese leaders sought changes to improve the conditions of their electorates in order to retain their power base. On the other hand, the Tamils felt neglected and dominated by the Sinhalese and, therefore, demanded a system of 'balanced representation' under which 50 per cent of the seats in the legislature should be reserved for the minorities as a safeguard. Minority safeguards in such a context, however, guaranteed constitutional barriers that would protect the advantageous positions of the Sri Lankan Tamils in the public services.[56] Consequently, the competition for representation between the Sinhalese and the Tamil political elites between 1920 and 1948 served as a barometer of their ethnic conflict. The overt political competition was underlined by economic competition between the middle classes of the Sinhala and Tamil communities for well-paying public service employment. By the time Sri Lanka was granted independence in 1948, the seeds of ethnic disharmony and conflict had already been sown, and were being fostered in the public and private sectors.

Soon after independence the Tamil Congress (T.C.) joined the U.N.P. government and was guided by the political formula of 'responsive co-operation'.[57] The T.C. mainly represented the Colombo-based public servants of Jaffna origin. Hence the T.C. saw that mutual co-operation would be the best means of preserving employment and the general interests of its supporters.[58] C.R. de Silva observes that this formula of responsive co-operation was a loosely knit political compromise based on the following four considerations. Firstly, the dominance of the English language was gradually replaced by the Sinhala and Tamil languages as the official languages; secondly, all minority groups were protected from discrimination by section 29 (2) of the 1948 Constitution;[59] thirdly, provision was made for proportional representation of the minorities in the electoral system; and, finally, government was founded on the concept of the secular state where all religions would enjoy equal status.[60]

An area of conflict was to soon emerge between the two communities over the citizenship and voting rights of the Indian Tamil plantation workers. The Citizenship Act of 1948, the Indian and Pakistani (Citizenship) Act of 1949, and the Parliamentary Election (Amendment) Act of 1949 were designed to confine the granting of franchise to those who were eligible by descent or by registration.[61] Eventually, what resulted from these legislative acts was that the vast majority of the Indian Tamils who were predominantly plantation workers became stateless and disenfranchised. Of the total of 825,000 Indian Tamils residing in Sri Lanka, 250,340 applications for citizenship were filed; of these applicants only 134,188 were successful, representing exactly 16.2 per cent of the total Indian Tamil population in Sri Lanka.[62] This disenfranchisement had significant implications for electoral politics in Sri Lanka. At an election held in 1947, the Ceylon Indian Congress (C.I.C.) had seven parliamentary candidates in the estate region, of whom six were of Indian origin. When a large proportion of Indian Tamils lost their voting rights, these seats were monopolized by the Sinhala majority.[63] For instance, the number of seats held by the Sinhalese in the Legislature rose from 67 per cent of all elective seats in 1947 to 73 per cent in 1952.[64] This situation paved the way for the emergence of a new Tamil political Party. The emergence and the development of the Federal Party as a considerable force in Sri Lankan politics since 1949 have further intensified the Sinhalese Tamil ethnic conflict.

4.9 The Role of the Federal Party

The issue of citizenship for Indian Tamils did not create a major conflict between the Sinhalese and the Sri Lankan Tamils. Its impact, however, was felt in the Tamil Congress when in 1949 a section of the Tamil politicians broke away and founded the Federal Party (F.P.), also known as the Ilankai Tamil Arasu Katchi (The Tamil State Party). A.J. Wilson gives a vivid explanation of this breakaway:

> The immediate pretext for the F.P.'s emergence in December 1949 was the objection of two T.C. M.P.'s and a T.C. Senator to the legislation of 1948 and 1949 against the Indian Tamils.[65]

The F.P. sought the creation of a new national flag, the solution of the citizenship problem related to the Tamil population of Indian origin in the plantation sector, and the abolition of the system of state-aided colonization by the Sinhalese people in the Northern and Eastern provinces as its objectives. These goals were reflected in the F.P.'s first pamphlet in which it also called for the demarcation of an autonomous state on the basis of language and an ethno-political framework in a "Federal Union of Sri Lanka".[66] In later years, however, the term 'autonomous Tamil State' was amplified to mean 'autonomous Tamil states'. As James Jupp points out, there was a degree of ambiguity regarding the specific aims of the F.P. The party vacillated between adopting a federal system similar to that of Switzerland versus that of India. In the eyes of the Sinhalese, the F.P.'s objectives represented efforts by the Tamil community to restore the independent Tamil Kingdom. The worst fears of the Sinhalese were rooted in an assumption that such a separate state would be merely a pawn of Tamil Nadu imperialism which was attempting to annex the Tamil areas of Sri Lanka.[67] Consequently, the founding and the development of the F.P. marked a significant landmark in the relationship between the Sinhalese and the Tamil communities.

The F.P. became the basis for political activity by the nationalist elements within the Sri Lankan Tamil community. The F.P. having adopted the rhetoric of Tamil nationalism, articulated a claim that the Tamils were a distinct nation distinguished by language, territorial demarcations, and a definite history and destiny. The main rudiments of the party's ideology were incorporated in the following resolution of 1951:

> The Tamil-speaking people in Sri Lanka constitute a nation distinct from that of the Sinhalese by every fundamental test of nationhood, firstly that of a separate historical past, in this island at least as ancient and as glorious as that of the Sinhalese; secondly by the fact of their being a linguistic entity, entirely different from that of the Sinhalese, with an unsurpassed classical heritage and a modern development of language which makes Tamil fully adequate for all present day needs; and finally by reason of their territorial habitation of definite areas, which constitute over one-third of the island.[68]

The F.P. was opposed to the links established between the T.C. and the U.N.P. Government on the basis of mutual co-operation which lasted from 1948 to 1956. On the other hand, the F.P. was committed to the cause of a nationalist movement based on Tamil ethnicity in the Northern and Eastern provinces. The F.P.'s opposition to the T.C.-U.N.P. alliance was, therefore, an obvious attempt to appeal to nationalism of the Tamil people and hark back to the days before the advent of the Portuguese, when there was a separate Tamil kingdom in Northern Sri Lanka. A.J. Wilson perceives that the F.P. was determined to safeguard the distinct identity of the Tamil people and concludes that:

> For the first time there had emerged a group which had begun to think in terms of an economic future for the Ceylon Tamils, not in the public service or in the common exploitation by Sinhalese and Tamils but in the preservation and development in isolation of a "Tamil homeland".[69]

Thus, the emergence of the Federal Party marked a significant change in the politics which had been followed hitherto by the Sri Lankan Tamils. From the time of the formation of the F.P. in 1949, four major issues formed the impetus for the party's agitations. These issues, as identified and discussed above, were the internal migration of the Sinhalese peasants in the Northern and Eastern provinces through state-sponsored resettlement schemes, the adoption of the vernacular languages as the official languages, and competition for public sector employment and admission to universities.

The F.P. viewed the Northern and Eastern provinces as the Tamil 'traditional homelands'. The F.P. was convinced, therefore, that any incursion into these areas by the Sinhalese was proof of Sinhalese designs to transform the predominantly Tamil areas into Sinhala areas.[70] The concept of a traditional homeland was derived mainly from the vague historical evidence of a Jaffna Kingdom. S.J. Tambiah interprets this rhetoric of a traditional homeland as a political move to reassure the security of the Tamil community.[71] Although the F.P. did not have the power to obstruct or prevent the colonization programme, it was successful in arousing an ethnic consciousness by using the concepts of a Jaffna Kingdom and a traditional homeland. K.M. de Silva assesses the role of the F.P. as a significant contribution to Tamil politics as follows:

> This was the Federal Party's great contribution to Tamil politics. Not only did they draw attention to the possession of a Tamil territorial unit, and the memory of an independent Tamil kingdom, (which survived from the thirteenth century to the beginning of the seventeenth), they also emphasized the role of language as the determinant of nationhood.[72]

When it was formed in 1949, the F.P. campaigned vigorously for a federal system of government to be instituted in place of the existing unitary system. These campaigns, however, were not met with much enthusiasm by the Tamil population itself. The English-educated Tamil intelligentsia, Tamil traders and the Tamil professionals in the Sinhalese provinces argued that more would be gained by the T.C.'s policy of co-operation with the U.N.P. Government. In addition, the Tamil Christians looked upon the F.P. with suspicion, fearing that if federalism became a reality they would be a minority within a minority and might suffer at the hands of a Hindu majority. Consequently, the Roman Catholic Church in the Tamil areas was hostile to the F.P. until 1956, while the Tamil Protestants were apathetic and at times even inimical to the F.P.'s objectives.[73] The lack of support for a federal system is indicated in the results of the second General Election of 1952 when the F.P. was successful in securing only two parliamentary seats.

It was the issue of official language which brought the F.P. to the forefront of Sri Lankan politics. Until then it had not been very successful in mobilizing the Tamil people to attain the F.P.'s objectives. The F.P., by virtue of its policies, felt compelled to express its opposition to the official language act. The F.P. viewed the new orientation of the vernacular movement, which emphasized Sinhala only, as a serious threat to the distinctive identity of the Tamil nation. The suspicions of the Tamil community are explained by Kearney:

> To the Tamil, the language controversy symbolized the threat of domination by the Sinhalese majority and appeared to endanger their existence as a unique and separate group.[74]

Given these circumstances, the F.P. found it necessary to take up the issue of the Tamil language, an issue which they felt had not received enough consideration. One F.P. Member for Parliament stated his reasons for taking up the language issue:

> We speak often and repeatedly about the language because that is so fundamental to us. Language today is the basis for our culture and our nationality.[75]

As these suspicions and fears gained momentum, the F.P. demanded parity of official status for the Tamil language along with the Sinhala language. The victory of the M.E.P. in 1956 not only brought hitherto suppressed layers of society to the fore but it also brought the F.P. into the mainstream of Tamil and national politics. From 1956 onwards the Tamil peasants, school teachers, and English-educated Tamil intelligentsia in the Northern and Eastern provinces became the solid base of the F.P. The Tamil Christian minority in these provinces turned to the F.P. for protection from the rising tide of Sinhalese-Buddhist revivalism. Tamil public servants, traders and professionals also switched their support to the F.P. Consequently, the F.P. won six of the nine Northern Province seats and four of the Eastern Province seats. During the five subsequent elections the F.P. succeeded in winning about two-thirds of the Tamil constituencies in the North and the East. As noted earlier, the language factor had an intrinsic link with state employment. The language issue, therefore, impacted on the wider Tamil community by politicizing them under the leadership of the F.P. After 1956, the F.P. as the chief spokesman for the Tamil community, was concerned with protecting and promoting the interests of the Tamil community throughout Sri Lanka. R.N. Kearney observes this situation as follows:

> The party's justification for existence rests on the assumption of the primary of communal identification and solidarity in politics and the belief that the common political interests of all members of the community by virtue of their ethnic bonds out-weigh political interests which internally divide the community.[76]

In 1956, the F.P. convened a conference in Trincomalee and passed the following resolutions to resolve the problems faced by the Tamil community in Sri Lanka. The F.P.'s demands were as follows:

1. The adoption of a federal constitution and the creation of one or more Tamil linguistic state or states enjoying the widest autonomous and residuary powers consistent with the unity and external security of Sri Lanka;
2. Recognition for Tamil, with absolute parity of status with Sinhalese as an official language;
3. Amendment of the relevant laws to grant citizenship on the basis of residence in Sri Lanka; and
4. The immediate cessation of colonization of the traditionally Tamil-speaking areas by the Sinhalese.[77]

The F.P.'s demands were made not to achieve political independence, but rather to secure some measure of devolution of national power. To achieve its objectives the F.P. employed a two-fold strategy. The first was to launch campaigns of non-cooperation and a full-scale satyagraha (non-violent resistance) and civil disobedience movements in the Tamil-speaking areas of the Northern and Eastern provinces. Secondly, the F.P. sought to bargain alternately between the S.L.F.P. and the U.N.P. in exchange for parliamentary support. It is evident from the following discussion that these strategies did have a significant impact. The demonstrations that they organized and other party activities intensified the political participation of Tamils, introducing an ethnic dimension which had hitherto been less overt. Consequently, the communalization of politics has certainly contributed to the increased political consciousness and participation of the Tamil community in Sri Lanka.

4.10 Government Response

Given these circumstances, the government's response to the Tamil demands were vital in terms of the integration of the Tamils into Sri Lanka's political system. There were two major efforts made by both the S.L.F.P. (1956-80) and the U.N.P. (1965-70) governments to arrive at a political accommodation with the Sri Lankan Tamils to ease the problem of ethnic conflict. The first attempt in this regard was the Bandaranaiake-Chelvanagam Pact (B-C Pact). The B-C Pact campaigned for legislation that would recognize Tamil as the language of the national minority and as the dominant language of the Tamil areas. The B-C Pact also included a plan for Regional Councils which would be empowered to resolve educational and agricultural issues and select colonists for state-sponsored colonization schemes. Moreover, the Prime Minister assured the F.P. that he would take the necessary steps to solve the problems involved with granting citizenship to the Tamils of Indian origin in Sri Lanka.[78]

Every concession to the Tamils, as K.M. de Silva points out, was bitterly fought over by forces within the S.L.F.P. led by Bhikkhus, as well as by opponents of the Government e.g. the U.N.P.[79] The U.N.P., in fact, opposed the B-C Pact largely on the grounds that it would prevent colonization by the Sinhalese in the Tamil areas.[80] The Buddhist clergy responded by staging a sit-in outside Bandaranaiake's home which exerted a great deal of pressure on the Prime Minister. Finally, he was forced to succumb to the pressures and the pact was withdrawn. S.J. Tambiah observes that this was a missed opportunity to settle the Tamil question forever.[81] The F.P., disillusioned by this withdrawal, reacted by obliterating the Sinhala letters 'SRI' which appeared on the number plates of automobiles registered in Sri Lanka. This campaign, which was directed at vehicles traveling to Northern Sri Lanka, climaxed in 1958 in an outbreak of ethnic violence. Thus, the years 1956 and 1958 were marked by turmoil and ethnic violence. The ethnic violence of 1956 and 1958, however, further strengthened the disharmony between the two communities and the F.P.'s demands for a federal state.

In spite of the repudiation of the B-C Pact by the Prime Minister, the pact still had a major impact on the Sinhala-Tamil relationship. By virtue of the federal policy contained in the B-C Pact, it gave both validity and recognition to the claim of the Tamil nationalists that the Northern and Eastern provinces were Tamil areas. From the F.P.'s point of view, the recognition of the Northern and Eastern provinces as Tamil areas was a strategic gain. Thereafter, the pact was a bargaining point between the F.P. and the moderate political parties such as the U.N.P. and S.L.F.P. Thus, the pact, though officially defunct, continued to provide the basic legitimacy and recognition for future agitation, first for federalism and later for separatism.

The Bandaranaiake Government made another attempt to address the language issue by ratifying the Tamil Language (Special Provisions) Act No. 28 of 1958. As a result of the Act, the use of Tamil in education, public service entrance examinations and administrative matters was granted in the Northern and Eastern provinces.[82] These concessions were recognition of the demands of the F.P. which fell far short of granting the Tamil language the parity of status with the official language, Sinhala. The drawback in these proposals was that although they were passed in 1958, to become effective, they first had to be gazetted, which was not done until January 1966.[83] Thus, the concessions had only a limited effect on the diffusion of both racial tension and Tamil agitation. Before the defeat in Parliament of the U.N.P. minority government in April 1960, the S.L.F.P. came to an understanding with the F.P. that they would implement minor modifications to the B-C Pact. This understanding, however, was not honoured after the S.L.F.P. came to power in July 1960.[84]

The Dudley Senanayake Chelvanayakam Pact (D-C Pact) was another attempt made by the Prime Minister of the later U.N.P. Government (1965-1970) to negotiate a settlement with the leader of the F.P., Chelvanayakam. The basic tenets of this pact were to provide specific guarantees pertaining to the status of the Tamil language, to establish district councils, and to set the conditions for repatriation of citizens of Indian origin.[85] The main outcome of the D-C Pact was the formation of a coalition government between the F.P. and the U.N.P. in 1965. For the first time since 1956, a member of the Tamil community was included in the Cabinet. In accordance with the demands of the D-C Pact, the Tamil Language Act in 1958 was gazetted as an official language in the Northern and Eastern provinces of Sri Lanka. Follow-up measures were also taken to draft a "White Paper" in June 1968 comprising the proposals to set up district councils. This proposition had to be abandoned due to opposition both within and without the coalition government. Not long thereafter the F.P. withdrew from the coalition government. Donald L. Horawitz observes these objections as follows:

> The U.N.P. feared that the left parties might take control of some localities if councils were set up. Members of parliament feared the district council chairman would become a rival local power. The Sri Lankan Moors, an important Muslim minority in the east, feared that local councils there would be Tamil dominated. The Tamil Congress remained wedded to a unitary state and argued that district councils could be used to oppress the Tamil minority in the South.[86]

Thus post-independent governments in Sri Lanka have not been willing to undertake necessary structural changes which were required to resolve the ethnic imbalance in the country.[87]

In the final analysis, it is evident that both pacts were futile because of pressure from a third force: the Sinhalese-Buddhists. There was widespread opposition from the Sinhalese-Buddhist sectors each time when there was a constructive attempt at compromise. This opposition was grounded mainly on fears and suspicions that any form of constitutional devolution would only lead to a separate Tamil state, which would subsequently be annexed by the South Indian Tamil state, a major force in the wider ambit of the region. The Sinhalese who constituted the minority group in the region were the majority in Sri Lanka. The Sinhalese-Buddhists viewed Sri Lanka as their land and believed that the future of the Sinhalese nation was linked with the survival and propagation of Buddhism. This vision is embodied in two concepts: the 'Dhammadipa' (island of the Dhamma or religion) and the 'Sinhadipa concept' (island of the Sinhala people or Sinhalese).[88] Consequently, the demand for Tamil political autonomy clashed with the Sinhalese aspirations to preserve the uncompromised political unity of the entire island of Sri Lanka. Hence, the Sri Lankan Tamils were viewed with suspicion by the Sinhalese. According to James Manor the failure of politicians on both sides to arrive at a political accommodation was due partly to the lack of political integration in Sri Lanka. Furthermore, he argued that the lack of a developed grassroots organizations made it impossible for any government party to mount a campaign to convince its followers of the need for accommodation.[89]

The failure of both the S.L.F.P. and the U.N.P. to reach a productive agreement with the F.P. led the Tamils to conclude that neither camp could fruitfully respond to Tamil interests and aspirations.[90] Thus, peaceful means of negotiation and co-operation were not satisfactory avenues for the greater Tamil community to achieve its goals. S.P. Huntington observes that the successful absorption of the Tamils into the Sri Lankan political system was far more problematic simply because the political elites of the country had no such highly developed and institutionalized procedures for handling the problem.[91] Furthermore, the Republican Constitution of 1972 gave a new dimension to the ethnic conflict in the country.

4.11 The 1972 Constitution

The 1972 Constitution was a triumph for the Sinhalese-Buddhist nationalists. The Constitution changed the name of

Ceylon to the indigenous name of Sri Lanka. The Constitution declared that "it shall be the duty of the state to protect and foster Buddhism". Article 29(2) dealing with the rights of minorities was replaced by a chapter entitled 'Human Rights'.[92] The Constitution, however, did not provide for the Tamils' longstanding expectations to share political power. It also ignored their main demands for a federal system of government and the parity of their language. The constitution further institutionalized the concentration of power at the central government and rationalized the unitary state system. As Donald L. Horowitz observes, the 1972 Constitution was a decisive symbolic rebuff to the Tamils.[93] The following statement summarises their reaction:

> The infamous constitution which was passed on the 22nd May 1972 brought an end to Tamil participation in the sharing of state power and created a condition of political alienation of a nation of people.[94]

The Tamils reacted to the 1972 Constitution by declaring a three day 'hartal' (general stoppage of work) and a period of mourning for the Tamil people. The Tamil M.P.'s who had supported the enactment of the Constitution in 1972 were publicly threatened with 'liquidation'. The degree of the intensity of communal conflict is determined by what Huntington has termed the 'autonomy' of the society's political institutions. To quote Huntington:

> Political institutionalization, in the sense of autonomy, means the development of political organizations and procedures that are not simply expressions of the interests of particular social groups. A political organization that is the instrument of a social group—family, clan, class—lacks autonomy and institutionalization.[95]

Nevertheless, in Sri Lanka, political institutions under both major political parties came to be identified with the interests of the Sinhalese-Buddhist community, thereby impairing their legitimacy in the eyes of the Tamil minority at both national and regional levels. Consequently, they lost their legitimacy and institutional effectiveness for the wider society. Robert Nelson and Howard Wolpe further observe that when political institutions lack institutional wholeness and appear to be manipulated by one communal group, the other groups which do not have equal access to power and position will begin to doubt the legitimacy of the institutional order and will be politically motivated to secede.[96]

There was no escape from the fact that the failure of two governments to accommodate the Tamils into the existing political system has made Sri Lanka's moderate ethnic demands far more extreme than it would otherwise have been. From its inception in 1949, the F.P. demanded a federal form of government for Sri Lanka and rejected the concept of separatism. The idea of separate statehood was dismissed as economically untenable because of the lack of resources in the Tamil areas.[97] These remained the F.P.'s views until 1972, their demands being confined to a fair share of power. The F.P., though a minor party in the wider arena of Sri Lankan national politics, was a strong force at a regional level in the Tamil areas. According to Duverger:

> If a party is clearly a minority in the country as a whole but in a majority in certain districts its attitude becomes autonomist or even secessionist, which may imperil the unity of the country.[98]

When the 1972 Constitution failed to recognize the significance of the concept of federalism for the Tamils, for the first time Tamil politicians postulated the idea of separatism. The idea of separatism represents the climax of Tamil nationalism. It introduced a new dimension of hostility between the Tamil community and the government.

4.12 Separate State

In May 1972, all Tamil political parties and organizations including the F.P., the T.C. and the Ceylon Workers Congress (C.W.C.) became untied. This merged force came to be known as the Tamil United Front (T.U.F.). The adoption of the 1972 Constitution was the immediate catalyst for the formation of the T.U.F. The goals of the T.U.F. were no longer based on federalism, but rather were based on an independent Tamil state for the Tamil-speaking people. For two decades, the F.P. had argued that the Sri Lankan Tamils were a distinct nation with a separate language, culture, traditional homeland and history. This nationalist rhetoric had succeeded in convincing the Sri Lankan Tamils that they had a history and tradition of their own which was not shared by the Sinhalese or the Indian Tamils. In this phase of Tamil nationalism the Tamils sought to opt out of Sri Lankan politics. R.N. Kearney observes that the shift in demands for separatism was followed by nearly two decades of frustrating efforts to secure concessions from a series of governments put in power by Sinhala voters.[99]

The slogan for a separate state taken up by the T.U.F. was later pursued with greater determination by the Tamil United Liberation Front (T.U.L.F.).[100] As the aims of the front strengthened it was indicated by means of the added identification with "liberation". Their strategy for separatism, however, was based on non-violent means. Nevertheless, this commitment to non-violence was fragile in the face of the unrest and frustration among the Tamil Youth.

4.13 Youth Radicalisation

By 1970 the most significant development in the Tamil areas was the emergence of a cadre of militant Tamil youth who were as deeply involved in the process of radical politics as were their counterparts in the South. Frustration and restlessness had captured the mood of the Tamil youth. Since 1970 these feelings have been a phenomenon to be reckoned with. The gradual transformation of the somewhat conservative and passive Tamil youth into violent radicals can be largely attributed to the competition for non-agricultural employment and to the general lack of employment opportunities produced by social modernization and the absence of a political settlement for the Tamil problem.

Moreover, the standardization of university admissions became a salient factor in the process of radicalization among the Tamil youth. The impact of the changes made in the system of admissions to universities that affected the Tamil youth is graphically explained by C.R. de Silva, as follows:

> Nevertheless, the question of university admission is clearly one which mobilized the youth in Jaffna and produced the Tamil United Front leadership to declare in favour of a separate state.[101]

The founding of a university campus in Jaffna in 1974 as a response to a demand by the F.P. came too late and was too little to satisfy the Tamil youth. For them, standardization was no more than a discriminatory measure. The only way to circumvent these discriminatory measures was to form a separate state. Just as a socialist state represented a multifaceted solution to the problems of the Sinhala radical youth, for the Tamil youth a separate state represented a panacea to the problems of language, education and employment. The process of radicalization and militancy escalated among the Tamil youth both within and without the confines of the T.U.L.F. youth organization. The Tamil youth had been exposed since the 1960s to the strategy of protest politics adapted by the Tamil leaders in the form of school boycotts, the picketing of government offices, the hoisting of black flags, and the performance of 'satyagraha' (passive resistance).

When protests proved futile the Tamil youth realized that their political leaders, with their party politics and parliamentary tactics, had failed to make any major inroads into the power politics of Sri Lanka. These views were shared by their counterparts in the South prior to the armed uprising of 1971. Although the Insurrection of April 1971 did have an impact on their future politics, the Tamil youth did not play a substantial role in the insurrection. The uprising, however, introduced political violence as an alternative approach to the problems caused by the oppression of the Tamils. The formation of a separate state in Bangladesh strengthened their convictions further and kindled a lingering hope of assistance from India in the event of a similar movement in Sri Lanka.[102] When the Dravida Munnethra Kazagam (D.M.K.) came to power in 1967, the Tamil political parties found sympathy and moral support for their oppositional political role. The Tamil militant youth had received some encouragement from expatriate Tamils. Therefore, the support extended by Tamil Nadu and the expatriate Tamils for the Tamil cause acquired an ominous significance, which will be further examined in Chapter 5.

Such was the context within which the Tamil youth pressured the T.U.L.F. for more swift and drastic action. The T.U.L.F.'s demands for a separate state, however, were confined to rhetoric as they had no viable strategy to achieve this goal. In the face of an overwhelming majority for the government in 1970, as well as in 1977, the Tamil youth could not depend on their parliamentary strength. As a result, the T.U.L.F. had to depend on an alternative strategy of extra-parliamentary means. The following statements by the leader of the T.U.L.F., A. Amirthalingam,[103] indicate that their extra-parliamentary tactics were well within the scope of parliamentary politics:

> If the government failed to take any meaningful steps towards the solving of the problems facing the Tamils within a reasonable period of time, then the T.U.L.F. would launch a struggle or start a civil disobedience campaign against the Government.[104]

Thus, the T.U.L.F. was totally committed to a policy of non-violence which depended heavily on demonstrations and satyagraha to prove their point but which in the long run had little impact. The T.U.L.F. failed to attract the impatient youth due to its inability to resolve any of the major grievances. This situation paved the way for more disappointment and loss of faith among the militant Tamil youth both within and without the T.U.L.F. The left-wing parties, which theoretically should have absorbed these disillusioned cadres, failed to do so because they too had been de-radicalized by this time. On the other hand, the left-wing movement had hardly made any impact either on the Tamil masses or on the political leadership.[105] The existing political parties were seen to be conservative and rigid in a situation where flexibility was needed. The impatient Tamil youth became restive. The commitment to a separate Tamil state was so deeply entrenched in the minds of the Tamil youth that they sought to attain their goal by means of an armed struggle. P. Wilkinson observes such a development as follows:

> When governments and majorities adamantly withhold or oppose such reforms, then aggrieved minorities may well lose faith and confidence in the democratic system and peaceful methods of opposition and turn to violence.[106]

Given these circumstances, what emerged was a polarization of radical youth who were closely linked with the youth league of the T.U.L.F. and were committed to organizing a political violence movement.

4.14 Summary

In summary, the preconditions for the origin of the Tamil political violence movement lie in the background of ethnic conflict between the Sinhalese majority and the major minority, the Tamils. The ethnic conflict, however, is not a clash of fundamentally different ethnicities rooted in the longstanding antagonisms of opposed political communities. The socio-economic changes initiated by the British Raj had a positive impact on the Tamil community, which benefited and was sustained by these changes. It was the policy innovations during the post-independence era, namely land settlement, the official language, state employment and university admission which had an adverse impact on the Tamil community. Consequently, the political participation within this community gained ground and broadened in terms of a demand for a federal state. Once again the government failed to introduce precise political reforms which would have eased the growing discontent among the Tamil community. Furthermore, unemployment and the lack of opportunities for university admission to science-oriented faculties which would ensure employment in the state sector alienated the Tamil youth. The result was an escalation of political participation by the Tamil youth based on a more radical demand for a separate state. The moderate Tamil political parties were unable to impress on the central government the significance of these demands which were made by legitimate and peaceful means. This progressive failure gave rise to underground groups comprised mainly of the youth cohorts of the Tamil population. They were committed to violent tactics.

The above-mentioned socio-economic and political changes formed the preconditions for the origin and development of the guerrilla organizations within the Tamil community. The political violence waged by the J.V.P. and the Tamil guerrilla organizations were precipitated by a combination of two factors. First, the propensity for political violence within these organizations made them volatile and susceptible to political violence. Second, the failure of successive governments to present a viable solution to the political problems and their determination to resort to counter violence triggered political violence. The author further examines these political organizations in Chapter 5 and their ideologies in Chapter 6 while the counter violence comes under further discussion in Chapter 7.

References

1. Martin O. Heisler, "Ethnic Conflict in the World Today: An Introduction", *Annals of the American Academy of Political and Social Science,* Vol. 433, (1977), p. 1.
2. K.M. de Silva, *Managing Ethnic Tension: Sri Lanka, 1880-1985,* (Lanham: University Press, 1986), p. 12.
3. S.P. Huntington, *Political Order in Changing Societies,* (New Haven: Yale University Press, 1968), p. 42.
4. Ted Robert Gurr, "Persistent Patterns of Repression and Rebellion: Foundation for a General Theory of Political Concern", in Margaret P. Karns, (ed), *Persistent Patterns and Emergent Structures in a Waning Century,* (New York: Praeger, 1986), p. 159.
5. Christopher Hewitt, "Majorities and Minorities: A Comparative Survey of Ethnic Violence", *The Annals of the American Academy of Political Science,* Vols. 429-434, (1977), p. 157.
6. Historically the first Sinhalese migrants led by Prince Vijaya and his 700 followers migrated from Northern India to Sri Lanka some 2,500 years ago. Given the myth of their early

migration from Northern India, as well as their belief in their royal descent the Sinhalese enjoy a sense of priority.

7. Although both the Moors and the Indian Tamils speak the Tamil language, they are in many ways different from the Sri Lankan Tamils. The Moors identify their ethnicity in terms of religion and culture and not language. The Indian Tamils, while sharing the common bonds of language and religion with the Sri Lankan Tamils, are different socially.
8. Sri Lankan Tamils formed a majority of the populations of the Jaffna, Mannar, Vavuniya, and Mullaitivu districts in the Northern Province. In the Eastern Province they were a majority in the Batticaloa district and were large minorities in the Trincomalee and Ampara districts. See, Appendix 5.
9. Arend Lijphart, *Democracy in Plural Societies – A Comparative Exploration,* (New Haven: Yale University Press, 1977), p. 88.
10. See, W.I. Siriweera, "The Dutthagamini-Elara Episode: A Reassessment", in The Social Science Association, (ed), *Ethnicity and Social Change in Sri Lanka,* (Colombo: Krunarathna and Sons, 1984), pp. 54-73.
11. W. Howard Wriggins, *Ceylon: Dilemma of a New Nation,* (Princeton: Princeton University Press, 1960), pp. 232-233.
12. Clifford Geertz, "The Integrative Revolution: Primordial Sentiments and Civil Politics in New States", in Clifford Geertz, (ed), *Old Societies and New States: The Quest for Modernity in Asia and Africa,* (New York: ?The Free Press, 1963), p. 123.
13. S.P. Huntington, Civil Violence and the Process of Development", in "Civil Violence and International System", *Adelphi Papers,* Part 2, No. 83, (1971), p. 11.
14. It should be noted that there is a controversy among scholars about the precise time and period during which the Jaffna Kingdom was founded, its boundaries, the nature and scope of its power and its level of independence. For the Tamil version of the Jaffna kingdom see, S.Pathmanathan, *The Kingdom of Jaffna, Part 1, Circa A.D 1250-1450,* (Colombo: Rajendran, 1978). For a Sinhalese version see, C.W. Nicholas and C. Paranavithana, *A Concise History of Ceylon, From the Earliest Times to the Arrival of the Portuguese in 1505,* (Colombo: Ceylon University Press Board, 1961), and K.M. de Silva, "Traditional Homeland of theTamils of Sri Lanka: A Historical Appraisal", *Paper presented at the International Centre for Ethnic Stuidies,* Kandy, (Sri Lanka, 1987)

15. G.C. Mendis, *Ceylon Under the British,* (Colombo: The Colombo Apothecaries, 1946), p. 34.
16. The Burghers are descendants of the Portuguese and the Dutch. They speak English and are Christians by religion.
17. The Sinhalese themselves are divided into low-country Sinhalese and up-country Sinhalese. The majority are low-country Sinhalese.
18. S.J. Tambiah, "Ethnic Representation in Ceylon Higher Administrative Services, 1870-1946", *University of Ceylon Review,* Vol. 13, Nos. 2-3, (1955), pp. 113-134.
19. *Ibid.,* p. 130.
20. W. Howard Wriggins, *Ceylon: Dilemmas of a New Nation, op. cit.,* (1960) p. 235.
21. S.P. Huntington, *Political Order in Changing Societies.* (New Haven: Yale University Press, 1968), p. 39.
22. Joseph Rothschild, *Ethnopolitics: A Conceptual Framework,* (New York: Colombia University Press, 1981), p.
23. B.H. Farmer, *Pioneer Peasant Colonization in Ceylon,* (London: Oxford University Press, 1953), p. 229.
24. C. Monogaram, *Ethnic Conflict and Reconciliation in Sri Lanka,* (Honolulu: University of Hawaii Press, 1987), p. 97.
25. W.H. Wriggins, "Impediments to Unity in New Nation, The Case of Ceylon", in T.S. Fuikle, and R.W. Gable, (eds), *Political Development and Social Change,* (London: John-Wickey, 1961), pp. 568-569.
26. English is spoken among the upper socio-economic strata in all ethnic categories and especially among the Sinhalese and the Sri Lanka Tamils.
27. Jane Russel, "Language, Education, and Nationalism – The Language Debate of 1944", *Ceylon Journal of Historical and Social Studies,* Vol. 8, No. 2, (1978), p. 47.
28. On the 18th of February 1955, the United National Party unanimously decided at its conference in Kelaniya that the Sinhala language alone should be the state language of Sri Lanka.
29. Tarzie Vittachi, *Emergency 58: The Story of the Ceylon Race Riots,* (London: Andre Deutsch, 1958), p. 33.
30. R.N. Kearney, *Communalism and Language in the Politics of Ceylon,* (Durham: Duke University Press, 1967), p. 77.

31. M.R. Singer, "National Government in Ceylon: A Year of Reconciliation", *Asian Survey,* Vol. 6, No. 2, (1966), p. 90.
32. Although passed by Parliament in 1956 the Official Language Act (No. 33) was not in fact enforced until 1961.
33. W.H. Wriggins, "Impediments to Unity in a New State: The Case of Ceylon", *American Political Science Review,* Vol. 55, No. 2, (1961), p. 317.
34. S.U. Kodikara, "The Separatist Eelam Movement in Sri Lanka: An Overview, *India Quarterly,* Vol. 37, (1987), p. 187.
35. R.N. Kearney, "Political Mobilisation in Contemporary South Asia", in Robert I. Crame, (ed), *Aspects of Political Mobilisation in South Asia,* (Syracuse: Maxwell School of Citizenship and Public Affairs, 1975), pp. 49-50.
36. N. Gunasinghe, "Open Economy and Its Impact for Rational Ethnic Relations in Sri Lanka", in Committee for Rational Development, *Sri Lanka: The Ethnic Conflict, Myths Realities and Perspectives,* (New Delhi: Navrang, 1984), p. 199.
37. Walter Schwarz, "The Tamils of Sri Lanka", London, *Minority Rights Groups Report,* No. 25, (1975) p. 13.
38. Ministry of Defence and Foreign Affairs, "Tamils in Sri Lanka", Colombo, Department of Government Printing, (1976).
39. The United Front consisted of the Sri Lanka Freedom Party, (S.L.F.P.), the Lanka Sama Samaja Party, (L.S.S.P.) and the Communist Party (M) C.P.M.).
40. D.L. Jayasuriya, "Development of University Education: The Growth of the University of Ceylon, 1942-1965", *University of Ceylon Review,* 23, Nos. 1-2, (1965), P. 84.
41. Ibid., pp. 91-92.
42. C.R. de Silva, "Weightage in University Admission, Standardization and District Quotas in Sri Lanka", Modern *Ceylon Studies,* Vol. 5, No. 2, (1974), p. 172.
43. C.R. de Silva, "The Politics of University Admission: A Review of Some Aspects of the Admission Policy in Sri Lanka, 1971-1978", *Sri Lanka Journal of Social Science,* Vol. 1, No. 2, (1978), p. 87.
44. C.R. de Silva, "The Impact of Nationalism on Education: The School Takeover (1961) and the University Admissions Crisis", 1970-1975, in Michel Robert, (ed), *Collective Identities Nationalism and Protest in Modern Sri Lanka,* (Colombo: Marga Institute, 1979), p. 488.

45. R.N. Kearney, "Language and Rise of Tamil Separatism", *Asian Survey,* Vol. 18, No. 5, (1978), p. 531.

46. According to the 'standardization system' science students in urban areas needed to obtain higher 'raw marks' than students in rural areas. According to the 'district quotas system' admission to the university from each area is according to a quota which was determined by its population.

47. C.R. de Silva, "Weightage in University Admissions: Standardisation and District Quotas in Sri Lanka, 1970-1975", *Modern Ceylon Studies,* Vol. 5, No. 2, (1974), pp. 165.

48. C. Manogaram, *op. cit.,* p. 125.

49. C.R. de Silva, "Impact of Nationalism on Education", *op. cit.,* p. 490.

50. Urmila Phadnis, "Ethnicity and Nation Building in South Asia: A Case Study of Sri Lanka", India Quarterly, Vol. 35, No. 3, (1979), p. 337.

51. S.P. Huntington, "Civil Violence and Process of Development", in "Civil Violence and International System", *Adelphi Papers,* (1971), p. 11.

52. In the Election of 1912, the Sinhalese-Govigama caste voted for Sir Ponnambalam Ramanathan who was from the Tamil-Vellala caste rather than for the candidate from the Sinhala-Karava caste, Sir Marcus Fernando. As Bryce Ryan has pointed out, from the end of the 19th Century until about 1925, some of the bitterest fulmination in Sri Lanka was not inter-communal but inter-caste. See Bryce Ryan, *Caste in Modern Ceylon: The Sinhalese System in Transition,* (New Brunswick, N.J.: Rutgers University Press, 1953), pp. 332-35.

53. W. Howard Wriggins, *Ceylon: Dilemmas of a New Nation, op. cit.,* pp. 83-84.

54. The Donoughmore Constitution was the outcome of a British Government investigation undertaken by a four-man commission from November 1927 to January 1928. These commissioners were as follows: The Earl of Donoughmore (The Chairman), Sir Geoffrey Butler, Dr. T. Drummond Shiels and Sir Mathew Nathan. For other pertinent studies see, Howard Wriggins, *Ceylon: Dilemmas of a New Nation,* (Princeton: 1960), pp. 85-90; S. Namasivayam, The Legislature of Ceylon. 1928-1948, (London: 1951), pp. 110-115; and T.P. Meththananda, *The Donoughmore Constitution in Ceylon, 1927-1931,* (Wxford University: 1974).

55. C.R. de Silva, "Sinhala-Tamil Ethnic Rivalry, from Independence to Statehood", in Robert B. Goldmann and A.J. Wilson, (eds), *The States of South Asia,* (London: France Printer, 1984), p. 112.
56. A.J. Wilson, "The Tamil Federal Party in Ceylon Politics", *Journal of Commonwealth Political Studies,* Vol. 4, (1966), p. 117.
57. The Tamil Congress was of the view that there were responsible members of the Sinhalese community who were willing to co-operate with the Tamils and give the latter a fair deal. Co-operation, therefore, was actually viewed as a two-way process, not merely as a subordination of the Tamils to the Sinhalese majority. Hence the term responsive co-operation'.
58. J. Jupp, *Sri Lanka: Third World Democracy,* (London: Frank Cass, 1978), p. 139.
59. Section 29(2) of the 1948 Constitution states that: "No law shall make persons of any community or religion liable to disabilities or restrictions to which persons of other communities or religions are not made liable; or...confer on persons or on any community or religion any privilege or advantage which is not conferred on persons of other communities or religions".
60. C.R. de Silva, "The Sinhalese Tamil Rift in Sri Lanka" in A.J. Wilson, and D. Dalton, (eds), *The State of South Asia: Problems of National Integration,* (London: C. Hurst and Co., 1982), p. 159.
61. I.D.S. Weerawardena, "Minority Problems in Ceylon", *Pacific Affairs,* (1953), p. 284.
62. S.U. Kodikara, *Indo-Sri Lanka Relations Since Independence,* (Colombo: Ceylon Institute of World Affair, 1965), pp. 113-114.
63. The Srima-Shastri Agreement in 1964, and the Sirima-Ghandhi Agreement in 1974 solved the problem of the disenfranchisement of the Indian Tamils. The main terms of the agreement of the Srima-Shastri Pact was that India would take bace 525,000 Indian Tamils over a period of 15 years during which Sri Lanka would admit another 300,000 to citizenship. A subsequent agreement in 1974 regarding the remaining 150,000 Indian Tamils conferred citizenship on 75,000 of them. See, S.U. Kodikara, *Indo-Sri Lanka Relations Since Independence,* (Colombo: Ceylon Institute of ?World Affair, 1965).

64. S.U. Kodikara, "Communalism and Political Modernisation in Ceylon", Modern Ceylon Studies, Vol. 1, (1970), p. 98.
65. A.J. Wilson, Politics in Sri Lanka 1947-1979, (London: The Macmillan, 1979), p. 151.
66. *Ibid.*
67. J. Jupp, "Constitutional Development in Ceylon Since Independence", *Pacific Affairs,* Vol. 41, (1968), p. 176.
68. "The Case for a Federal Constitution for Ceylon: Rsolution Passed at the First National Convention of the Federal Party" [Ilankai Tamil Arasu Katchu], (Colombo: Federal Party, 1951), p. 1.
69. A.J. Wilson. "The Tamil Federal Party in Ceylon Politics", *op. cit.,* p. 118.
70. C.R. de Silva, "Tamil Ethnic Rivalry from Independence to Statehood", *op. cit.,* p. 120.
71. S.J. Tambiah, *Sri Lanka, Ethnic Fratricide and the Dismantling of Democracy,* (London: I.B. Tauris, 1986), p. 80.
72. K.M. de Silva "Nationalism and Its Impact", *The Ceylon Journal of Historical and Social Studies,* Vol. 4, Nos. 1-2, (1974), p. 69.
73. A.J. Wilson, *op. cit.,* p. 130.
74. R.N. Kearney, "Nationalism Modernisation and Political Mobilisation in a Plural Society", in Michael Roberts, (ed), *op. cit.,* 1979, p. 452.
75. Parliamentary Dbate, Vol. 39, Col. 409, cited in R.N. Kearney, op. cit., (1967), p. 97.
76. R.N. Kearney, *Communalism and Language in the Politics of Ceylon,* (Durham: Duke University Press, 1967), p. 94.
77. The Federal Party of *Ceylon, Ceylon Faces Crisis,* (Colombo: Sutantiran Press, 1957), pp. 31-32.
78. The Text of the Bandaranayike-Chelvanayagam Pact of 1957 is contained in R.N. Kearney, *Communalism and Language in the Politics of Ceylon,* (Durham: Duke University Press, 1967)
79. K.M. de Silva, *Managing Ethnic Tensions in Multi-Ethnic Societies: Sri Lanka 1880-1985,* (Lanham: University Press of America, 1986), p. 179.
80. B.H. Farmer, *Ceylon: Divided Nation,* (London: Oxford University Press, 1963), p. 179.

81. S.J. Tambiah, *Sri Lanka: Ethnic Fratricide and Dismantling of Democracy,* (London: I.B. Tauris and Co. Ltd. Publishers, 1987), p. 71.
82. James Manor, *The Expedient Utopian: Bandaranaike and Ceylon,* (Cambridge: Cambridge University Press, 1989), p. 269.
83. S.U. Kodikara, *op. cit.,* p. 197.
84. Robert N. Kearney, "The New Political Crisis of Ceylon", *Asian Survey,* Vol. 19, (1962), p. 21.
85. The Senanayake-Chelvanayakam Pact of 1965, in S. Ponnambalam, *Sri Lanka: National Conflict and the Tamil Liberation Struggle,* (London: Zed Books Ltd., 1983), pp. 257-258.
86. Donald L. Horawitz, *Ethnic Groups in Conflict,* (Berkeley: University of California Press, 1985), p. 390.
87. W.H. Wriggins, "Problems of Communalism in South Asia", *Ceylon Journal of Historical and Social Studies,* Vol. 4, (1974), p. 138.
88. Michael Roberts, "Ethnic Conflict in Sri Lanka and Sinhalese Perspectives: Barriers to Accommodation", *Modern Asian Studies,* Vol. 12, (July 1978), p. 383.
89. James Manor, "The Failure of Political Integration in Sri Lanka (Ceylon)" *Journal of Commonwealth and Comparative Politics,* Vol. 17, No. 1 (March 1979), pp. 21-46.
90. R.N. Kearney, "Political Mobilisation in Contemporary Sri Lanka", in Robert I. Crane, (ed), Aspects of Political *Mobilisation in South Asia, (Syracuse, N.Y.: Syracuse University Press,* 1978), p. 48.
91. S.P. Huntington, *Politcal Order in Changing Societies, op.* cit., p. 599.
92. *The Constitution of Sri Lanka,* Colombo, Department of Government Press, (1972).
93. Donald L. Horowitz, "Patterns of Ethnic Separatism", *Comparative Studies in Society and History,* Vol. 23, (1981), p. 183.
94. A. Balasingham, *Liberation Tigers and Tamil Eelam Freedom Struggle,* Political Committee, Liberation Tigers of Eelam, Book Publication, No. 4, (1983), p. 22.
95. S.P. Huntington, *op. cit.,* p. 20

96. Robert Nelson and Howard Wolpe, "Modernisation and the Politics of Communalism", *The American Political Science Review,* Vol. 64, No. 4, (1970), p. 1120.

97. A.J. Wilson, *op. cit.,* p. 119.

98. Maurice Duverger, *Political Parties,* (London: Methuen and Co. Ltd, 1967), p. 294.

99. R.N. Kearney, "Ethnic Conflict and Tamil Separatist Movement in Sri Lanka", *Asian Survey,* Vol. 25, No. 9, (1985), p. 905.

100. The Ceylon Workers Congress left the T.U.F. before the general election in 1977. The faction of the T.C. split over the selection of candidates in the 1977 election and left the T.U.F. under the leadership of Kumar Ponnambalam.

101. C.R. de Silva, "The Impact of Nationalism on Education: The School Takeover (1961) and the University Admission Crisis 1970-1975", in Michael Roberts, (ed), *op. cit.,* 1979, p. 497.

102. S. Arasaratnam, "Nationalism in Sri Lanka and the Tamils" in Micheal Roberts, (ed), *op. cit.,* p. 515.

103. A. Amirthalingam became the leader of the Federal Party and the Tamil United Liberation Front (T.U.L.F.) in 1976. From 1977 to 1983 he was the leader of the opposition. In 1989 he was assassinated by the L.T.T.E.

104. The Scribe, "Party Round Up: The T.U.L.F." Tribune, Ceylon News View, Vol. 22, No. 23, (1977), p. 16.

105. Edward Appathurai, "Communal Politics and National Integration in Sri Lanka", in Milton Israel, (ed), *National Unity: The South Asian Experience,* (New Delhi: Promila and Co., Publishers, 1983), p. 231.

106. P. Wilkinson, Terrorism and the Liberal State, (London: Macmillan, 1986), p. 120.

5

Origin, Development and Form of Guerrilla Organisations

5.1 Introduction

In analyzing political violence in Sri Lanka the socio-economic and political factors are intrinsically significant, but limiting of this study to such factors would be inappropriate and misleading. The very origin and development of political violence movements are a stage of political violence. According to Lucian W. Pye, the organizational form of an insurrectionary movement is another major factor that determines the pattern of the struggle.[1] Furthermore, the author contends that the nature and composition of an insurgent organization affects the pattern of political violence that it commits. Therefore, the author contends that it is necessary, amidst other aspects, to examine the origin, development and form of any organization which resorts to political violence in order to broaden the understanding of such a phenomenon. Consequently, this chapter focuses on the organized political groups that on a protracted basis deliberately plan and engage in acts of political violence.

The genesis of the organization that staged the insurgency of 1971 dates back to the mid 1960s. This period was marked by a proliferation of underground political violence movements among the Sinhala youth. The main organizations were the Gini Pupura (Iskra) group, the Peradiga Sulaga (East Wind) group, the Revolutionary Communist League (R.C.L.), Sumith Devinuwara group, The Janatha Vimukthi Peramuna (J.V.P. or the People's Liberation Front) and the Mathrubhumi Arakshaka Sangamaya (the Society for the Protection of the Motherland). These clandestine organizations were splinter groups of either the C.P. (P), or the L.S.S.P. (R.). The Ginipupura, the Peradiga Sulaga, Sumith Devinuwara and the J.V.P. in the mid 1960s broke away from the C.P.(P). The R.C.L. was a splinter group of the L.S.S.P. The Matthrubhumi 'Arakshaka Sangamaya (Motherland Protection League) was a breakaway group of the J.V.P. The proliferation of such groups led to keen competition amongst them for supremacy in the sphere of underground activity in Sri Lanka. In spite of the competition for hegemony, however, these groups shared three common factors: the first was the common objective of achieving socialism; the second was their opposition to parliamentary government and to orthodox left-wing parties, though for different reasons; and finally was their perception that a violent struggle was the means of achieving state power. The J.V.P. emerged as the most significant and active group that was capable of attracting a wider membership. The other groups were not only politically less attractive, but were also less active in terms of political violence. In addition, a number of Tamil guerrilla organizations also engaged in political violence, thus widening the effect throughout Sri Lankan society.

Due to the complexity of this area of study, and for purposes of lucidity, this chapter is sub-divided into two main parts: the first deals with the pattern of organization and related factors inherent in the movement which was responsible for the insurgency of 1971; while the latter examines the nature of the Tamil guerrilla organizations. Therefore, in the first part of this chapter the author concentrates on the study of the J.V.P. as an organization by mainly focusing on the following aspects: the origin and the development of the organization, background of the membership, infrastructure of the organization, background of leadership, division of labour, of activities funding and international links.

5.2 Origin and the Development of the J.V.P.

The J.V.P, in its origin, has a background similar to those of the other contemporary underground groups in Sri Lanka. The founder of the J.V.P., Rohana Wijeweera,[2] claimed that the initial stages of the organization were formulated on the 21st of May 1964.[3] The authentic origin of this organization, however, can be traced back to the Marxist Study Circle at the People's

Friendship University (Lumumba University) in Moscow during the early 1960s. A.C. Alles confirms that Wijeweera was the architect and moving force behind the J.V.P.[4] Furthermore, Janice Jiggins also credits Wijeweera as having been undoubtedly the chief theoretician and the most mature political mind in the J.V.P.[5] Therefore, in order to examine the origin and the development of the J.V.P., it is necessary to examine Wijeweera's political background.

Wijeweera came from a left-oriented family which had its roots in the Southern city of Matara, which is also a stronghold of the C.P.(M).[6] Influenced by his father who was a supporter of the C.P., Wijeweera became a member of the C.P. Youth league. S.A. Wickramasinghe, who was the leader of the C.P.(M), was his political mentor.[7] This left-oriented background enabled him in 1962 to obtain a scholarship to study medicine at the Lumumba University in Moscow. Apart from pursuing his education, Wijeweera was exposed in Moscow to the radical political trends which were being advocated by students from Asia and Africa. Other than the, radical political atmosphere at Lumumba, certain individuals appear to have had a significant impact on Wijeweera's political philosophy. Among them were: Murad Aidith, Kassim Hanga, and Sheikh Abeld Karume.[8]

The other noteworthy influence on Wijeweera's future political thought and activities was exerted by Professor Metropolski of Lumumba University. Wijeweera himself admits that "it was this great man's ideas that helped me to give up my love for medical science and become a revolutionary rather than a doctor".[9] Thus, the cumulative political influences which were operational at the Lumumba University had a significant impact on Wijeweera.

As a student he became involved in the activities of the union of Sri Lankan students in Moscow, and was elected as its deputy secretary.[10] Together with another fellow Sri Lankan student activist named Dharmakeerthi, who was a keen supporter of the C.P. of Sri Lanka, Wijeweera organized the Marxist Study Circle.[11] The student organization later proved to be the pioneer group which gradually developed and expanded into the J.V.P.

The immediate political background which influenced Wijeweera, however, was permeated by the wider circle of international politics in the context of the Sino-Soviet dispute of the 1960s. This dispute was to have a lasting impact on Wijeweera's political destiny. He perceived this dispute to be more of an ideological struggle between reformism and revolutionism than a national or border dispute. Due to the influence of Murad Aidith, Wijeweera became a keen supporter of the stand taken by the Chinese Communist Party. Wijeweera was convinced that the Chinese interpretation of Communism was more in accordance with the teaching of Marx and Lenin than the stand taken by the Soviet Government, which was deteriorating in favour of a capitalist form of government.[12] Thus convinced, and while still at Lumumba University, he established contact with the Maoist faction of the Sri Lankan C.P. through an ex-M.P. Premalal Kumarasiri, who in turn happened to be an admirer of the North Korean leader Kim-11-Sung. When the Maoist faction broke away from the C.P. and formed the C.P.(P) in late 1963, Wijeweera extended his support to the breakaway faction. Wijeweera's continued support and association with the C.P.(P) had repercussions when he applied for a visa to return to the Soviet Union after a short visit to Sri Lanka in 1964. His application was turned down by the Soviet Embassy on the basis of his involvement in anti-Soviet propaganda and his links with the C.P.(P) in Sri Lanka.[13] This was a turning point in his political activities as he changed his relationship with the C.P.(P) from that of a mere sympathizer to that of an active candidate of the party.[14] Thus in tracing the origin of the J.V.P. it becomes necessary to focus next on Wijeweera's participation and involvement within the C.P.(P).

5.3 Activities Within the C.P.(P)

In 1965 Wijeweera became a full-time activist for the C.P.(P) and was later appointed as the assistant secretary of the party's Youth League. As assistant secretary, he came into close contact with the party's youth cadre some of whom he succeeded in converting to his own political philosophy. His converts later joined him in forming the J.V.P. Wijeweera's ambitions within the C.P.(P) were more far-reaching, and he had obvious motives for gathering a group of followers. From the initial stages of membership he was governed by an ambition to assume power within the C.P.(P) by ousting its leader, N. Shanmugadasan.

When Wijeweera joined the party, there were internal conflicts and strife over issues of authority and ideology. One of the primary conflicts was between the leadership and the youth membership of the party. Wijeweera used these internal rivalries and crises to his advantage by stressing certain shortcomings and deficiencies which would be most useful in ousting the party's leader. The main issues capitalized upon were: the defeat of the party's candidates including its leader in the General Election in 1965;[15] the emphasis and priority given to trade union activities rather than to general political activity; and the special attention paid to the Indian plantation workers rather than to the peasantry. On the strength of these issues he succeeded in organizing a rival group which supported the removal of N. Shanmugadasan from the leadership of the C.P.(P). Wijeweera's faction, however, was not the only political group which flourished within the C.P.(P) during this period. There were three other such groups as follows: the Ginipupura (Iskra) led by Kalyananda Thiranagama; the Peradiga Sulaga (East Wind) led by Gamini Yapa; and the Samajavadi Sangamaya (Socialist League) led by Nihal Dias and Sarath Wijesinghe.[16]

Within this framework of factionalism, Wijeweera and his followers in 1966 attempted to capture power in the party's Youth League Federation, but the attempt proved futile. He and his followers were soon expelled from the party. The overt reasons given by the C.P.(P) for their expulsion were that of establishing and running two youth farms without informing the party leadership, and that of participating in a demonstration without prior permission from the leadership. The expulsion was yet another step in the formation of the underground movement which came to be known as the J.V.P. Having been expelled from the C.P.(P), Wijeweera and his followers in 1967 held a meeting in Kalaththawa an isolated dry zone village near Anuradhapura.[17] The focal point of the discussion was their future as a political faction. It was decided that they should continue their political activities as an independent political movement. This decision was crucial, in the sense that it marked the beginning of an underground movement which would later resort to political violence. For the next three years the J.V.P. operated and functioned as a clandestine movement.

5.4 The J.V.P.'s Underground Period: 1967-1970

From 1967 to 1970 the movement pioneered and organized by Wijeweera, did not display a distinct identity and was rather secretive in its activities. Until the General Election of 1970 there was no name for this underground movement. It was identified by its members as the 'Viyaparaya' (movement) rather than by an acronym. Some newspapers identified it as the "Che Guevara" group, in spite of the fact that it was not entirely founded on Che Guevara's political ideology. The movement's association with Che Guevara's name, however, was attractive to the Sinhala youth who perceived him as a revolutionary hero.

During this period, the J.V.P. initiated a series of indoctrination classes and acquired a definite strategy. In these early stages, the J.V.P. contemplated mobilizing the support of the peasantry and the working class, mainly through the Trade Union of the Land Development Department.[18] While their attempts to mobilize the participation of the working class and the peasantry were futile, the response of the Sinhalese youth was enthusiastic and widespread. Consequently, the J.V.P. made rapid progress as an underground movement with support from all the Sri Lankan university student organizations. The main supporting organizations were the Socialist League of the University of Peradeniya, a substantial section of the C.P.(M)-oriented student society of the University of Vidyalankara, headed by D.I.G. Dharmasekera,[19] and a breakaway faction of the C.P.(M) from the University of Vidyodaya led by M. Wijesekara.[20]

During this period the "Viyaparaya" focused its attention on mobilizing those rural youth cadres who were most responsive to the prospects of a radical clandestine movement. It was really nothing more than a concentrated effort toward ideological indoctrination and crude military training. The clandestine nature of the J.V.P., however, did not last long. This early period in the J.V.P.'s development is paradoxical in the sense that although it was said to have been secretive and undercover, the methods by which the J.V.P. actually conducted political debates, contested student council elections, and organized student strikes, were quite contrary to the supposedly clandestine nature of the movement.[21] As a result, the first police report of the existence of the underground movement was presented to the Cabinet as early as 1968.

As the J.V.P. movement expanded, not only was its clandestine and secretive nature become subject to metamorphosis, but also its cohesion. Thus, internal rivalries and factionalism flourished and by 1969 a split was imminent. The breakaway occurred later that year. The new group was called the Mathrubhumi Arakshaka Sangamaya (the Society for the Protection of the Motherland).[22] The increasingly overt nature of the J.V.P. movement soon became a primary concern of the police. Wijeweera and some other members of the movement were taken into custody on the eve of the Parliamentary Election of 1970.[23] In order to secure their release, the J.V.P. applied a strategy of arousing public awareness by means of a widespread poster and leaflet campaigns under the name of the Janatha Vimukthi Peramuna (J.V.P.). Another strategic measure was the unanimous support extended by the J.V.P. to the U.F. coalition against the U.N.P. in its campaign for the General Election of 1970. The J.V.P. had serious reservations regarding the post-election role of the U.N.P., believing that even if the incumbent U.N.P. Government was defeated, the U.N.P. would resort to a military-aided dictatorship rather than relinquishing power. On the basis of this assumption, the J.V.P. prepared for an armed confrontation with an anticipated dictatorship. Furthermore, the J.V.P. conducted a propaganda campaign in which it urged the Sri Lankan masses to make ready for an uprising.[24] After the 1970 elections, however, there was a peaceful transfer of power without any of the anticipated resistance, and Wijeweera and his followers were released by the U.F. Government.[25] This was the beginning of yet another stage of the transition of the J.V.P. from a clandestine movement to a semi-clandestine organization.

5.4 The J.V.P.'s Semi-Clandestine Period 1970-1971

During this period the J.V.P. assumed a dual role of continuing its illegal and underground activities in preparation for an armed struggle. At the same time, the J.V.P. undertook overt activities such as mass meetings and poster campaigns to gain public support, and held public meetings in most of the major cities in Sri Lanka.[26] As a result, the J.V.P.'s capacity to expand its membership was enhanced during this period. The rapid expansion of the J.V.P.'s cadres and the increased extent of its activities can be largely attributed to two main factors: first, the rather overwhelming defeat of the U.N.P. in the General Elections of 1970 and the resulting disarray within their ranks reduced the effectiveness of the U.N.P. as an opposition party. Secondly, the U.F. Government failed to fulfill their campaign promises, especially those effecting the youth population. Thus, the vacuum created by the lack of a strong opposition to the U.F. was filled by the J.V.P. and led to the increasing hostility between the U.F. Government and the J.V.P. On the whole, this hostility was more advantageous to the J.V.P. in recruiting new members. This phase of the J.V.P.'s existence was confined to increased political mobilization which involved the building up of a disciplined, dedicated revolutionary cadre, and the organizing of mass support. There is no evidence that the J.V.P. used violence prior to April 1971. In order to gain a detailed insight into the J.V.P. the author wishes to examine the background of the group's membership and it is necessary to examine the recruitment procedure of the J.V.P. to understand the background of the membership.

5.6 Recruitment Procedure of the J.V.P.

The clandestine nature of the organization necessitated that the methods of recruitment be confined to individual trust and friendship. Thus, there were no formal applications for membership. The recruitment of new members was done on the basis of personal relationships. The following statement made by a prominent member of the J.V.P. clarifies the procedure of recruitment:

I know one Chandrasena, who was in a lower class to mine in college. Somewhere in September 1968 Chandrasena met me in Ambalangoda town and spoke to me of the left-wing movement in the country and made out that they were not true to the policies they preached. Later one day, Amaradasa met me. He was a member of our youth league. He told me that there was a movement trying to organize a socialist party and suggested that we join it... Later again Chandrasena met me and I told him that I was keen on joining this movement. He then told me to come for a class to his house. I went for this class with Amaradasa to the house of Chandrasena.[27]

Thus, the procedure of recruitment was on the basis of personal contact and friendship channeled through existing members of the organization. Those seeking membership were initially involved in an elementary discussion which dealt with the prevailing political situation in Sri Lanka. Potential members were then eligible for further indoctrination classes which were held in secret. The J.V.P.'s ideology was explained at the first four of five indoctrination classes.

If the potential recruits shared the views expressed in the four initial lectures, they were admitted to the fifth lecture which dealt with the J.V.P.'s "strategy of revolution". After the course of classes had been completed, the prospective members were observed in order to verify their allegiance to the organization. Once their loyalty was proven satisfactory, the recruits were entitled to formal membership in the organization. Thereafter, the new members were assigned the task of propagating the views of the organization for further recruitment of prospective members. In light of this recruitment procedure, it is evident that ideological conviction was not the only criterion employed during the recruitment and training of members. Trust and dedication were characteristics of equal importance in expanding the J.V.P.'s membership and were reflected by the way in which membership was structured. All members of the J.V.P. were classified into two lists: List A and List B. List A contained the names of the most trustworthy and loyal members, all of whom had completed the five indoctrination classes. They were assigned to combat units, and were generally more active than prospective members.[28] In terms of the analysis of Eric Hoffer, List A J.V.P. members should be seen as the true believers, men of fanatical faith ready to sacrifice their lives for what they considered a holy cause.[29]

List B, on the other hand, contained the names of the would-be or prospective members who the J.V.P. utilized mainly for propaganda activities, such as poster campaigns. Both lists were compiled by the secretary of the regional committee. Wijeweera, in defining the role of the two categories within the organization, stated that those on List A were entitled to all rights within the party as well as the privilege of presenting their views and ideas regarding the organization and its decision-making process. The members on List B were totally excluded from the deliberative process.[30] In practice, however, the members on List A were not given the opportunity to express their views or participate in decision making. Furthermore, contact between members was totally discouraged in order to prevent information from being leaked to the police and to otherwise ensure secrecy. The anonymity of the J.V.P.'s members was maintained by the use of the blanket word 'Mahaththya' (Gentleman) instead of individual names. This word replaced the popular word 'Sahodaraya' (Brother) used by the left-wing parties. The leader of the movement was referred to as 'Loku Mahaththya' (Boss).

Once recruited, the functions of the J.V.P.'s members were similar to those of any left-wing underground movement. They were to contact and recruit new members, finance the organization, and popularize the ideology and activities of the organization by means of propaganda. In addition to these common requirements, all members received physical training and crude military instruction in preparation for the forthcoming armed struggle. Each member was instructed to collect a uniform and a kit consisting of a gun, box of cartridges, boots, stockings, black trousers, blue shirt with pockets, an army belt, black running shorts, black vest, steel helmet, knife, torch, lighter, haversack, first aid box, and canvas cloth.[31] Another aspect of the training was the rather rigid discipline imposed on members. The consumption of alcohol, smoking, viewing of films, and emotional attachments between the sexes (except those in which both partners were involved in the activities of the J.V.P.) were strictly prohibited.

The members of the J.V.P.'s hierarchy were drawn from both the full-time and part-time membership. This categorization was derived mainly from the extent of commitment and dedication of the members. The full-timers devoted their lives entirely to the operational aspects of the organization, and to its expansion through the popularization of the movement.[32] They were usually members of List A and were merely identified by pseudonyms. According to Wijeweera, at the beginning of 1970 there were 500 such full-time members, each capable of delivering the indoctrination classes.[33] These members, in spite of their total commitment to the organization, were not entitled to any remuneration for their services, but rather were supported and maintained by other members and sympathizers. The part-time members, on the other hand, were either employed or were pursuing their studies, and devoted their spare time to the activities of the group. As a whole, irrespective of the extent of their commitment, these members played a vital role in the organization and functions of the J.V.P.

The accurate number of total membership is subject to conjecture. The conspiratorial and secretive nature of the organization eludes exact figures. It is known that prior to 1970 the membership was confined to a mere 2,000, but by 1970 it had increased to about 3,000. Loku Athula, who was a leading figure in the J.V.P., claims that in spite of the 8,000 names appearing on List A in 1971, approximately 50,000 had actually participated in the political classes conducted by the J.V.P.[34] Contrary to these claims a former cabinet member estimates the number of members, based on their participation in the 1971 Insurrection, as having been between 5,000 and 7,000.[35] There are further claims that the number of people associated with the J.V.P. might have been 10,000 or higher.[36] These figures are also contradicted by Urmila Phadnis, who claims that the J.V.P.'s membership varied from 20,000 to 80,000, excluding sympathizers who numbered about 30,000.[37] From the contradictory statistics given above, it is evident that there is no consensus regarding the number of people who have been involved in the J.V.P. It is manifest in this context, however, that the J.V.P. had a fairly widespread membership. Therefore, it becomes increasingly important to examine the socio-economic background of this membership.

5.7. Socio-Economic Background of the J.V.P.'s Membership

The socio-economic background of the membership of the J.V.P. not only gives an insight into the subsequently violent nature of this organization, but also sheds light on the factors which led to the mobilization of the youth cadres in Sri Lanka. Different aspects of their socio-economic background such as sex, ethnicity, religion, age, caste, education and profession will be examined. Most of the relevant factors will be derived from a study conducted by Gananath Obeysekara on the social background of the participants of the 1971 Insurrection. Obeysekara based his study on a sample of 10,192 suspected members of the J.V.P.[38]

It is obvious from an examination of Obeysekara's sample that the participation of women in the J.V.P. was marginal due to the overwhelming number of male members. Of the 10,192 suspected insurgents, 9,976 were male and the remaining 216 were female. Hence, like other underground movements in the Third World, the J.V.P. was male dominated. It is a reflection of the social norms of the wider Sri Lankan society where females were assigned a secondary role. The role of the female members of the J.V.P. was confined to supporting duties such as couriers, tailors and nurses. In terms of ethnicity, there is no specific data upon which one can statistically analyze ethnic participation. Religion in this context, however, serves as an indicator of ethnicity. The following Table 5.1 further clarifies the religious background of the J.V.P. membership.

Table 5.1. J.V.P. Membership Based on Religion

Religion	*Number*	*Percentage*
Buddhist	9597	94.2
Hindu	82	.8
Muslim	57	.5
Christian	382	3.8
Unspecified	74	.7
Total	10,192	100.0

Source: Gananatha Obeysekara, "Some Comments on the Social Background of the April 1971 Insurgency in Sri Lanka (Ceylon)", *Journal of Asian Studies,* Vol. 33, No. 3, (1974), p. 370.

According to Table 5.1, approximately 94 per cent of members were Buddhist and, therefore, were Sinhalese. The next largest group, the Christians, were more or less Sinhalese; less than one per cent were Hindus and, therefore, were Tamils. The Muslims who are ethnically either Moors or Malays were only 0.5 per cent of the membership. Overall, the data reveals that less than six per cent of those involved in the activities of the J.V.P. were non-Buddhists and were non-Sinhalese. Considering the orientation of the above-mentioned data one could safely infer that the J.V.P. was dominated and activated by the Sinhala-Buddhists. This Sinhala-Buddhist dimension of the J.V.P. aroused criticisms that it was a communally chauvinistic organization which was largely governed by a hostile approach to the minorities. Another significant aspect was the age distribution of the J.V.P.'s membership. Table 5.2 highlights the rather obvious weighting of the organization towards the youth population.

Table 5.2. Members of the J.V.P. by Age

Age	*Number*	*Percentage*
0-14	36	4.4
15-24	7330	71.9
25-34	2349	22.1
35-44	375	3.0
45-54	141	1.0
55 and over	61	.6
Total	10,192	100.0

Source: Gananath Obeysekara, *op. cit.,* p. 377.

As indicated in Table 5.2, 98 per cent of the J.V.P. membership was under 36 years of age while about 72 per cent were between the ages of 15-24. The average age of the J.V.P. members was around 20 years, thus emphasizing the significant role of youth within the movement. Ethnically 98 per cent were Sinhala, while on the basis of age 98 per cent came within the purview of the youth population in Sri Lanka. A combination of these factors clearly indicates that the J.V.P. was an organization dominated by Sinhala-Buddhist youth.

In this context, education appears as a pertinent factor which requires further examination. Table 5.3 concerns the levels of education attained by the membership of the J.V.P. The sample data indicates that only a mere 19 per cent of the membership was poorly educated. The majority had attained an average standard of education while some others had achieved a much higher standard. A. Arasarathnam, however, disputes the representation of university students within the sample. He contends that more of them were involved in J.V.P. activities than is shown in Table 5.3[39]

Table 5.3. Membership by Level of Education

Level of Education	*Number*	*Percentage*
No Education	250	2.5
Grade 1-4	1739	17.1
Grade 5-8	4315	42.3
G.C.E. (O/L)	3282	32.2
G.C.E. (A/L)	419	4.1
University	158	1.6
Unspecified	29	0.2
Total	10,192	100.0

Source: Gananath Obeysekara, *op. cit.,* p. 377.

Apart from mobilizing radical youth cadres from the universities, the J.V.P.'s potential membership was drawn from the radical young secondary school teachers, and students from the rural-based high schools, the Maha Vidyalayas or the Madya Maha Vidyalayas (Central Colleges). Although data on the representation of the urban/rural-based population within the J.V.P. is not available, Table 5.4 gives an insight into the urban/rural-based membership in the J.V.P. by type of school attended.

Table 5.4 indicates that almost 85 per cent of the J.V.P.'s members were educated either in Maha Vidyalayas or Madya Maha Vidyalayas which are mainly located in the rural sector and provide an education in social sciences, with the indigenous language serving as the medium of instruction. These schools were deprived of the facilities to provide an education in science and technology, which were the major areas within which employment was available. Table 5.4 also indicates that those who had received an urban elite education were hardly attracted to the J.V.P. Rather, the J.V.P. held allure for those from the Sinhalese rural background. This trend is further, clarified in the occupational status of the membership as shown in Table 5.5.

Table 5.4. Members of the J.V.P. by Type of School Attended

Educational Institution	*Number*	*Percentage*
Unspecified	23	.2
No schooling	240	2.4
Private Schools, Tutory,	210	2.1
Maha Vidyalaya	8081	79.3
Madya Maha Vidyalaya	652	6.4
Technical, Training Colleges	189	1.9
Universities	02	1.9
Others	595	5.8
Total	10,192	100.0

Source: Gananath Obeysekara, *op. cit.* p., 376.

Occupations in administration, medicine, engineering, and law, which fell mainly within the elite category, together represent a mere 0.2 per cent of the J.V.P. membership. Thus, the participation of the urban intelligentsia in the J.V.P. was insignificant. The rural-based nature of the J.V.P. deterred the urban intelligentsia from participating. S.P. Huntington, states that a peasant or rural-based revolutionary movement may have difficulty in appealing to the urban intelligentsia.[40] The middle-class categories which include the Ayurvedic (indigenous) physicians, the middle grades in government service, the clerks, teachers, and other grades in government service, were poorly represented in the J.V.P.

The lower to middle positions, at 20% of the total membership, were well represented in the J.V.P. This category is comprised of minor grade government employees, technicians, fishermen, traders and security personnel. It was the low income category which includes workers, labourers and cultivators that had a significant presence in the J.V.P. membership.

Table 5.5. Occupational Status of the Members in the J.V.P.

Occupational Status	*Number*	*Percentage*
Administrative positions in Govt. and private sector	10	.1
Doctors (Western trained)	2	.0
Engineers	1	.0
Lawyers	2	.0
Officers-police and security services	6	.1
Ayurvedic physicians	9	.1
Middle grade in govt.	247	2.4
Govt. clerks	117	1.1
Teachers	214	2.1
Other ranks in security services	26	.3
Minor grades in govt.	660	6.5
Technicians and artisans	698	6.8
Fishermen	25	.2
Estate labourers	198	1.9
Traders	434	4.3
Cinnamon peelers	55	.5
Barbers	63	.6
Washermen	20	.2
Textile weavers	47	.5
Beedi wrappers	205	2.0
Casual labourers	1091	10.7
Cultivators	2737	26.9
Students	1270	12.5
Unemployed	1783	17.5
Others	110	1.1
Clergy (Buddhist)	34	.3
Unspecified	128	1.3
Total	*10,192*	*100.0*

Source: Gananath Obeysekara, *op.cit.*, p. 373.

Statistically, the unemployed were also fairly well represented at 17.5 per cent of the J.V.P. membership. It was this proportion which served as a basis for contradicting the argument of the spokesmen of the U.F. Government, who denied the impact of the high rate of unemployment in Sri Lanka on the armed uprising of 1971.[41]

What these statistics fail to account for is that the number of students involved in the J.V.P. represented potentially a separate unemployed or underemployed category. As noted earlier, the underemployed had a higher level of education or developed skills, but were forced by unfavorable socio-political factors to seek employment below their qualifications. The majority of J.V.P. members were Sinhala-Buddhist rural youth. (Tables 5.1 and 5.2), including a significant proportion who were unemployed or underemployed. The tension and frustration within these two groups contributed substantially to J.V.P. militancy. The following Table 5.6 on occupational status of fathers of the J.V.P. members reinforces the above-mentioned socio-economic background.

Table 5.6. Occupational Status of the Fathers of the J.V.P. Members

Occupational Status	*Number*	*% of Total*
High positions	47	.4
Middle positions	553	5.4
Lower Middle	1979	19.4
Underemployed	4969	49.7
Unemployed	260	2.8
Unspecified	2214	21.7
Unspecified but employed	168	1.6
Clergy (Christian, Hindu)	2	.0
Total	*10,192*	*100.0*

Source: Gananath Obeysekara, *op. cit.*, p. 375.

Table 5.6 indicates that a majority of fathers of the J.V.P. membership came from the low income strata and held correspondingly low-status occupations. The socio-economic background of the J.V.P. membership, however, cannot be confined to the analysis of the above-mentioned factors. In the context of the Sri Lankan society, where class stratification coexists with a less overt stratification of caste, the caste factor too is a significant aspect. Furthermore, the caste dimension of the movement has been brought to the fore by a widespread belief that the J.V.P. was mainly motivated and stimulated by the 'oppressed' castes. This argument is correct when it is applied to the leadership of the J.V.P. This contention, however, does not apply to the movement as a whole especially as depicted in Table 5.7.

Table 5.7 refutes the argument that the J.V.P. was a lower caste-based movement as over 50 per cent of its members belonged to the Govigama caste, which is at the apex of the caste structure. As W.A.W. Warnapala contends, however, there is valid evidence that the so-called 'oppressed' castes were mobilized in certain areas where their demographic strength was the highest. According to Warnapala, within the Kegalla district, where the J.V.P. influence was widespread, the caste factor was fully exploited and young men belonging to the 'oppressed' castes[42] constituted a sizeable segment of the support base.[43]

In the final analysis, the socio-economic base of the J.V.P. seems to further establish the author's contention that factors which gathered momentum over a long period of time, especially in the rural sector, culminated in the formation, expansion and mobilization of the rural youth into a revolutionary organization. The social and economic context of the movement which appears to be crucial permeated all aspects of the movement.

Infrastructure in this context denotes the internal organizational structure of the J.V.P. including its informal and formal network. Due to the J.V.P.'s clandestine nature, until 1970, it did not have a formal politico-military structure and contacts between members were made on a personal basis within limited confines. Consequently, the J.V.P., in its initial years of existence, was loosely organized, and was centred on dominant personalities. The foundations of a formal politico-military organization were laid after the General Election of

1970, and were ordered from top to bottom on the basis of Lenin's model of the Bolshevik party.

Table 5.7. Caste Background of the Members in the J.V.P.

Caste	*Traditional Occupation*	*Number*	*Percentage*
Govigama	Farmers	5962	58.9
Karava	Fisheries	636	6.2
Salagama	Cinnamon Peelers	193	1.9
Vahumpura	Juggery Makers	1038	10.2
Dhoby	Washermen	204	1.9
Hunu	Lime Burners	35	.3
Batgama	Servants to govigama	944	9.3
Nawandanna	Smiths	159	1.6
Rodiya	Untouchable beggars	2	.0
Durava	Toddy Tappers	267	2.6
Berava	Drummers	156	1.5
Kumbal	Potters	27	.2
Paraiyar	Tamil Castes	17	.1
Vellala	-do-	16	.1
Pandaram	-do-	2	0
Kaunda	-do-	1	.0
Nadar	-do-	1	.0
Harijan	Untouchable	10	.1
Unspecified		520	5.1
Total		**10,192**	**100.0**

Source: Gananath Obeysekara, *op. cit.,* p. 371.

5.8 Infrastructure of the J.V.P.

At the lowest level of the structure were the primary organizations called 'cells'. The cells were popularly known as the 'pahe committees' each of which consisted usually of five members. These committees were sometimes expanded, however, to include a maximum of nine members. The head of each committee was appointed by the local leader of the J.V.P. The committee heads were responsible for maintaining links with the higher echelons of the organization. Only the most hardworking and trustworthy members were selected as committee leaders. It was compulsory for these committees to meet at least once a month and for their members to train and willingly participate in an armed struggle. The meetings also served as a forum for criticism, including self-criticism. The operating areas of the committees were confined to the immediate environment such as a sub-area, school or work place. The narrow confines of scope and the isolated nature of these cells largely contributed to the anonymity assured to the members and served as a safeguard against betrayal and police infiltration. The cell-system kept members not only isolated but also ignorant of the J.V.P.'s overall plans.

Within the hierarchy of the organizational structure of the J.V.P. the village committees were comprised of the five secretaries of the 'pahe committees' and, therefore, ranked above the 'pahe committees'.[44] Each village committee was headed by the most active full-time or part-time member of the J.V.P. in the village, and its activities were confined to the village area. The local committees which came next in the order of ascendancy were also known as "police committees". Although the J.V.P. emulated the structure of a political party, its regional base was not organized on an electoral level but rather on the basis of the police divisions in Sri Lanka. Each police committee was formed by the full-timers in the local or police area, and by the secretaries of the village committee. The police committees were each led by a secretary appointed by either a district secretary or the higher echelons of the J.V.P. leadership. The secretary was charged with preparing an armed attack on the local police station, and organizing and co-ordinating the activities of the cells and village committees.

The district committee which was next above the police committee in the J.V.P.'s hierarchy was the important nucleus of the organizational structure. Except for the Tamil-dominated districts of Jaffna, Trincomalee and Batticaloa, the J.V.P. had succeeded in organizing the other districts. The district committees were formed by the most active secretaries of the police committees. Hence, the members of the district committees varied according to the numbers of police committees within the district, and were led by a secretary who was appointed by the leadership of the J.V.P. He was the medium of communication between the leadership and the secretaries of the police committees.

Neither a central committee nor a politbureau existed within the formal memorialized structure of the J.V.P. Therefore, the number of members and the method of selection were matters of controversy. Loku Athula claimed that there were 25 members on the central committee, and 12 members on the politbureau.[45] Rohana Wijeweera, the leader of the J.V.P., however, disagreed with Loku Athula and declared that the politbureau had only eight members.[46] The members of the central committee and politbureau were selected from amongst the district secretaries and other senior members of the J.V.P. It can be stated with certainty that members were not elected by means of a party congress but on the strength of their personal friendships and contacts with the higher echelons.

According to Feliks Gross, secrecy is an important element in any underground movement. The leader at the top of the underground hierarchy know more about the whole organization than do members of the individual cells, and only a few members of the central committee know all the details. The cadres are informed as to their own responsibilities in strengthening the ranks of the organization, and spreading the ideology of the resistance, but beyond that they can ask no questions.[47] The J.V.P. too followed this universal procedure as outlined by Gross. The structure of the J.V.P. leadership was not disclosed to its members as exemplified in the following statement made by a leading member:

The Janatha Vimukthi Peramuna in principle refused to disclose in full the nature of its party organization even to its members. It was only after I came to prison, that I myself came to know, that the Janatha Vimukthi Peramuna had a politbureau. The four who were the party's leaders for life were the first to decide on all issues..... [the J.V.P.'s] members were made to act as mere puppets of the four.[48]

The members of the central committee and politbureau were not empowered to make decisions. As shown above, it was not only the lower level cells, but also the higher echelons of the central committee and the politbureau that were undemocratically constituted. Almost all the appointments and decisions within the J.V.P. were made by the secretarial committee, which was composed of four senior members including Wijeweera who was the general secretary and leader of the J.V.P.[49] The nature of this self-appointed leadership is explained by Wijeweera himself in his statement to the C.I.D. in 1971.

I was the chief secretary. If any of you gentlemen question me as to who elected me the chief secretary...I accepted that office sir, once I was released. Mr. Wicramanayake, asked me whether I knew that we would be suppressed, taken to task one day. I knew. As they gave me that office. I told them that they were putting the noose around my neck. I knew what I was in for. Understand. When the party decided to make me the chief secretary, I knew that I would be held responsible for everybody's actions. But there should be someone to do it....There was no election of chief secretary as such. Do you know where it was announced first of all, that I was chief secretary? At that....press conference. A *Daily News* editor, or a reporter, asked me in which capacity I was speaking. Sanath and I knew that the question would arise; so we decided beforehand. We thought of saying, party leader. But in a Marxist-Leninist party it had to always be a chief secretary. That was the system. So I said 'chief secretary'. Sir, this was the first reference to myself as the chief secretary. You question anyone under arrest as to who was elected the chief secretary. No one did so. What I mean is, it was a self-appointment.[50]

Thus, the system of decision-making was taken from the top and flowed to the bottom and this pattern of appointment and decision-making accounts for the authoritarianism exerted by the leadership over the members of the J.V.P.

Martha Crenshaw, in discussing the models of terrorist organizations, finds that there are two such organizational structures which are widely applied. The first is a cellular structure within which decisions are made at the apex of the pyramid and communicated downwards through subordinates in compartmentalized units. Only the top echelon has any knowledge of the comprehensive organizational structure or the identities of the leaders. The second form of structure resembles a wheel with central leadership at the hub in direct contact with the encircling units.[51] The organizational structure of the J.V.P. came within the purview of the first structure, which is pyramidical.

In the context of the organizational structure it becomes necessary to examine the distribution of activities within the J.V.P. Therefore, the author next focuses on the division of labour within the organization as it has existed since 1970. The activities of the J.V.P. were divided mainly between four divisions. Wijeweera explained that each division was assigned the task of dealing with one particular aspect of activity. The four divisions were propaganda education, organization and arms, with each division being headed and supervised by one of the four members of the secretarial committee.[52]

The propaganda division was in charge of organizing and carrying out the propaganda activities of the J.V.P., and was the only division which conducted its activities overtly. The propaganda activities varied from publishing newspapers and organizing public meetings and speeches, to conducting poster campaigns. For these activities the J.V.P. used its auxiliary bodies such as the Samajavadi Shishya Sangamaya (Socialist Student League), the Bikku (Buddhist Clergy) also known as the Deshapremi Bikku Peramuna (Patriotic Monks Front), and the Women's organization. The educational division was assigned the task of politically indoctrinating the members at training camps in preparation for the series of five classes, especially recruits who were willing to work for the movement either as part-time or full-time members. The educational division was also responsible for co-ordinating the continued indoctrination of members within the J.V.P. The weapons division also was assigned the crucial task of supplying arms to the J.V.P., including self-manufactured ordnance if necessary. The personnel were also charged with safely accumulating the material in secure locations, and with training the members in the manufacture and use of weaponry such as hand-grenades and Molotov cocktails. Thus, the preparation for armed violence was an inherent part of the J.V.P.'s organization. The weapons sections were assigned a crucial role which, due to extraneous factors and weaknesses inherent within the organization, was unsatisfactorily fulfilled.

5.9 Background of the Leadership of the J.V.P.

In order to understand the socio-economic background of the district and national leadership in the J.V.P. the author will examine the following variables: sex, ethnicity, religion, education, area of residence occupation and political background. As previously noted in section 5.7 herein, a small number of women were accepted into the J.V.P. membership. None, however, appeared among the district or national leadership. Consequently, the district and national leadership of the J.V.P. was male-dominated. The author has also shown in section 5.7 above that nearly all of the J.V.P.'s members came from the Sinhalese ethnic majority, and were Buddhists. Table 5.8 gives an insight into the occupational status of the members of the district committees. It shows that a majority of the district committee members were either students or unemployed youth.

Table 5.8. The Status of the Members of the District Committees

District	*Student*	*Unemployed*	*Employed*	*Total*
Kandy	9	4	3	16
Badulla	5	3	1	9
Galle	9	6	2	17
Kegalle	14	4	1	19
Polonnaruwa	-	13	2	15
Trincomalee	9	-	2	11
Kurunegala	2	10	-	12
Anuradhapura	6	3	3	12

Source: Janatha Sangamaya, (People's League) *71 April Nagiteema, (71 April Uprising)* (Dehiwela: Allen Printing Press, 1980), p. 20.

The high representation of students and unemployed on the district committees is further reflected in the occupational status of the district secretaries, a majority of whom were also on the central committee. Most of the district secretaries were students or unemployed. A close examination of Table 5.8 and other statistics clarifies the occupational distribution of members by district. Of the 23 district secretaries within the J.V.P. fifteen were students, three were unemployed, two were government clerks, two were teachers and one was a farmer. In terms of age, 16 secretaries were between the ages of 20-24 years and eight were between 25-30 years of age.[53] S.P. Huntington observes that students are the most coherent and effective revolutionaries within the middle class in most modernizing countries.[54] According to Leiden and Schmitt, students are frequently the centre of revolutionary ferment because they are anxious about their own future with its limited opportunities, and moved by a sense of responsibility as an educated elite in backward societies, and are motivated by nationalism in economically dependent countries.[55]

In terms of socio-economic background, there is no visible difference between the J.V.P.'s membership and leadership. In terms of ethnicity, all were Sinhalese; and in respect of religion, all were Buddhist. Furthermore, twelve of the politbureau members belonged to the Karava caste, which was also the caste of the J.V.P. leader, Wijeweera. As Janice Jiggins points out, of the 41 alleged leaders appearing before the Criminal Justice Commission (C.J.C.) fourteen belonged to the Karava, eleven were Govigama, four were Vahumpura, and only one belonged to the Batgama.[56] The educational background of twelve of the 14 members of the politbureau was recorded, and was as follows: one medical student, one science graduate, two social science undergraduates, four advanced level students, three G.C.E. (O./L.) students, and one who was educated up to secondary school level. Five were from the same school,[57] and seven had belonged to the C.P. (P) prior to joining the J.V.P. Further examination of the politbureau members shows that eleven of them were less than 30-years old. In terms of occupation, one politbureau member was a teacher, one a clerk, one an engineer, one a labourer, one a lino operator, six were students, and two were unemployed.[58] All of them were based in urban areas either by birth or education. Consequently, it may be concluded that the J.V.P. leadership was comprised of Sinhalese-Buddhist youth who were primarily urban based. According to S.P. Huntington, the urban middle class provides revolutionary leadership in modernizing countries.[59] When considering the social forces represented in the J.V.P., however, it is evident that in contrast to the rural background of the wider membership, the leadership originated from the urban petit bourgeois and not the urban middle class.[60]

5.10 Sources of Funds of the J.V.P.

An analysis of the financial support extended to a clandestine organization such as the J.V.P. is vital in understanding its operational aspects, and determining whether such an organization can achieve its goals. At the outset it should be noted that no definite avenues of financial assistance to the J.V.P. have been established. Therefore, it remains a matter of conjecture as to how the J.V.P. financed its activities. There is no evidence of financial assistance from any foreign governments or formal organizations. Closer investigation reveals that funds were raised through several legitimate and illegitimate means within Sri Lanka. One source was donations collected from members and sympathizers. In a press conference given on the 20th of September 1970, Wijeweera explained that every employed member of the J.V.P. contributed from three to 30 per cent of his earnings depending on his income level.[61] In addition, university students who were either members or sympathizers were also expected to make contributions from their scholarship or bursary funds.[62] The few female members also contributed a portion of their income, and donated their jewelry to the organization. Funds were also raised at political meetings and public gatherings conducted by the J.V.P.

Apart from these fairly legitimate sources, a considerable amount was raised from robberies and thefts. The J.V.P. was unconcerned about the legality of the means of fund raising, and thus sanctioned any method of acquiring funds for its activities.

A.C. Alles compiles the following account of the number of thefts and robberies committed by members of the J.V.P: in November 1970, a rural bank robbery in Okkampitiya netted the sum of Rs.65,000; in November 1970, a mail bag robbery at the Badulla Station yielded an undisclosed amount; in February 1971, a bank clerk employed at a Bank of Ceylon misappropriated a sum of Rs. 57,000.[63] Victor Ivan, a prominent activist in the J.V.P., provides the following list of robberies committed by the J.V.P. to raise funds.

Table 5.9. Number of Robberies Committed by the J.V.P.

Year	*Place*	*Amount (Rs.)*
1970, April	Urubokka sub-post office	6,000
1970, September	Rural Bank	65,000
1970, November	Post-Mail Train	10,000
1971, January	Peoples Bank	30,000
1971, February	-do-	2,000
1971, February	Bank of Ceylon	57,000
1971, March	C.T.B. Depot.	8,000

Source: Victor Ivan, *71 April Keralla, (71 April Insurrection,)* (Colombo: Lake House Investments, 1978), pp. 180-181.

The total commitment of its members thus resulted in several major sources of funds for the J.V.P. through legitimate and more often illegitimate means. Finally, the author wishes to identify and analyze the international links of the J.V.P.

5.11 International Links

The international links maintained by the J.V.P. were vague and thus raised controversy and debate amongst scholars. The J.V.P. leadership convinced their followers that supplies of arms and moral support would be forthcoming from governments or insurgent groups in foreign countries. There was evidence that the J.V.P. made serious attempts to secure arms and support from overseas during the crucial period 1970-71. The J.V.P., by virtue of its ideology, was not an ally of the C.P. Chinese Wing, or the C.P. Moscow Wing and therefore, could not expect aid from those powers. Instead, the J.V.P. tried to establish contact with the Palestine Liberation Organisation (P.L.O.), the Naxalite Movement in India, the Communist Party of Kerala in south India, and Vice-President Karume of Tanzania. These attempts at establishing international contacts proved futile with the exception of the sympathetic hearing extended by South Yemen, which promised to deliver arms indirectly through another source of supply.[64]

Paradoxically, the U.F. Government in their propaganda denounced the J.V.P. as C.I.A. agents while the C.P.(P.) accused them of being agents of the K.G.B. Investigations before and after the 1971 Insurrection, however, failed to produce any supporting evidence for either claim. The involvement of North Korea and the People's Republic of China had been subjects of considerable speculation both within and outside Sri Lanka. During the 1971 Insurrection, the Sri Lankan Government ordered the North Korean Government to withdraw its diplomatic representatives and temporarily terminated foreign relations with the said state. Despite the measures taken by the Sri Lanka Government, there was no valid evidence that the J.V.P. maintained contacts with the North Koreans. The official explanation given by the Prime Minister was that the North Koreans had indulged in overenthusiastic and indiscreet propaganda which had not been curbed, despite being cautioned by the Sri Lankan Government.[65] The propaganda in question was the full-paged advertisements in Sri Lankan newspapers featuring the revolutionary thoughts of Kim II Sung and the distribution of literature on guerrilla warfare. As Anthony Burton points out, however, the exact nature and extent of the North Korean involvement could have exceeded the mere boundaries of propaganda.[66] The J.V.P. had attempted to establish links with the People's Republic of China through the P.R.C.'s embassy in Sri Lanka, but these attempts also proved futile.[67] Other than the thwarted efforts at establishing links with the North Koreans and the P.R.C., there is no evidence of the J.V.P.'s having had links with any other foreign governments. The evidence of the J.V.P.'s negligible contacts with foreign governments or organizations led the Sri Lankan Prime Minister to conclude that there had been no outside support or interference.[68] The crude weapons and equipment utilized in the 1971 Insurrection and the poor military training of its members were further evidence of the absence of foreign assistance to the J.V.P. In summary, it could be said that the J.V.P. was an entirely home-grown guerrilla organization.

5.12 The Tamil Guerrilla Movements

While the J.V.P. was gaining ground as a clandestine movement among the Sinhala-Buddhist rural youth, another major strand of political activity began to emerge among their Tamil counterparts. Precisely when the Tamil underground movement came into existence, however, remains a subject of debate. The Tamil guerrilla organizations were collectively identified as the "Tamil Tigers" in formal terms, but the Tamil community referred to them as the 'boys'. From the outset this political strain was never a monolith, but rather was a proliferation of over 30 uncoordinated groups.[69] Although some of these groups were rather insignificant in the sense that they had few members, all were actively involved in political violence at one time or another.

By the early 1980s, five of these groups emerged as the dominant underground movements, as follows: the Liberation Tigers of Tamil Eelam (L.T.T.E.), the Tamil Eelam Liberation Organisation (T.E.L.O.), the People's Liberation Organisation of Tamil Eelam (P.L.O.T.), the Eelam Revolutionary Organisation of Students (E.R.O.S.), and the Eelam People's Revolutionary Liberation Front (E.P.R.L.F.). Of the five groups, the L.T.T.E. claims to have been the pioneer group. Whatever it's past, the L.T.T.E. developed it self into the most organized, cohesive, and powerful guerrilla organization, with an expansive membership and particularly ruthless tactics. Unlike the Sinhalese youth-dominated underground organizations the Tamil guerrilla organizations, especially the L.T.T.E., from their inception have been more action-oriented than theory-oriented. Therefore, the author finds it necessary to focus in particular on the L.T.T.E. There is little or no detailed information available regarding the L.T.T.E. compared to the J.V.P. because its guerrilla activities are still on-going. Perhaps the most important factor contributing to the information gap is that while members of the J.V.P. were captured or surrendered, the L.T.T.E. guerrillas have followed a code of suicide to avoid capture. Furthermore, several of the founders of the Tamil groups and their associates have been killed in action. Hence the data on the Tamil guerrilla organizations is often sparse and vague. In this study the author wishes to focus attention on the following aspects: the origin and growth of the Tamil guerrilla groups, background of the members, organizational structure, background of leaders, source of funds, and international links.

5.13 The Origin and Growth of the Tamil Guerrilla Movements

The origin of the Tamil guerrilla groups is a complex web based mostly of circumstantial evidence. Unlike the J.V.P. it is not possible to clearly trace the origins of the Tamil groups nor can they be linked with the left-wing movement in Sri Lanka. Instead they have their roots either in the Federal Party or the T.U.L.F. student or youth organizations. These major groups, therefore, either belonged to the Tamil Ilanar Iyakkam (Tamil Youth Movement), which was the youth wing of the F.P., or to the Tamil Manavar Peravai (Tamil Student Union), which was the student wing of the F.P. and the T.U.L.F. These organizations could thus be characterized as the nurseries within which the entire strand of Tamil guerrilla activity was nurtured and fostered.

As mentioned above, the L.T.T.E. was the foremost Tamil group that had indulged in political violence. It's origins can be traced to the Tamil Student Movement (T.M.P.) which gained publicity, or perhaps more appropriately notoriety, during the early 1970s by burning buses and national flags, destroying public property, organizing protest marches, and hoisting black flags as signs of protest. As a result by 1974, 41 Tamil youth had been detained under the emergency regulations, but they were released to appease the T.U.L.F. before the by-election for Kankesanturai.[70]

In 1975, a faction calling itself the Tamil New Tigers (T.N.T.) or the Liberation New Tigers broke away from the T.M.P. The T.N.T. was the precursor of the Tamil guerrilla movement;

most of the other Tamil guerrilla organizations emerged later.[71] Three pioneer members of this Tamil youth group, Vallupillai Prabakaran, Pathmanathan, and Chetti Thanabalasingham, gained stature throughout the various groups in the Tamil guerrilla movement. Prabakharan was the chief architect of the future L.T.T.E. Just as Wijeweera pioneered and led the J.V.P., Prabakharan proved to be the driving force of the L.T.T.E.

Prabakharan was born in 1956 to a middle-class family from Velvetithurai, which was a fishing village in Northern Jaffna notorious for smuggling goods from Southern India. He apparently dropped out of school after grade five, and by the age of sixteen was involved in guerrilla activities. He began operating undercover when he was 19-years old. To his fellow members in the L.T.T.E., he was more fondly known as "thambi" which means young brother. His earliest involvement with the Tamil guerrilla groups began when he and other Tamil youth formed T.N.T. Soon after the formation of T.N.T., Prabakharan assassinated the original leader, Thanabalasingham, and assumed the leadership of the group.[72] Prabahkaran also became the *de facto* leader of the Tamil guerrillas. As Rohan Gunarathna points out, the T.N.T. was the first Tamil separatist group to have indulged in fierce violence.[73]

From 1972 to 1975, the T.N.T. was a relatively anonymous group. Nevertheless, it came to the centre of attention when Prabahkaran masterminded and participated in the assassination in 1975 of Alfred Dureppa, the Mayor of Jaffna, the capital of the Northern Province. This episode resulted in notoriety for the Tiger movement in general and for Prabahkaran in particular.[74] The T.N.T. renamed itself the Liberation Tigers of Tamil Eelam (L.T.T.E.) in 1976. It gained popularity in the Tamil community as the L.T.T.E. when, in 1979, it began to claim responsibility for a number of assassinations.[75] Under the Prevention of Terrorism Act (P.T.A.) imposed in 1979, the L.T.T.E. and other Tamil underground movements were proscribed, thus compelling them to function as fully clandestine organizations. After the implementation of the Act, the L.T.T.E. began actively operating as a guerrilla movement in the Tamil community. By 1980, the L.T.T.E. was cooperating with T.E.L.O., another major guerrilla group. This coalition, however, did not last long due to the capture in 1982 of the prominent leaders of T.E.L.O. by the police. As S. Ponnambalam observes, from July 1982, the Liberation Tigers came into their own in the Tamil areas of Northern Sri Lanka, and attended the first "World Eelam Tamil Conference" which was held in New York in 1982.[76] The L.T.T.E. could not make significant inroads in terms of recruitment until mid 1983, perhaps because the escalation of its activities was only gradual. The ethnic violence in 1983, however, was a landmark in the growth and expansion of the entire Tamil guerilla movement.

Apart from the ethnic violence of 1983, there are two other factors which contributed to the growth of the L.T.T.E. and similar organizations. First, the military intervention in Northern and Eastern Sri Lanka heightened ethnic tension and created an ambience for the growth of the guerrilla movement, which was based on ethnicity of the Tamil community. The L.T.T.E. decried this situation as the occupation of the Tamil motherland by a foreign army. Secondly, the Sixth Amendment to the Sri Lankan Constitution placed M.P.'s of the moderate T.U.L.F. in a vulnerable position, and so they sought to exclude themselves from Parliament.[77] Once the legitimate political forces were excluded from the mainstream of political activity, the environment was conducive for the L.T.T.E. and similar organizations to flourish.

It was first necessary, however, for the L.T.T.E. to gain dominance over the other guerrilla groups which had previously proliferated. Towards this end the L.T.T.E. began to eliminate any group which posed a threat to their supremacy. Their first victims were the moderates within the T.U.L.F. in 1985. Soon thereafter, they entered into an alliance with the T.E.L.O., the E.P.R.L.F. and the E.R.O.S., all of which came to be known as the Eelam National Liberation Front (E.N.L.F.).[78] After the formation of the alliance, the L.T.T.E. pursued a strategy of gaining international recognition by applying some tactics pioneered by the P.L.O. The E.N.L.F. soon fell apart, however, as had previous alliances. The L.T.T.E. again began to systematically liquidate other guerrilla groups with the objective of emerging as the foremost guerrilla group in the Tamil community. The T.E.L.O. was singled out as the first victim in this process of elimination. Between April and May 1986, nearly 150 members of T.E.L.O. including its leader, Sri Sabarathnam, were killed by the L.T.T.E. The operations of P.L.O.T. were banned by the L.T.T.E. in Jaffna, and the E.P.R.L.F. was disbanded and systematically destroyed. Once these major groups had been subject to the 'process of elimination', the L.T.T.E. was left with a clear field. From then on, the L.T.T.E. was recognized as the *de facto* representative of the Tamil guerrillas. Consequently, from 1985 onward, the L.T.T.E. took virtual control of the Jaffna peninsula.

The author at this point finds it necessary to further describe some of these major groups. The T.E.L.O. was founded in 1975 by Thangadorai and Kuttimani, and from its formation competed with the L.T.T.E. for seniority. Thus the T.E.L.O. was one of the pioneer guerrilla groups in the Tamil community. Until 1983, it was second to the L.T.T.E. in terms of membership and military strength. The death of its founders and leadership in the prison massacre of 1983 was the beginning of its deterioration.[79] The intense struggle with the L.T.T.E. for supremacy in 1986 further debilitated the group. The breakaway of the Tamil Liberation Army (T.E.L.A.) and the Tamil Eelam Army (T.E.A.) was almost the final blow to its survival.

The P.L.O.T. was also a breakaway group from the L.T.T.E.[80] It was formed in 1980 by Uma Maheswaren, the former chairman of the central committee of the L.T.T.E., but was not proclaimed as a group until 1981. With the deterioration of T.E.L.O., the P.L.O.T. assumed a position second only to the L.T.T.E. in terms of strength and power. As Dissanayake observes, however, the P.L.O.T. had the highest casualties of all the guerrilla groups within the Tamil community.[81] Internal rivalries led to a split in 1985 and this greatly reduced the political activities of the group. Thereafter, the P.L.O.T. continued to operate in alliance with several smaller guerrilla groups such as the T.E.L.A., the Tamil Eelam Liberation Front (T.E.L.F.), the Tamil Eelam Republican Army (T.E.R.A.), and the National Liberation Front of Tamil Eelam (N.L.F.T.).

Another major component of the Tamil guerrilla movement was E.R.O.S. which originated in 1975 in London and, therefore, was the only externally-based Tamil guerrilla group. E.R.O.S. was formed by the Eelam Research Organisation, which comprises a powerful secretive student body. Furthermore, E.R.O.S. was the only group which had been closely associated with the L.T.T.E. E.R.O.S. also had the distinction of masterminding violence outside the Northern and Eastern provinces of Sri Lanka. As a result, E.R.O.S. had sometimes been tagged as 'the mouthpiece of the L.T.T.E.' in the South. The publication *Frontline*, on the other hand, had identified E.R.O.S. as the dark horse of the Tamil militant groups.[82]

Another significant Tamil guerrilla organization was the E.P.R.L.F. which broke away from E.R.O.S. and was a relatively new group compared to the others. The E.P.R.L.F. became widely known when in 1984 its members kidnapped an American couple working in Jaffna.[83] This group was distinctive ideologically in the sense that it was more militant and had an ethnically-mixed membership. Whereas the other groups emphasized terrorist and guerrilla tactics, the E.P.R.L.F. emphasized the ideological orientation of the movement.

Thus, the Tamil underground movement was rife with disputes about authority, responsibility and ideology. In short, internal rivalries for power had flourished. Despite the differences, however, all the groups shared common objectives which shall be discussed in detail in Chapter 6. Their common beliefs may be summarized at this point as follows: all the groups believed strongly that the Sri Lankan Tamils have been penalized; that a separate state was their solution to the Tamils' problems; and that violence was the primary means of achieving that end. It was widely accepted that the shared objectives of this movement supersede the rivalries and factionalism within.

5.14 Recruitment and Training of the Tamil Guerrillas

The Tamil guerrilla groups were operating as underground movements. Therefore, recruitment was conducted in secret and was restricted. This earnest secrecy was maintained mainly to prevent the infiltration of police informers. In this section the author will address the L.T.T.E.'s methods of recruitment, and the training and duties of its membership.

The process of gaining membership was long and drawn out, and the criteria were selective. A person seeking membership in any of these groups had to prove himself bona fide. In this context the L.T.T.E. checked the background of its potential members for criminal records or anti-social activities. A clear record and high moral standards were expected of its members.[84] It was also mandatory for a prospective member to undertake a task as a test of his good faith. Once these requirements had been satisfactorily accomplished, a member was eligible for training in guerrilla warfare and handling weapons.[85] Thus recruitment to the Tamil guerrilla movement was said to be voluntary, and it was open to both sexes and persons of all ages. Despite the emphasis on voluntary mobilization, there was evidence that forced recruitment was also implemented.[86] There had been speculation that the L.T.T.E. made demands on the Tamil people to enlist at least one member of each family into the guerrilla movement.[87]

The training of L.T.T.E. members, which was much more sophisticated than that of the J.V.P., was conducted in camps where members were exposed to instruction in the use of weapons and to physical endeavours. The extent and type of teaching, however, varied from group to group. The training programmes of the L.T.T.E. emphasized the use of weaponry such as AK-47, M-63, M-16, SLR .303 and other riflery, revolvers and grenades. In addition to the training in handling of firearms, members were also instructed in the basic practices of guerrilla warfare. This aspect was comprised of training in military tactics and operations such as field craft, ambush, frontal attacks, raids, handling of explosives, radio communication and basic first aid. The period of instruction varied from six months to one year. Select members were also given specialized training in communication, intelligence, advanced first aid and politics.

Once the military training was completed, the full-fledged members were assigned duties depending on his/her ability, choice and preference e.g., in research, political literature, social work, political propaganda or social welfare. Irrespective of their choices and aptitudes, all members were required upon completion of training to participate in military action when called for by the regional commander. The L.T.T.E. deemed it imperative that its members participate in armed violence. During the days of relative calm the cadres participated in shramadana (volunteer) activities like the laying of roads, or engaged themselves in cultivation or political propaganda. They also worked in the L.T.T.E.'s food production units such as bakeries or helped run the numerous shops in the villages.[88] In a broad sense, the members of any Tamil guerrilla movement including the L.T.T.E. could be divided into three main categories as follows: the fighting cadres, the propaganda units and reservoir of sympathizers. The first two categories are the active members of the movement who were directly involved in the violence and who used pseudonyms.

According to the code of discipline imposed in most if not all guerilla groups, it was compulsory for members to adhere to the code of conduct and ethical principles which bound them to the organization. In this respect the L.T.T.E. also imposed an iron discipline on its members and leaders. Accordingly, cigarettes, liquor, drugs and casual relationships with the opposite sex were diligently prohibited. In addition to these demands, it was mandatory that members take an oath swearing total allegiance to the leadership, even staking their very lives for the cause of the 'Liberation of Tamils'. The L.T.T.E. imposed additional rules on those who were in the combat cadre.

Members of the L.T.T.E. were compelled to carry their identity cards with them at all times and to wear cyanide capsules around their necks in the form of a pendant. The features of a suicide squad were most evident in their preference to death rather than capture.[89] The discipline imposed on its members by the L.T.T.E. was so rigid that the group did not accept any dissidents or breakaway factions from other guerrilla groups. To complement this policy, similar rules applied to those leaving the L.T.T.E. The members of the L.T.T.E. could leave the group only with prior consent. Members who left the L.T.T.E. were not permitted to join another group or organize a new group.[90]

Characteristically as in most underground movements, it is not possible to ascertain accurate figures on the number of members; the Tamil guerrilla groups are no exception. Furthermore, there are several factors which obfuscate the true strength of these groups. First, for security and propaganda reasons none of the groups have ever divulged their true strength. Second, due to the clandestine nature of these groups most members operated undercover and in secret, thereby exposing their very existence to only a few individuals. Finally, due to the armed attacks and counter-attacks, the number of recorded casualties varied as did the number of deserters. Furthermore, the membership of these groups fluctuated, thereby eluding specific statistics. On the whole, it was a complex area within which data was hardly ascertainable.

As Bruce Matthews aptly points out, the membership figures for these organizations vary, and are dynamic in the sense that membership oscillated with the level of activity and the amount of governmental counter-insurgency.[91] It was widely known, however, that at the inception these groups were comprised of very few members. Prior to 1975, the number of hard core activists in all Tamil guerrilla organizations was confined to a mere 50 members. According to Marshal R. Singer, during the interim period from 1975 to 1983, before the 1983 ethnic violence, the conditions were not conducive for mobilization. Consequently, as of 1983 the membership had expanded to only 200 hard core members.[92] In 1986, however, ***The Economist*** estimated the total membership within the entire Tamil guerrilla movement at 10,000.[93]

Numerically, the L.T.T.E. has always been the largest group within the Tamil guerrilla movement. In 1985, it was estimated that the L.T.T.E. had around 2,500 trained guerrillas and 5,000 untrained recruits.[94] One of the local guerrilla commanders claimed in 1986 that there were about 1,500 guerrillas from the L.T.T.E. operating within the Jaffna peninsula.[95] Kittu, the L.T.T.E. military commander of Jaffna, claimed in 1987 that his group had mobilized more than 10,000 regulars throughout Sri Lanka.[96] It is noteworthy that a majority of the L.T.T.E. members were from the Northern Province rather than the Eastern Province of Sri Lanka. Jaffna, the capital of the Northern Province, was the nucleus of the L.T.T.E. The T.E.L.O. had about 800 trained members and another 3,000 poorly trained members before its confrontation with the L.T.T.E. in 1986. According to the ***Economist*** the E.P.R.L.F. had, as of mid 1988, around 1,500 guerrillas.[97] The E.R.O.S. now had approximately 500 trained members. The membership of the P.L.O.T. had not been divulged though it was known. As mentioned earlier, that the P.L.O.T. had the highest casualties amongst the Tamil guerrilla groups.

5.15 Socio-Economic Background of the Tamil Guerrillas

As mentioned previously, literature pertaining to the Tamil guerrilla movement was limited, and the author adds the observation that the literature regarding the socio-economic background of the membership was also minimal. Ethnically, nearly all members of the surviving Tamil guerrilla groups were Sri Lankan Tamils. There was no evidence of Sinhalese participation in the L.T.T.E. The ideology of the L.T.T.E. was such that it never did, and still does not permit Sinhalese participation.[98] There were indications, however, that a minor percentage of Muslims and Indian Tamils have participated in L.T.T.E. activities. The P.L.O.T. too was said to have a few Muslims among its membership, and a low percentage of Indian Tamils have been involved with the E.P.R.L.F. and E.R.O.S. On the other hand, the E.P.R.L.F. and P.L.O.T. were believed to have some connections with certain Sinhala radical groups. The E.P.R.L.F. had associated itself with the Vikalpa Kandayama (Alternative Group) while P.L.O.T. had become linked with the J.V.P. Nava Pravanathawaya (New Tendency).[99] It is obvious that both groups were open to Sinhala involvement in the Tamil guerrillas' movement. Despite the contacts maintained with the Indian Tamils, Muslims and Sinhalese, however, none have ever been represented in the regional or local leadership of Tamil guerrilla groups. Thus, one can conclude that the involvement of the other communities had been rather tepid and that the Tamil guerrilla movement was in fact dominated by the Sri Lankan Tamils.

In Sri Lanka, ethnicity reveals the religion of the various communities. Consequently, Hinduism is the main religion followed by the Sri Lankan Tamils, and thus a majority of the members of the Tamil guerrilla groups were Hindus. There was evidence of the involvement of Tamil Christians in the movement though they were not represented in significant numbers.

The age range of the Tamil guerrillas was similar to that of the J.V.P. members. A majority were said to be between 18 and 25 years of age with only a few in their thirties.[100] Thus, most of the current Tamil cadres were young teenage men and women. The youthfulness of these members was further indicated by the word the Tamil people still use to identify the guerrillas: 'thambi' (boy). As the overall composition of this movement had always been youth based, these groups could be identified as youth guerrilla organizations.

The educational attainment of the Tamil guerrillas reflected another similarity with the J.V.P. membership. A majority of the guerrilla fighters had passed their G.C.E.(O/L) or G.C.E.(A/L) examinations, while a few had obtained a university education. R.N. Kearney points out that most of them had been educated in their indigenous language 'Tamil' and, therefore, were unfamiliar with the English language.[101] The J.V.P.'s members had received a similar education which had ensured fluency in the mother tongue and a very limited knowledge of the English language.

By comparison, the urban/rural-based nature of the J.V.P. and the Tamil guerrillas was quite different. An overwhelming proportion of the J.V.P. membership was from the rural sector while the Tamil guerrillas seem to hail from both the urban and rural sectors. The ethnic orientation of the Tamil guerrilla movement obfuscates the class, caste and economic base of its members. Since 1983, it had been increasingly evident that the guerrilla groups represent almost all strata of Tamil society. A sizeable proportion appeared to come from an affluent middle-class background and a fairly large number were from families of higher socio-economic status. The majority of the rank and file, however, belonged to the lower middle class or its economic equivalent.

The caste structure, which was an inherent part of Tamil society, was of significance when considering the background and social composition of the Tamil guerrilla groups. Few scholars have focused on caste as it was manifest in these groups, perhaps because little information was available. It was known, that the caste base varies from group to group. The L.T.T.E. and T.E.L.O. have drawn their membership mostly from Velvetithurai, Vadimaratchi and Point Pedro, which were major fishing villages in the Northern Province of Sri Lanka. Hence, the leadership and a majority of the members in these two groups were from the Ḳaraiyars or the fishermen's caste. A significant number of Mukkuvar (fisherman) and Koviyar (domestic servant) castes were also represented in the L.T.T.E. The T.E.L.O. was said to contain a large number of members from the Karaiyars, Mukkuvars and Koviyars castes. Most members of the P.L.O.T. were drawn from Vavunia, an area devoted primarily to agriculture, and as a result, a majority of its leaders and members were from the Vellala (cultivators) caste, which was one of the highest castes in the Tamil caste structure.[102] The majority of members of the E.P.R.L.F. were apparently from the Vellala and Mukkuvar castes. It is not possible at this point, however, to establish the exact figures of caste origin in the Tamil guerrilla movement as no definite pattern has yet emerged.

5.16 Organisational Structure of the Tamil Guerrilla Groups

The internal structure of Tamil guerrilla groups gives insights into the operational nature of these groups. As mentioned earlier, these groups were primarily, action-oriented rather than theory-oriented. Therefore, the basic structure of a majority of these groups was that of a guerrilla force rather than a political party. The organizational patterns of these groups were not uniform. Of all the groups, the L.T.T.E. was the most tightly structured and autocratically-led group. At the same time, the internal structure of the L.T.T.E. had remained intact without any visible fissures.[103]

As mentioned above, the L.T.T.E. was organized as a liberation army. Although the organization was divided into political and military sections, the two wings did not operate separately. The political wing was subordinate to the military wing. The L.T.T.E.'s organizational structure did not permit a separate political party structure independent of the military wing because of its Guevarist orientation rather than a Leninist or Maoist approach. The P.L.O.T. and T.E.L.O. were similar organizationally to the L.T.T.E. The E.P.R.L.F. and the E.R.O.S., however, had adopted a contrary approach by establishing separate political and military wings, with the military wing subordinate to the political wing.[104]

The military wing of the L.T.T.E. was mainly confined to the Northern and Eastern provinces of Sri Lanka. The L.T.T.E. had subdivided the two provinces into five military districts: Jaffna, Mannar, Vanni (including Vavunia) and Mulathivu, Trincomallee and Batticaloa. Each region was under the charge of a regional commander who was appointed by the L.T.T.E.'s supreme leader on the basis of seniority and merit. There is evidence that these commanders were usually the most trusted and closest associates of the supreme leader. Feliks Gross aptly observes that relations between the leaders in underground organizations are based to a high degree on personal confidence and often on personal friendship.[105] In a broad sense these regional commanders enjoy a degree of autonomy within the group, and were in a position to make local decisions which affect their regional commands. This is particularly the case with decisions pertaining to military action such as attacks on Sri Lankan military personnel and convoys. Once such operations were completed, the regional commanders reported the results to a superior officer or perhaps to the supreme leader himself. In the case of political issues concerning the ethnic crisis, the leader of the L.T.T.E. had to be consulted and his approval must be obtained before any decision was taken.[106]

Generally the regional council in each of the five districts was further subdivided into smaller military and political units which were commanded by the local guerrilla leaders. Thus, the council in each regional district was equipped with a regional army and political structure.[107]

The organizational structure of the group was further divided downward to the local and cell levels. The local councils of the L.T.T.E. were under the regional council, and were headed by the local commanders who were appointed by the regional commanders. Furthermore, there were twenty local committees under each of the five regional councils of the L.T.T.E.

The L.T.T.E.'s military wing had military bases and sub-bases which were assigned code names. By 1986, the L.T.T.E. had set up 25 military bases and many more sub-bases within the Northern Province. Each of the major military bases was manned by about 60 to 70 members while 25 to 30 members operated from each of the sub-bases.

As mentioned earlier, the political wing of the L.T.T.E. was dominated by the military wing. The leader of the political wing was appointed by the supreme leader of the organization. The main function of this wing was propaganda, and the political adviser was the key figure in assuring its successful operation. The political wing also controlled the front organizations such as student groups and foreign lobbies. In late 1986, the L.T.T.E. organized a political party named the Tamil Eelam People's Organisation (T.E.P.O.). The main objectives of this party were to inform and educate the masses on the political developments occurring in Sri Lanka and worldwide. The hierarchical structure of the Tamil guerrilla groups was also vertically divided into separate units on the basis of the division of labour into specialized fields. The L.T.T.E., for example, contains the following units: military, science, research, communications, medical, social, economic and cultural.[108]

Within the organizational structure of the L.T.T.E. there was a central committee and a polit bureau. The central committee was composed of the military commander, regional commanders and senior members of the organization. These sub-bodies, however, existed more in theory than in practice. There was no uniformity in the pattern of leadership in the Tamil guerrilla groups. Thus, the leadership structure varied from group to group. The L.T.T.E. and T.E.L.O., though do share the common characteristic of a heavy dependency on personal leadership. Most of the major guerrilla groups have a very charismatic leader who provided the driving force behind the organizations. The E.P.R.L.F. and the E.R.O.S., however, were said to have an elected leader from a central committee. The E.R.O.S., on the other hand, was the only Tamil guerrilla group with a collective leadership made up of a three-member executive committee.[109] Thus, the L.T.T.E. and some of the other key groups were dominated by strong personal leadership and were strictly hierarchical in structure.

5.17 Background of the Leaders of the Tamil Guerrilla Groups

In order to achieve a comprehensive understanding of the structure and operation of the Tamil guerrilla organizations, it is also necessary to examine the socio-economic and political background of their leaders. The Tamil guerrilla leaders shared a similar socio-economic background with the exception of their different caste origins. All of the top leaders were Sri Lankan Tamils and Hindu, as were all or most of their followers. On the other hand, like the J.V.P., the Tamil guerrilla groups were strictly male-dominated. Tamil women have been ascribed a secondary role in the political violence movements in Sri Lanka and therefore, none had succeeded in assuming the leadership of any of the movements which come within the purview of this study. The leaders of the Tamil guerrillas were, on the whole, in their late twenties and tend to be fairly well-educated. Nearly all the leaders of the major Tamil guerrilla groups came from a particular area in Jaffna, namely Velvettiturai, an urbanized area in the Northern Province. Their professional backgrounds, however, varied. Uma Maheswaran, the leader of P.L.O.T. was a surveyor, but Prabahkaran, the leader of the L.T.T.E., did not have any professional experience prior to forming the L.T.T.E. The founding leaders of T.E.L.O., Thangadorai and Kuttimani, were smugglers. It is significant that none of these Tamil guerrilla leaders were exposed to the left-wing movement before joining the respective guerrilla organizations.

As mentioned earlier, the caste background of the Tamil guerrilla leaders varied. The leaders of the E.P.R.L.F. were from either the Vellala or Karaiyar castes. The leaders of E.R.O.S. were from the Karaiyar caste. The L.T.T.E., which was the most powerful Tamil guerrilla group, was led by V. Prabahkaran who was from the Karaiyar caste. The P.L.O.T., the L.T.T.E.'s major rival group, was led by Uma Maheswaren who was from the Vellala caste. It was evident, however, that there was no significant link between the caste differences and the conflicting political ideologies of the groups.

5.18 Sources of Funds

The Tamil guerrilla organizations had diverse and varied sources of funding. A consistent source of funds, for example, had been the expatriate Tamils based in the United Kingdom, the United States of America, the Middle East, West Germany, Australia, Canada and other countries.[110] Another source was donations collected from sympathizers and supporters in Sri Lanka. The T.E.L.F. has collected funds by selling lottery tickets, a unique fund-raising method for a guerrilla group.[111] Illegal sources, however, such as the kidnapping of wealthy businessmen and collection of ransom money, have provided far more funds.

There was convincing evidence that, as with many guerrilla groups throughout Asia, the Sri Lankan Tamil guerrillas had resorted to narcotics trafficking as a means of fundraising.[112] For example, the Indian Narcotics Bureau in 1985 detected ten cases of opium and heroin smuggling by Tamil guerrillas.[113] The L.T.T.E. and P.L.O.T. were said to be the two main groups involved in this trade. The Tamil guerrillas had little or no control over or involvement in the production and processing of drug-yielding crops as do the Karen guerrillas of Burma, or the Afghan guerrillas who fought the Soviet Union. Rather the

Tamil guerrillas acted as couriers, as part of a link in the wider narcotics trade of the "Golden Crescent" which extends from North West Asia to Europe. Thus European drug addicts had unwittingly become an important source of funds for Sri Lanka's Tamil guerrillas.[114] The Sunday Times further confirmed that members of the Sri Lankan Tamil guerrilla movement were trafficking in drugs in order to raise funds.[115]

Several daring but sporadic bank robberies had served the same aim by generating substantial sums for guerrilla activities. The banks located in the Northern and Eastern provinces where most Tamil guerrilla operations occur, had been especially subject to this threat. It had become the most lucrative method of finance for the Tamil guerrilla groups. The following Table 5.10 illustrates the number of robberies known to have been committed by the Tamil guerrilla groups between 1976 and 1984.

Table 5.10. Robberies by Tamil Guerrilla Groups 1976-1084

Year	*Group*	*Place*	*Amount (Rs)*
1976	-	People's Bank, Puttur	668,000
1976	-	Co-operative society, Pulaly	350,000
1978	LTTE	Post-office, Thinnaveli	10,000
1978	-	People's Bank	1,080,000
1978	-	People's Bank, Nallur	1,120,000
1979	-	Kilinochchi mail bags	20,000
1980	-	M.P.C.S., Thunakai	20,000
1981	TELO	Urembasiddi Pawnshop	80,000
1981	PLOT	Neeraveli People's Bank	8,000,000
1982	-	Chavakachcheri Rail Station	35,000
1982	-	Killinochchi Peoples Bank	4,400,000
1983	-	Jaffna mail bags	20,000
1983	-	Mankulam petrol station	45,000
1984	TEA	Kattankudy (Batticaloa) Bank	50,000,000

Source: T.D.S.A. Disanayake, *Agony of Sri Lanka,* (Colombo: Swastika Press 1984), pp. 29-73, and *Tamil Terrorist, A Record of Murder and Robbery,* Ministry of State Publication, Colombo, Government Press, [no date].

In summary, donations from Tamil expatriate supporters and sympathizers, but more importantly illegal means such as ransom demands, drug trafficking and robberies, had become the major sources of funding for the Tamil guerrilla groups.

5.19 International Links

Any analysis of the Tamil guerrilla movement would not be complete without focusing on their international links with foreign state and non-state institutions and organizations. At the outset the author admits that the true nature and full extent of this network of international links remains undiscovered, although some literature provides limited insights into its possible scope. There is no doubt that foreign support in terms of funding, arms, training bases and sanctuary was essential for the successful operation of any guerrilla movement. Furthermore, the Tamil guerrilla groups have been seeking international assistance not only for funding and material, but more importantly for acknowledgement equal to that of the P.L.O., Namibia and Polisario movements as a prelude to diplomatic recognition should the Tamil guerrillas come to political power in Sri Lanka. Hence, contrary to the J.V.P. which had been comparatively isolated, the Tamil guerrillas had established international ties. Evidence of these associations was best traced through the sophisticated weapons and equipment and thorough guerrilla training that the Tamil groups had received from foreign sources.

The main international links had been with the expatriate Tamils, who have played a vital role in furnishing the Tamil guerrillas with financing, and also with propaganda which emphasized racial discrimination and the plight of the Tamil people in Sri Lanka. The Tamil expatriates were responsible for the build-up of a global network of Eelam bodies particularly in the U.K., the U.S.A., Australia, West Germany, and Canada.[116] The post 1983 Tamil Diaspora has experienced the separatist war as well as ethnic riots and was therefore more easily mobilized for fund raising and propaganda activities. Thus the major Sri Lankan Tamil guerrilla groups had established front organizations in many countries in collaboration with their expatriates. According to the publication, ***Frontline***, the L.T.T.E. had bases in more than 100 countries.[117] The T.E.L.O. also had a powerful branch force in France. The author admits that there is no systematic study regarding the role of the expatriate Sri Lankan Tamils in the phenomenon of political violence. The following passage by A.J. Wilson provides some insight into the objectives and strategies of the propaganda campaign masterminded by the expatriate Tamils, as follows:

> There are militant Tamil expatriate groups in India, West Germany, Britain, Canada, and the United States and they have achieved a measure of success. Their principal tactics are to expose discrimination by successive Sinhalese-dominated governments against the Tamils in Sri Lanka, bring to the world's attention violation of the Tamil human rights, lobby government, and international lending agencies against providing economic aid to Sri Lanka, invite the attention of foreign investors and tourists to the political instability in the island and popularize the cause of Eelam.[118]

The Tamil guerrillas had not confined their international links only to Tamil expatriates. There is overwhelming evidence of their contacts with international guerrilla and terrorist organizations. In an interview, the leader of the L.T.T.E., V. Prabahkaran, admitted that the L.T.T.E. maintained relationships with other liberation movements throughout the world.[119] The L.T.T.E. established contact with the P.L.O. in order to obtain military training for its members.[120] Both the L.T.T.E. and the P.L.O.T. had central fighting cores that have been trained by the P.L.O.[121] The other international guerrilla groups which had been actively linked with the L.T.T.E., were the Zimbabwe African People's Union (Z.A.P.U.), and the African National Congress (A.N.C.).[122]

The P.L.O.T., on the other hand, established ties with the Popular Front for the Liberation of Palestine (P.F.L.P.), a breakaway faction of the P.L.O.[123] Rohan Gunarathna observes that the Dera camp in Damascus was a popular training base for P.L.O.T. members.[124] Sri Lankan intelligence sources had confirmed that several top Tamil guerrillas had received training in guerrilla warfare at P.L.O. camps based in Lebanon.[125] Sri Lanka's C.I.D. investigation into the Liberation Tiger Movement had revealed that at least 20 Tamil guerrillas had received training abroad as had some members of international terrorists groups such as the I.R.A. and the Baader-Meinhoff group.[126] Thomas Marks believes that Libya was also aiding the Tamil guerrilla movement. It was not known, however, whether any of the Tamil groups have had any contact with the Soviet Union or with its current or former proxies.[127]

The role of the Indian national and state governments particularly that of the Indian state government of Tamil Nadu, within the guerrilla movement will not be explored in detail. Despite the well-established links between the Sri Lankan guerrillas and the various Indian state governments, the complexity and extensiveness of those links would not permit an in-depth analysis within the confines of this study. The examination of such links is confined here primarily to those with other guerrilla organizations. This study would not be complete, however, without at least a brief overview of the links between the Tamil guerrilla movement and the Indian Federal and state governments.

While the Indian Federal Government on second occasions acted as mediator with the Tamil guerrillas on behalf of the Sri Lankan Government, that representation was both paradoxical and ambivalent in nature in view of the fact that the Indian governments had always been deeply involved in assisting the Tamil guerrillas. The mediation offered by the Indian Federal Government, therefore, can hardly be viewed as a disinterested effort. During the rule of Indira Gandhi (1979-1984), the Tamil guerrillas were considerably indulged by the Indian national authorities.[128] Prime Minister Indira Gandhi acknowledged in 1983 that the Research and Analysis Wing (R.A.W.), India's foreign intelligence agency, had established contacts with a number of Tamil guerrilla groups.[129] The T.E.L.O. and the P.L.O.T. were closely linked with India at the initial stages of that intelligence operation. Moreover, *The Times* reported that in 1982, R.A.W. agents recruited T.E.L.O. members and brought them to India for training in espionage and sabotage.[130] The T.E.L.O. had achieved notoriety as India's 'little soldiers' because the T.E.L.O. had been, in major part, funded, trained and armed by the R.A.W. Sri Sabarathan, the leader of T.E.L.O., clearly revealed the nature of those ties with India when he said: We will be soldiers, let India decide out politics.[131]

The complexity of India's involvement was further accentuated by the guerrilla training camps in India, whose existence had been reported in foreign and local magazines and newspapers. The following Table 5.11 depicts the locations of Tamil guerrilla military training bases in Northern India and the number of guerrillas trained.

Table 5.11. Military Training of Tamil Guerrilla Groups in Northern India

Group	*No. Trained*	*Location of the camp*
TELO	Not Known	The camp near Great Kailas 11, in New Delhi
TELO	Not Known	Sadtagen development area adjoining Cannal Park in New Delhi
TELO	300	At a location about 2 hours journey by bus from New Delhi Railway Station
TELO	362	A camp in Uttar Pradesh close to the Himalayan foothills
TELO	60	Green Park, New Delhi, close to the medical College
TELO	Not Known	A camp in Uttar Pradesh close to the Himalayan foothills
PLOT	Not Known	The army camp close to the International Airport, New Delhi
EROS	56	A camp in Uttar Pradesh close to the foothills of Himalaya

Source: Denzil Peiris, *Colombo Rides the Tigers,* Overseas Information Series, No. 30, Colombo, Department of Government Printing, Sri Lanka, (1985), p. 12.

The Indian Government, however, had diligently denied the existence of training camps and related facilities for Tamil guerrillas. The Indian Government's continued denials was especially ironic in light of Indian journalists' extensive coverage of these camps and bases.[132] It was claimed that the Indian Government's first involvement preceded May 1983 with the training of P.L.O.T. and T.E.L.O. insurgents at a camp close to the New Delhi International Airport.[133] The Indian Government had also permitted the Tamil guerrilla groups to establish bases in southern India, which had served as the nucleus of their operations. Thus, the Tamil guerrillas had been allowed to amass arsenals of sophisticated arms in India and ship them to Sri Lanka, operate training camps, install communication facilities, create 'Eelam' information centres, and move freely between India and Sri Lanka.[134] Moreover, the Indian Government had refused to undertake military operations to dislodge the Tamil guerrillas from India's Tamil Nadu Province.

Although the links between the Tamil guerrilla groups and the Indian Government were varied and complicated, the guerrillas' links with the Tamil Nadu state government were more readily discernible. The long-standing ethnic, cultural and religious ties between the Sri Lankan Tamils and the Indian Tamils in Tamil Nadu, have reflected a strong tradition of open support and sympathy for the Sri Lankan guerrilla movement. Consequently, the guerrillas' links with Tamil Nadu were sustained by the local sympathizers who were sometimes motivated by deeper political ambitions. In view of these circumstances it was no surprise that most of the major Tamil guerrilla groups were based in Southern India. When the Sri Lankan Government declared an emergency situation in the Northern Province in August 1979, the Tamil guerrilla groups took refuge at their bases in Southern India.[135] Since then, the headquarters of all Tamil guerrilla groups had been based in the Tamil Nadu capital of Madras which had been transformed into a breeding ground for and haven of Tamil guerrillas.

In addition to this sanctuary and continued support provided in India before and after the ethnic violence in Sri Lanka in 1983, the Tamil guerrillas in Tamil Nadu had been trained by retired Indian army officers.[136] Thus Tamil Nadu has been the cite of several training facilities for T.E.L.O., P.L.O.T. and T.E.L.A. Table 5.12 below illustrates the location of the military training camps and the identity of each guerrilla group trained in Tamil Nadu.

Table 5.12 Military Training of Tamil Guerrillas' in Tamil Nadu

Group	*No. Trained*	*Location of the camp*
TELO	Not Known	Large house at No. 777, or 977
TELO	Not Known	Parangimali and at a place about 40 km. From the Madras Airport
TELO	300	Salem, Kollimalai, Kanjipuram
TELO	Not Known	Kollimalai, Kanjipuram
TELO	360	Kollimalai, Kakavel
TELO	24 1st visit	Anna Nagar, Parangimalai in close Proximity to Meenambakkam Airport
	700	Salem
TELO	50	Kanchipuram
PLOT	Not Known	Sengalpattu, Presawakkam
PLOT	Not Known	Sengalpattu, Thanathur, Kongurukolam in Erode
TELA	300	Valachchari and Thenikramam

Source: Denzil Peiris, *op. cit.* pp. 6-7.

The Tamil guerrilla links with Tamil Nadu, however, were maintained not as a collective front but rather on the basis of the personal contacts established by each group. The Anna Dravida Munnethra Kazagam (A.D.M.K.), which formed the Tamil Nadu state government, supported the L.T.T.E., while the opposition party, the Dravida Munnethra Kazagam (D.M.K.), supported T.E.L.O. In 1987 the Tamil Nadu state government announced that it had granted aid to the L.T.T.E. worth U.S. $ 2,300,000.[137]

The overt support extended to the Tamil guerrillas by both the Indian federal and state governments led K.M. de Silva to conclude that the Sri Lankan Tamil guerrillas operated in Tamil Nadu with an amount of freedom and publicity for which the only parallel was the P.L.O. and its various factions in the Arab world.[138]

5.20 Summary

The origin and development of guerrilla movements represent the most crucial phases of political violence. The organizational aspects of the J.V.P., therefore, were as important to this study of political violence as those of the Tamil guerrilla movements. Consequently, from the above discussion it is evident that although these two strains of political violence movements have displayed some similarities, their organizational differences have been far more profound.

The J.V.P. broke away from the left oriented C.P. (P.) in 1966. Except for a very brief period in 1970-1983, the J.V.P. had operated as a clandestine organization. The J.V.P.'s members had been under the continued close supervision and scrutiny of its leaders and were mainly drawn from the Sinhalese-Buddhist, rural, and fairly well-educated young Sri Lankans. The participation of the peasantry and the middle class in the J.V.P. was insignificant. Its organizational structure was characterized by an informal and personal dimension under a pyramidical structure where decisions and authority converge at the top and filter down through the cadres to the lower ranks. Like many guerrilla organizations in the Third World, the J.V.P. was primarily a paramilitary organization, following such guerrilla practices as assumed names, a secret language, weapons training and rigid discipline. Moreover, it had displayed all the characteristics of an indigenous guerrilla organization where foreign support had been almost non-existent.

Unlike the J.V.P., the Tamil guerrilla groups originated in the student movement of the moderate T.U.L.F. in the 1970s. They have abided by a rigid procedure of recruitment, with the membership having been drawn mainly from the Sri Lankan Tamil-Hindu youth, who represent both the rural and urban sector, and who like the Sinhala guerrillas, were fairly well-educated. A majority of the Tamil groups had been organized Unlike the J.V.P., the Tamil guerrilla groups originated in the student movement of the moderate T.U.L.F. in the 1970s. They have abided by a rigid procedure of recruitment, with the membership having been drawn mainly from the Sri Lankan Tamil-Hindu youth, who represent both the rural and urban sector, and who like the Sinhala guerrillas, were fairly well-educated. A majority of the Tamil groups had been organized as armies geared for combat rather than as politically-motivated factions. As a result, their membership was well trained and equipped for military operations against the Sri Lankan Government and competing guerrilla factions. The response of the Tamil community, both within and without Sri Lanka, had been supportive and enthusiastic. Nearly all the groups had secured international networks of contact and support, including covert assistance from the Indian Federal and state governments, especially that of Tamil Nadu. The limited features akin to the J.V.P. were their clandestine nature, their youthful membership and their secret procedure of recruitment. The covert and tightly structured nature of these guerrilla organizations has had an impact on their ideologies, programmes and strategies. Their different ideologies had played a key role in determining the nature of each group's attitudes and doctrines as well as their programmes and strategies regarding the use of political violence. Therefore, the author devotes the following Chapter 6 to an examination and comparison of these aspects in both the Sinhalese and Tamil guerrilla movements.

References

1. Lucian W. Pye, "The Roots of Insurgency" in Harry Eckstein, ed. *Internal War: Problems and Approaches,* (New York: The Free Press, 1964), p. 163.

2. His proper name is Ptabandige Don Nadasiri Wijeweera.

3. Rohana Wijeweera, *"Janatha Vimukthi Peramuna C.I.A. Karayo," (J.V.P. C.I.A. Agents),* speech given on the 14th July, 1970, to the Sri Lanka Vidyodaya (Nugegoda) University Socialist Society, in Gangodawila, p. 4.

4. A.C. Alles, *The Insurgency 1971,* (Colombo: Apothecaries, 1976), p. 1.
5. Janice Jiggins, *Caste and Family in the Politics of Sinhalese, 1947-1976,* (London: Cambridge University Press, 1979), p. 139.
6. James Jupp, *Sri Lanka: Third World Democracy,* (London: Frank Cass, 1977), p. 297.
7. Rohana Wijeweera, "Speech Given to the Criminal Justice Commission", in Robin Blackburn, (ed), *Explosion in a Subcontinent: India Pakistan, Bangladesh and Ceylon,* (London: Penguin Books, 1975), p. 225.
8. Murad Aidith was a brother of the chairman of the Indonesian Communist Party who died in the abortive military coup in 1965, Sheikh Hassim Hanga was a former student of the London School of Economics, who happened to be at Lumumba in the 1960s. Sheikh Abeid Amani Karume was a student from Zanzibar, who later led the one-day revolution in January 1964, and became President of the People's Republic of Zanzibar.
9. Rohana Wijeweera, *op. cit.,* p. 226.
10. Victor Ivan., *71 Aprel Keralla (The '71 April Insurrection),* (Colombo: Lake House Investment Ltd. Co., 1978), pp. 3-4.
11. In 1962 Dharmakeerthi was killed in a plane crash near Moscow.
12. A.C. Alles, *op. cit.,* p. 5.
13. Rohana Wijeweera, *Statement to the Police on 24th September,* 1971, unpublished, p. 2
14. Victor Ivan, *op. cit.,* p. 4.
15. The C.P.(P) contested four seats in the General Election of 1965, but all of its candidates lost.
16. Kalayananda Thiranagama was a graduate of the University of Colombo, and later became an attorney of law. Gamini Yapa, whose real name was Wimal Ranasinghe, was a science graduate from the University of Colombo. Nihal Dias and Sarath Wijesinghe were social science students at the University of Peradeniya. The latter died in April 1971 while instructing fellow members on how to use a shotgun.
17. The other attendees were Sanath Boralucatiya (Wijesena G. Vithana), W.T. Karunarathna, and Nimalasiri Jayasinghe (Loku Athula). Sanath who was a teacher, W.T. Karunaratna

who was a clerk at a government department, and Loku Athula who was unemployed, were on the Board of Secretaries in the J.V.P. Sanath died in the 1971 Insurrection, and the other two left the J.V.P. during the subsequent trial.

18. The J.V.P.'s dependence on this particular trade union was based on the support extended by D.B. Danapala, the secretary of the Trade Union who was also a founding member of the J.V.P.

19. D.I.G. Dharmasekera, more popularly known as Castro Dharme, for his advocacy of a Cuban-style revolution, broke away from the J.V.P. in 1969.

20. Mahinda Wijesekara, left the J.V.P. after the trial related to the 1971 Insurrection and became an attorney at law. A short time later he led a party called the Mahajana Vimukthi Pakshaya (People's Liberation Party) and then joined the S.L.F.P. In the General Election of 1989, he was elected to the National Assembly.

21. The pro-J.V.P. students were behind the clash in 1968 between the army and the students at the University of Peradeniya.

22. Later known as the Mao Youth Front (M.Y.F.), it was the group responsible for the attack on the 6th of March 1971 on the U.S. Embassy in Colombo during which a police inspector was killed.

23. Fred Halliday, "The Ceylon Insurrection", *New Left Review,* No. 69, (1971), p. 190.

24. *Wijeweera Athulu Deshapremi Tharunayan Vaha Nidahas Karanu,* (Release Wijeweera and all other Patriotic Youths immediately) [no date], a cyclostyled leaflet.

25. A J.V.P. activist named P. Siriwardena, however, was tried for an attempted coup d'etat.

26. The J.V.P. held 16 public meetings between August 1970 and February 1971. See, Victor Ivan, *op. cit.,* p. 186.

27. W.T. Cicil Chandra, *Statement Given to the C.I.D.,* (1971), unpublished pp. 1-2.

28. A.C. Allas, *op. cit.,* p. 33.

29. Eric Hoffer, *The True Believers: Thoughts on the Nature of Mass Movements,* (New York: Harper and Row Publishers, 1951), p. xii.
30. Rohana Wijeweera, Statement to the C.I.D., *op. cit.,* p. 132.
31. B.A.R. Kurukulasuriya, Statement to the Police, (no date), unpublished, p. 8.
32. A.C. Allas, *op. cit.,* p. 33.
33. *Ibid.,* p. 33
34. Nimalasiri Jayasinghe, (Loku Athula), "Evidence In the, Criminal Justice Commission, (C.J.C.)", *Ceylon Daily News,* (18 January 1973).
35. Felix R. Dias Bandaranayake, "The Recent Events in Ceylon", *Ceylon Today,* Vol. 20, (1971), p. 54.
36. Robert N. Kearney and Janice Jiggins, "The Ceylon Insurrection of 1971", *Journal of Commonwealth and Comparative Politics,* Vol. 13, (1971), p. 54.
37. Urmila Phadnis, "Insurgency in Ceylon", *Economic and Political Weekly,* (May 1971), p. 967.
38. Gananatha Obeysekara, "Some Comments on the Social Backgrounds of the April 1971 Insurgency in Sri Lanka (Ceylon)", *Journal of Asian Studies,* Vol. 33, No. 3, (1974), pp. 367-383.
39. S. Arasarathnam, "The Ceylon Insurrection of 1971: Some Causes and Consequences", *Pacific Affairs,* Vol. 45, No. 3, (1972), pp. 356-372.
40. S.P. Huntington, *Political Order in Changing Societies,* (New Haven: Yale University Press, 1968), p. 304
41. N.M. Perera, *Budget Speech, 1971-72,* Colombo, (1971), p. 1, cited in Robert N. Kearney and Janice Jiggins, *op. cit.,* p. 48.
42. In Table 5.7 all other castes than Govigama, Karava, Salagama and Vellala are known as oppressed castes in Sri Lanka.
43. W.A.W. Warnapala (Politicus) "The April Revolt in Ceylon", *Asian Survey,* Vol. 12, No. 3, (1972), p. 268.
44. B.A.W. Kurukulasuriya, *Statement Made to the Police on 20 April, 1971,* (unpublished), p. 30.
45. (Loku Athula) Nimalasiri Jayasinghe, Statement to the C.I.D. cited by R.N. Kearney and Janice Jiggins, *op. cit.,* p. 53.
46. Rohana Wijeweera, *op. cit.,* p. 310.

47. Feliks Gross, *Seizure of Political Power, in a Century of Revolution,* (Westport, Conn: Greenwood Press, 1979), p. 353.
48. S.A. Piyatilake, Statement Made to the Criminal Justice Commission (C.J.C.), (1973), [unpublished], p. 2.
49. The other three members were Sanath, Karunaratna and Loku Athula.
50. Rohana Wijeweera, Statement to the C.I.D. *op. cit.,* pp. 106-107.
51. Martha Crenshaw, "An Organisational Approach to the Analysis of Political Terrorism", *Orbis,* Vol. 29, No. 3, (1985), p. 469.
52. Rohana Wijeweera, Statement to the C.I.D. op. cit., p. 107.
53. Janatha Sangamaya, (People's League), *71 April Uprising: Background and Politics,* (Dehiwela: Allen Printing Press, 1980), pp.
54. S.P. Huntington, *op. cit.,* p. 290.
55. Carl Leiden and Karl M. Schmitt, *The Politics of Violence: Revolution in the Modern World,* (Englewood Cliffs, N.J.: Prentice-Hall, Inc, 1968), p. 87.
56. Janice Jiggins, *op. cit.,* p. 127.
57. G.B. Keerawella, "The Janatha Vimukthi Peramuna and the 1971 Uprising", *Social Science Review,* (1980), p. 52.
58. *Ibid.,* p. 127.
59. S.P. Huntington, *op. cit.,* pp. 288-290.
60. The gap between the middle class and petit bourgeois is obvious in a country like Sri Lanka. The middle class is a social class between the capitalist and working class. Petitbourgeois is the class between the middle class and the working class. Generally the lower middle class is assumed to be a petit bourgeois.
61. A.J. Wilson, "Ceylon: The People's Liberation Front and the Revolution that Failed", *Pacific Community,* Vol. 3, No. 2, (1972), p. 371.
62. A.C. Allas, *op. cit.,* p. 40.
63. *Ibid.,* p. 41.
64. James Manor, and Segal Jeralad, "Sri lanka and Indian Ocean Strategy", *Asian Survey,* Vol. 25, (1985), p. 1169.
65. *Ibid.,* p. 1169.

66. Anthony Burton, *Revolutionary Violence: The Theories*, (London: Leo Cooper, 1977), p. 96.
67. A.C. Allas, *op. cit.*, pp. 76-83.
68. *Text of Broadcast to the Nation by the Hon. Prime Minister Sirimavo Bandaranaike, on April 24, 1971,* (Department of Information Press Release, 24 April, 1971), cited in Kearney and Jiggins, *op. cit.*, p. 42.
69. See, Appendix. 1.
70. T.D.S.A. Dissanayake, *The Agony of Sri Lanka,* (Colombo: Swastika Press, 1983), p. 32.
71. "Tamil Struggle: The Origin", *India Today,* (31 March 1984), p. 91.
72. Robert c. Oberst, "Sri Lanka's Tamil Tigers", *Conflict,* Vol. 8, Nos. 2-3, (1988), p. 191.
73. Rohan Gunarathna, *War and Peace in Sri Lanka,* (Kandy: Institute of Fundamental Studies, 1987), p. 14.
74. T.d.S.A. Disanayake, *op. cit.*, p. 33.
75. S. Ponnambalam, *Sri Lanka: The National Question and the Tamil Liberation Struggle,* (London: Zed Books Ltd. 1983), p. 200.
76. *Ibid.*, p. 219.
77. The Sixth Amendment requires members of the National State Assembly and Government to swear allegiance to a Unitary State.
78 . Degenhardt W. Henry, (ed), *Revolutionary and Dissident Movements: An International Guide,* (London: Longman, 1988), p. 349.
79. During the ethnic violence of July 1983, 52 detainees belonging to the Tamil guerrilla groups were killed by other prisoners in the Velikada prison in Colombo. Most of the dead belonged to the T.E.L.O. See, Sinha Ratnatunge, *Politics of Terrorism: The Sri Lanka Experience,* (Melbourne: Global Press Ltd., 1988), pp. 49 and 54.
80. The underlying motivations behind this faction are not known.
81. T.D.S.A. Disanayake, *op. cit.*, p. 40.
82. *Frontline,* (28 June-11 July 1988), pp. 18-19.
83. See, Chapter 7.
84. *Frontline,* (10-23 January 1987), p. 21.

85. *Frontline,* (15-28 November 1986), p. 119.
86. *Far Eastern Economic Review,* (20 June 1985), p. 8, and Sinhja Ratnatunge, *op. cit.,* p. 262.
87. *The Economist,* (3-9 November 1990), p. 78.
88. "Spotlight on the L.T.T.E.", *Frontline,* (10-13 January 1987), p. 21.
89. As of 1987, about 300 L.T.T.E. guerrillas had committed suicide by swallowing cyanide capsules. *Sri Lanka News,* (11 March 1987), p. 1.
90. *Frontline,* (15-28 November 1986), p. 119.
91. Bruce Matthews, "Radical Conflict and Rationalization of Violence in Sri Lanka", *Pacific Affairs,* Vol. 59, No. 1, (1981), p. 34.
92. Marshal R. Singer, "Report on the Pressures and Opportunities for a Peaceful Solution to the Ethnic Conflict in Sri Lanka", *Journal of Developing Societies,* Vol. 11, (1986), p. 14.
93. *The Economist,* (August 1986), p. 16.
94. *The Economist,* (August 1985), p. 43.
95. *The Economist,* (9 August 1986), p. 40.
96. *Asia Week,* (8 February 1987), p. 25.
97. *The Economist,* (3 August 1988), pp. 43-44.
98. See, Chapter 6.
99. Robert C. Oberst, *op. cit.,* p. 194.
100. R.N. Kearney "Youth Protest In Sri Lanka", *Sociological Focus,* Vol. 13, (1980), p. 306.
101. *Ibid.,* p. 306.
102. Bryan Pfaffenberger, "Fourth World colonialism: Indigenous Minorities and Tamil Separatism in Sri Lanka", *Bulletin of Concerned Asian Scholars,* Vol. 16, (1984), p. 21.
103. "Spotlight on the L.T.T.E.", *Frontline,* (10-13 January 1987), p. 21.
104. The military wing of the E.P.R.L.F. is called the People's Liberation Army (P.L.A.).
105. Feliks Gross, *op. cit.,* p. 353.
106. *Frontline,* (10-13 January 1987), p. 21.
107. *Ibid.,* p. 21
108. *Frontline, op. cit.,* p. 21.

109. "E.R.O.S. the Dark Horse", *Frontline,* (11 July 1987), p. 19.
110. "No End in Sight", *Far Eastern Economic Review,* (20 September 1984), p. 27.
111. Rohan Gunarathna, *War and Peace in Sri Lanka, op. cit.,* p. 25.
112. K.M. de Silva, *Managing Ethnic Tensions in Multi-Ethnic Societies: Sri Lanka, 1880-1985,* (Lanham, NY: University Press of America, 1987), p. 352.
113. *The Island,* (6 April 1986), p. 9.
114. John Harris, "Drugs, Guns, and Tamil Terrorism", *The Asian Wall Street Journal,* (9 September 1985), p. 8.
115. *The Sunday Times,* (30 August 1987), pp. 1-3.
116. *India Today,* (31 March 1984), p. 90.
117. *Frontline,* (10-20 January 1987), p.21.
118. A.J. Wilson, "Sri Lanka and Its Future: Sinhalese Versus Tamils", in A.J. Wilson, and D. Dalton, (eds), *The States of South Asia: Problems of National Integration,* (London: C. Hurst and Company, 1982), pp. 300-301.
119. Anita Pratap, *Sunday,* (11-17 March 1984), pp. 86.
120. Thomas Marks, "People's War in Sri Lanka: Insurgency and Counter-insurgency", *Issues and Studies,* (1986), p. 92
121. *India Today,* (31 march 1984), p. 90.
122. *Ibid.,* p. 90.
123. *The Sunday Telegraph,* (14 April 1985),
124. Rohan Gunarathna, op. cit., p. 34.
125. K. Pathmanaba, the general secretary of the E.P.R.L.F., is said to be one of the members who received training in Lebanon. See, *The Economist,* (19 May 1984), p. 59.
126. W.I. Siriweera, "Sinhala-Tamil Relations", *Asian Survey,* Vol. 20, No. 9, (1980), p. 907.
127. Thomas Marks, *op. cit.,* p. 92.
128. *Far Eastern Economic Review,* "Tamil Separatists Also Fight Among Themselves", (12 June 1986), p. 29.
129. Thomas Marks, *op. cit.,* p. 91.
130. *The Times,* (8 October 1987), p. 16.
131. *Vityal Etu,* (June 1986), p. 3.
132. See, *India Today,* (March 1984), pp. 88-94.

133. Rohan Gunarathna, *op. cit.*, p. 50.
134. P. Venkateahwar Rao, "Ethnic Conflict in Sri Lanka: India's Role and Perception", *Asian Survey,* Vol. 28, No. 4, (1988), p. 424.
135. A.J. Wilson, *op. cit.*, p. 301.
136. *The Economist* (7 April 1984), and *The Guardian* (3 April 1984).
137. W. Henry, *op. cit.*, p. 350.
138. K.M. de Silva, *op. cit.*, p. 347.

6

Ideologies, Strategies and Programmes

6.1 Introduction

The main objective of this chapter is to explore the ideologies, strategies and programmes of the left-wing J.V.P. and the Tamil-underground organizations which have indulged in political violence in Sri Lanka. According to Chalmers Johnson, revolutionary ideology supplies the answers to the questions what, how and why in respect of political violence. That is to say, it offers a critique of the socio-political conditions which lead guerrilla groups to resort to political violence in order to change those conditions and implement their vision of an improved society.[1] According to Rex D. Hopper, the following elements are usually present in the ideology of a revolutionary movement: a statement of the objectives, purposes, and premises of the movement; a body of criticism and condemnation of the existing social order which the movement is attacking and seeking to change; a body of defense doctrine serving to justify the movement; and a belief system dealing with policies, tactics, practical operations and the myths of the movement.[2]

None of these aspects have been explicitly memorialized by those organizations, nor for that matter have scholars bothered to delve deeply into these areas. Yet a comparison of the various ideologies offers invaluable insights into the goals and motivational factors behind those guerrilla movements, their methods of achieving their goals, and their plans of action thereafter. In this context the author has found it necessary to examine closely their indoctrination classes, training camps, public lectures, and publications such as papers, pamphlets and wall posters in order to achieve an understanding of their ideologies, strategies and programmes. As in the previous chapter, this chapter is also divided into two main parts: the first deals with the J.V.P. and some of its contemporary organizations; and the second are devoted to a closer examination of the L.T.T.E. and some of its related organizations. Guided by the above observations, the author focuses on the following aspects of guerrilla procedures and operations: political objectives, origin, indoctrination classes, social views, and guerrilla strategy, tactics and programme.

6.2 Political Objectives

According to P. Wilkinson, the long-term objectives of any guerrilla movement are naturally determined by its ideological alignment.[3] The original political objectives of the J.V.P. were based on its perception of Sri Lankan politics and society. The J.V.P. characterized Sri Lanka as a typical new colony of Anglo-American "imperialism", and also claimed that the country was increasingly coming under the influence of "Indian Expansionism".[4] Consequently, the declared main objective of the J.V.P. was to "liberate the oppressed people from Anglo-American new-colonialism and "Indian Expansionism" and to "usher in a socialist society according to the principles of Marxism-Leninism and the thought of Mao Tse Tung."[5] Thus the J.V.P. and the other left-wing organizations shared a common objective of overthrowing the capitalist system in Sri Lanka and replacing it with an independent socialist system. The socialist nature of this objective through national liberation was explicitly stated by the J.V.P. in its newspaper:

The J.V.P., which was born out of the suffering of the masses, is pledged to redeem the mother land and her children from the darkness of subjugation and march them towards the light of socialism.[6]

Thus, the overthrow of the constitutionally elected government and the transition to a socialist system was an attractive option. The transformation of the political system was to be achieved by means of an armed struggle or revolution. The J.V.P. firmly believed that such a change could not be achieved within the confines of Sri Lanka's existing constitutional framework. The J.V.P.'s ideology, however, had several dimensions which elude a straightforward analysis. The political origins of this ideology further explicate its influences and orientations.

6.3 Political Origins

The ideological orientations of some of the J.V.P.'s underground groups were strongly influenced by the ideological trends in the international Marxist movement. The Peradiga Sulanga (The East Wind), the Ginipupura (the Spark), and the Sumith Devinuwara group adhered to Maoism and were especially impressed by Mao's strategy of a protracted people's war. The Mathrubhumi Arakshaka Sangamaya also was ideologically influenced by Maoism but preferred the Cuban strategic model. The Revolutionary Communist League (R.C.L.) was committed to both Trotskyism and the Soviet model. The J.V.P., on the contrary, developed its own distinct political ideology, programme and strategy which were manifested in many facets of the organization.

The J.V.P. claimed that the nucleus of its ideology was Marxism-Leninism adapted to Sri Lanka's own indigenous political and cultural ethos. Rohana Wijeweera, the J.V.P.'s leader, sought to explain these adaptations in the following context:

> Marxism-Leninism is a universal truth. It has a common utility all over the world, irrespective of land, race, nationality, caste, and area. But every country has special and peculiar conditions. We should adapt Marxist-Leninism to suit these special conditions.[7]

This definition of the J.V.P. ideology as an adaptation of Marxism-Leninism, however, has been disputed. A close analysis of the J.V.P.'s ideology strongly indicates that it was more an eclectic mixture of various elements of Marxism ranging from Stalinism, Maoism, and Guevarism to nationalism, mainly Sinhala-Buddhist nationalism. The manifestations of Stalinism were most evident in their antipathy towards Trotskyism. The international debate between Stalinism and Trotskyism created a rift in Sri Lanka's left-wing movement after 1939. The J.V.P.

in developing its own ideology, adopted a strong anti-Trotskyism stand claiming Trotskyism to be a reactionary ideology. In spite of the J.V.P.'s tendency to support Stalinism, there is little doubt that the crux of the J.V.P.'s ideology was heavily influenced by Mao's interpretation of Marxism-Leninism. Consequently, the J.V.P. actually found Soviet-Communism to be decadent and, therefore, supported China against the Soviet Union in the Sino-Soviet dispute. The Soviet interpretation of Communism as it had developed from the post revolutionary period of the Soviet Union was considered by the J.V.P. to be lacking in the fundamentals inherent in the revolutionary concept of Marxism. The Soviet system was perceived by the J.V.P., therefore, as a transition from a socialist system to a capitalist system rather than to the anticipated advanced socialist system. Viewed in this context, the J.V.P. found the then existing version of Soviet Marxism-Leninism to be a modern version of revisionism. The essence of the J.V.P.'s attitude toward Soviet socialism is summarized thus:

> Soviet Russia is reverting back to capitalism-socialist imperialism. It is an imperialist country which has used great ingenuity to absorb the neighboring countries like Mongolia into colonies. It owns colonies.[8]

Thus the J.V.P.'s ideology vehemently opposed the "modern revisionism" and "social imperialism" of the Soviet Union. Consequently, the J.V.P.'s ideology remained closer to Maoism in holding that revisionism in the Soviet Union began after Stalin's death, rather than subscribing to the Trotskyist tradition that the Soviet Union's departure from Marxist-Leninist Communism began with Stalin's defeat of Trotsky in the 1920's. While the J.V.P. censured the Soviet Union, its members were strongly attracted to Maoism and believed Mao's dictum that political power was developed through the barrel of the gun. The emphasis on the suppressed position of the peasantry seems to have been largely derived from Maoism. Quite contrary to the J.V.P's concern for the peasantry, the orthodox left-wing parties in Sri Lanka were preoccupied with how to radicalize the working class. The J.V.P emphasizes the agitation of the rural sector under the tutelage of the already enlightened urban working class, in an excerpt from the J.V.P.'s newspaper:

The rural population represents a considerable proportion of the entire population. Of this rural population the majority belong to the oppressed classes. Due to the vastness of the number of the rural poor, they are the moving force of the Ceylonese revolution. The socialist revolution would succeed in Sri Lanka only when the oppressed peasantry become politicized and, under the leadership of the working classes, begin their class struggle.[9]

By adopting the peasantry as the vanguard of the Sri Lankan revolution, the J.V.P. divorced itself from the ideology of the orthodox left-wing parties. While other left-wing parties in general were pre-occupied in mobilizing the urban working class as a revolutionary vanguard, the J.V.P. acted on the conviction that the peasantry was the true revolutionary force. In stressing the revolutionary role of the peasantry in the ideology of its organization, the J.V.P. moved away from the ideology of the long-established Marxist parties in Sri Lanka. Thus convinced, the J.V.P.'s ideology focused on the plight of the peasantry and the many problems they encountered.

The capitalist economic system had swallowed up the fertile land in the up country and in the wet zone areas creating a great shortage of land for the Ceylonese people. Liptons, Brooke Bonds and other white imperialist companies owned thousands of acres. Ninety per cent of the local families share one acre. (sic) The so-called left-wing leaders of our country have said that the peasantry is not revolutionary and that they are against socialism. These leaders can never understand the problems of Ceylon. There has been no attempt to establish a worker-peasant alliance and no attempt to unite all the oppressed classes and to work towards a socialist revolution. It was only socialism that could permanently liberate the up country landless peasant, the peasant of the wet zone whose crops are constantly destroyed by floods, the Dry Zone peasant who is the victim of drought, the agricultural labourers, chena cultivators and the share croppers.[10]

The J.V.P.'s reliance on the peasantry as a revolutionary force was expressed as follows:

The joy of emancipation will rise tomorrow from the peasantry of the up-country and the dry zone who on this day shed tears and cry through immense suffering without food and water.[11]

The nature of the revolutionary forces thus determined, the J.V.P. once again rejected the ideology of the orthodox left in the country. In spite of being influenced by Leninism, Maoism, and Guevariaism, however, the J.V.P. contrived to formulate its own distinct ideology,.strategy and programme. One of its theorists summarized the limitations of foreign influences exerted on the J.V.P.'s ideology as follows:

"We are definitely admirers of Che, Mao and Ho Chi Minh, but we have our own plans and theories."[12]

Therefore, to ascertain an insight into any of the aspects discussed in this chapter it becomes necessary to examine closely the J.V.P. and its related groups. The ideology of the movement was best expressed in their indoctrination classes, more popularly known as the five political lectures. These lectures were mainly derived from the J.V.P.'s perception of the country's socio-economic and political problems and the alternative solutions offered by them.

6.4 Classes of Indoctrination

The J.V.P.'s five indoctrination classes were geared mainly as an effective means of attracting potential cadres to the J.V.P. and convincing them to join the J.V.P.'s fight to bring about a socialist system in Sri Lanka. Hence, the fundamentals of the J.V.P.'s ideology, which were a fusion of ideas derived from other theorists as well as their own indigenous adaptations, were imbibed in these five classes. The session was entitled "the Present Political Conditions" and divided under the following headings: "Economic Crisis", "Independence", "Indian Expansionism", "the Left-wing Movement" and finally "the Path of Sri Lankan Revolution".[13]

The J.V.P. strongly believed that the five lectures contained the essence of Marxism-Leninism in so far as it could be adapted to indigenous conditions. The headings of the classes coincided with the major socio-economic and political issues in Sri Lanka. Moreover, the content was contrived to mobilize potential cadres, and to educate the masses on the current socio-economic and political problems confronting them. The political consequences of these classes were assessed by Wijeweera when he said:

We had to first deal with day to day problems, the socio-economic problems of the masses, the problems, the root causes of which were not known to the masses—the problems for which no solutions had been sought. (sic) We had to enlighten the masses on Marxism-Leninism and through that to interpret the causes of their problems and to win them over to Marxism by showing them a scientific solution to their problems.[14]

The five classes which in effect served in place of a policy document or manifesto for the J.V.P. will be viewed in particular at this juncture as they contain the very essence of its ideology.

6.5 On Economic Crisis in Sri Lanka

As would any other Marxist adherents, the J.V.P. too felt that the economic dynamics in any society were crucial in the analysis of social forces. The J.V.P. viewed the Sri Lankan economy as a crisis area in which socio-economic deficiencies were having severe repercussions on the wider society. This crisis was largely attributed to the adverse impact of colonialism and neo-colonialist capitalism.[15] The J.V.P. perceived the plantation economy, which had been introduced and firmly established by the British Raj at the expense of the indigenous rural sector, as the root cause of the economic deterioration which loomed large in Sri Lanka. The J.V.P.'s views were thus expressed:

The primary root of the burning economic problems of the country is the collapse of a simple self-sufficient economy. The birth of the tea plant at the expense of the Kurakkan (Millet) plant is the main cause of the economic crisis.[16]

The focal point of the J.V.P.'s argument was the crisis in the agrarian sector where landlessness, drought and lack of irrigation facilities for agriculture beset the dry zone while the wet zone was faced with acute soil erosion and floods. The agricultural areas, upon which a large part of the population depended, were a nerve centre of Sri Lanka's society. The problems which were acute in this sector affected a wider population and, therefore, were of added significance. Thus, according to the J.V.P., the introduction and stabilization of the plantation economy not only destabilized the agricultural sector but also led to a process of pauperization of the peasantry. Lastly, the J.V.P. concluded that the frustration and crisis prevailing in the agrarian sector had transformed an economic crisis into a political crisis which could be overcome only by means of a class struggle.[17] The J.V.P.'s proposed solution to the economic crisis in Sri Lanka will be discussed in section 6.11 entitled "programme".

6.6 On Independence in Sri Lanka

The second of the five lectures focused on and analyzed the impact of colonialism before and after independence from a social, political and cultural perspective. The J.V.P. viewed the independence granted on the 4th of February 1948 as a pseudo-independence void of full-fledged political and economic freedom.[18] The J.V.P. considered the independence conferred by the British more as a maneuver to protect the colonial system of property ownership from the anti-British political trends that had evolved in Sri Lanka during the Second World War.[19] The other ties which reinforced the colonial representation within Sri Lanka were said to be certain clauses in the Sri Lankan Constitution of 1948, the structure of governmental institutions, the legal system, the cultural ties and more significantly the post-independence reliance on a plantation economy. The J.V.P.'s perception of Sri Lanka's independence and its significance began with the following blunt statement:

> We have no independence. What we still have is the Queen's government. If we consider the constitution, the legal system, the cultural field, the colonial system of education which prevails up to date all this show that this thing called independence is a mere farce. In other words, it is a colonial device.[20]

Viewed in this context the J.V.P. found Sri Lankan independence a pretence contrived by the British to appease the clamour for independence by Sri Lankan nationalists. The J.V.P. maintained that authentic independence could only be achieved by means of an armed struggle. Their method of achieving total independence was described in the following terms.

> It was under the cannon fire of the imperialists that we lost the freedom of our motherland, which had been kept guarded with lives and blood. The way to win that freedom lost through the power of the gun also lies in the barrel of the gun.[21]

In this context, the J.V.P.'s views on colonialism and independence were quite similar to the views expressed by Frantz Fanon.[22]

6.7 On Indian Expansionism

Of the five classes, the lecture on Indian expansionism was one of the most controversial and debatable. The different aspects discussed by the J.V.P.'s indoctrinators under this heading were the Indian plantation workers in Sri Lanka, the Federal Party, and the role of the neighboring Indian Federal Government. The J.V.P.'s ideology pertaining to this particular area was strongly influenced by the stand taken by the Chinese Communist Party during and after the Indo-China Border War of 1962. The People's Republic of China viewed India with suspicion claiming that the Indian Government was motivated by territorial ambitions as well as by its economic prowess. It was further argued that India planned to subjugate the smaller states within its immediate environs. The Chinese communists attributed India's alleged expansionary ambitions to its dependency on foreign investment and aid, and consequently on India's supposed need to market the products of the capitalist monopolists. The Chinese communists designated the process as 'Indian expansionism'.[23]

The J.V.P., having found these ideas ideologically appealing, borrowed them and integrated them into its lecture on Indian expansionism. The J.V.P. further reasoned that India had interfered in Sri Lanka's domestic affairs, and was a threat to the Sri Lankan economy, its political sovereignty and its survival as an independent state. One reason given by the J.V.P. to justify its accusations of Indian expansionism was the apparent monopoly of Indian business interests within Sri Lanka. The J.V.P. gave several other reasons as follows: the smuggling to and from India, the role of the Sri Lankan Federal Party, the organization known as "We are Tamils" (Nam Tamilar), the cultural influences exerted by Southern India, illicit immigration and the Indian plantation workers.[24]

The J.V.P.'s fears regarding Indian expansionism were not, as of the 1960s, of recent origin but dated back to ancient times when invaders from Southern India had dethroned the Sinhala Kings and destroyed their kingdoms, though the remnants of the Sinhala kingdom later regained some of the lost territory in the Elara-Dutugamunu War in the first century B.C. Viewed in this historical context, the strong element of Sinhala nationalism inherent in the J.V.P.'s ideology appeared to have been at least partly responsible for its accusations against the Indian Government.[25]

The crucial part of the lecture, however, focused on the Indian plantation workers. The left-wing parties in Sri Lanka looked upon the plantation workers as part of the proletariat which according to Marxism-Leninism was the revolutionary force. The J.V.P. did not accept this reasoning, but instead maintained that the problems of the plantation workers were an integral part of Indian expansionism, and that the workers themselves were more a reactionary element than a revolutionary force. The J.V.P. further argued that the Indian plantation workers had not integrated themselves into the Sri Lankan society and culture, but rather had adhered to their Indian identity, and continued to think of India as their motherland and of its leaders such as Gandhi and Nehru as their own.

The J.V.P. instructors also compared the plight of the Chena cultivators (shifting cultivation) in the dry zone with that of the plantation workers. They found that the plantation workers enjoyed considerably improved living conditions compared to the former. The plantation workers not only lived in the more fertile wet zone but also had greater access to housing, education and health facilities than did the dry zone cultivators who were deprived of many of these basic facilities. The dry zone was not only malaria endemic but also was an area of limited facilities. Thus, the J.V.P's stand on the Indian plantation workers was negative and uncompromising, and highlighted the relative advantages whose workers enjoyed compared to other sections of the peasantry.

The major ethnic minority, the Sri Lankan Tamils, were another segment of society which the J.V.P. found necessary to analyze. The J.V.P. perceived the Tamils' major political party, the Federal Party of Sri Lanka, to be a pawn of Indian expansionism and possibly a medium by which the Tamil state of South India and Tamil-dominated Northern Sri Lanka would merge. As a whole the J.V.P. not only adopted an unfavorable approach to the influences exerted by the Indian and Sri Lankan Tamils as an ethnic minority but also, as a policy, opposed India.

6.8 On the Left-Wing Movement in Sri Lanka

The J.V.P.'s class on the left-wing movement in Sri Lanka sought to emphasize the failure of that movement and the supposed causes of such a failure. The J.V.P.'s instructors began the lecture with an examination of the movement from its inception in the 1930s and traced its growth and activities thereafter. Rohana Wijeweera himself stated that the purpose of this lecture was to draw a lesson from the unpleasant experiences of the old left-wing movement and to understand the reasons for its failure, so that the J.V.P. could avoid similar mistakes and achieve the proletariat aim of building a new left-wing movement.[26]

The J.V.P. asserted that by the mid-1960s the traditional left was on the wane, and stressed the need for a new left-wing movement to attain the aspirations of the impoverished masses. This decline of the traditional left was mainly attributed to the switching of strategies from the revolutionary path to a parliamentary course, and to the formation of coalitions with the capitalist parties. In this context, the J.V.P. viewed the orthodox left-wing movement as having more of a revisionist than socialist nature. These ideas were further elaborated in the J.V.P.'s newspaper in the following passage:

> The left-wing movement was born in December 1935 and was congenitally a social revisionist movement. It was not a haphazard event. It was the beginning of a lamentation.[27]

The J.V.P.'s criticisms were not confined to the policies and activities of the left-wing movement; its leaders also were subject to strong criticism. The J.V.P. launched personal attacks on the leaders of the orthodox left-wing parties maintaining that the leaders of those parties had failed in Sri Lanka not because the masses were less revolutionary but because those leaders were not true Marxists. The substance of this criticism was as follows:

> What did these old leaders do? They entered the law courts in the morning adorned in black cloaks and served the capitalist for money they earned through the Roman Dutch law. Arguing that the mortar or the haystack was responsible for the murders committed by the affluent murderers, they saved them from the gallows and went home and changed their clothes to white trouser and red shirts, approached the workers and incited them to struggle to win their cup of gruel, and finally went home fully drunk after enjoying ball room dancing with Colombo seven (socialite) ladies, at the Otters club or the Eighty club and returned home drunk and unsteady. Marx wrote "Capital" against the (the power of) capital. But our leftist leaders destroy themselves because of capital.[28]

It is evident that the J.V.P's lecture on the left-wing movement in Sri Lanka was not only an indictment of the existing left-wing parties but also of their leaders. The J.V.P. used this opportunity to present itself as an alternative.

The fifth lecture dealt with the crucial subject of a Sri Lankan revolution and the strategies that should be adopted for such an event. To facilitate a clear explication of the above matter the author discusses the fifth lecture on strategy separately in section 6.10. From the indoctrination classes hitherto discussed it is evident that they were more action-oriented and agitational than concerned with issues of theory and ideology. This dimension was carefully construed to appeal to the indigenous rural masses, which at the time were faced with many of the problems discussed during the lectures.

6.9 Views of Society

The J.V.P.'s views on contemporary society were based on the Marxist interpretation of society derived from the concept of the mode of production. From this perspective, it was observed that Sri Lanka represented a neo-colonial social structure riddled with class stratifications. The J.V.P. identified the predominant social classes in Sri Lanka as follows: proletariat, petit-bourgeoisie, middle class, national bourgeoisie and comprador-bourgeoisie. This was analogous to Mao's analysis of China's pre-revolutionary society.[29] By definition, however, there was a difference between the J.V.P.'s identification of the working class and that of Marxism-Leninism. According to the Communist Manifesto, the proletariat was composed of the wage earning class or the working class.[30] The J.V.P., on the other hand, defined the proletariat as comprising the peasants, the students and unemployed youth. In the following passage Rohana Wijeweera explained this interpretation further:

> Some people don't like when we call them the proletariat class. They say we should call them the working class? What is meant by the working class? Isn't that a part of the proletariat? It is a part of this proletariat class who are employed all over the country and sell their labour. There are yet others all over the country that doesn't have any chance to sell their labour and earn their living. Take for example the unemployed youth in the villages, the chena cultivators and share croppers. To which class do they belong? What means of production do they have? I do not know whether there is another proletariat class in Sri Lanka if they, these poor people, do not belong to this proletariat class.[31]

Thus, the J.V.P. by virtue of its social base could not ignore the other deprived segments of society and, therefore, were compelled to deviate from orthodox Marxism and recognize the complexity of such a definition. Their adaptation of the

Marxist-Leninist approach was further evident in their sympathetic attitude towards the peasantry rather than the working class.

The J.V.P's lack of concern for the working class was due mostly to its perception that the Sri Lankan working class was passive and lethargic. Consequently, the J.V.P.'s neglect of the working class was reflected in their attitude towards the trade unions and strikes. Strikes were dismissed by the J.V.P. as feeble struggles for equally insignificant demands and were often called "kanda koppa satana" which means 'struggles for a cup of porridge'. Moreover, strikes were viewed as a device to protect the capitalist system, rather than as a means by which the working class could safeguard its rights. In a speech given by Wijeweera, he explained the J.V.P.'s indifferent approach to the working-class trade unions and strikes as follows:

> At first Goonesinghe[32] and his like started forming trade unions. Later, all the revisionists started forming trade unions. What did they do? They organized the workers in factories. They placed the carrot of economic demands for a full thirty years? Every year there were hundreds of strikes for a better standard of living. It is a universal truth that the working class cannot get relief within the prevailing social system – this capitalist system. To obtain relief within the prevailing system the working class demand greater pay. When demands are made some of them are granted. But a hundred times more than what is given is taken back.[33]

It is obvious that the J.V.P's ideology sought to deviate from Marxism-Leninism according to indigenous conditions in Sri Lanka. In their endeavour to adapt Marxism to their own ideology the J.V.P. absorbed a strong nationalist dimension, which was wrapped in socialism. Nationalism was evident in the J.V.P's ideological use of the word "patriotism" which often appeared in their literature. The J.V.P. interpreted the patriotism as:

> The aggregate of the class hatred against the imperialist enemy in all the structures oppressed by imperialism

> and old and new colonialism...In its struggle against imperialism, Marxism-Leninism is nothing but patriotism.[34]

The J.V.P. often referred to the peasants and workers as 'patriotic peasants and workers', and its student front was a 'patriotic students' front'. Furthermore, the J.V.P.'s Bikku (Buddhist Clergy) organization was called the 'Patriotic Bikku Front', while the women's front was named the 'Patriotic Women's Front'. The armed uprising for which the J.V.P. was preparing was called a 'patriotic struggle'. The concept of patriotism was emphasized over and over again by the J.V.P. in every possible way. The J.V.P.'s meaning of this concept was explained as follows:

> The colonial economy, the Queen's government, the Roman-Dutch law and the imperial traditions which arrived in the country through the guns and bullets of foreign imperialists will be chased out of the country by the patriotic traditions and the guns and bullets of patriotic people.[35]

The strong nationalist element inherent in the J.V.P.'s ideology was evident in all its endeavours. This patriotic stance was carried still further in their slogans such as 'Mathrubima Nathnam Maranaya' ('Motherland or Death'). The historical heroes who strongly represented the Sinhala-Buddhist images were idealized in the J.V.P. literature. Some of these heroes were those who had agitated in the 19th Century against foreign occupation, such as Keppetipola and Puran Appu, and who were thus held in high esteem as those who had struggled for freedom.[36] The J.V.P.'s nationalism did not, however, embrace the diverse ethnic and cultural entities within Sri Lankan society, but merely represented the predominant Sinhala-Buddhist image. Hence, the J.V.P. has been accused of advocating Sinhala-Buddhist chauvinism rather than Sri Lankan nationalism. This chauvinistic element is further evident in their approach to minority problems in Sri Lanka, as well as in their conception of Sinhala culture and the manner in which they practiced Buddhism.

Viewed from such a perspective it is apparent that the J.V.P.'s attitudes and political vision concerning the grievances of the Sri Lankan minority communities were biased and rather hostile. Consequently, on the question of Sri Lanka's official language, the J.V.P. maintained that the Official Language Act of 1956, which pronounced Sinhala as the official language, was justified, and totally disagreed with the C.P. and the L.S.S.P. on their advocacy of parity of status for the Sinhala and Tamil languages. Furthermore, the J.V.P.'s views of the peasant resettlement schemes in Northern and Eastern parts of Sri Lanka were a strong indication of their lopsided approach. Peasant resettlement has been represented as a panacea for social and economic evils by successive post-independence governments. The Tamils, however, had contrary views and posed counter arguments for such a programme. Their main contention was that resettlement represented a state-sanctioned threat to their territorial and linguistic identity. The J.V.P. totally disregarded these counter arguments. As Kumari Jayawardena observes, the J.V.P.'s strategy was to resettle the Sri Lankan Tamils in such a manner that they would be widely scattered throughout Sri Lanka rather than being concentrated in strong regional pockets. Such a resettlement would strike a strong blow to the Tamils' territorial claims and distinctive ethnic identity.[37]

The J.V.P.'s emphasis on Sri Lanka's culture was mainly confined to the Sinhala-Buddhist tradition and ethos. Their disciplinary code was derived from Buddhist ethics, and its leadership and membership were bound to adhere to this code. As mentioned in Chapter 5, the main guidelines were based on the prohibition against smoking tobacco, consuming alcohol, viewing films of a pornographic or violent nature, adopting western habits and fashions, and finally, getting involved in casual emotional attachments between the sexes. The J.V.P. manifested particularly strong opposition to the infiltration of western culture and insisted that its members strictly adhere to the tenants of the indigenous culture. In this context what was really meant by 'indigenous culture' was the Sinhala-Buddhist culture. The J.V.P.'s approach to Buddhism was not explicitly stated in any of their literature, nor was it discussed during any of the five political classes. Wijeweera, however, offered his personal concept of Buddhism in his statement to the C.I.D. He said:

> I do not accept Buddhism as a religion but as a philosophy - of course I definitely accept it. It is a progressive philosophy.[38]

It is thus evident that the J.V.P.'s political ideology had a Sinhalese-Buddhist nationalist flavour. Furthermore, this aspect of the J.V.P.'s ideology again emerges in the selection of pseudonyms which were adopted to protect the true identity of its leaders and full-time members. The pseudonym adopted by Wijeweera, the J.V.P.'s leader, was "Rohana", which happened to be the historical name of the present Southern Province, the heartland of Sinhala nationalism. Gananatha Obeysekara observes that Rohana not only represented the nucleus of Sinhala-Buddhist nationalism but also presented itself as the centre of resistance to Tamil nationalism.[39] Legend has it that whenever the threat of foreign invasion loomed, especially from India, a Sinhala hero emerged from the 'Ruhuna' or Rohana to resist the invaders. The basic sentiments of this legend were embodied in the historical annals of the Dutugammunu-Elara War which was fought by the Sinhala King Dutugamunu to regain the lost kingdom of Anuradhapura from the Tamil King Elara in the first century B.C. The second ranking member of the J.V.P. assumed the name 'Athula', which was derived from a historical novel by Martin Wickramasinghe based on the Dutugamunu-Elara war. The novel describes one of its characters, Athula, as King Dutugamunu's most trusted lieutenant. Thus, some of the J.V.P.'s appeal was derived from Sinhalese-Buddhist history and mythology.

The J.V.P.'s choice of a flag in 1971 was another symbolic indication of its culturally chauvinistic approach. The flag depicted a lion on a red background – the lion being the symbol of the Sinhala nation. Members were ordered to hoist this flag at all the captured police stations.

The ideological orientation of the J.V.P. discussed thus far strongly indicates that it was action-oriented, concentrating on agitational issues rather than grappling with theoretical issues. Consequently, as *The Economist* observes, it was "richly compounded, variously spiced an unmistakably home-made".[40] Moreover, the violent nature of the J.V.P.'s ideology was further elaborated in the following excerpt from a cross-examination in 1973 of Loku Athula (Nimalasiri Jayasinghe) at the Criminal Justice Commission (C.J.C.) trial at bar. The text clarifies that the J.V.P. was concentrating on an armed struggle rather than developing and expanding a broad-based political ideology which could cover wider socio-economic and political problem in Sri Lanka:

> Q. Was it an armed struggle or a political philosophy that the J.V.P. presented as a socialist Revolution?
>
> A. Both, a political philosophy and an armed struggle.
>
> Q. Were these two correlated
>
> A. Yes.
>
> Q. Did the J.V.P. give the first place to the political philosophy or to the armed strategy?
>
> A. Actually, it gave first place to the armed struggle.[41]

In this context it was obvious that the J.V.P. endeavoured to form its ideology for an armed uprising within a short gestation period. The action-orientation was conducive to the mobilization of rural youth toward the capture of state power by means of political violence.

The basic elements of the J.V.P. ideology clearly indicate that it incorporated most of the pressing problems in the rural sector and emphasized a practical rather than a theoretical or abstract approach. This appealed to those among the Sinhalese community who were most disadvantaged by indigenous socio-economic and political conditions? The rather sparse information on the alternative political system proposed by the J.V.P. indicated that they concentrated more on capturing state power and had no intention of seeking to change the existing political structure through legitimate means. The J.V.P.'s ideology was not easily identifiable either with Marxism-Leninism, Stalinism, Maoism, or Guevaraism.[42] Their ideology on the whole was eclectic, incorporating the concepts of Marxism-Leninism, a

Maoist urge for violent action, a Che Guevaraist obsession with instant revolution, and last but not least Sinhala-Buddhist ethnocentrism. In other words, the J.V.P. wanted to develop a wholly Sri Lankan character as they saw all other modes tainted by outside influences or peculiar to those other cultures. What emerged as a result of this fusion of ideology and concepts was, as Urmila Phadnis observes, an anti-capitalist, anti-western, anti-traditional leftist and anti-Indian ideology.[43] Many of the J.V.P.'s beliefs and perceptions were indigenous, and it preached a variety of National Socialism. Consequently, the J.V.P.'s ideology was not influenced by Western radical thinking. Rather it was an oriental ideology viewed through rural Sinhalese-Buddhist eyes. This ideology had the necessary power to mobilize the Sinhalese-Buddhist rural youth to political violence against the government. Their strong opposition to the established order and system were thus made obvious, and the fusion of ideology was further exemplified in their strategy.

6.10 Strategy and Tactics

The J.V.P.'s pre-planned strategy to capture state power was embodied in the fifth and final lecture of their indoctrination classes, titled "the Path of the Sri Lankan Revolution". Revolutionary warfare was the ultimate means for the J.V.P. of achieving state power and they totally rejected the electoral process which, they maintained, was futile. According to Wijeweera, the fifth lecture dealt with a theoretical explanation of the path to a socialist revolution. In this context it dealt with issues which were then under debate within the left-wing movement in Sri Lanka. The first was the anticipated Sri Lankan revolution, which, the orthodox left espoused, should be completed in two stages. The orthodox left held that in the absence of a democratic revolution as in Europe, a democratic revolution and then a socialist revolution should be launched in Sri Lanka.[44] The Sri Lankan C.P. (P) and its breakaway groups such as the 'Peradiga Sulanga' (East Wind) and the 'Ginipupura' (Spark) having been influenced by Maoism, also advocated this programme. The J.V.P. rejected this two-phase revolution and favoured a single-phase path, i.e., an instant revolution. Likewise, as regards to tactics the J.V.P. rejected an idea of a popular front approach.

The second aspect combined the strategy and tactics of a socialist revolution. In this context it was contended that socialism could not be achieved by applying a strategy which had been successful elsewhere, but that it had to be achieved by an indigenous strategy devised according to the given conditions. Considering the historical experience of the international revolutionary campaign, Wijeweera concluded that the Sri Lankan revolution had to be achieved after considering the conditions peculiar to Sri Lanka.[45] It was evident that the J.V.P. did not accept a universal strategy of revolution but firmly believed that the course of revolution taken in one country at a particular time, given specific conditions, would differ from the revolutionary process in another country. They totally rejected the idea of accepting the Leninist, the Maoist or the Cuban strategies. The Maoist model of guerrilla warfare, which advocated a 'protracted people's war' launched against the urban centers from the rural areas, was rejected due to demographic and topographic restrictions in Sri Lanka. The Soviet and the Cuban models were also found to be unsuitable as Sri Lanka is a comparatively small country, with a contrasting geo-physical environment. The accepted revolutionary strategies thus found to be inapplicable; the J.V.P. set about devising its own strategy which they believed was in accordance with the indigenous conditions.

The J.V.P. planned a strategy which depended on a one-day armed attack accompanied by a general strike by the working classes. The general strike was intended to destabilize the politico-economic system in synergy with the attack for maximum disruption. Hence, if the general strike did not take place, the J.V.P. devised an alternate plan to disrupt the system of communications, including the telephone lines and the supply of electricity. The basic strategy of a one-day revolution was to launch simultaneous night-time attacks on the police stations and military bases throughout Sri Lanka. Thus, the strategy of the J.V.P. was an island-wide armed insurrection which depended on a single swift blow, designed to capture political power within a very short time frame. In spite of their advocacy of a one-day attack, the J.V.P. was aware that strategically such an attack would be far from viable unless it was launched in two stages. In the first stage the aim would be to capture arms and ammunition for a major attack on stronger bases. By virtue of this strategy the smaller police stations were to be the first targets. When launching their attack, their main tactic would be to overpower the opposition by the sheer strength of numbers rather than superiority in weapons and ammunition. It was also deemed necessary to cut off all forms of communication including the supply of electricity in order to totally isolate the police stations before launching the initial attack. Parallel to their attacks on police stations, the J.V.P. planned to seize the important state institutions and capture significant members of state. The final stage of the strategy was the mobilization of the masses for the final attempt to secure state power after capturing arms and ammunition from the police and the military.[46]

The theoretical concepts which defined the J.V.P. strategy determined that an army of professional revolutionaries could mobilize the masses for political action and the seizure of power. The J.V.P. from thereon, however, tested theoretical concepts such as those of the Maoist or the Cubans models which said that if the initial attack was unsuccessful the revolutionaries were advised by theory to retreat to the main natural reserves and forests. In the J.V.P.'s case that would have meant hiding in the Wilpattu near the Anuradhapura district, the Sinharaja in the Kalutara district and the Nacules range in the Matale district, as a means of self-preservation. Conventional Marxist theory would have further instructed the launching of a protracted struggle from the hinterland. The J.V.P.'s strategy, however, did not contain an alternative strategy for a protracted struggle in the event the one-day attack failed. The J.V.P. reasoned that as Sri Lanka is a small island, its police unpopular and its military services weak, a one-day armed revolution could succeed.

According to the J.V.P.'s interpretation of the Marxist-Leninist theory, revolutionary pre-conditions were not imperative conditions for a revolution. Despite the lack of emphasis on pre-conditions they believed that the mere ambience created by the government's repression of the J.V.P. would ferment a revolution. Wijeweera further explained this belief when he said:

> We will strike when we are provoked to do so by the armed forces.... We caution the government not to send us underground. The revolution will commence on the day that our group is banned as we would have no alternative but to retaliate.[47]

The J.V.P. was nonetheless devoid of logical consistent tactics. Before 1970, total secrecy and armed attack was the hub of their tactics, and they declined mass mobilization as part of their strategy. The General Election of 1970 marked a change in their strategic course. Thereafter, the J.V.P. launched a campaign of overt agitation by means of mass rallies and propaganda. Theirs was a dual strategy in which open incitement would be accompanied by a serious stepping up of recruitment for their clandestine activities. The J.V.P.'s strategy, like those of other Marxist revolutionaries, was a conspiratorial one amongst a few professional revolutionaries who would lord over the masses both throughout the anticipated revolutionary process and after they had seized political power. It was not to be a Maoist people's war, but rather a left-wing putsch. The J.V.P.'s plan for a one-day struggle was not a unique strategy as it was derived from the Zanzibar Uprising of 1964. The Zanzibar Uprising was carried out by about 600 trained rebels under the command of Field Marshal John Okello. Okello's revolutionaries seized the armouries and swiftly over powered the military within twenty-four hours.[48]

The J.V.P. was also heavily influenced by the Castro-Guevara revolutionary tradition as elaborated by Regis Debray. Pursuant to Guevaraist theory, the J.V.P. anticipated that a band of determined revolutionaries could overthrow the existing state apparatus, capture state power, and subsequently convince the masses of their legitimacy. Thus, Guevara's theoretical postulation that popular guerrilla forces could resist and overcome the military was assimilated into the J.V.P. ideology. Moreover, they agreed with Guevara's idea that limited conditions conducive to a revolution could be created and would not require further development before launching the revolution. As a result, the J.V.P. drew away from and put the least emphasis on the mass-mobilization approach, opting instead for the quick one-day revolution. After the events of 1971, the J.V.P., in reviewing its past political performance, assessed the impact of these political thoughts in the following perspective:

> There is no doubt that the fact that the revolution in Cuba triumphed without a revolutionary party, had been in our minds when the capitalist class was suppressing the J.V.P. and there was also no doubt that it influenced our activities. It is clear that, particularly because of the Cuban experience, the concept of the necessity of a Bolshevik party was, to a certain extent, denied.[49]

Consequently, just as the J.V.P.'s ideology was eclectic, so too were their tactics, which were pragmatic and opportunist. Another aspect intrinsically linked to the J.V.P.'s ideology, was their proposed programme for a socialist state and a socialist society in Sri Lanka.

6.11 Programme of the J.V.P.

The proposed programme of the J.V.P.'s future state was based mainly on the issues discussed in the five indoctrination classes. The J.V.P. aspired to establish an egalitarian socialist society and for this purpose they endeavoured to frame a programme of action. The J.V.P. failed, however, to produce a definite programme. They had no firm notion of what the future socialist state would be like, nor any conviction as to how they would replace the existing parliamentary system of government or the administrative apparatus.

Nonetheless, it was obvious that the J.V.P. was influenced by the Cuban and the Chinese models of a socialist state espousing a one-party system with the abolition of the multi-party parliamentary form of government.[50] Their strong opposition to the parliamentary system was explained as follows:

People must realize that parliament is an agency of the bourgeoisie, intended to confuse the people and divert their attention from the real problems of our country.[51]

In spite of their opposition to the existing system, the J.V.P. had paradoxically promised some of their member's positions similar to those within the existing parliamentary system. Hence, their proposal of a one-party dictatorship with little participation of the people did not evince a tendency for radical changes in the system. The J.V.P. further implied that they would adopt an anti-western foreign policy which would include the closure of the U.S. and the British embassies in Sri Lanka, and the termination of all ties with foreign donor agencies such as the P.L. 480 and the West German Ebert Foundation.[52] The J.V.P.'s strong nationalist ideology urged an unfavourable approach to the problem of the Indian plantation workers. The J.V.P. proposed a solution which called for forced repatriation and the prevention of further migration from South India. The J.V.P. also outlined an alternate economic model for Sri Lanka, as they found the existing system to be degenerated and a failure. They proposed a planned socialist economy which would revolve around systematic industrialization and the collectivization of agro-industries. The existing trade-based economy, which depended heavily on the export of tea, rubber and coconut, was to be replaced by a system which would liquidate individual enterprise and in its place sponsor collective production. The traditional tea industry, which was considered a colonial legacy, and the newly developed tourist industry were specifically criticized. The tea plantations which were concentrated in the central highlands were found to be the cause of several ecological problems. Hence, in the J.V.P.'s plans for economic reconstruction it was suggested that the tea plantations should be uprooted and replaced with reforestation to ensure an adequate rainfall and prevent soil erosion. Tea and rubber plantations would be cultivated only to cater to Sri Lanka's own needs. The J.V.P. further advocated a programme of new irrigation which would prevent floods in the wet zone and drought in the dry zone. This alternate economic policy was further clarified by Wijeweera when he said:

> We should change the entire economy. The neo-imperialist economy should be changed to a socialist economy. The basic aim is to do away with the plantation industry, the hill slopes should be reforested, reservoirs should be built, and rivers should be tapped to harness electricity and diverted to the Dry Zone.[53]

The rural-based support for the J.V.P. rendered it necessary to address Sri Lanka's agrarian crisis. To counter the existing economic policy which depended mainly on foreign aid and loans, and the import-export system, the J.V.P. advocated a policy of utilizing the indigenous resources and 'know-how'. Their antipathy to the plantations had become so bitter that one youth who captured an estate superintendent in 1971 stated that they would uproot the tea and rubber estates and plant yams instead.[54] The J.V.P., however, did not have a coherent outline for the political future. As J.M.Van Der Kroef observes, in a general sense the J.V.P. programme did not significantly deviate from that of the Sri Lanka Communist Party (P). Some salient points mentioned by Van Der Kroef were: the severing of the remaining ties with the Commonwealth; the completion of the nationalization of foreign enterprises and banks; the implementation of an extensive agricultural subsidy and price support programme; the creation of workers' councils in industrial establishments; support for all national liberation movements against American "imperialism"; and the distribution of state-owned lands to the landless.[55] As James Jupp observes much of this was vague utopian rhetoric.[56]

6.12 Ideologies of the Tamil Guerrillas

The author concentrates next on the ideology of those Tamil guerrilla groups which never explicitly outlined their ideologies, strategies and programmes. These groups, like the J.V.P., stressed the importance of military tactics rather than ideological goals. The volatile situation in Sri Lanka as a result of the continued political violence did not permit a widespread exposure of their different ideologies. The Tamil guerrilla organizations, however, did share the common characteristic of concentrating on military action rather than theoretical issues. Moreover, while the J.V.P. relied on indoctrination and conviction to mobilize the Sri Lankan masses, the Tamil guerrillas depended on armed violence to mobilize the Tamil youth in particular. The L.T.T.E., the most powerful of these groups, strongly believed that what was necessary was action rather than words.[57] None of the guerrilla groups has systematically documented any of these relevant aspects, but their literature, within certain limits, contained the basic rudiments of their political ideologies.

In studying the basic structure of the political ideologies, strategies and programmes of these groups, the author found it necessary to make the following divisions for a clear explanation: objectives, origins of ideology, views of modern society, programmes, strategies and tactics. Towards this end, the author has relied on newspapers, journals, pamphlets, interviews and articles.

6.13 Objectives

The objectives of all the Tamil guerrillas were generally the same despite their internal and inter-group rivalries, and were mainly related to domestic matters. Their primary objective was to break away from the existing unitary Sri Lankan national state and form an independent Tamil or 'Eelam' state mainly in the Northern and Eastern provinces where a majority of the Tamil population was still concentrated.[58] The Tamil guerrillas based this objective on the following assumptions: the rights of the Tamil people for self-determination, the recognition of Tamils as a distinct nationality and the calls among the Tamil community for the formation of a new Tamil state.[59]

These groups further aspired to an independent socialist state rather than to a democratically-elected provincial form of government. A.S. Balasingham, a political adviser to the L.T.T.E., summed up their common objective of a socialist state in the following way:

> The political objective of our movement to advance the national struggle along with the class struggle or rather our fundamental objective is national emancipation and socialist transition of our social formation.[60]

They were unanimous in their common objective which was the establishment of a separate socialist Tamil state by means of an armed revolutionary struggle.[61]

The political objectives of the Tamil guerrilla groups were a mixture of Tamil nationalism and Marxist ideology. The nationalistic element was mainly derived from the historic glory of a Tamil Kingdom, while the Marxist ideology was more an influence of Marxism-Leninism than orthodox Marxism itself. Their ideological framework and strategies were designed to explain, achieve and justify their objectives. Dissimilar for the most part in their objectives, the guerrilla groups did not share a common ideology, programme and strategy. These differences were minor compared to the strength of their main common objective- that of the liberation and establishment of a separate socialist Tamil state. Prior to focusing on these ideologies the author wishes to trace their origins and sources.

6.14 The Origins and Sources

The sources of the ideologies of the Tamil guerrilla groups had been an issue of controversy and debate. Yet it was widely accepted that the various groups derived their ideological framework from Marxism-Leninism. The depth of this influence, however, was questionable as the incorporation of Marxist concepts in the ideology of the Tamil guerrillas was exaggerated. Concepts and rhetoric which proved to be useful in justifying their objectives were borrowed from Marxism and utilized widely. For example, the concept of self-determination was a concept much overused by scholars to justify the Tamils' common objective of a separate state. The differences in ideology between the groups were mainly attributed to their different interpretations of Marxism. The E.P.R.L.F. advocated an orthodox Marxist-Leninist Approach irrespective of any embellishments. The P.L.O.T. adhered to a socialist revolution of the workers and peasants based on a strong Marxist line. The E.R.O.S. on the contrary advocated an even firmer Marxist view of the struggle. The T.E.L.O., on the other hand, adopted an indifferent attitude towards a theoretical approach. Its leader Sri Sabarathnam presented T.E.L.O's position when he said that:

> Our people want Eelam immediately. They are not concerned with Marxism or any other "ism". It (ideology) is only the next step after Eelam is achieved.[62]

The L.T.T.E. had its own distinct approach to Marxism which was also mixed with the goal of achieving Eelam. In reply to questions posed by N. Ram of *The Hindu*, the leader of the L.T.T.E., V. Prabakaran, explained that socialism and Tamil Eelam formed the nucleus of the L.T.T.E. ideology.[63] The aim, of forming a separate state, however, subsumed their socialist commitment. Anton Balasingham explained this twist of ideology as a commitment to being socialist revolutionaries who uphold democracy rather than being totally committed to dogmatic Marxism.[64] Within this context it was indicated that the Tamil nationalism of the L.T.T.E. took some ideological support from a loose synthesis of Marxism-Leninism. Thus, it was the L.T.T.E. which took up the cause of Tamil nationalism and emerged as the rallying force of all nationalistic elements within the Tamil community. This trend was further exemplified by the L.T.T.E.'s views pertaining to modern society and the would-be Tamil state.

6.15 Perceptions

A major part of the various Tamil guerrilla ideologies were based on the influence of Tamil legends and ethnic lore which had been imbibed into their culture over the years. One of their major perceptions which, was fundamental to all of their ideologies was that of a traditional homeland. The concept of a traditional Tamil homeland was inextricably linked with the political ideologies of the Tamil guerrilla groups. The L.T.T.E. and the other guerrilla groups perceived that the Northern and Eastern provinces of Sri Lanka were in fact the traditional homeland of the Tamil people. The L.T.T.E. expressed this belief to a representative of the Tamil Nadu state government.

> This "homeland" is a clearly identifiable, contiguous, single region composed of the Northern and Eastern provinces. This region is the historically constituted homeland of the Tamil speaking people and therefore indivisible. The recognition of the territorial integrity of the region as the "homeland" of the Tamil is cardinal to any meaningful lasting solutions to the Tamil national question.[65]

The L.T.T.E. found it imperative to demarcate a territorial base to foster and nurture a separate Tamil state where the Tamils' own cultural identity could flourish. Thus, the concept of a homeland was associated with the claim to constitute a community based on language, culture and tradition. Within this context, the ethnocentric orientation of the L.T.T.E. heightened the intensity of their demand for a separate state and the depth of their claim of the right to the land where generations of Tamils had been born. The Tamils felt strongly that any attempts to settle Sinhalese in these areas should be resisted. They further emphasized and exaggerated the importance of the language, culture, tradition and level of achievement of the Tamil people to arouse nationalistic fervour in the Tamil populace. Their ultimate aim was to gain support for their armed struggle for a separate state.[66] Their concept of a separate state was based mainly on the historical Jaffna Kingdom which the L.T.T.E. perceived to have been the golden age of the Tamil culture in Sri Lanka.

According to the L.T.T.E., a Tamil Kingdom had flourished in Sri Lanka between the 13th and the 17th centuries wherein the Tamil people had been ensured a stable national existence. The Portuguese annexed these predominantly Tamil areas in 1619, but governed them as a separate national entity. The Dutch who later annexed these areas adhered to the Portuguese system. It was the British who integrated this territory to the unitary system of government thus amalgamating the Sinhala and Tamil kingdoms. This integration, claimed the L.T.T.E., was the beginning of a bitter and long drawn out ethnic conflict. The L.T.T.E. summed up its views on this amalgamation as follows:

> Until 1833, there existed separate states in Sri Lanka. After 1833 these separate states were brought under one central administrative organization for reasons of administrative convenience and disregarding the opposition of the Tamils and Sinhalese.[67]

The L.T.T.E. was influenced by the historical past in formulating its ideology rather than by more current socio-economic and political developments. According to Eric Hoffer, preoccupation with the past stems not only from a desire to demonstrate the legitimacy of a new movement and the illegitimacy of the old order but also to show the present as a mere interlude between the past and the future.[68] As a result, the L.T.T.E.'s ideology was exclusively nationalist and ethnocentric as reflected in their approach to the ethnic conflict in Sri Lanka. The L.T.T.E. extended to post-independent Sri Lanka its ideological vision in which the granting of independence was viewed as a transfer of power from the British to a Sinhala national bourgeoisie.[69] This transfer of power, according to the L.T.T.E., marked the beginning of a state-sponsored system of genocide which continued into the post-independent period. The examples cited for this genocide were: the Sinhala Only Act of 1956, the ethnic riots in 1956 and 1958, the government intervention against the Satyagraha campaign in 1961, the new constitution in 1972, and the ethnic violence in 1977, 1981 and 1983.[70]

The ideological sustenance of the L.T.T.E. was derived from Tamil nationalism and was expressed in their views regarding S.J.V. Chelvanayagam, who was referred to as 'Tantai Selva' which means 'Father Selva'.[71] The L.T.T.E. was the only guerrilla group which, acknowledged Chelvanayagam as the father figure and believed that they had taken up his cause for separatism and therefore, were the authentic successors of Chelvanayagam and the Federal Party he represented. Their support for him was expressed publicly as follows:

> The gun in their hands, the fire of freedom in their hearts, arises the third generation: Tantai Selva's (Father Selva) heroic policies cannot be bartered away, in strength his heirs rise up ...L.T.T.E. members have come into his heritage on the battlefield.[72]

It is thus evident that the L.T.T.E. viewed itself as part of a long tradition of nationalism whose task was to succeed and pursue the goals of prior nationalists. The L.T.T.E. alone among the Tamil guerrilla groups had the distinction of adhering to the ideological traditions of the Tamil nationalist politicians and further developing and adapting their ideas.

Just as the J.V.P.'s choice of the emblem of a lion on its flag was symbolic of its ideological emphasis, so too was the choice of the L.T.T.E.'s emblem of a tiger. According to the L.T.T.E.'s leader Prabakaran, the tiger had deeper connotations of an historic Tamil patriotic resurgence, and was derived from the royal emblem of the ancient Chola Empire.[73] D.B. Jeyaraj concluded that the symbol aroused a deep-seated nostalgia for a golden age which was said to have existed during the Chola Empire.[74] Furthermore, it also represented a counterpart to the Sinhala emblem of a lion.

The strong influence of Tamil nationalism was further evident in the code of discipline adapted by the L.T.T.E. This disciplinary code was based on the ethics advocated by Hinduism and those which were inherent in the traditional Tamil culture. Thus, the L.T.T.E. was committed to a resurgence of Tamil culture thereby rejecting the influences of western culture. Consequently, its ideology was one that depended heavily on the glory of the past and culture which had gradually been eroded.

The L.T.T.E.'s nationalist image called for an ideologically anti Sinhala stand, and so they opposed the Sinhalese community as a repressive majority community. Though the E.P.R.L.F. and P.L.O.T. were willing to cooperate with the left-wing movement and socialist groups of the Sinhalese community, the L.T.T.E. was not open to any form of dialogue with the Sinhalese. For the L.T.T.E. the primary contradiction in Sri Lanka was not capitalism but nationalism.[75] Viewed from this perspective, any form of cooperation with the Sinhalese was to be rejected. The extent of this rejection was indicated in the L.T.T.E.'s shooting in 1985 of the headmaster of St. John's College in Jaffna after he organized a cricket match between the government army and the students.[76] The L.T.T.E.'s extreme stand was not shared by either the E.P.R.L.F. or the P.L.O.T. which were ideologically more Marxist-oriented than the L.T.T.E. The P.L.O.T. expressed its ideological orientation on the subject of the Sinhala majority as follows:

> Our propaganda is not only intended to prepare people for armed combat, but also to let the Sinhalese people know that we are not its enemies, that our fight is one against imperialism and that for this fight we want to help the Sinhalese.[77]

The L.T.T.E.'s approach to other minority communities within the country was quite contrary to that of the Sinhala majority. Due to linguistic bonds, the Sri Lankan Muslims were also considered to be part of the Tamil community irrespective of the marked differences in religion. The Muslim community was given priority over the Indian Tamil plantation workers because the L.T.T.E. aspired for a merger between the Tamil-dominated Northern Province and the Eastern Province where a large part of the Muslim population was still concentrated.[78] Although the Indian Tamil plantation workers were not considered as an integral part of the Tamil guerrillas' liberation struggle, they were to be accommodated in the state of Eelam.[79] E.R.O.S., however, did not share the views of the L.T.T.E. on the role of the plantation workers. To E.R.O.S., the plantation workers of Indian origin also represented part of the proletariat which was crucial to achieving the concept of an Eelam.[80]

In addressing some of the pressing social problems prevalent in Sri Lankan Tamil society, the L.T.T.E. was faced with the conflicts of caste and class. According to its ideological convictions, the L.T.T.E. strongly believed in a classless, casteless society which would ensure equality for all. It was known that they favoured the lower castes to eradicate any discrimination.[81] Another significant social consideration was the status of women in the Tamil society. In a society where women were culturally bound by traditions of dowry and castes their position was perceived to be vulnerable and suppressed. The L.T.T.E. failed, however, to present a definite perception of how such conditions would be changed. The L.T.T.E. obviously failed to come to grips with the social and economic problems of Sri Lankan Tamil society. The L.T.T.E. addressed a few obvious grievances, but not the ones which were the crux of the socio-economic fabric. The L.T.T.E. strove for reforms but not for radical social changes; changes were not an inherent part of the L.T.T.E.'s ideology.

The analysis of the L.T.T.E's ideology thus far strongly indicates that they not only rejected the unitary political system in Sri Lanka, which they believed was against their socio-economic and political interests, but also rejected the more moderate Tamil political stand which was represented by the T.U.L.F. To the L.T.T.E., the T.U.L.F. represented the Tamil bourgeoisie who had made futile attempts to secure an egalitarian position for the Tamil people. Prabakaran, the L.T.T.E.'s leader, found the "opportunistic" politics of the T.U.L.F. a barrier to the Tamil liberation struggle in Sri Lanka. He perceived the T.U.L.F. to be governed by motives of self-advancement rather than a party structured to achieve the "liberation" of the oppressed Tamil people. Furthermore, the T.U.L.F. failed to grasp the realities of a revolutionary force which was motivated by a political desire to achieve a state of Eelam, and, therefore, its members were seen as traitors to the revolutionary cause.[82] The L.T.T.E.'s disillusionment regarding the policies and strategies of the T.U.L.F. were indicated in the following statement:

The political structure of the Tamil United Front, founded on a conservative bourgeois ideology, could not provide the basis for the articulation of revolutionary politics. It became very clear to the Tamil masses and particularly to the revolutionary youth that the Tamil national leaders, though they fiercely championed the cause of the Tamils, have failed to formulate any concrete practical programme of political action to liberate the oppressed Tamil nation. Having exhausted all forms of popular struggle for the last three decades, having been alienated from the power structure of the Sinhala state, the Tamil politicians still cling to parliament to air their disgruntlement which went unheard, unheeded like vain cries in the wilderness.[83]

The Tamil guerrillas not only opposed the Sinhala-dominated government but also any of their own political leaders who failed to support their demands.

Just as the J.V.P. stressed the word 'patriotism' in its indoctrination classes and propaganda literature, so too did the L.T.T.E. rely on this word over and over again, defining it as follows:

> If a national race loves its history, filled with greatness and its language and culture, its traditions and ancient customs, that, we call patriotism. One who discards this progressive patriotism, this love of the nation and calls for cosmopolitanism, is not a true socialist. People like these are bourgeois cosmopolitans.[84]

The absolute commitment which the L.T.T.E. demanded from its members was indicative of its ideological orientation towards extremism. The cyanide capsules which were worn around the necks of their fighter cadres were seen as a symbolic expression of the commitment, determination and courage of its members.[85] The symbolic revival of the ancient tradition of the warriors following their chieftain to the battlefield and death appear to have been assimilated by the L.T.T.E. from the legendary accounts of the Tamil kingdoms. K. Subramaniam concludes that the Tamil Tigers were inculcated with a "Masada" type cult which was manifest in the cyanide capsules.[86]

The basic framework of the L.T.T.E. ideology was dependent on the search for causes and explanations of the repression of the Tamils by the Sinhala-dominated governments, which they felt was extreme enough to annihilate the Tamil people. The result was an eclectic body of thought which was geared to a liberation struggle. In spite of its extreme nationalistic strain and predominantly anti-Sinhala feelings, the L.T.T.E.'s ideology was pragmatic and subtle in comparison with that of some of the other Tamil guerrilla groups. Most of the other groups derived support for the state of Eelam from the existence of a Tamil kingdom in Jaffna prior to being conquered by the Portuguese. The territorial base of the Jaffna Kingdom, however, was complex: there was strong evidence that the Eastern Province had been excluded from the said kingdom. Hence, the L.T.T.E. used a more subtle argument harking back even further in history to the powerful Chola Empire whose territorial limits remained vague. Furthermore, there was evidence of a mutual antagonism between the people of the Vellalar caste in Jaffna and the Mukkuar caste of Batticaloa. With such an ambience of conflict, the argument for a Jaffna Kingdom could not possibly have served as a truly uniting factor. Therefore, the L.T.T.E. had more subtly adapted the supposed idea of a glorious 'Chola Kingdom' in order to unite and mobilize the Tamil people in the Northern and the Eastern provinces. The pragmatic character of the L.T.T.E.'s ideology was further obvious in the following statement by an area leader:

> Well I do have some political principles. Basically, it is what the L.T.T.E. stands for, I adhere to it fully. I am a practical man, more of a pragmatist. I also prefer practical action to merely talking or discussing theory. That is what is important. I don't talk about ideology. I don't know ideology, I believe in action.[87]

The ideological differences apart, the L.T.T.E. emerged as the most prominent guerrilla group due to its strong nationalist stand and action-oriented approach. The guerrilla groups differed in their approaches to the socio-economic aspects, which they discussed at a superficial level and which were superseded by the more blatant differences in their strategic and tactical approaches to a revolutionary struggle. This was a crucial area of controversy.

6.16 Strategy and Tactics

The military strategies of the Tamil guerrilla groups were a topic which had received scant attention though they were a crucial area of the phenomenon of insurgency. Of all the Tamil guerrilla groups, only the L.T.T.E. ever formed a definite strategy of political violence to achieve its ends. The L.T.T.E. in their literature claimed to stand for national liberation and socialist revolution. Their aim was to overthrow the Sri Lankan national government through a protracted armed struggle or at least to gain control in the Tamil areas. According to the L.T.T.E., guerrilla warfare marked the beginning of a people's war which was one of the most effective means of gaining a separate state. They believed that unrelentless guerrilla warfare would eventually rally the mobilization of the general populace, and that until the final war of liberation united the guerrilla factions they should continue with a protracted guerrilla war, based mainly on hit-and-run tactics.[88] Thus, the final goal of urban guerrilla warfare was to politicize the broader masses for a war of national liberation and socialist revolution.[89] The L.T.T.E. claimed that this particular strategy was adapted to suit the specific political conditions in Sri Lanka.[90]

The L.T.T.E.'s interpretation of a people's war, did not actually include the active participation of the people, but rather only the moral support of the populace. This strategy of urban guerrilla-cum-rural guerrilla warfare was complex and multi-faceted. Dagmar found it necessary to view this complex strategy under the following three stages: (1) individual terror; (2) armed confrontation with the police, state symbols of repression and Tamil collaborators; and (3) armed confrontation with the military forces.[91] The L.T.T.E. further adopted, when necessary, some of the tactics advocated by Mao and Che Guevara namely that of confusing the enemy, attacking unexpectedly, and destroying one's targets.[92]

The L.T.T.E.'s strategy was found to be unacceptable by the other Tamil guerrilla groups. Notably, the P.L.O.T. viewed a guerrilla war as useless and counter-productive, especially when considering the vulnerability of the Tamil civilians to army reprisals after each guerrilla attack. The P.L.O.T.'s fundamental argument was that the strategy of an armed struggle should be closely related to the indigenous conditions. On the basis of these premises, the P.L.O.T. rejected the idea that strategies which were successful in one state could be applied in another without modification or adaptation.[93] In this way it was similar to the

J.V.P. which had great antipathy to outside influences, even revolutionary ones. According to the P.L.O.T., the strategy which would be most successful in Sri Lanka would be one which stressed mass mobilization and a full-fledged battle once this mobilization was complete.[94] The P.L.O.T.'s interpretation of a mass base was as follows:

> Extending mass bases means creating grassroots party branches in villages, towns and districts and strengthening the alliance with important population groups and classes like landless peasants, students, artisans etc.[95]

The E.R.O.S. too was committed to deriving an indigenous revolutionary strategy rather than importing one.[96] They further found the L.T.T.E.'s hit-and-run strategy to be redundant as such a strategy was only effective at the beginning of a guerrilla war.[97] According to the strategy of the E.R.O.S., the sensitive areas of the economy would be destabilized, to be followed by an attack on military targets. As a result, although some of its guerrilla operations particularly in Southern Sri Lanka were concentrated on sabotage and subversion of economic targets, those in the Northern and Eastern provinces were directed at military personnel and installations in the form of ambushes, landmines, bombings and raids.[98]

The E.P.R.L.F. was influenced by Leninism rather than Guevaraism and, therefore, attempted to mobilize the masses, especially the lower classes in the Tamil areas. They rejected guerrilla warfare as a strategy but accepted such methods as mere tactics.[99] The strategy of the T.E.L.O.was generally vague and undefined, but did include hit-and-run tactics especially when its members were unable to engage the enemy in open confrontation. The T.E.L.O. advocated a strategy of a protracted war of national liberation which would be fought by all factions in a united effort.

From the above discussion it becomes increasingly evident that the Tamil guerrillas differed in their strategic and tactical approaches. They were influenced by Maoism, Guevaraism and the strategies of Margihella, typifying the strategies of other politically violent groups in the Third World.

6.17 Programme of the Tamil Guerrilla Groups

The various revolutionary programmes of the Tamil guerrilla movements revolved around the groups' shared and envisaged strategy for an independent Tamil state, Eelam. At this juncture the author will concentrate on the political aspects, the foreign policy and the economic proposals of the said state of Eelam, as proposed by the Tamil guerrilla groups. Despite their deeply committed demands for a separate state, none of the Tamil groups presented a precise alternative to the existing socio-economic and political system in Sri Lanka. Their various programmes were vague, unformulated and ambivalent. The L.T.T.E., for example, discussed its own programme at a superficial level in its propaganda literature. On the basis of this literature, and in order to facilitate a clear explication, the author focuses on the following aspects: the proposed boundaries or territorial limits of the state of Eelam, the nature of its government, its foreign policy and economic programme.

Regarding the territorial limits, the Tamil guerrilla groups failed to reach an agreement and engaged in a constant debate. Nor was there a consensus as to the ideology of the proposed state. The only factor they agreed upon was that a separate state should be established in the area claimed to be the traditional homeland. There was disagreement, however, as to the historical boundaries of the imagined homeland. The nucleus of the Tamil state was generally comprised of the Northern and Eastern provinces but again the peripheral limits were subjectively defined. The L.T.T.E., for instance, while accepting the Northern and the Eastern provinces as the foundation of a Tamil state, extended the territorial limits to Puttlam in Western Sri Lanka and Potuvil in the East.[100] The T.E.L.O. and the P.L.O.T., on the other hand, did not define the boundaries precisely but rather signaled that they were in agreement with the L.T.T.E. in this respect. The E.R.O.S. and the E.P.R.L.F. devised a more ambitious plan which also included the central highland areas, populated by the Indian plantation workers. Accordingly the E.R.O.S. claimed that an area ranging from Point Pedro to Badulla in the central highlands, and from Mannar to Batticaloa including Potuvil in the East should be included in the state of Eelam.[101]

Just as the territorial limits of an independent Eelam state were open to controversy, so too was the political nature of the said state. The L.T.T.E. had a more precise format for the political and constitutional elements of the independent Tamil state, and claimed that it would be an egalitarian socialist state. Prabakaran explained the L.T.T.E.'s conception of the character of an Eelam socialist society in the following excerpt:

> By socialism I mean the construction of an egalitarian society where there is no class contradiction and exploitation of man by man, a free rational society where human freedom and rights are protected and progress enhanced.[102]

The L.T.T.E. rejected parliamentary democracy based on a multi-party system, and instead advocated the advantages of a one-party system. Prabakaran claimed that the necessary socio-economic and political changes would actually be accelerated under a socialist constitution based on a one-party system. Within such a system, the L.T.T.E. said, priority would be given to the needs of the people.[103] The L.T.T.E.'s rejection of a British-oriented parliamentary democracy as bourgeois, however, did not mean a preference for the Russian one-party model. The L.T.T.E.'s peculiar form of socialist orientation opposed the Russian model on the premise that the party becomes the state. Rather, the L.T.T.E. selected a one-party state similar to that of the Yugoslavian model. The L.T.T.E. called it a 'socialist democratic' model, but a closer review of their literature strongly suggests that their aspirations for an egalitarian state were more along the lines of a benevolent dictatorship. The other Tamil groups gave scant attention to this aspect of their ideologies although all expressed a basic belief in a socialist state rather than a parliamentary democracy.

The foreign policies of all the Tamil guerrilla groups were also vague and ambivalent. At first the L.T.T.E. claimed that they had been strongly influenced by the socialist block, but then claimed that they were not partial to any international ideology and were committed to non-alignment.[104] Due to Sri Lanka's geographical proximity to India, the L.T.T.E. adapted a pro-Indian stand and supported proposals to declare the Indian Ocean a 'zone of peace'.[105] Their partiality to India, in general, compelled them to adopt a stand in opposition to Pakistan and the People's Republic of China. The L.T.T.E.'s propaganda, however, was rife with attacks on the U.S.A. and Israel. The U.S.A. was branded as an 'imperialist force' and Israel was condemned as an 'international Zionist force'. These aspersions were merely rhetoric meant to signify a preference for a purely indigenous solution to the ethno-political conflict in Sri Lanka, but were not intended to incite physical attacks against those foreign powers or their interests.

The ultimate commitment to guerrilla warfare and political violence distracted the major groups from discussing their programmes theoretically and explicitly. Economics was perhaps the most neglected area, with little or no attention given to economic issues in the groups' propaganda literature. Nevertheless, the author has derived his insight from the activities of the L.T.T.E. from 1985, when they began a parallel administration in Jaffna. During this period the L.T.T.E. strove to develop local industries based on the available agrarian and other local resources. Their primary focus was on maximizing the utilization of those resources in the manufacture of Palmyrah syrup, jams, soft drinks and soap. The L.T.T.E.'s economic programme also concentrated on reforms rather than on revolutionary changes.

The L.T.T.E.'s organizational structure offers an insight into the proposed political pattern within a state of Eelam. As mentioned in Chapter 5, the L.T.T.E. was the most tightly structured, disciplined and autocratically-led group with an absolutely committed membership. It also had the reputation for being the most intransigent of the Tamil groups, and thus would have imposed a benevolent dictatorship rather than a democracy despite its claimed preference for a socialist state. After the L.T.T.E.'s takeover of Jaffna in 1985, the L.T.T.E. did not disturb the existing administrative and judicial structure, but actually adopted the same direction and style of the existing system. What emerged was a mere *de facto* government void of any significant changes.

6.18 Summary

The discussion so far has revealed distinct differences between the ideologies, strategies and programmes of the Sinhala-dominated left-wing J.V.P. and the Tamil guerrilla organizations. The objectives of the J.V.P. were basically anti-government and non-capitalistic. Its ideology was a mixture of Marxism-Leninism, Maoism, Guevaraism and Sinhala-Buddhist nationalism. The complexity and fusion of diverse sources reduced its ability to postulate a coherent ideology, effective strategy and a viable programme for waging guerrilla warfare and installing a distinctly strong socialist state. The ideologies of the Tamil guerrillas too were diverse and incoherent due to the proliferation of factions, though they shared a common inspiration of Tamil nationalism rather than Marxism. Hence, all the ideologies of the Tamil guerrilla groups were preoccupied with the survival and preservation of the Tamil race, nation, language, culture and traditional homeland. Moreover, they believed that the supposed racial superiority of the Tamils justified their ethnic prejudice against the Sri Lankan Sinhalese majority. Thus, their ideology was limited to the confines of their own community and lacked a wider societal perspective.

Neither the J.V.P. nor the L.T.T.E. and other Tamil groups fit into either of the ideological categories of hard-line leftists or communists. Rather all may be categorized as hard-line nationalists with leftist leanings. This fundamental nationalism which was fused with the revolutionist theories of the major Marxist-Leninist thinkers was common to other underground movements in many Third World countries. Finally, in Chapter 7 the author will examine the pattern and sequence of political violence waged by the organizations discussed above.

References

1. Chalmers Johnson, *Autopsy of People's War*, (Berkeley: University of California Press, 1973), p. 104.
2. Rex D. Hopper, "The Revolutionary Process: A Frame of Revolutionary Movements", *Social Forces*, Vol. 28, No. 3, (1959), p. 276.
3. Paul Wilkinson, *Terrorism and Liberal State*, (London: Macmillan, 1986), p. 110.
4. Bertie Gajameragedera, "Internal War and International Intervention: A Study in Theory and Practice", *Seminar for Asian Studies*, University of Peradeniya, No. 20, (1985), p. 14.
5. *Janatha Vimukthi (People's Liberation)*, The Newspaper of the J.V.P., (1 August 1970). Translated from Sinhalese.

6. *Ibid.,* p. 5.
7. Rohana Wijeweera, Statement to the C.I.D. [unpublished], (1971), p. 4.
8. *Ibid.,* p. 336.
9. Janatha Vimukthi, (30 September 1970).
10. Janatha Vimukthi, (5 September 1970).
11. *Janatha Vimukthi,* (30 September 1970).
12. A.J. Wilson, "Ceylon: The People's Liberation Front and the Revolution that Failed", *Pacific Community,* Vol. 3, No. 2, (1972), p. 369.
13. Rohana Wijeweera, *op. cit.,* p. 57.
14. Rohana Wijeweera, *op. cit.,* p. 62.
15. *Judgment of the Criminal Justice Commission, (Insurgency Inquiry),* No. 1, (Colombo: Department of Government Printing, 1976), p. 118.
16. Janatha Sangamaya (Peoples' League), *71 April Negiteema (71 April Uprising),* (Dehiwela: Allen Printing Press, 1980), p. 96.
17. Judgment of the C.J.C. *op. cit.,* p. 118.
18. Rohana Wijeweera
19. Judgment of the C.J.C. *op. cit.,* p. 118.
20. Rohana Wijeweera, Statement to the C.I.D., *op. cit.,* p. 38.
21. A.C. Alles, *Insurgency-1971,* (Colombo: The Apothecaries, 1976), p. 50.
22. See Frantz Fanon, *The Wretched of the Earth,* (London: Penguin, 1986).
23. This concept of Indian Expansionism was further discussed in two articles published by the editorial board of the Chinese Communist Party's daily newspaper Renmin Rebao, and entitled "The Chinese Indian Border Struggle" and the "Nehru Doctrine". The articles were exposes on the Indian capitalist class and its basic philosophy which accordingly was to spread its economic and political hegemony over India's much weaker and smaller neighbour states. Rohana Wijeweera, Speech to the C.J.C. *op. cit.,* p. 238. See, Neville Maxwell, *India's China War,* (London: Penguin, 1970), pp. 277-309.
24. Janatha Sangamaya, *op. cit.,* p. 90.
25. Kumari Jayawardana, *Ethnic and Class Conflict in Sri Lanka,* Centre for Social Analysis, (Dehiwela: Navamaga Printers, 1985), p. 86.

26. Judgment of the C.J.C. *op. cit.*, p. 120.
27. *Janatha Vimukthi*, (20 January 1970).
28. G.B. Keerawella, "The J.V.P. and the 1971 Uprising", *Social Science Review*, No. 2, (1980), p. 35.
29. See, Mao Tse-Tung, "Analysis of the Classes in Chinese Society", in *Selected Reading from the Works of Mao-Tsetung*, (Peking" Foreign Language Press, 1971), pp. 11-19.
30. See, Karl Marx and Friedrich Engels, *The Communist Manifesto*, (London: George Allen and Unwin, 1948), p. 124.
31. Rohana Wijeweera, *Rathu Lanka (Red Ceylon)*, A Paper of the J.V.P., (15 March 1971), p. 4.
32. E.A. Goonesinghe is a pioneer of the Trade Union movement in Sri Lanka.
33. Rohana Wijeweera, "Trade Union Politics and Workers Union Politics", speech given on 13th September 1970 at the New Town Hall. In Colombo, Quoted in G.B. Kerawella, *op. cit.*, 1981, p. 37.
34. Patriot (Deshapremi), a newspaper of the J.V.P. (8 August 1970), p. 1.
35. *Janatha Vimukthi*, (1 August 1970).
36. Keppetiapola was a Kandyan chieftain who in 1818 led an armed rebellion against British Colonial rule. Puran Appu was a leader of the peasant uprising in 1848 against British rule.
37. Kumari Jayawardena, *op. cit.*, p. 88.
38. Rohana Wijeweera, *op. cit.*, p. 229.
39. Gananatha Obeysekara, "Sinhala Nationalism and Culture in Relation to the April 1971 Insurgency in Sri Lanka", [unpublished], (1975), p. 2.
40. *The Economist*, (3 July 1971), p. 33.
41. Loku Athula (Nimalasiri Jayasinghe), "Evidence to the C.J.C.", *Daily News*, (15 February 1973).
42. James Jupp, *Sri Lanka – Third World Democracy*, (London: Frank Cass, 1978), p. 306.
43. Urmila Phadnis, "Insurgency in Ceylon Politics: Problems and Prospects", *Defense Studies and Analyses Journal*, Vol. 13, No. 4, (April 1971), pp. 596-597.
44. Rohana Wijeweera, Statement, *op. cit.*, pp. 57-59.
45. A.C. Alles, *op. cit.*, p. 45.
46. Anura Kurukulasuriya, "*Statement to the Police*", 1971, (unpublished), p. 36.

47. Rohana Wijeweera, "Speech at Hyde Park Meeting", (27 February 1971), *Daily Mirror*, (28 February 1971).
48. *Keesings Contemporary Archives*, (14-24 March 1964), pp. 19951-3.
49. *Niyamuwa* (The Pilot) newspaper of the J.V.P. (29 May 1977), cited by G.B.Kerawella, *op. cit.,* pp. 42-43.
50. A.J. Wilson, "Ceylon: The People's Liberation Front and the Revolution That Failed", *Pacific Community*, Vol. 3, No. 2, (1972), pp. 372-376.
51. *Janatha Vimukthi*, (20 January 1971).
52. A.J. Wilson, *op. cit.,* p. 372-73.
53. Rohana Wijeweera, Statement to the C.I.D., *op. cit.,* p. 235.
54. *The Nation*, A Paper of the L.S.S.P., (22 April 1971).
55. Justus M. Van Der Kroef, "The Sri Lanka Insurgency of April 1971: Its Development and Meaning", *Asia Quarterly*, Vol. 2, (1973), p. 114.
56. James Jupp, "The JVP Insurrection of 1971 and Its Impact on the Marxist and Socialist Movements in Ceylon", *A Paper for the Conference on Sri Lanka*, (London University, March 1974), p. 10.
57. "Making of a Militant Leader: An Interview with V. Prabakaran, *Lanka Guardian*, Vol. 9, No. 11, (1986), p. 13.
58. From the 10th century A.D. onward there was three Dravidian or Tamil Kingdoms in South India. Among these the Chola was the mightiest, having conquered Sri Lanka. Eelam was the name given by the Chola Empire to what is now the island of Sri Lanka.
59. These objectives were put forward by the Tamil guerrilla groups at the Thimphu Talks.
60. A.C. Balasingham, "Liberation Tigers and Tamil Eelam Freedom Struggle", No. 4, Political Committee, Liberation Tigers of Eelam, (1983), p. 42.
61. Political Committee of the L.T.T.E., *Towards Liberation*, Selected Political Documents of the Liberation Tamil Tigers of Eelam, (1984), p. 7.
62. "The Terrorist Scourge Puts up the Ante", *Far Eastern Economic Review*, (12 June 1986), p. 29.
63. "Making of a Militant Leader: An Interview with V. Prabakaran", *Lanka Guardian*, Vol. 9, No. 10, (15 September 1986), p. 10.
64. *Frontline*, (10-23 January 1987), p. 22.
65. L.T.T.E., "Tamil Militants' Position on Government's Proposals: L.T.T.E. Comments", letter to M.G. Ramachandran Chief

Minister of Tamil Nadu", *Frontline*, (15-28 November 1986), p. 116.

66. Cociyalicat Tamil Ilattai Nokki, (Towards a Socialist Tamil Eelam), L.T.T.E. publication, p. 32, cited in Dagmar Hellmann-Rajanayagam, "The Tamil Tigers in Northern Sri Lanka: Origins, Factions, Programmes", Internationals Asienforum, Vol. 17, No. (1986), p. 74.
67. "Makkalin Vitutalaiyai Venretuppom. (We Will Obtain People's Liberation)", P.L.O.T. publication, p. 2, cited in Dagmer, *op. cit.*, p. 76.
68. Eric Hoffer, *The True Believer: Thoughts on the Nature of Mass Movements*, (New York: New American Library, 1958), p. 71.
69. Towards Liberation, *op. cit.*, p. 4.
70. *Ibid.*, pp. 4-5.
71. S.J.V. Chelvanayagam was the leader of the Federal Party who pioneered the demand for a federal government and later for a separate state. From 1949 to 1976 he led the demands for a federal state, but afterwards he abandoned his demands for federalism and opted for a policy of separatism based on the concept of Eelam.
72. Putiya Patai [New Path], (January 1986), p. 5.
73. Interview with V. Prabakaran, in *Sunday*, (11-17 March 1984), reprinted in Towards Liberation, *op. cit.*, p. 80.
74. S.B. Jeyaraj, "How Strong are Boys", *Frontline*, (23 March-5 April 1985), p. 62.
75. Viravenkai, [Brave Tiger], L.T.T.E. publication, (October 1986), p. 3.
76. The reason was that he organized a Cricket match between the students and the armed forces. See *Daily Telegraph*, (28 June 1985).
77. *Putiya Patai [New Path]*, P.L.O.T. publication, (June-July), 1985), p. 2, cited in Dagmar, *op. cit.*, p. 73.
78. The Ethnic composition in the Eastern Province is as follows: Tamils 41%, Muslims 31%, and Sinhalese 21%.
79. T.S. Subramaniam, "Spotlight on the L.T.T.E.", *Frontline*, (10-23 January 1987), p. 22.
80. T.S. Subramaniam, "Eros, the Dark Horse", *Frontline*, (28 June-4July 1986), p. 18.
81. Diary of Combat, p. 44, cited in Dagmar, *op. cit.*, p. 73.
82. Towards Liberation, *op. cit.*, p. 84.

83. A. Balasingham, *Liberation Tigers and Tamil Eelam Freedom Struggle*, Political Committee, Liberation Tigers of Eelam Book Publication, No. 4, (1983), p. 25.
84. *Cociya licit Tamil Ilattai Nokki*, p. 32, cited in Dagmar, *op. cit.*, p. 74.
85. *Lanka Guardian*, (October 1986), p. 12.
86. Frontline, (14-27 November 1987), p. 23.
87. *Frontline*, (15-28 November 1986), p. 117.
88. S.B. Jeyaraj, *op. cit.*, p. 65.
89. "Liberation Tigers and Tamil Eelam Freedom Struggle", *op. cit.*, 1983, p. 42.
90. *Ibid.*, p. 42.
91. Dagmar, *op. cit.*, pp. 70-71.
92. Diary of Armed Combt, L.T.T.E. publication, p. 11-13, cited in Dagmar, *op. cit.*, p. 71.
93. *Putiya Patai*, (September 1984), p. 10, cited in Dagmar, *op. cit.*, p. 70.
94. *Putiya Patai*, (June-July 1985), p. 6, cited in Dagmar, *op. cit.*, p. 74.
95. *Ibid.*, p. 70.
96. *Putiya Patai*, (March 1985), pp. 4-5, cited in Dagmar, *op. cit.*, p. 70.
97. T.S. Subramanyam, "EROS the Dark Horse", *Frontline*, (28 June-11 July 1986), p. 18,
98. *Frontline*, (23 March-5 April 1985), p. 65.
99. *Ibid.*
100. *Frontline*, (25 March-5 April 1985), p. 65.
101. See Appendix 6 for a map of proposed Eelam state.
102. *Frontline*, (28 June-11 July 1986), p. 18.
103. *S.O.L.T.*, a magazine of the Student Organization of the L.T.T.E., (1986), p. 16.
104. *India Today*, (30 June 1986).
105. Towards Liberation, *op. cit.*, p. 87.

7

Patterns of Political Violence : 1971-1987

7.1 Introduction

Political violence in Sri Lanka during 1971 and 1987, as characterized by its divisive social, economic and political conflicts, was organized and pre-planned, and was a potent development of the country's prolonged modernization process. The form of organization and manifestation of this violence, was dependent on the contrary ideologies, strategies and tactics adopted by its various perpetrators. The author has already examined these aspects of political violence as experienced in Sri Lanka. Nevertheless, the two main strains of political violence as organized by the left-wing J.V.P. and the Tamil guerrilla groups have featured their own distinct patterns and sequences of commission.

The primary objective of this chapter is to examine the overall patterns and consequences of political violence in Sri Lanka from 1971 to 1987. The first half of the chapter addresses the unmitigated violence resorted to by the J.V.P. in 1971. The latter half examines the political violence generated and prosecuted by the Tamil guerrilla groups through 1972 to 1987. Therefore, the author has subdivided this chapter under the following headings which contributes to a more lucid analysis of the political violence as follows: short-term factors, aims and planning, modes of warfare or forms of warfare, the governmental response, magnitude of violence, the patterns and outcomes.

7.2 Short-term Factors

The first major manifestation of political violence in post-independent Sri Lanka was the left-wing guerrilla insurrection of April 1971. It was a pre-planned armed attack which was motivated and launched by the J.V.P. The combination of two immediate factors impelled the J.V.P. to plunge into an armed struggle against the Sri Lankan Government. The first was the inherent propensity for political violence which was deeply entrenched in the J.V.P.'s political ideology. As a result of the method of indoctrination and mobilization practiced by the J.V.P., its members held the conviction that a socialist society, would be ushered in through an armed struggle. As discussed in Chapter 6, the J.V.P. had prepared for armed resistance prior to the General Election of 1970, anticipating a prospective dictatorship of the incumbent U.N.P. Government with military backing.[1] Although the election of 1970 brought the U.F. Government to power, the U.N.P.'s defeat did not stall the J.V.P.'s preparation for armed confrontation. Instead, the J.V.P. began criticizing the U.F. Government for its delay in bringing about major and constructive changes. Furthermore, at a rally in Colombo on the 28th of February 1971, the J.V.P. vehemently criticized the U.F. Government and promised to commence an armed revolt if police persecution of the J.V.P. did not stop.

Consequently, the continued process of preparation for an initial offensive resulted in a growing restlessness and an urgency among the J.V.P.'s members. By 1971 the members of the J.V.P. were impatient to launch an armed attack, having secured a ready supply of weaponry, ammunition and uniforms, and many of them having sacrificed their jobs and careers to become full-time members of the J.V.P. In light of their presumed preparedness, there was a growing clamour among the J.V.P.'s members to begin the violent campaign to capture power as quickly as possible. According to Chalmers Johnson, the belief held by an insurgent group that it can succeed in overcoming the elite's armed might is an accelerator of revolution.[2]

The second manifestation of the violence to come was the disposition of government forces to prepare for a military solution to the J.V.P.'s armed threat. Generally, the government's counter-offensive was based on reports submitted by the local police and the intelligence services. The U.N.P. during its term of government from 1965 to 1970, had studied the changes in Sri Lanka's political climate and compiled a report on the subversive movement, its pattern of activities and the key players involved. The first such report was compiled on the basis of information procured in 1967; the next was compiled in 1969.[3] Though the U.F. Government initially adopted a liberal attitude towards the J.V.P., this posture was soon replaced by a policy of repression.

In 1970 the U.F. Government set up a special police unit nicknamed the 'Guevara Bureau', through which all intelligence pertaining to the subversive movement was channeled. The government also prepared for legal action which would be crucial in the event of the outbreak of political violence. The laws then were far from adequate for dealing with guerrilla warfare. A proposed law entitled "The Prevention of Violent Insurrection Act" was submitted to the Cabinet for consideration. The Act bestowed the police with special powers of custody, arrest and trial of insurgents on charges of sedition.[4] The initial outcome of this pre-insurrectionary measure was the immediate arrest of about 500 members and sympathizers of the J.V.P.[5] Regardless of the new legal measures, the government's programme for counter violence depended most heavily on the strength and ability of the military and the police forces. An additional 1,500 men were recruited to the police service, which already had a man power strength of about 11,000 regulars.[6] Furthermore, in early March 1971 army units were deployed in Anuradhapura, Matara and Kandy.

While the U.F. Government was preparing for its own military offensive, the government launched a political programme under the direction of a parliamentary committee to counter J.V.P. propaganda and reduce the guerrilla group's channels of mobilization. This programme was a mixture of slander and theory, rather than a viable politico-economic programme. The government's propaganda campaign sought to discredit the J.V.P. by accusing them of responsibility for a right-wing plot supposedly backed by the C.I.A.[7] The potential channels of dialogue between the U.F. and the J.V.P. were thus blocked by the government's unwillingness to consider the deep seated factors and gain an understanding of the nature of the J.V.P.'s movement. The gap, thus breached, widened even further, and continued to do so even after the government's quelling of the J.V.P.'s armed struggle later in 1971. The military approach to the J.V.P.'s uprising was one of well-planned tactics and overwhelming superiority of combatants and material, while the political approach lacked coherence, co-ordination and strategy. It was evident that the government's counter-insurgency programme before the eruption of the armed struggle was characterized by a lack of genuine socio-economic and political measures.

The main action taken by the U.F. Government to deter violence before the uprising began was the declaration of a state of emergency on the 6th of March 1971, including the enforcement of a strict curfew. Two major incidents led the government to make the declaration: first, was the discovery of large stocks of hand bombs, arms and ammunition in some parts of the island; second, was an attack earlier that day on the U.S. Embassy.[8] Then on the 10th of March 1971, a bomb exploded at Dedigama in the Kegalle district; and on the 16th of March 1971 another explosion occurred at the University of Peradeniya.[9] These incidents alerted the government to the likelihood of an imminent concerted guerrilla attack. The police began to arrest more members of the J.V.P., sowing further fears of suppression within the J.V.P. movement. Nearly 500 members of the J.V.P. were already in custody, including Rohana Wijeweera, the leader of the movement. The J.V.P. leaders encountered with the ominous threat of provocative acts of the police directed the movement into violent retaliation.

7.3 Aims and Planning

The J.V.P.'s long-term political objectives in the uprising were to overthrow the ruling regime and to capture state power. The strategy that had been devised to capture state power was based on the strength and effectiveness of a one-day armed struggle, which the J.V.P. referred to as the 'socialist revolution'. The J.V.P. was convinced as to the feasibility of its strategy because of the government's meager military presence throughout Sri Lanka and its relatively ill-equipped apparatus for internal security. Consequently, the primary objective of the J.V.P. was to launch a vast frontal attacks on the state apparatus and thereby seize power.

In order to achieve this long-term objective, the J.V.P. had to fulfill certain immediate aims, the first of which was to capture and amass weapons and ammunition from police stations and military bases. Their second objective was to rescue their leader, Wijeweera, who had been confined in Jaffna Prison in the Northern Province of Sri Lanka.[10] Given the pre-insurrectionary objectives of the J.V.P., it was evident that its strategy was based on limited political objectives.

The decision to launch an armed struggle was arrived at by the politburo of the J.V.P. on the 2nd of April 1971 when they met at the hostel for the Buddhist clergy at the University of Vidyodaya.[11] The date and time of attack were set for the 5th of April 1971 at 11 p.m. The decision to attack and the date and time of the attack were communicated to the district cadres and local leaders, and through them were transmitted to all other members of the J.V.P.

7.4 Mode of Attack

The J.V.P.'s strategy for mounting the insurrection against the U.F. Government in April 1971 was developed in three phases. The first phase of the attack was focused on overpowering the police stations and military bases. The regular police forces in 1970 numbered 10,605, and were assigned to 266 police stations of which 53 were regional headquarters, 172 were staffed by 20 or fewer policemen, and 41 were smaller offices.[12] There were five major military bases widely dispersed throughout Sri Lanka in the following areas: Panagoda and Galleface in the Western Province, Diyatalawa in the Uva Province, Kandy in the Central Province, Matara in the Southern Province, and Anuradhapura in the North Central Province. In addition, there was an Air Force base located at Katunayake in the Western Province. Since the J.V.P.'s leader, Wijeweera, was then imprisoned in Jaffna, it was deemed necessary to attack concurrently that police station, the naval base and the prison in Jaffna in order to rescue him. The Prime Minister and other key officials were considered important targets for capture.

What was significant in their strategic plans was that the rural-based police stations, rather than the more strategically-based targets within the capital, were marked as prime targets.

The J.V.P.'s preoccupation with rural-based targets may be attributed to their assumption that the government was more unpopular in the rural areas, and that a larger stock of arms and ammunition could be procured with greater ease within those areas.[13] According to J.M. Van Der Kroef, the J.V.P.'s tactics appeared to call for a series of ever more violent confrontations with the police designed for the following two objectives: (*i*) to create the impression that the government was losing control; and (*ii*) to win new recruits in the aftermath of the government's suppressive measures.[14]

The plan of attack devised for the police stations and military bases did not differ. Accordingly, the attack was preceded by collecting shotguns which were available within the vicinity. The attackers were outfitted in home-sewn dark blue uniforms and were armed mainly with shotguns, locally-made hand bombs and 'Molotov cocktails'.[15] Groups of youth ranging from 40 to 50 in number were responsible for launching the respective attacks on police stations on the 5th of April 1971. First, all communications were disrupted and electricity supplies were disconnected. Their approach in attack varied. Some launched frontal attacks arriving in buses and lorries which had been forcibly commandeered, while others resorted to more surreptitious approaches. The overall method of launching surprise attacks, under the cover of darkness, was a valid form of guerrilla warfare.

Consequently, on the night of the 5th of April, the J.V.P. was responsible for the tumultuous violence, on a scale of which had never been experienced in Sri Lanka. The J.V.P. did not, however, successfully implement its full plan of action as its members failed to launch attacks in the following districts: Ampara, Nuwara Eliya, Baddulla, Rathnapura and Monaragala. Their failure to launch attacks within those districts was largely attributed to the curfew imposed by the government after being alerted earlier that day by a premature attack on the Wellawaya police station in the Monaragala District of the Uva Province. More importantly, the J.V.P.'s entire plan of attack had been revealed to the security forces by an informant. Likewise, the J.V.P. failed to attack any of the military bases as anticipated in their strategy. The number of police stations attacked was an area of dispute amongst scholars. A.C. Alles states that the J.V.P. attacked 74 police stations in the initial stage of the insurrection.[16] J. Jupp maintains that 93 police stations were attacked within the first two days.[17] Fred Halliday states that at the height of the armed struggle, between 90 to 100 police stations were abandoned or fell under the pressure of repeated attacks.[18] The J.V.P. was able to capture a mere five police stations in the initial wave of the attacks perhaps because a majority of these police stations were based in the rural sector and thus were dispersed over a vast area.[19] This may have led to the thin application of J.V.P. fighters across a wide line of attack.

The aftermath of the overall failure of the initial attack was characterized by a series of unfulfilled short term objectives. The J.V.P. had failed to capture a single major police station which would have been vital to the overall realization of their strategy. Second, they had failed to seize the Prime Minister or key members of her cabinet; nor had they succeeded in causing any disruption in the capital. Third, their feeble attempt to rescue their leader, Wijeweera, foundered. The J.V.P. not only failed to meet their immediate objectives, but also failed to ignite the mass uprising which had been anticipated in their military strategy.

The failure of the initial attack on the 5th of April 1971, gave rise to a second phase which was confined to the following districts: Anuradhapura and Polonnaruwa in the North Central Province, Kurunegala in the Central Province, Monaragala in the Uva Province, Kegalle in the Sabaragamuwa Province, and Matara, Galle and Hambantota in the Southern Province. Long-term occupation and open fighting with the military was confined to those areas. The earlier tactics, which had depended on a one-day attack to deal a single swift blow, were changed in favor of a protracted guerrilla warfare within the districts mentioned above. The police stations within those areas were either attacked or were likely to be attacked. Therefore, it was prudent if not necessary for the Sri Lankan Police to abandon their more isolated stations. Until about the 11th of April the police stations continued to be the most likely targets, especially in the rural areas. Several stations were either seized or destroyed, main roads and rail tracks were damaged, and communications were disrupted by the guerrillas. The J.V.P. assumed command in areas where the police had withdrawn and the civil administration was in disarray. They implemented the basic functions of distributing food, running post offices, and in some areas, conducting the judicial functions.[20]

During the first few days of the insurrection, the armed forces were not equipped to launch a significant counterattack as they lacked the military strength for such an operation. As a result they were on the defensive during the first two weeks of the uprising.[21] Consequently, the J.V.P. took advantage of this low resistance from the police and military forces, and thus occupied several major towns in semi-urban and rural areas. In these and in other towns which the J.V.P. successfully occupied, the police and public servants were besieged in public buildings. In some cases the J.V.P. passed over towns to instead secure the surrounding countryside, thereby isolating the government forces in the town centres. For instance, an army officer reported that on the 10th of April within the Kegalle District in the Sabaragamuwa Province, an area of about three acres where the Kachcheri (District Office), the police station and the Courts of Law were located was held by the armed forces while the J.V.P. dominated the rest of the district.[22] Once the J.V.P. had taken over these areas they successfully disrupted the transport system, telecommunications, power supplies and food distribution. The Inspector General of Police explained the situation as follows:

> As police stations were withdrawn and civil administration collapsed in these areas the insurgents took over. They distributed food from cooperative stores and even held their courts of Justice.[23]

The J.V.P.'s immediate objective during the first few weeks of the insurgency was to consolidate their power in areas where they had already gained a foothold, and then to launch attacks from these power bases. As a result they were engaged in fierce confrontations in some areas along the main road from Kegalle to Colombo, in a few areas in the Anuradhapura District, and in the South mainly centred around the small towns of Elpitiya and Deniyaya. Elpitiya was controlled for nearly three weeks by the J.V.P. The districts of Matara, Galle and Kegalle provided the J.V.P. with the most consistent and hard fighting support from the populace.[24]

The J.V.P. failed, however, to achieve its objectives during the second phase as it had in the first phase of its armed struggle. They not only failed to organize or mobilize mass support, but also neglected to launch an extensive propaganda to explain their ideology and objectives to the Sri Lankan people. Hence, when the Sri Lankan military forces launched their counter-attacks in the areas which the J.V.P. had occupied, the less-committed guerrillas retreated to areas of refuge in the hills and forests for lack of local assistance. Subsequently, the hard core members of the J.V.P. were also forced to retreat to the remote jungle areas and national parks with the aim of conducting protracted rural guerrilla warfare. The retreat itself was the third and the final phase of the armed struggle.

The guerrillas retreated to the jungles or national parks nearest to the areas they had formerly occupied. The steadfast members in the South made their way to the Sinharaja Rain Forest which was a Strict Natural Reserve of about 24,000 acres. The members in the Anuradhapura, Kegalle and Kurunegala districts decided upon either the Wilpattu Sanctuary (National Park) or the Ritigala Mountains, which are about 2,500 ft. high. Those based in Dambulla and Polonnaruwa retreated to the vast surrounding jungles. A group of 103 members from the South who intended to retreat to the Sinharaja Forest failed to do so largely due to their ignorance of the terrain and environs. By the 30th of June the few who had made it to this forest were either captured or surrendered.[25]

On the other hand, the retreat from the Kegalle and Kurunegala districts assumed a different dimension. On the 23rd of June the 200 guerrillas from those two areas decided to retreat to the Wilpattu National Park, and made their way there in two lots. The retreat took place under the cover of darkness and along unpopulated tracks to avoid any major confrontation with the armed forces. During the day they camped in isolated areas either on the mountains or in the jungles. A.C. Alles observes that this retreat was marked by murder, arson and looting commonly associated with terrorist activity.[26] This could only have offset their attempts at surreptitiousness and created new informants to tip the armed forces as to the guerrillas' whereabouts. Of the 200 who set out, only about 30 reached their destination. By the end of August 1971, 69 guerrillas were hiding in Wilpattu and about 50 in the forest surrounding Dambulla. Although these guerrillas intended to continue rural guerrilla warfare, the J.V.P. was not in a position to support such a protracted struggle for the following reasons: lack of manpower due to arrest of cadres, desertion or defection; lack of mass support; the recapturing of base areas by the Sri Lankan armed forces; lack of adequate food supplies, weapons and ammunition; lack of adequate training for such warfare; and the poor knowledge of the terrain and environs to which the remaining guerrillas had retreated.

According to V.I. Lenin, an insurrection should have two capabilities: the physical ability to overthrow a government; and the political ability to retain power for the insurgents.[27] Neither of these aspects was evident in the Insurrection of 1971. Moreover, there were several factors which subsequently resulted in the entire collapse of the J.V.P.'s armed struggle. One of the main reasons behind the J.V.P.'s defeat was the lack of a revolutionary environment. Charles Tilley asserts that revolution depends on the following proximate conditions:

(*i*) The appearance of contenders, or coalitions of contenders, advancing exclusive alternative claims to the control over the government currently exerted by the members of the polity;

(*ii*) Commitment to those claims by a significant segment of the subject populations (especially when those commitments are not simply acknowledged in principle, but activated in the face of prohibitions or contrary directives from the government);

(*iii*) Formation of coalitions between members of the polity and the contenders advancing the alternative claims; and

(*iv*) Incapacity or unwillingness of the agents of the government to suppress the alternative coalition or the commitment to its claims.[28]

None of these conditions were prevalent when the J.V.P. launched its armed attacks. Nevertheless, by attacking the police and security forces, the J.V.P. attempted to create a revolutionary ambience. Moreover, there was a lack of widespread mass discontent aimed at the U.F. Government and no visible erosion of its legitimacy when the J.V.P. decided to launch its armed attack. Ernesto Che Guevara categorically stated:

> Where a government has come into power through some form of popular vote, fraudulent or not, and maintains at least an appearance of constitutional legality, the guerrilla outbreak cannot be promoted, since the possibilities of peaceful struggle have not yet been exhausted.[29]

Another reason for the rapid failure of the insurrection was the J.V.P.'s omission of strategic provision for a sustained protracted military effort. The members who were engaged in the insurrection were not physically or psychologically prepared to continue an armed struggle, largely due to their scanty and inadequate training in military tactics and weapons use, and after their initial defeats, to their inadequate supply of arms and ammunition. The supply of arms to which the J.V.P. gained access was inferior and often out-dated. The shotguns and locally made hand-thrown bombs were not only inferior in quality but were in short supply, thereby placing the guerrillas in a vulnerable position as compared to their adversaries, the Sri Lankan armed forces who had superior training and fire power. The guerrillas' poor military training was clearly exemplified in their armed attack on the Polonnaruwa police station in the North Central Province where 39 activists of the J.V.P. were killed and many were wounded compared to few government casualties.[30]

According to Andrew C. Janos, the existence of a potential mass base that lends itself to mobilization through organizational channels or through mere physical concentration, affect the feasibility and success of insurrectionary warfare.[31] As in Guevara's theory of guerrilla warfare, an inherent part of the J.V.P. strategy was to mobilize the support of the masses once the insurrection had been initiated. The J.V.P. anticipated the support of the urban working class, the rural peasants and even the armed forces. In spite of the J.V.P.'s critical reliance on the masses, however, it did little or nothing to inform the general populace about its ideology or objectives. Its failure to launch an effective propaganda campaign against the government not only resulted in the non-mobilization of the masses during the insurrection, but also placed the J.V.P.'s sympathizers in a vulnerable position and inhibited new recruitment before the attack. The final outcome was that the masses were suspicious of the J.V.P.'s motives and opposed its activities, while the trade unions, including that of the Indian origin Tamil workers employed in the plantations, pledged their support to the U.F. Government. The left-wing unions in the Joint Council of Trade Union Organization (J.C.T.U.O.) also pledged their full support to the government and began organizing vigilance committees. Furthermore, T.H. Green observes that the guerrillas attacked local villages and isolated peasants in order to steal food and money, thereby alienating the population on which they depended and signaling the imminent defeat of the guerrillas by the government forces.[32] Consequently, one of the fundamental characteristics of the Maoist and Guevaran lines of guerrilla warfare, namely mass base, mass support and mass involvement, was not manifest in the case of the 1971 uprising.

The J.V.P. failed to gain the support of army and security forces as anticipated. The left-wing parties too were opposed to the armed attacks of the J.V.P. As Chalmers Johnson observes, the activists of the 1971 uprising hoped for intervention by international socialist forces.[33] As it would be discussed in detail later in this chapter, the socialist countries such as the Soviet Union and China assisted the U.F. Government instead of the J.V.P. Johnson suggests that the socialist countries did not come to the J.V.P.'s aid probably because the U.F. Government was already sufficiently left-oriented to suit both Moscow and Peking.[34] Although the Sri Lankan Government denied external involvement, the North Korean Embassy was ordered to close down, on the premise that its propaganda activities encouraged insurgency.[35] As a result the J.V.P.'s insurrection was almost totally isolated.

The lack of smooth co-ordination was another salient factor in this context. The armed attack was insufficiently co-ordinated to overawe the government security forces. The curfew and emergency imposed by the government and the suspension of public transport crippled the J.V.P.'s own communication network with their fighting units. The organizational structure which was based on a hierarchical system of cells not only isolated its members into pockets but also prevented vital interaction. Although its conspiratorial structure excelled for surprise armed attack, it was too fragmented for long drawn-out guerrilla warfare.

The low morale of the J.V.P. membership was another cause of the failure. The first surrender of nearly 4,000 members in response to an amnesty granted by the government from May 1st to May 4th shook the faith of the more committed members. The second request for surrender was issued on the 5th of June and was aimed at the guerrillas who had retreated to bases in secluded jungles. Finally, the failure to rescue their leader from prison left the J.V.P. hierarchy in disarray and ill-equipped to continue a protracted struggle. Considering the overall weaknesses inherent in the J.V.P.'s organizational structure and in their bid to capture state power, it was apparent that they were not authentically prepared to launch such an attack. Therefore, these cadres achieved only sporadic raids which continued until August 1971, and thereafter only occasional raids and hold-ups until mid-1972.[36] The insurrection was concentrated in terms of effort, but failed because it wasn't broad in actual force. According to Jupp, the failure of the single concentrated attack became such a liability that effective long-term guerrilla warfare did not follow the initial defeat.[37]

In spite of the defeat of the J.V.P., its last guerrilla fighters were not captured until 1976. The overwhelming defeat of the J.V.P. within three months of the initial attack did not mean that the impact of the uprising had abated. It not only left an indelible mark on Sri Lankan politics but marked the advent of a new trend in political violence.

7.5 U.F. Government's Response

Gurr surmises that a regime's basic options in the face of political violence are to increase coercive measures or to meet some or all dissident demands.[38] In the case of the 1971 insurrection, the J.V.P. mad no immediate demands other than state power. Thus, the U.F. Government's response to the uprising could be broadly perceived from two main aspects: the military and legal response, and the political response. The response had been planned since 1969 by the U.N.P. and then by the U.F., as has been discussed above. Therefore, the author broadly examines the government's counter offensive in early April 1971.

When the J.V.P. attacked on the 5th of April the government forces were ill-prepared to cope with the ensuing anarchy and disruptions in some areas. As mentioned earlier, during the first two weeks the armed forces were on the defensive, and the police stations in remote areas were temporarily closed. Consequently, 43 police stations in Kegalle, Anuradhapura, Polonnaruwa and Galle Districts were abandoned.[39] An all-island curfew was declared on the 6th of April and lasted until mid-July, except in the Western Province where it continued through November 1971. The J.V.P. as a political organization was proscribed and their publications including their newspapers were banned.[40] This ban also included any publications of other left-wing groups which propagated revolution.

The police force was far from equipped to confront the J.V.P. Therefore, the onus of combating the J.V.P. was undertaken by the Sri Lankan Army and the Air Force. A breakdown of manpower of the military and police as of April 1971 was as follows: Police, 12,500; Army, 7,000; Navy, 1,900; and Air Force, 1,500.[41] The security forces were small in number and the army commander stated that he had fewer than 7,000 trained men to crush the uprising.[42]

Realizing their weakness in numbers of trained men, the government sought volunteers for the military forces from amongst persons between the ages of 35 and 55 years because people in that age range were considered poor candidates for J.V.P. infiltration. Furthermore, the existing government forces were not adequately equipped to confront a mainly local-based uprising. The government, as a result, appealed to foreign governments for assistance in the form of military equipment and advisers. The United Kingdom, the United States, the Soviet Union, India, Pakistan, Yugoslavia and Egypt responded to this appeal by providing arms, ammunition, other material and personnel. The strength of their response was significant, for they not only supplied military equipment but also gave legitimacy to the Sri Lankan Government's counter-insurgent policies. The assistance of the external powers, however, was designed to sway the U.F. Government due to Sri Lanka's strategic importance in the world and regional balances of power.

The U.K. was the first foreign state to respond positively to the Sri Lankan Government's request for military assistance. During the early period of the insurrection, small arms and ammunition were provided from the British bases in Singapore. The British Government mediated to enable the Sri Lankan Government to purchase six Bell helicopters from the U.S.A. Several scout cars, evidently in the range of 12-18, were supplied between the 20th and 25th of April.[43] Nevertheless, in spite of Britain being Sri Lanka's historical defense partner and the traditional source of military supplies, it was evident that the degree of British assistance was very limited.

The assistance from the U.S.A. during the early period of the insurrection was tepid. In addition to the six Bell helicopters supplied through the U.K. on a commercial basis, the U.S.A. shipped spare parts in mid-April. In early May the U.S.A. contemplated supplying several additional Bell helicopters, as well as mortars, small arms and ammunition, and a large amount of medical supplies from U.S. bases.[44] The very limited nature of the assistance offered by the U.S.A. indicated its reluctance to get involved in the counter-insurgent operation in Sri Lanka.

The Sri Lankan Government received more significant military assistance from the U.S.S.R., including five Mig-17 fighter air-craft and six helicopters, 60 pilots and air-craft technicians, an unspecified number of ground maintenance crew, and 20 armoured cars and transport facilities for delivering police communication equipment from the German Democratic Republic.[45]

Of these countries, no other country was more deeply involved in the April 1971 insurrection than India whose intervention was partly based on the Indian Government's assumption that the People's Republic of China stood behind the

J.V.P. insurrection.[46] India dispatched a large quantity of small arms and ammunition, six helicopters with crew, 150 Gurkha soldiers, and four naval frigates reportedly carrying 2,500 other military personnel.[47] The Gurkha forces were deployed to guard the international airport at Katunayake. The four naval frigates patrolled Sri Lanka's coastal waters to prevent the smuggling of arms to the J.V.P.[48] Furthermore, had an extreme movement gained power in Sri Lanka, it was believed that India was prepared to invade the island and that plans to that effect had been drawn by the Indian Army staff.[49]

Pakistan not only supplied arms but went further in offering military experts and forces. There was widespread belief in Sri Lanka that Communist China was linked to the J.V.P.'s insurrection as it had been to some of the other Asian insurrections. It was obvious in any case, that Communist China was not as willing as Britain or the U.S.A. to come to Sri Lanka's aid. During the first week of the insurrection, a Communist Chinese ship carrying small arms to Tanzania entered Colombo Harbour. The Sri Lankan Government sought, without success, to persuade the Chinese and Tanzanian governments to release a portion of the arms for the U.F.'s counter-offensive against the J.V.P.[50] The Communist Chinese later announced full support for the Sri Lankan Government, offered an interest free long-term loan of Rs. 150 million in convertible currency, and provided five patrol boats. In spite of the J.V.P.'s apparently Maoist nature, the J.V.P., given its rejection of Maoist theory, would never have been acceptable to communist Chinese. Consequently, as James manor and Gerald Segal observe, Sri Lanka became the only state to have received military aid simultaneously from the U.S.S.R., the U.S.A., the U.K., India and Communist China.[51] There is no evidence, however, of any foreign personnel being used in the military operations against the J.V.P. guerrillas.

The military aid was received by the Sri Lankan Government within three weeks of the J.V.P.'s first attack. Thus reprovisioned, the U.F. Government was prepared to launch its counter-offensive with the objective of total capitulation by the J.V.P. This objective was further specified in the statement made by a Sri Lankan Army official:

> We have learned too many lessons from Vietnam and Malasia. We must destroy them (the insurgents) completely. We have no choice.[52]

The primary outcome of the counter-attack was the recapturing of the abandoned police stations by the armed forces. Military co-ordinators were appointed to govern the districts where political violence was intense, and the armed forces had to assist the police in safeguarding police stations. Then the J.V.P.'s camps were attacked by air and land, the air attacks serving as a means of preliminary attack before the army moved in. The army used mortars before proceeding en masse to confront the J.V.P. bases. There were many reported instances of the military and the police using dissenters and captured insurgents to further the government's counter-insurgent warfare. Consequently, by the end of April, the government forces had recovered from their initial set backs. According to T.H. Green, the isolation of the guerrillas reinforced effectiveness of the government's counter-insurgent programme.[53] The Prime Minister offered an amnesty between the 1st and 4th of May to those who were willing to surrender.[54] It was reported that 3,978 surrendered in response to this amnesty. Yet another amnesty was offered from the 7th to the 9th of June when 236 surrendered.[55] The J.V.P. members who surrendered and those who were captured were kept in detention without trial.

7.6 Magnitude of the Violence During the 1971 Insurrection

For Gurr the magnitude of political violence is likely to be greatest when regimes and their rebellious opponents are more or less evenly matched in coercive control and institutional support.[56] In this context the author wishes to focus attention on how and where the violence originated and spread; its duration and its perpetrators. The political violence that broke out in April 1971 was mainly confined to certain predominantly rural areas. The centers of insurgent violence were: Matara and Galle Districts in the Southern Province; Kurunagala District in the North Western Province; Kegalle in the Sabaragamuwa Province; Anuradhapura and Polonnaruwa Districts in the North Central Province.[57] The areas mentioned above include some of the least urbanized areas in Sri Lanka, which shows the rural dimension of the insurrection. It was further evident that the uprising was not confined to any particular region but was a phenomenon which was scattered throughout Sri Lanka, polarizing the rural sector. The fact that insurgent violence was concentrated in Sri Lanka's rural areas during the 1971 insurrection contradicts Huntington's observation that in the poor nations, acts of political violence may very well occur in the more prosperous regions.[58] The 1971 uprising, however, failed to gain ground in the more urbanized or modernized Western Province which according to Huntington's modernization theory should have proven to be the most susceptible region.

The duration of political violence, it is contended by Gurr, is a factor which determines the final outcome of violence. The history of Third World insurgencies since the Second World War has indicated that guerrilla conflicts which were terminated in less than three years were often unsuccessful. The duration of a war for three to nine years meant that there was a fifty-fifty chance of success. Conflicts which lasted beyond ten years demonstrated a perceptible decline in the prospects for a successful revolution, though the chance of a compromise settlement was high.[59] The insurrection of 1971 did not last for more than three months and thus, according to empirical evidence, was doomed to failure.

The level of participation in the political violence of 1971 varied according to the ethnic distribution throughout Sri Lanka. It was evident that ethnically, the Sri Lankan Tamils, the Indian Tamils and the Muslims excluded themselves from the armed struggle. The Sri Lankan Tamils dominated the Northern Province, while the Indian Tamils had settled in the up-country plantation areas, and the Muslims and some Sri Lankan Tamils resided in the Eastern Province. All of these areas were totally free from the J.V.P.'s armed struggle. Examined demographically in terms of religion, the Hindus, the Muslims or the Christians (mainly Catholics) who dominated the west coast of Sri Lanka, did not take pat in the political violence. The insurrection was instigated and perpetuated only by secular Sinhalese and Sinhala-Buddhists.

In terms of occupations, the non-participation of the urban working class in the 1971 insurrection was evident. S.P. Huntington observes that the participation of the peasantry in political violence in the Third World is also crucial.[60] Nevertheless, data pertaining to the participants in the uprising in terms of occupations indicates the clear exclusion of the rural peasantry from the armed struggle. The uprising was exclusive not only to the J.V.P.; the dominant youth representation within the J.V.P. meant that the insurgents and their collaborators were mainly limited to the Sinhala-Buddhist youth from the rural sector.

In the absence of accurate data pertaining to the number of participants in the uprising, defining accurate figures has become a matter of conjecture. The statistics which have been made available were subject to dispute and contradictory. The most reliable indicators may be the total casualties during the period of insurrection from early April to August 1971, and the number taken into custody by the police and armed forces. As in most armed conflicts, the method of determining the deaths in the field may be deemed flawed as deaths are often merely assumed. As for the number of detainees, a differentiation must be made between the J.V.P. members who were captured before the attack, those who surrendered during the two amnesty periods and thus may never have even participated in the attack, and the guerrillas who were taken prisoner in the field. It is widely believed, therefore, that the true number of attackers and the human toll of the 1971 insurrection may never be known.

The government version of the number of deaths from the 1971 uprising was exemplified in the statement of the Prime Minister, which revealed that 1,200 guerrillas, civilians and government forces had been killed as a result of the uprising.[61] The following Table 7.1 is an official estimate of the number of deaths and casualties based on the total number of known participants.

According to Table 7.1 the death ratio between the government armed forces and the J.V.P. fighters was 1:19. There was no doubt regarding the government estimates of the number of deaths among the security forces. As mentioned earlier, the number of deaths among the J.V.P., however, could be highly inaccurate. Some of the figures that have been suggested in this context are discussed below.

Table 7.1 Number of Deaths and Wounded in the Events of 1971

Persons	*Number Killed*	*Casualties*
Guerrillas	1096	Not Known
Civil	41	193
Police	37	87
Army	19	15
Air Force	4	28
Navy	3	—
Total	1200	323

Source: A.C. Alles, Insurgency 1971, (Colombo: The Colombo Apothecaries Co. Ltd., 1976), p. Appendix l. p. (iii).

Tillman Durdun, the political correspondent of *The New York Times,* reported that the death toll reached a figure of 6,000 deaths.[62] Rene Domount, who was in Sri Lanka at the time of the insurrection, estimated that 8,000 were killed by the government forces.[63] Rohana Wijeweera, the leader of the J.V.P., issued a statement from prison in 1972 arguing that nearly 15,000 members of his movement had been killed as a direct result of the government's campaign to suppress the violence.[64] The major reason for the government's understatement of the casualties was to avoid national political and security implications, and international accusations of human rights violations.[65]

The contradictory statistics declared to these sources indicate the ambiguous nature of the statistics pertaining to the 1971 uprising. It has been noted that these unofficial statistics do not stipulate a breakdown in numbers according to the role of the participants, either as guerrillas, civilians or the branches of the armed forces and the police. In spite of these ambiguities, it could be safely claimed that the actual number of deaths ranged between a minimum of 6,000 to a maximum of 8,000.

As discussed earlier, the number of deaths and the number of J.V.P. members and sympathizers in custody indicate, as closely as possible, the number of participants in the 1971 uprising. When the uprising was curbed in August 1971, there were a total of 17,953 in custody as a result of the violence. This total was subdivided as follows: 11,748 arrested and 6,025 surrendered.[66] Not all of those prisoners were members of the J.V.P. On the contrary, it was obvious that some of them were never involved in the armed struggle. Therefore, the author assumes that only about 20,000 to 25,000 actually participated in the insurrection.

7.7 Pattern and Outcome

As discussed in Chapter 2, the theoretical analysis of the insurrection of 1971 varies according to the theoretical orientation of each theorist.[67] Chalmers Johnson's typology of violence places the insurrection of 1971 within the typology of mass insurrection. According to Gurr's analysis this insurrection represents an internal war, while S.P. Huntington's typology perceives it to be a revolutionary war conforming to the eastern pattern. The macro perspective of these theories limits their applicability to the specific pattern and sequence of political violence in Sri Lanka.

The main objective of this chapter is to examine the pattern of the 1971 armed uprising. In this context the author has thus far examined its aims, mode of warfare, magnitude of violence and government response. All of these aspects of the uprising indicate the revolutionary objective and the pre-planned strategy of the armed struggle. On the other hand, the insurrection was also one of exclusivity and isolation in terms of the lack of mass participation or awareness. As discussed in Chapter 5, the inherent emphasis on the participation of Sinhala-Buddhist rural youth defines the insurrection of 1971 as a rural insurrection launched by the Sinhala-Buddhist youth from the semi-urban and rural sector.

There were no systematic studies based on the outcome of the 1971 insurrection. Therefore, the author wishes to examine its consequences from the following two aspects: the fate of the participants of the armed struggle, and its impact on the country's socio-economic and political fabric. In the aftermath of the armed struggle of 1971, the U.F. Government devoted itself to the process of liquidating the J.V.P. as a movement and dealing with its known members. The ban on the J.V.P. was enforced with more vigour after the insurrection, and the movement was suppressed to an extent that it was forced to go completely underground. The government devised a dual approach in dealing with the participants of the armed struggle in 1971. There were approximately 18,000 supposed J.V.P. members and collaborators in custody by the end of 1971. Of this total, charges were brought against 3,872 persons who were believed to have been involved in armed attacks on police stations and other acts of political violence. A special court called the Criminal Justice Commission (C.J.C.) was set up in May 1972 to try those prisoners. There were nearly 140 inquiries which led to the identification and prosecution of 41 leaders at the main trial. In addition, another 139 inquiries were in progress involving nearly 3,000 defendants of whom 2,536 had pleaded guilty. When the C.J.C. trials concluded in 1975, 92 of the accused had been acquitted, 2,519 had been released on suspended sentences, and 365 had been sentenced to prison terms.[68] Those who were not formally charged were subject to rehabilitation programmes.

According to Sri Lankan Government statistics, about 12,000 suspects were placed in rehabilitation camps, including two universities which were temporarily converted into rehabilitation centres. At the same time, the government began releasing detainees, but as Douglas Hyde has observed, this process, was slow.[69] Nevertheless, compared to release rates in other Third World countries, the rate of release in Sri Lanka was quite fair and timely. Table 7.2 below illustrates this process of release over the period between 1971 and 1975.

Table 7.2 The Number in Custody: 1971-75

Year	*Number in Custody*
1971	14,000-18,0000
1972	10,000
1973	4,600
1974	600
1975	295

Source: R.N. Kearney, "Note on the Fate of the 1971 Insurgents in Sri Lanka", *Journal of Asian Studies,* Vol. 37, No. 3, (1977), pp. 515-519.

Those who were never taken into custody went underground with the objective of re-organising the J.V.P. Their further clandestine existence, however, was short-lived. When the U.N.P. Government offered yet another amnesty in 1977 the remaining detainees, including the J.V.P.'s leader, Wijeweera, was released, and the J.V.P. entered the mainstream of Sri Lankan politics.

The immediate economic cost of the armed uprising was high. According to the Minister of Finance in 1971, the total economic cost was estimated to be Rs. 333 million.[70] Another significant economic outcome of the political violence in April 1971 was the Land Reform Act of 1972 (L.R.A.) which established a Land Reform Commission (L.R.C.) with the power to expropriate privately-owned agricultural land above a ceiling of 50 acres per person.[71] The economic cost and land reform apart, the insurrection also had far reaching political consequences for the political parties within the government, the S.L.F.P., the L.S.S.P. and the C.P. The insurrection marked the beginning of conflicts within the coalition government and subsequently led to its break-up.[72] The L.S.S.P. broke away from the S.L.F.P. coalition government in 1975, while the C.P. did so in 1977.

Moreover, the insurrection had an adverse effect on those parties in the General Election of 1977. The S.L.F.P., L.S.S.P. and C.P. suffered a severe defeat in the areas where the insurrection had spread in 1971. As a more long-term impact, the insurrection seriously challenged the legitimacy of the centre-left and orthodox left-wing political parties in Sri Lanka. The more immediate outcome was the increased attention paid to the armed forces and their expansion. There was not only a significant rise in enlistments but also an acceleration of the expenditure for arms and equipment. Consequently, the Sri Lankan military establishment which until then had remained in the political background gained significance and came to the fore after the uprising.

According to Fred Halliday, the uprising revealed to the left-wing parties that left-wing-orientated armed struggle is possible in colonial and former colonial countries.[73] Whether or not insurgents could succeed in such an ethnically-mixed social and multi-party political environment is another matter. The uprising also unintentionally influenced the emergence of the Tamil guerrilla organizations who were opposed to the Sinhalese aims of the J.V.P. In the long run, the insurrection of 1971 raised a question about the continuing viability of political institutions in Sri Lanka.

7.8 The Tamil Guerrilla Warfare

The second part of this study concentrates on the political violence which gathered momentum among the Tamil community during the year following the abortive armed struggle in 1971. There are certain significant factors which should be considered in studying the Tamil guerrilla warfare which did not apply in the case of the J.V.P.'s insurrection. First, the political violence committed by the Tamil groups was protracted, unlike the uprising of April 1971 of which the government was in total control within a few months. The Tamil political violence continued to assume additional diverse facets and dimensions which cannot be included in this study. Secondly, the Sri Lankan Government imposed a censorship on news items and other information pertaining to the guerrilla organizations and their activities. To circumvent these limitations, the author has limited the scope of this study to a period between 1972 and July 1987 when the Indo-Sri Lanka Peace Accord was reached, although some observations on the more recent developments are included in the conclusion. As in the study of political violence in 1971, the author concentrates on certain aspects, which are as follows: short-term factors, aims and objectives, forms of warfare, magnitude of violence, government response and outcome.

7.9 Short-term Factors in Tamil Guerrilla Warfare

The political violence waged by the Tamil guerrilla organizations like that of the J.V.P. insurrection of 1971 was pre-planned and organized. Unlike the J.V.P. insurrection which was staged solely by one organization, the Tamil violence was motivated and launched by factional groups such as the L.T.T.E., the T.E.L.O., the E.P.R.L.F., the P.L.O.T. and the E.R.O.S. The L.T.T.E. has nevertheless emerged as the most potent of the surviving groups. The possibility of a violent confrontation between these groups and the government forces had been imminent since 1972.

A combination of two strategic features is cited as the short-term factors which heightened the potentiality for Tamil-inspired political violence and confrontation in Sri Lanka. The first is the commitment to, and planning and preparation for guerrilla warfare. The strategy adopted by those underground groups was multi-faceted. Government property and Tamil politicians who supported the political party in power were prime targets. A campaign of assassination was launched against Tamil politicians who were deemed to have 'collaborated' with the Sinhala-dominated U.F. Government. Another aspect of this strategy included large-scale bank robberies which were apparently intended to finance the purchase of arms for the guerrilla movement. The violation of state property on the Republican Day anniversary in 1973 was yet another example of this campaign. On that day, 49 buses were attacked resulting in six being completely burned, and an attempt was made to derail a train. Chalmers Jonson postulates that guerrilla warfare serves as a short-term factor for political violence.[74] A detailed analysis of the strategy of the Tamil groups is examined in section 7.11 on their forms of warfare.

The second factor was inherent in the political and security policies adopted by the U.F. Government to counter the Tamil guerrilla violence. In applying those policies, the government failed to address the legitimate demands for redress among the Tamils' grievances, namely: language, land, unemployment and university education. The government's approach led to the further escalation and militarization of an ethnic conflict which had hitherto depended on agitation, political negotiation and other non-violent activities. The U.F. Government launched a political campaign spearheaded by the mayor of Jaffna, Alfred Durayappah, to secure a party base in Northern Sri Lanka. There, he utilized attractive incentives, such as state employment and other material benefits to expand party cadres and organizations. These policies, however, clashed with the objectives and demands of the Tamil youth underground organizations for an independent Tamil state. Furthermore, when the leader of the moderate T.U.L.F., S.J.V. Chelvanayakam, resigned his parliamentary seat to crusade for a mandate calling for a sovereign 'Eelam Tamil state', the by-election was delayed until February 1975.[75]

The military intervention was comprised mainly of the deployment of police and armed forces, and the revival of the state of emergency from the previous year, 1971. A more overt military campaign, came into effect after 1972, when the Tamil underground movements became increasingly active. The heightened activity of the Sri Lankan security forces only deepened the tension between the Tamil youth and the police in the Northern Province. The Sinhala-dominated police came to be identified as an enemy of occupation. In this context, two incidents were recounted here as events which generated a fear of further repression amongst the Tamil youth and led directly to the first Tamil guerrilla violence. The first was the role of the police at the fourth meeting of the International Association of Tamil Research (I.A.T.R.) held in Jaffna in 1974. On the final day of this conference a speaker from India, whose application for an entry visa had been rejected by the Sri Lankan Government, appeared on stage. The police intervened to disperse the crowd, resulting in the death of nine people and many were wounded. The other incident concerned the death of the Tamil pioneer guerrilla activist, Ponnadurai Sathyaseelan, who committed suicide while in police custody, having been accused of numerous bank robberies. His death had an emotional impact on the other Tamil activists. The initial acts of political violence by the Tamil guerrillas in retaliation against the police, marked the beginning of a protracted guerrilla warfare led by the Tamil youth.

In addition, the following two factors influenced the Tamil youth to resort to political violence. The first was the left-wing insurrection by the J.V.P in April 1971, which indicated the weakness in the security organization of the country. The insurrection also gave insights to the credibility of an armed struggle to achieve political objectives. The second was the birth of Bangladesh, former East Pakistan, through an armed struggle of Mukti Bahini, which indicated the importance of the involvement of the Government of India in creating a separate state in South Asia.[76]

7.10 Aims and Objectives

The major long-term political objective and driving force of the Tamil guerrilla movement was always clear: the creation of an independent sovereign socialist state of Tamil Eelam. The primary means of achieving this goal was the mobilisation of a people's war of national liberation and socialist revolution. There were also certain secondary, more immediate objectives which had to be achieved before the final aim could be realized. Some of those short-term objectives were as follows: to provoke terror upon the Tamil population in Northern Sri Lanka so that no one would extend any co-operation to the government; to assassinate Tamil politicians and their political supporters as a warning against interference; to paralyze the government administrative apparatus in the Northern Province; to politicize the Tamil population; and to publicize their cause to gain grass root support throughout Sri Lanka toward a people's war. To determine the nexus between such short term objectives and the growth and development of political violence among the Tamil community, the author examines the forms of warfare adopted by the Tamil guerrilla organizations.

7.11 Forms of Warfare

The political violence which gained ground among the Tamil community throughout the 1970s assumed a different dimension from that of the armed struggle of 1971. Whereas the insurrection in 1971 had concentrated on an intense confrontation with the government, the Tamil guerrillas rejected that strategy in favour of protracted attacks over many years. Consequently, in spite of their insurrectionary orientation they depended on terrorism and guerrilla warfare as their prime strategy. According to Brian Crozier, whatever the country or the circumstances, insurrection tends to follow a sequence of three stages; terrorism, guerrilla warfare and full-scale war.[77] T.P. Thornton made a related observation that a rigid classification is not valid, and terror can extend throughout all three stages.[78] The Tamil guerrilla violence, however, did not follow the third phase completely. The initial attacks were activated by the Tamil guerrillas as early as 1972. Although these attacks were sporadic, they were carefully planned against selected targets of strategic importance. As the scope of their activities expanded, a distinct pattern began to emerge as the guerrillas moved from seemingly haphazard attacks to more structured operations. This pattern of political violence can be broadly divided into three phases in chronological order as follows:

(*i*) The first phase: 1972-1976

(*ii*) The second phase: 1977 through ethnic violence of 1983

(*iii*) The third phase: 1983 to the Indo-Sri Lanka Accord in July 1987

It was evident that the objectives, targets and mode of attack varied from one phase to another. Nevertheless, due to the factors mentioned earlier, this aspect of the study is confined to sources which deal with the subject in general.

7.12 The First Phase: 1972-1978

When the Tamil guerrillas committed their first acts of political violence in 1972, their intention, at first, was confined to arousing nationalism and a consciousness among the Tamil community of the need for political organization. On the basis of those initial objectives, the Tamil guerrillas concentrated on symbolic targets such as government buildings and public transport. The guerrillas' first attacks, and the U.F. Government's harsh response to them, widened the implications of non-cooperation with the government. The guerrillas sought to use the government's counter violence to their advantage by mounting an immediate propaganda campaign through the foreign press to embarrass the Sri Lankan Government internationally. They also hoped to obtain foreign assistance by demonstrating the urgency of the ethnic problem.

The Tamil guerrillas resorted to terrorism in the form of sabotage and robbery without the appearance of a coordinated plan.[79] According to T.P. Thornton, terrorism may gain political ends in one of two ways: either by mobilizing forces and reserves sympathetic to the cause of the insurgents; or by immobilizing forces and reserves that would normally be available to the incumbents.[80] Terrorism in this phase was aimed at immobilizing pro-government forces, which will be discussed below in detail. The post-1975 period was not a profoundly active period for the Tamil guerrilla organizations, but rather was an intermediate interval devoted to strengthening their operational capacity. This does not mean to imply that they were inactive during those years. In 1972 alone, 22 terrorist incidents were reported mainly confined in the Jaffna peninsula.[81] Tamil politicians who cooperated with the government in office were deemed to be collaborators with a repressive system and thus became the targets of assassination. Alfred Duraippah, the mayor of Jaffna, in 1975 was the first Tamil politician to be assassinated. His death marked the beginning of organized political terrorism in the North[82]

This assassination of Duraippah also signaled a new trend in political violence in which the emphasis shifted from symbolic targets to practical ones such as political personalities. Organized gang robberies of public institutions served not only to weaken the government's position, but also as a means of gathering resources and gaining much needed domestic and international publicity. The Tamil guerrillas also assassinated a number of other Tamil politicians of the S.L.F.P. and U.N.P. in the Jaffna Peninsula.[83] According to S.P. Huntington, the elimination of prominent members of the target group who refuse to cooperate with the rebels convinces other members of the group that the only prudent course is to buy safety by contributing money to the rebels, furnishing them with information, or cooperating with them in other ways.[84]

The weapons which were utilized during this first phase of violence were self-manufactured hand bombs and time bombs, shotguns and pistols.[85] According to P. Wilkinson, the symbolic and propagandist functions of terrorist acts may be rather more important in the early stages of insurgency, and should be recognized by the governmental authorities as key indicators of immediate danger and of the likely escalation of violence to come.[86]

7.13 The Second Phase: 1977-1983

During the second phase of Tamil political violence, the guerrillas' scope of activity expanded, accompanied by the use of more and more sophisticated weaponry. Of the many factions which emerged during this second period, the L.T.T.E., the T.E.L.O. and the P.L.O.T. gained supremacy. The main aims of their guerrilla activities were to block all police investigations pertaining to terrorist acts, accumulate arms and ammunition, collect funds, and provoke the Sinhalese population into ethnic-based violence which would create the appropriate ambience for

Tamil agitation for a separate state. In this context the most likely targets were the police and other armed forces, banks and police informers.

At the outset, the assassinations were confined to Tamil police officers who were responsible for investigating the Tamil Terrorist acts in the North. The L.T.T.E. was responsible for the murder of four C.I.D. officers in 1978. Until 1980, the L.T.T.E. and T.E.L.O. were responsible for most of the attacks against members of the Sri Lankan forces.[87] With the expansion of their scope of activity, the nature of the targets widened to include Muslim and Sinhala members of the police force. From 1977 to July 1983, 50 police officers and servicemen, 11 Tamil politicians, 13 police informers and 16 civilians were killed.[88] These attacks triggered the ethnic violence of 1977 and 1981.[89] The outbreaks of ethnic violence, which followed the Tamil guerrilla assaults, heightened national and international support for Tamil separatism. According to government sources, during the seven years from 1971 until the introduction in 1978 of the bill proscribing the Tiger movement, the total number of crimes attributed to terrorist activity amounted to 75. During the following year this total rose to 84.[90]

The L.T.T.E., which had established itself as the foremost guerrilla group, planted a bomb in a civilian aircraft which was due for an internal flight on September 7th 1978, the date on which the new constitution was promulgated.[91] Other than the overt manifestations of such violent incidents, the sensationalism achieved by the sheer magnitude and intensity of these episodes was crucial to the international attention drawn to the question of Tamil Eelam. From August 1979 the Tamil guerrilla groups had the ability to operate from base areas located in the sanctuary of the state of Tamil Nadu in Southern India. This provided a safer refuge than did Sri Lanka's jungle and national reserves which had been the only haven for left-wing J.V.P. guerrillas after the 1971 insurrection. The bases in Southern India also gave the Tamil guerrillas ample opportunity for continued para military training, and offered them a secure location for weapons storage. According to S.P. Huntington, the existence of an external base of support beyond the territory of the target government is obviously a major aid to revolutionary forces.[92]

From 1981 the scope of activity of the Tamil guerrillas expanded to include attacks in the North on police stations and on military convoys and patrols, which proved to be vulnerable targets for hit-and-run attacks. For example, the police station at Anaicodai was attacked by the P.L.O.T. in 1981, and in 1982 the police station at Chavakachcheri was attacked by the L.T.T.E. Yet, the guerrilla groups failed to coordinate their actions despite their similar tactics.

The following Table 7.3 illustrates the extent of the terrorist activities from 1977 to 1983.

Table 7.3 Summary of Terrorist Incidents from 1977-1983

Year	*Casualties of Forces*	*Casualties of Civilians*	*Murders of Politicians*	*Attacks on Police Stations*
1977	03	03	1	-
1978	08	04	-	-
1979	03	03	-	-
1980	00	-	1	-
1981	09	04	1	1
1982	09	10	1	1
1983	18	05	7	-
Total	50	29	11	2

*Source: This is the Truth...*The Associated Newspapers of Sri Lanka Ltd. (Colombo 1983), pp. 6-9.

Table 7.3 clearly indicates that the political violence generated by the Tamil youth acquired other diverse facets as they strengthened in numbers and military supplies. During this period the civilian targets were confined to police informers who were perceived to be traitors to the Tamil cause.[93] Government statistics for the period from 1978 to 1983 credit the Tamil guerrillas with more than 265 bombings, robberies, assaults and other criminal activities.[94]

Following their attacks on the police stations, the Tamil guerrillas widened their activities against the Sri Lankan military units. From July 1982 to July 1983 several major attacks were launched against the security forces, the most crucial of which was the ambush of an army patrol by the

L.T.T.E. which killed 13 soldiers.[95] Although the attack was not decisive in magnitude or intensity, it triggered an outbreak of ethnic violence which had been imminent for sometime. From the perspective of the Tamil guerrillas, the ethnic violence of July 1983 proved to be a much anticipated opportunity to internationalize their cause. Thereafter, the Tamil guerrillas, particularly the L.T.T.E., stepped up their raids at an alarming rate and as K.M. de Silva observes, concentrated their attacks on the security forces and carefully selected targets.[96]

7.14 The Third Phase: 1983 to 1987

The third and the final phase which began with the acceleration of guerrilla attacks, ended with the Indo-Sri Lanka Accord of 1987. The significance of this period in terms of Tamil political violence lies in the determination and purpose with which the Tamil guerrillas intensified their activities. The attacks were primarily motivated by the increasing demand amongst the Sri Lankan Tamil community for a separate state. As a result, a new wave of armed attacks was launched against police stations, army convoys and civilian targets. There was not only a sharp increase in political violence in terms of scope and frequency but it also became an all-encompassing phenomenon. Although the Tamil guerrillas confined their operations mainly to the Northern and Eastern provinces, they also made their impact felt beyond those administrative boundaries. As mentioned before, the imposition of censorship by the government has put serious constraints on studying the entire scope and depth of the activities of the Tamil guerrillas. Nevertheless, the author delves further into the recorded incidents and the likely motives which determined the extent of the political violence.

After the ethnic violence of 1983, it is evident that the pattern of political violence took yet another turn. From 1984 to 1985 the hit-and-run guerrilla strategies adopted by the L.T.T.E., the P.L.O.T., and the T.E.L.O., and the newer factions, the E.P.R.L.F. and the E.R.O.S., resulted in attacks on police stations in the Northern and Eastern provinces, with the specific intention to capture arms and ammunition. Large guerrilla units numbering between 50 and 250 participated in these attacks. Table 7.4 displays the number of police stations which were subject to attack and the number of weapons which fell into the hands of the Tamil guerrillas.

Table 7.4 Police Stations Attacked by Tamil Guerrillas

Year	*No. of Police Stations Attacked*	*No. Killed*	*No. of Weapons Removed*	*Groups Responsible*
1981	01	02	23	P.L.O.T.
1982	01	03	30	L.T.T.E.
1983	—	—	—	—
1984	12	29	103	LTTE.PLOT.TELO
1985	12	17	316	LTTE.EROS
1986	08	01	—	TMPP
1987	01	—	—	—
Total	34	53	453	—

Source: Sri Lankan Research Centre, *Tamil Terrorists Destroy Police Stations in the North and East,* [leaflet, no date].

Accordingly, 34 police stations in the Northern and Eastern provinces were attacked by the Tamil guerrillas, resulting in the death of 53 police officers and the loss of 453 weapons. Other than the single attack on the Nikawaratiya police station in the North Western Province in April 1985 by the P.L.O.T., the other attacks were confined to police stations in the Northern and Eastern provinces. The attack on the Chavakachcheri station was significant because it was the largest single armed operation launched by the Tamil guerrillas since they had begun their campaign of violence in 1972.[97]

As indicated in Table 7.4, a majority of the attacks on police stations were master-minded by the L.T.T.E. These sporadic attacks compelled the government to withdraw personnel from nine police stations in the Northern Province. After 1984 the activities of the existing police stations were seriously curtailed. The Jaffna police ceased patrolling and instead relied on the army for protection.[98]

The assassination of police informers was intrinsically linked to the attacks on police stations. The guerrillas branded the informants as traitors to the Tamil cause for an independent state.[99] These killings came to be known as 'lamp post' killings because most of the victims were tied to lamp posts before they were executed. A note was pinned to each of the bodies identifying them as collaborators. The primary objective of these murders was to prevent any information from being leaked to the police and armed forces; the second objective was to warn potential collaborators of their fate and to prove the certain reach of guerrilla justice. According to government sources there were about 60 lamp post killings in 1985, and 80 to 120 in 1986.[100]

The successful attacks on police stations gave sufficient confidence to the Tamil guerrillas to engage the Sri Lankan Army, Navy and Air Force. The dates of these confrontations were often marked as 'confidential' information and, therefore, the author is confined to the incidents which have been made public. At the initial stages, the attacks on the armed forces were aimed at army convoys by means of landmines, ambushes and booby traps. A majority of the army casualties were attributed to landmine attacks. Edgar O'Balance has recorded 14 landmine attacks from 1983 to 1986.[101]

The army and navy camps within the Northern and Eastern provinces were also vulnerable targets for the Tamil guerrilla attacks. By early 1984, encouraged by their initial successes, the guerrillas had escalated their operations against military bases, prompting vigorous counteraction by the Sri Lankan armed forces. Of the attacks launched by the guerrillas, three attacks were significant because they show that the guerrillas had overcome their previous divisive attacks. The attacks which took place between January and February 1985 were launched against the Karainagar Naval Centre, the Kokkilai Army Camp and the Kilinochchi Police/Army Camp. The naval centre was attacked by the E.P.R.L.F.[102] The T.E.L.O. was responsible for the attack on the Kokkavil army camp in May 1985.[103] The land-based attacks launched by the major factions were followed by confrontations at sea between the Sri Lankan Navy and the guerrillas enroute to their own bases. The navy sought to halt the smuggling of arms and the increased mobility of the guerrillas to and from their bases in the South Indian state of Tamil Nadu completely. In 1987 the guerrillas, in another combined operation, attacked the army camp in Kankasanthurai, killing 18 soldiers.[104]

The overriding objective of the guerrillas' persistent attacks on military bases was to compel the government to withdraw the armed forces from the Northern and eastern provinces. The procurement of arms and ammunition was an important, but, at that stage, only a secondary objective. The guerrillas also hoped to provoke the armed forces into making indiscriminate assaults on the civilian population thus inducing a mass uprising against the government in those provinces.[105]

The attacks were also geared at a more long-range strategy to transform a political crisis concentrated in the Tamil areas in Sri Lanka into a broader military confrontation with the government, and thereby secure the support of the Tamil masses in the fight for a Tamil state. By July 1985 the government forces considered the northern part of the Jaffna peninsula an area to be avoided. The guerrilla strategy and tactics thus achieved half of the desired effect.

Another major development during the third phase was the attacks on Sinhala civilians residing in isolated villages in and around the Northern and Eastern provinces. The first of successive attacks occurred on the 30th of November 1984, when Tamil guerrillas attacked and killed Sinhala civilians residing on the Kent and Dollar farms in the Mullaitivu district. In December 1984, guerrillas killed 80 Sinhala civilians in the fishing communities of Kokilai and Nayaru in the North Central Province. Fourteen Sinhala fishermen and their families were killed by the Tamil guerrillas in early 1985 in the Eastern Province.[106] Other incidents of political violence resulting in the death of Sinhala civilians were reported throughout 1985 in the Eastern Province. The obvious objective was to drive out all Sinhala settlers from the 'traditional homeland' claimed by the Tamils. In addition to the direct attacks on civilians, in August 1984 a bomb which was planted aboard an Air Lanka flight to Colombo exploded at a terminal of the Madras Airport in India killing 29 people.[107] This was the first terrorist attack outside Sri Lanka attributed to the Tamil guerrillas and was carried out by the Tamil Eelam Army (T.E.A.), a breakaway faction of Tamil Eelam Liberation Army (T.E.L.A.).

As the activities of the Tamil guerrillas became more assured and daring, their terrorist activities began to impinge on the lives of the Sinhala civilians residing outside the Northern and Eastern provinces. The first such attack took place in May 1985 in Anuradhapura, the historical capital of the North Central Province.[108] A group of Tamil guerrillas belonging to the L.T.T.E. disguised themselves as government soldiers and fired their weapons indiscriminately killing 146 civilians within the city centre.[109] In April 1987 the L.T.T.E. stopped three buses, two lorries and a private automobile within the Trincomalee district and shot the passengers, amounting to 126 deaths.[110] Carrying their terrorist onslaught still further, members of E.R.O.S. exploded a car bomb in May 1987 in Colombo, killing nearly 200 people.[111] On the 2nd of June 1987, 33 Sinhala passengers on a bus, 29 of whom were Buddhist monks from the Eastern Province were killed.[112] From 1984 to 1987, irrespective of the urban/rural dichotomy or any other differences, Sinhala civilians were targeted for Tamil terrorist attacks.

Table 7.5 illustrates the number of civilian deaths as a result of terrorist attacks from 1984 to 1987. As depicted in Table 7.5, the L.T.T.E. and E.R.O.S. were responsible for all of those terrorist activities.

Table 7.5. Deaths of Civilians As a Result of Terrorist Activity

Year	*Place*	*Number Killed*	*The Group Rsponsible*
1984	Mulativu	70	LTTE
1984	Kokilai	80	LTTE
1985	Anuradhapura	132	LTTE
1986	Colombo	200	EROS
1987	Colombo	200	EROS
1987	Eastern Province	175	LTTE

Source: Penelope Tremayne, "Sri Lanka Chronology of a Conflict", in Defence Year Book 1988, The Royal United Services Institute for Defence Studies, (London: Brassey's Defence Publishers, 1989), pp. 387-431.

The objectives of the attacks on Sinhalese were threefold. First the attacks on Sinhala civilians residing within the

Northern and Eastern provinces and in the peripheral areas were carried out with the purpose of establishing the dominance of the Tamils within the areas deemed to represent the 'traditional homeland'. The second objective was to provoke the Sinhala population into resorting to ethnic violence which would boost the Tamil propaganda-mill and create an appropriate ambience for their agitation. Finally, the acts of political violence in Southern Sri Lanka were expected to compel the government to concede and negotiate. As observed in *The Economist,* the Tamil guerrillas had to persuade more Tamils of the need for a separate state. The most effective mode of persuasion was to provoke ethnic violence against the Tamil populace and the best way of doing so was to murder large numbers of ordinary Sinhalese.[113]

The sabotage of economic targets was another aspect of the violence organized and carried out by the Tamil guerrillas. Until 1984, public property, including the transport service, was sabotaged only in the Northern and Eastern regions. After 1984, attacks on public property spread to other areas in Sri Lanka. The first attack on property outside the Northern and Eastern provinces occurred on January 28 1984, when the E.R.O.S. detonated a bomb in the Hotel Oberoi in Colombo. The intention of the E.R.O.S. was to disrupt the "All Party Conference" convened by the government as a preliminary step towards negotiations.

In October 1984, the E.R.O.S. was responsible for blowing up an oil pipeline in the north of Colombo.[114] The E.R.O.S. launched a similar bombing attack on the 3rd of May 1986, against an Air Lanka Tristar Jet at the Katunayake International Airport killing 21 people, seventeen of whom were foreigners, and injuring forty-one.[115] The incident was the first in which non-Sri Lankans were the victims. The E.R.O.S. carried out another attack that day at the Central Telegraph Office in Colombo, killing 14 people.[116] By mid-1986 the Tamil terrorist attacks which had previously been confined mainly to the Tamil-dominated areas had become a grim reality in the city of Colombo. In June 1986 the Tokyo Cement Factory in Trincomalee was yet another target. The factory was jointly owned by the Japanese Mitsui Cement Company and a group of Colombo investors.[117] The Tamil guerrillas thus expanded their terrorist activities to deter any foreign investors from investing within Tamil-dominated areas. The strategy to debilitate the Sri Lankan economy not only encompassed the tourist industry; the tea industry was also vulnerable. Rumors that Sri Lankan tea had been poisoned alarmed foreign buyers, leading them to apply more stringent tests before purchasing Sri Lankan tea.[118] The E.R.O.S. was intent on sabotaging the economy, thereby touching the nerve centre of power.[119]

Public transport and communications were two other relevant functions which came under terrorist attack. A train was blown up on the 19th of January 1985 resulting in 34 deaths.[120] In addition, main bridges, including five in Jaffna, were blown up. The magnitude of this sabotage campaign was partly concealed by censorship and the reluctance of the government to divulge the exact nature of the problem. Although the sabotage was aimed primarily at economic targets, however, ironically, it resulted in more civilian casualties than did any other form of guerrilla violence in Sri Lanka.

The Tamil guerrillas also expanded their activities to include kidnapping for ransom as a source of funding for their operations. According to Penelope Tremayne, the Tamil guerrillas kidnapped 120 civilians during 1986. A majority of the kidnapping incidents ended in the release of the hostages despite the rejection of the ransom demands. Kidnapping was also a means of gaining national and international attention, as for example in the kidnapping of an American couple in 1984 and a British journalist in 1985. The American couple, Stanley and Mary Allen, was seized from their home in Jaffna on May 10th 1984. The kidnappers, who threatened to kill them, demanded a ransom of 50,000,000 rupees in gold (U.S. $2,000,000) and the release of 20 guerrilla suspects. The government rejected those demands and the couple was released on May 14th 1984.[121] Mrs. Penelope Willis was seized in Mullaittivu sometime between January 17th and the 22nd 1986, by the E.R.O.S. She was accused by her captors of being a British spy working in collusion with the Sri Lankan Government. She was released on the 18th of February 1986, following negotiations between British diplomats and the Tamil guerrillas and the intervention of the

International Red Cross.[122] Thus kidnapping proved to be, at least for the Tamil guerrillas, an unfruitful strategy.

The third phase of political violence strongly indicates that the Tamil guerrillas widened the scope of their activities further with ever more sophisticated and lethal weapons. In tracing the steady growth of violence Mastrangelo reports that from 1974 to 1982 only seven incidents of terrorist activity were reported; in 1983 the total rose to 13 incidents; in 1984 it escalated considerably to 92 events; and in 1985 the level of political violence rose further to 110 incidents.[123]

This phase is also significant as the period during which the Tamil guerrillas resorted to conventional warfare and comparatively open armed confrontations with the Sri Lankan military forces and police. The L.T.T.E. emerged as the dominant force both amongst the other Tamil guerrilla factions and in the fight against government units. The L.T.T.E. succeeded literally in confining the government troops to their barracks. The L.T.T.E. was largely responsible for limiting the activities of the government forces to the Central and Southern provinces.[124] Consequently, by July 1985 the northern part of Jaffna had been abandoned by the Sri Lankan forces. The L.T.T.E. assumed the functions of civil administration as the U.N.P.'s influence receded. By 1986 Jaffna was totally controlled by the L.T.T.E., who had successfully outmaneuvered the government. Their civil duties included collecting taxes and promoting primary education. As a prelude to declaring an independent Tamil state, and to ensure law and order, the L.T.T.E. 'assumed judicial responsibilities' by establishing 116 national courts.[125] While engaged in civil administration, however, the L.T.T.E. was still committed to an all-out war against the Sri Lankan Government. Hence, until July 1987 there were intermittent confrontations with the armed forces. The L.T.T.E.'s intention to declare the Jaffna peninsula as an independent region on the 1st of January 1987 failed.[126] Ultimately the L.T.T.E. failed in its objective to defeat the army in successive battles and to compel the government to negotiate for peace. A.S. Balasingham exemplifies these objectives in the following statement:

> We will force the government to negotiate on our terms when we are able to break the backbone of the Sri Lankan (Sinhala)

Army. The negotiations will be over the demarcation of boundaries for Eelam.[127]

The Tamil guerrillas' goal proved to be overly ambitious. The security forces were able to recapture most of the areas conceded to the L.T.T.E. There are several reasons for this set back, the complexity of which prevents the author from delving very deeply. The following factors, however, are salient in surmising the guerrillas' failure to realize their main objective. The first was the lack of unity and the keen competition for dominance amongst the Tamil guerrilla factions. They fought amongst themselves for supremacy over the Tamil community. In 1986 the L.T.T.E. eliminated the T.E.L.O. all together and dispersed the E.P.R.L.F. by murdering its leading hierarchy. The P.L.O.T. was also compelled to suspend its activities after its leader died under mysterious circumstances. Secondly, as Bruce Matthews observes, there was a profound lack of coordination amongst the various factions pertaining to ideology and strategy.[128] As a result, the Tamil guerrillas were eventually outclassed by the security forces. Thirdly, the guerrillas were unsuccessful in obtaining the support of the Tamil masses. The Tamils of Sri Lanka have never been a coherent community. Nor did a majority of them ever embrace Marxism-Leninism or support the concept of socialist Eelam. The moral support for the Tamil guerrillas in Northern Sri Lanka, however, was generally high. It was mainly derived from both the failure of the government to reach an equitable solution and the repression by the government security forces in the Tamil areas. Furthermore, the fierce ethnic attacks on the Tamil community in the South in July 1983 converted many Tamils in the Tamil-dominated North into guerrilla sympathizers. The Sri Lankan Tamils residing outside the Northern Province, however, were in the minority and thus were unsupportive of the guerrillas' objective of a separate Tamil state. The Indian Tamils in the plantation sector and the Muslims in the Eastern Province mainly supported the U.N.P. Government rather than the guerrilla organizations.[129]

Finally, the Indian Federal Government did not intervene as anticipated by the Tamil guerrilla organizations. According to the Tamil insurgents, the indiscriminate abuses by the Sri

Lankan armed forces against both the guerrillas and the civilians, combined with the refugee problem in the Indian state of South India, were supposedly adequate reasons for an Indian intervention on the side of the guerrillas. They also hoped to appeal to India on the basis of its protective image as 'mother India'.[130] As Bruce Matthews observes, none of these appeals for Indian assistance worked to the advantage of the guerrillas.[131] Moreover, the assistance provided by the Indian state of South India proved inadequate, and was eventually thwarted by the Indian and Sri Lankan national governments. The author concludes that the Tamil guerrillas were heavily though unrealistically dependent on the Indian national government, and particularly the state government of South India. Their dependency went unfulfilled, thus contributing to their eventual long term defeat at the hands of the better trained and equipped Sri Lankan military forces.

7.15 Government Response

The response of the Sri Lankan Government was critical in the context of the Tamil guerrilla warfare. According to S.P. Huntington, the reaction of the government in a revolutionary war goes through two phases: first, the government tends to treat the insurrection as a traditional problem for the police and military, and minimizes the threat of the revolutionary forces; second, the government recognizes that the revolution requires not only a much larger and different military effort to suppress it, but also demands an integrated politico-economic effort to counter the appeals of the revolutionaries to the masses. It also recognizes the need to overhaul its organizational structure dealing with the rebellion and to merge political and military responsibilities in a single individual.[132]

As in the insurrection of 1971, however, the government's initial response relied on coercive measures, which could be broadly divided into two periods: The first was before 1983; and the second was after the ethnic violence of 1983. All of these measures were conditional upon the following factors: the strength and the competence of the armed forces, the availability of foreign military aid, the ideological orientation of the government's domestic and foreign policies, and the nature and the changing magnitude of the Tamil insurrection.

At the initial stages of the guerrilla violence in 1972 the Sri Lankan Government dealt with each incident individually as an act of political violence. Therefore, the police were responsible for dealing with the acts of violence in the North and were empowered by emergency laws to do so. As the level of political violence gradually escalated through 1971 the police were incapable of dealing with an organized campaign of violence. Consequently, the government was compelled to deploy the Sri Lankan Army and the Navy around the Northern Province to assist the police. Simultaneously, Brigadier Tissa Weeratunga was commissioned by the government as the Commander of the security forces in Jaffna. The Prevention of Terrorism Act (Temporary Provision) of 1979 empowered the police and the armed forces with the capacity to search and seize people and property, and to internment those arrested. The act also declared kidnapping and abduction punishable offences entailing life imprisonment.[133] The other measures taken to discourage the growth and expansion of political violence were as follows: abolishing the standardization rules pertaining to university admissions; according the Tamil language the status of a national language in the Constitution of 1978[134]; and decentralizing local political structures with the District Development Councils (D.D.C.) Act in August 1981. The D.D.C. Act was intended to decentralize local administration and devolve powers to the 25 districts in Sri Lanka. Within two years of its implementation, however, the D.D.C. scheme proved to be a failure due to the lack of finances and the absence of an authentic devolution of power.[135] Following ethnic violence of 1983, the government response was an ill-defined mixture of political and military approaches.

The following discussion views first the military measures, and subsequently the political measures. The military measures were taken in conjunction with legal action to counter the guerrilla violence. The state of emergency imposed in 1983 was subsequently extended monthly until December 1988. The introduction of the state of emergency imposed censorship of domestic media coverage of both guerrilla activities and the government's counter measures. The Sixth Amendment to the Constitution in July 1983 prohibited the public expression of the separatist cause.[136]

The Sri Lankan security forces, too, were found to be ill-equipped and ill-trained to confront the Tamil guerrilla forces. The security forces were also overwhelmingly Sinhalese-Buddhist. Consequently, the Tamil guerrillas, who were predominantly Hindu, came to regard them as an alien army of occupation. Hence, the structure of the forces was reorganized, the enlistment was increased, and the quality of the training improved. By the end of 1983, however, the government had changed its approach to the ongoing violence and had assimilated a new institutional structure and new policies to face it. As a result, in May 1984 a new Ministry of Defense was established to coordinate the activities of the security forces and the police in activating the counter-insurgent and counter-terrorist programme.

In addition, two auxiliary militia units were formed in an effort to awaken the public to the dangers of complacency. The two services were the National Security Services under the direction of the Prime Minister, and the Man Power Mobilisation Office which came within the purview of the Ministry of Youth Affairs. The security services were deployed at the district level in collaboration with the police and the office of the local government agent. These forces were ascribed a surveillance role involving the collection of information and the protection of public institutions. They came under the direct supervision of the Minister for Transport in his role as Chief of Industrial Security. The 'mobilisation of manpower' meant that the youth were being trained in military combat in order to supplement the armed forces. In a further move towards consolidation, in 1985 the government initiated new operational arrangements which brought together all three forces, the Sri Lankan Army, Navy, Air Force and police under one command under a merged unit called 'Combined Operations'.[137] Appendix 8 further illustrates this organizational structure which was meant to counter the Tamil guerrilla warfare.[138]

In order to adequately strengthen and reinforce the Sri Lankan armed forces, the government had to appeal to foreign governments for assistance, as it had done during the 1971 insurrection. This dependency provided yet another opportunity for foreign states to become directly involved in Sri Lankan internal affairs, and thus to compete again for the strategic advantages offered by Sri Lanka's geographic location. The Sri Lankan Government's request for foreign assistance internationalized the Tamil conflict. S.P. Huntington aptly observes that the longer the domestic violence continues in a society, the more likely are foreign governments to become involved on one side or the other.[139] Moreover, according to George Modelski, the search for outside aid and the effort to counteract that search make every internal war of international concern.[140] Modelski further observes that given an internal war in one state, the foreign policy of the second state faces the following three choices:

(*i*) helping the weaker party—usually, but not invariably, the insurgents, and thus embarking on subversion.

(*ii*) helping the stronger party—usually but not invariably, the incumbents, and thus engaging in foreign aid; or

(*iii*) working for a conciliatory solution to the conflict by attempting mediation.[141]

The response of foreign governments to the renewed appeals for military aid, however, was rather limited when compared to the aid extended in 1971. The U.S. and British governments were reluctant to become involved overtly in the Sri Lankan conflict as they had in 1971.[142] In spite of that reluctance, however, covert aid was forthcoming. Former British Special Air Services (S.A.S.) commandos who, while ostensibly working for a private security organization called the Keenie Meenie Services Ltd (K.M.S.), helped train the Sri Lankan anti-terrorist forces.[143] The Sri Lankan Government was also successful in contacting the Israeli Government through the U.S. Government to request further military training. The Israeli Secret Service, Mossad, was invited to train the Sri Lankan security forces in counter-insurgency.[144] For this purpose the Israel Foreign Service set up an Interest Section at the U.S. Embassy in Colombo. On the other hand, the Soviet Union expressed no interest in supporting the Sri Lankan Government. This was in sharp contrast to the aircraft, weapons and the military advisers the U.S.S.R. had supplied during the 1971 Insurrection. The pro-government media in Sri Lanka alleged that the Soviet Union was supporting the Tamil guerrillas although there was no evidence to support that claim. Pakistan, however, not only supplied arms but was also involved in training Sri Lankan security personnel. The other countries that supplied arms were Communist China, South Africa, Singapore and Malaysia.[145] In July 1984, Communist China agreed to supply new military equipment, some of which was designed for sophisticated counter-terrorist operations.[146] The Communist Chinese support seemed meager in light of their much expanded global arms-export drive to earn foreign currency. The following Table 7.6 shows arms purchases by Sri Lanka from 1983 to 1988.

Table 7.6. Arms Purchases by Sri Lanka: 1983-1988

Country	*1983*	*1984*	*1985*	*1986*	*1987*	*1988*
U.S.A.	3	1	28	29	10	-
USSR	-	-	-	-	-	-
China	-	-	-	2	8	-
Italy	-	-	-	5	-	-
U.K.	-	-	15	15	-	-
Israel	-	31	26	-	9	44
Singapore	-	38	-	4	-	-
South Africa	-	-	12	10	-	10
Total	3	70	81	65	27	54

All figures are in millions of U.S. dollars at constant 1985 prices.
Source: Deepak Tripathi, *Sri Lanka's Foreign Policy Dilemmas,* The Royal Institute of International Affairs, (1989), p. 33.

No other external power was more deeply involved in Sri Lanka's ethnic conflict than India. The role of India is undoubtedly important, but is not a subject of detailed inquiry in this study due to its complexity and magnitude. Nevertheless, the Indian response was a crucial factor in moulding the Sri Lankan Government's counter-insurgency policies pertaining to the Tamil insurgency. Therefore, the author wishes to examine the salient aspects of India's role in the conflict.

The Indian response, unlike that of the other external powers, was neither automatic nor inevitable. Two factors determined India's involvement and limited her options vis-à-vis the Tamil insurrection. The first factor virtually constituted the basis of India's security doctrine. India's perception of South Asia as a security zone, which India alone was entitled to dominate and manipulate, did not in the opinion of the Indian Government, permit the involvement of other external forces within the region. India's regional doctrine for South Asia was best articulated by the following statements:

> India will neither intervene in the domestic affairs of any states in the region, unless requested to do so, nor tolerate such intervention by an outside power. If external assistance is needed to meet an internal crisis, states should first look within the region for help.[147]

Secondly, there was growing unease in the South Indian state of Tamil Nadu especially among more than 50 million Indian Tamils who had traditionally been close to the Sri Lankan Tamils regarding the political developments there. Therefore, the government and political parties in Tamil Nadu pressurized the Indian central government to mediate with Sri Lanka. As in the Insurrection of 1971, India chose to assist the Sri Lankan government not in terms of military aid, but rather as a mediator with the Tamil guerrillas and as a regulator of the stability of the crisis. The nature and extent of India's involvement in the conflict, however, varied substantially throughout the 15-year period under study. It is also noteworthy that the governments of the U.S.A., the U.K. and the U.S.S.R., chose not to extend at least overt military assistance during the Tamil insurgency as those states had during the J.V.P. insurrection in 1971. As previously observed, other powers such as China and Pakistan provided limited assistance. Consequently the Sri Lankan Government was left with no other option than to depend heavily on the Indian Government as a mediator.

From 1983 onward, the security forces were enlarged. The police service employed 14,500 personnel in 1983; this increased to 24,000 by 1988. The following Table 7.7 indicates the expansion of the security forces in Sri Lanka between 1983 and 1988.

Thus by 1987 the total strength of the Sri Lankan security forces stood at about 60,000.[148] The number of security forces was also bolstered after 1984 by the establishment of para-military forces for internal security.[149] In addition to the growth of the security forces, the Ministry of National Security in 1985 created a special 'Naval Surveillance Zone' under the purview of the Sri Lankan Navy within Sri Lankan waters encompassing the north western, northern and eastern coasts. The purpose of this surveillance zone was to curb the activities of the Tamil guerrillas who were receiving training and equipment from the South Indian state of Tamil Nadu.[150] Another significant step was the formulation of a new government policy on peasant resettlement in 1985 within the boundaries of the Tamil-dominated provinces. Its main objective was to confine the Tamil guerrillas to Jaffna.[151] The policy initiated the programme to resettle 200,000 peasants, including 150,000 Sinhalese and 50,000 peasants of mixed descent in the Northern Province. The settlement of these peasants was a security-cum-development strategy which aimed at creating a security cordon across the North. What the Sri Lankan Government did not foresee, however, were the fierce attacks inflicted upon these migrants by the Tamil guerrillas. The attacks not only halted any subsequent resettlement but drove away those who had already recolonised the area.

Table 7.7. The Security Strength of Sri Lanka

Forces	*1983/1984*		*1987/1988*	
	Regular	*Reserves*	*Regular*	*Reserves*
Police	14,500	-	21,000	28,000
Army	11,000	14,000	40,000	
Navy	2,960	582	4,000	
Air Force	2,600	1,000	3,700	
Home Guards		5,000		
Special Task Force			1,500	
National Auxiliary Volunteer Force			5,000	
Total	31,060	25,582	75,200	28,000

Source: IISS, *The Military Balance, 1983-1984,* p. 99 and *The Military Balance,* 1987-1988, p. 172.

By the end of 1985, however, the government had reinforced its position sufficiently to launch a counter-attack in the Northern and Eastern provinces.[152] The government relied heavily on the army for the forces and material needed to launch the offensive. By then 111 army camps had been dispersed in the Northern and Eastern provinces. Twenty-three camps were concentrated around the town of Trincomalee in the east which was the scene of a major military confrontation later.[153] Thus, the counter-insurgency policy relied on small unit warfare.

In late 1986 the government launched an enhanced offensive from land, air and sea putting the guerrillas on a defensive position and into retreat.[154] The Sri Lankan Government was soon forced to abandon the offensive due to the pressure from the Indian Government to find a non-military solution to political violence. Hence, the Sri Lankan Government sought to arrive at a political solution through peaceful negotiations while apparently rejecting the military course. P. Venketeshwar Rao observes that both domestic and international pressure compelled the Sri Lankan Government to concede the necessity to negotiate with the Tamil political parties and to accept the role of India as mediator.[155] Consequently, the government followed a two-pronged policy: pressuring the guerrillas surreptitiously by military means, while negotiating concurrently with them through the Indian mediators.

The Sri Lankan Government called for an All Party Conference (A.P.C.) to discuss the crisis of ethnic conflict and terrorism. R.N. Kearney, on the other hand, interprets the A.P.C. as a response made to appease the Indian Government by showing that the Sri Lankan Government was striving to arrive at a negotiated settlement.[156] Sixteen political, religious and ethnic organizations participated in the A.P.C.[157] The areas set for negotiation had been predetermined and memorialized in a document known as 'Annexure C' during late 1983 after talks between the Sri Lankan President, J.R. Jayawardena, and the Indian Prime Minister, Indira Gandhi, and her special envoy, G. Parthasarathy.[158] Jayawardena's proposals for the devolution of a limited measure of autonomy to regional councils were abandoned, however, due largely to the opposition from both the Tamil and the Sinhalese communities in Sri Lanka.[159]

Until the end of 1984, the government refused to negotiate with the Tamil guerrilla organizations.[160] Nevertheless, the Sri Lankan President and the new Indian Prime Minister, Rajiv Gandhi, met on four occasions during the next two years to forge a political settlement. The first decisive measure to emerge from these talks was the scheduling of the Thimphu (Bhutan) Talks in June 1985. The Sri Lankan Government and representatives of the Tamil guerrilla groups met on the 18th of June 1985, for introductory discussions.[161] Those discussions were also made possible by agreement between the Sri Lankan Government and the Tamil guerrillas to cease hostilities for three months. The two groups of representatives met twice in Thimphu for talks, the first time in July and the second in September 1985. The talks ended in deadlock, however, when the Tamil guerrillas rejected the government's offer to devolve more power and authority to the District Councils, and the government refused the Tamils' request for a separatist charter.[162]

The failure of the Thimphu Talks, which had been seen as a breakthrough in negotiations toward a peaceful settlement, gave the Sri Lankan Government no alternative than to resume its course toward a military solution. The government perceived the Tamil problem as an illegitimate armed threat which had to be tackled by the Sri Lankan military services. With the failure of the Thimphu Talks, the government and the guerrillas resumed their military confrontations. By the end of 1985, the government was in a much stronger position to launch more intense military operations against the Tamil guerrillas in the Northern and Eastern provinces.[163] Initially, the military operations were launched in the Eastern Province. As previously noted, later that year Trincomalee became the site for a major confrontation with the Tamil guerrillas.[164] Thus, the confrontations which became a cycle of terror and counter-terror soon developed into a full-blown internal war. By September 1986, more than 100,000 civilians both Sinhala and Tamil, had been rendered homeless in the Northern and Eastern provinces as a result of these subsequent developments.

In March 1986, the government launched an all-out offensive against the guerrilla bases in Jaffna.[165] The Indian response to these operations, however, was negative. The Sri Lankan

Government was once again compelled by the Indian Government to negotiate with the T.U.L.F., which represented the Tamil moderates. Once again there was deadlock with the T.U.L.F. and the guerrilla groups rejected the government proposals. The second breakdown of negotiations was decisive for the Sri Lankan Government as they hoped to launch 'Operation Liberation', which was to be the final all-out offensive. The three-pronged attack was coordinated to simultaneously shell the guerrilla bases by sea and air from the north, and mount a land invasion by the army from the south. The fact that the army and other forces were almost entirely composed of Sinhalese proved to be a major barrier in mobilizing the support of the civilians behind the government forces. This was contrary to the experience of 1971, and due mainly to the earlier reprisals of the armed forces against civilians. By 1986 the army camps were under siege, and were isolated by guerrilla mines and booby traps also on the roads and trails.[166] The government's full-scale operations did not yield its anticipated results due to international pressure on the Sri Lankan Government to withdraw its forces and accusations of brutality to civilians. Yet again an attempt was made to summon a Political Party Conference (P.P.C.). The guerrillas again rejected the government's proposals leading to the launching of the government's third major offensive in 1986, this time concentrated in the Jaffna Peninsula. In January 1987 the Sri Lankan Government imposed a total economic blockade on the peninsula.[167] This action effected the civilian population more than the Tamil guerrillas, and thus hardened the resistance of the Jaffna populace to the government's position.

All military operations came to a standstill in April 1987 when a unilateral cessation of hostilities was announced by the government, to be effective from the 11th to the 21st of April 1987. Nevertheless, the acceleration of guerrilla activities activated the government's plans for 'Operation Liberation' which had been held in abeyance. The main objective of the government's plan was to recapture the areas which the L.T.T.E. had occupied. The army succeeded in reaching the Jaffna Peninsula. Once more the Indian Government decided to intervene, this time more directly in the form of air drops of relief supplies to Jaffna in June 1987 to end the blockade.[168] Following India's aid to the

Tamils, 'Operation Liberation' collapsed. According to George Modelski there are three types of endings to civil wars: an outright win by one party, a lasting separation or a negotiated settlement.[169] What the Indian intervention achieved was a denial of victory for the government and a separate state for the Tamil guerrillas. Consequently, the final outcome was a negotiated settlement agreement signed by the Sri Lankan President and the Indian Prime Minister in June 1987 in Colombo. The agreement which came to be known as the Indo-Sri Lanka Accord marked the end of the third phase of Tamil political violence, and was followed by yet another phase of the Tamil insurgency in Sri Lanka.[170]

7.16 Magnitude of Political Violence

The author now focuses on the following aspects of political violence activated by the Tamil guerrilla groups: duration, area of expansion and participation. The duration of the Tamil guerrilla warfare eludes accurate assessment as their activities were not divulged by the Sri Lankan Government until about 1975. Although the Tamil guerrillas had been active since 1972, they did not emerge as a *bone fide* threat to the central government until the eruption of the ethnic violence in 1977. The ethnic violence in 1983 served to further expand their activities. The subsequent Indo-Sri Lanka Accord in June 1987 succeeded in disarming the P.L.O.T., the T.E.L.O., the E.P.R.L.F. and the E.R.O.S., but failed to disarm the L.T.T.E., the major guerrilla group. As a result, the L.T.T.E.'s guerrilla-cum-terrorist activities did not cease and are still on-going. The author notes again that this study is limited to a period of 15 years, beginning in 1972 and ending in 1987.

The guerrilla activities which were initiated within the Jaffna Peninsula in 1972, had by 1982 gradually spread to the Tamil–dominated districts in the Eastern Province. The districts in which these activities occurred are: Vavunia, Mannar, Trincomalee, Batticaloa, Jaffna, Ampara and Mulativu.[171] It should be noted that this strain of violence spread in areas which had remained undisturbed during the 1971 insurrection. For example, after 1984 civilian targets in Colombo and Anuradhapura were also vulnerable to attack. In spite of their bases in Tamil Nadu, the Tamil guerrilla movement was regionally-based in Northern Sri Lanka, unlike the 1971 insurrection which had been nationwide.

The undercover nature of the Tamil movement restricts an assessment of the actual number of guerrillas who were mobilized. Yet it is clearly evident that the overwhelming majority were, in terms of ethnicity, from the Sri Lankan Tamil community. The participation of Muslims or Indian Tamils was marginal while the Sinhalese remained totally aloof from the Tamil guerrilla movement. In terms of religion, a majority were Hindus with only marginal representation of Christians. Although the contribution by expatriate Tamils was significant in terms of their financial aid and public protests, there was no evidence of their having had direct participation in the armed struggle. Nor was there any evidence of the involvement of mercenaries or of the Tamil peasants.[172] The role of women in the guerrilla movement was viewed ambiguously in spite of some evidence of their direct involvement in the guerrilla groups. There was no tangible evidence of their involvement in any armed warfare at the early stages, reflecting the traditional role ascribed to women within the Tamil society. However, this situation was changed by the latter period where the participation of women was evidenced in attacks and as suicide bombers. In contrast to the rural-based Sinhalese youth who perpetrated the armed struggle of 1971, the Tamil youth who participated in the political violence during the period 1972-87 were drawn from both the rural and urban sectors.

Like the number of guerrillas in the insurrection of 1971, the number of participants in the Tamil guerrilla warfare has been hard to assess. It was evident that the number of guerrilla fighters and sympathizers varied from one stage to another. Prior to 1977 there were less than 50 Tamil guerrillas, but by July 1983 the total membership had risen to nearly 200. The number of participants increased after the ethnic violence of 1983. By 1987 the total had seemingly exploded to between 5,000 and 10,000.[173]

The human costs of the Tamil political violence in terms of the number of deaths have also been ambiguous and difficult to determine. As in the 1971 insurrection, the casualties in the long drawn out Tamil campaign were high but never accurately assessed. According to Bruce Matthews, by 1984 over 2,500 Sri Lankans had been killed as a result of this conflict.[174] Sri Lankan Government statisticians have arrived at 6,000 deaths broken down as follows: 600 Sinhala civilians, 500 military and police personnel and 5,000 Tamils.[175] Pro-Tamil human rights organizations claimed that the number of deaths was closer to 10,000[176] Sinha Ranatunga also claimed that over 7,000 were killed from 1983 onward.[177] Other sources have assessed the number killed between 1983 and 1987 to be 5,000.[178] Considering the conflicting assessments it could be safely estimated that numbers ranging from 6,000 to 10,000 persons had been killed as a result of this political violence. There were also 6,000 to 8,000 political prisoners. These statistics further indicated that the Tamil guerrilla violence was a protracted struggle of a magnitude and intensity hitherto unsurpassed in post-independent Sri Lanka.

7.17 Pattern and Outcome

In the final part of this section of the analysis, the pattern of violence, the subsequent development of the Tamil guerrilla groups, and the short-term socio-economic and political impact of the violence will be viewed. The protracted nature of the Tamil political violence in Sri Lanka makes it difficult to define a distinct pattern. Certain salient features, however, have emerged which indicate a general pattern of violence. First, the objective of the political violence was primarily secessionist. Almost all of the participants in the violence were Tamil-Hindu youth. Moreover, it was an ethnic insurgency which depended heavily on urban terrorism and rural guerrilla warfare to achieve its objective. In comparison to the insurrection of 1971, the political violence perpetuated by the Tamil guerrillas was not a mere domestic conflict. Apart from foreign aid, the Tamil conflict also had an international dimension given the guerrilla bases located in South India and arms training in the Middle East. It was thus secessionist guerrilla warfare heavily influenced by external factors.

In addition to the human toll, the socio-economic and political impact of the Tamil guerrilla warfare was high. The devolution of power was a major political outcome, which resulted from the Indo-Sri Lanka Accord of 1987. Thus, eight autonomous provincial councils were created in Sri Lanka.[179] Four of the guerrilla groups which had been actively involved decided to support the Indo-Sri Lanka Accord and surrender their arms. The L.T.T.E., which had been the most overtly involved group, continued their guerrilla warfare against the Indian Peace Keeping Force (I.P.K.F.) despite the agreement. The conflict gave rise to a dramatic increase of human rights violations such as torture, disappearances, extra-judicial killings, detention without trial and reprisal killings of civilians. The violation of human rights both by the Sri Lankan Government and the Tamil guerrillas has been heavily criticized by human rights organizations.[180] More than 150,000 Sri Lankans fled to India and other foreign countries, and the prolonged state of emergency created an environment that constricted all civil liberties.

Furthermore, the rapid deterioration of relations between the Sinhalese and the Tamil communities was evident. The degree of the rift between the two communities was clearly reflected by the outbreaks of ethnic violence in 1977, 1979, 1981 and 1983. Tourism, which at its peak had attracted over 400,000 visitors annually, had generated about U.S. $150 million in foreign exchange, and had provided about 64,000 jobs.[181] The monetary cost of the civil war amounted to some 15 billion Sri Lankan rupees (U.S. $500 million) annually.[182] By 1986, 17 per cent of the national budget was allotted to defense expenditure, leading to curtailment of other infrastructural expenditure in Sri Lanka. The increasing intrusion of military issues into politics resulted from the urgency of the Tamil guerrilla warfare. The rapid militarization of the country led to an increased centralization of power and a constitutionally authoritarian state. To this extent the sphere of party politics was made less significant. The democratic processes which had functioned undisturbed were gradually eroded with the centralization of power. Consequently, a veritable authoritarian state was established.

The role of the Indian Government was transformed from a diplomatic function to a force that was directly involved in Sri Lanka's internal affairs. Moreover, the Tamil insurgency provided a good opportunity for India to assert its superiority over Sri Lanka and its dominance in South Asia to any outside power interested in the region. The conflict also paved the way for the Indian Peace Keeping Force (I.P.K.F.) to be deployed in June 1987 in Sri Lanka causing much concern to the Sinhalese population. This concern led to the revival of the J.V.P.'s insurrection in 1987 which upheld the sentiments of the Sinhalese-Buddhist people. Finally, Indian intervention led to the prolonged civil war developing new complexities, which must be studied separately. Political violence was subsequently institutionalized. The immediate impact of the guerrilla war was the consequences mentioned above; but the long-lasting effects were yet to be assessed. It was too early yet to examine the long-term outcome of the Tamil political violence. As perceived from the above discussion, the socio-economic and political fabric of the country has been permeated by the effects of an intense and protracted struggle quite different from the insurrection of 1971. The immediate objective of this struggle was confined to the Northern and Eastern provinces but its national and regional impact has been more far-reaching. This aspect will be further examined in the concluding chapter.

7.18 Summary

Since 1971 the political developments in Sri Lanka have been characterized by political violence. The first overt manifestation of such violence was in April 1971. The armed struggle of 1971 was a textbook case which was pre-planned and organized with the objective of capturing state power. This uprising which marked the culmination of the J.V.P. activities assumed three stages.

During the first stage, in spite of the J.V.P. succeeding in capturing only five police stations, they were able to control a much wider area due to the total unpreparedness of the Sri Lankan Government and the armed forces and police. Forty police stations were abandoned during this stage as the government forces were put on the defensive. This trend of events, however, was not to last as the government received military assistance from foreign governments thereby strengthening the Sri Lankan Government's forces to launch a counter-offensive.

During the second stage, the J.V.P. planned to continue their armed assault by converting the abandoned police areas, and the few other areas they had successfully captured, into base camps. These plans proved futile, however, and the guerrillas were compelled to seek refuge in the jungles of the dry zone with the intention of continuing protracted guerrilla warfare. The members of the J.V.P. were ill-prepared and ill-equipped to resort to long-term guerrilla warfare and, as a result, the armed uprising collapsed.

Given these circumstances it was not long before the Sri Lankan Government crushed the uprising with the aid of foreign assistance. The government, on the other hand, adopted a dual policy for the participants of the uprising. Some members were brought to trial before the Criminal Justice Commission (C.J.C.) while others were rehabilitated. The significance of the armed struggle lay in its short duration of three months, and in the exclusivity of its membership: the J.V.P. was predominately Sinhala Buddhist youth from the rural sector. Contrary to the compressed nature of the rural guerrilla warfare of 1971, the political violence which gained ground among the Tamil community developed into a prolonged and intense struggle. Its long-term objective was to establish a separate Tamil state. At the initial stages from 1972 to 1977, these activities were confined to political terrorism. During the second phase of violence which covers a period from 1977 to 1983, however, the guerrilla activities expanded to include terrorist bombings, assassinations and bank robberies. Other than the expansion of activities, their territorial limits of action also expanded to include occasional terrorist attacks on targets outside the Northern and Eastern provinces. During the third phase from 1983 to 1987, there was a marked escalation of terrorist activity and guerrilla warfare.

The initial stages of Tamil political violence were confronted by the army and the police who were intent on crushing this movement. The ethnic violence of 1983 introduced an alternate course of political negotiations, with the Indian Government acting as a mediator. This dual approach failed as well, and the Sri Lankan Government was incapable of successfully controlling the guerrilla activities. The continued thwarting of the government's efforts subsequently led to the agreement between India and Sri Lanka, better known as the Indo-Sri Lanka Accord. This accord succeeded in disarming the E.P.R.L.F., the E.R.O.S., the T.E.L.O. and the P.L.O.T., but failed to disarm the most fundamentalist and hard-core group, the L.T.T.E.

The common characteristic shared by the political violence of 1971 and the protracted guerrilla struggle of the Tamils was the dominance of the youth component. The Tamil youth took up arms in 1972 for the cause of a separate Tamil state, while the Sinhala youth did so in 1971 with revolutionary objectives for Sri Lanka as a whole. The differences also lie in the nature of the warfare. Where the uprising of 1971 was a rural guerrilla warfare, the struggle of the Tamil youth assumed the dimensions of both urban guerrilla warfare and insurgency in the rural areas.

References

1. See, Chapter Six.
2. Chalmers Johnson, *Revolutionary Change*, (Boston: Little, Brown, 1966), p. 99.
3. Those reports were prepared by General John Attyagale who later became Advisor to the Ministry of Defence.
4. *Ceylon Daily News*, (3 March 1971).
5. Fred Halliday, "The Ceylonese Insurrection", in Robin Blackburn, (ed), *Explosion in a Sub-Continent*, (Harmondsworth, Penguin Books Ltd., 1975), p. 195.
6. *Ceylon Daily News*, (10 January 1971)
7. *Ceylon Observer*, (9 August 1971).
8. The Maoist Youth Front was responsible for the attack on the U.S. embassy during which a police inspector was killed.
9. The accidental explosion at Nelundeniya in the Dedigama electorate took place in a thatched mud hut which was the venue of manufacturing hand bombs. It thus claimed the lives of five youths. The explosion in the university took place in a room at Mars Hall.
10. Rohana Wijeweera, the leader of the J.V.P., was taken into custody by the police on the 12th of March 1971, and kept in the Jaffna prison under the emergency regulations. At the trial of suspected J.V.P. members in 1972 Wijeweera received a life

sentence. He was released in 1978 when the United National Party, which was elected in 1977, abolished the Criminal Justice Commission Act under which Wijeweera had been tried. He contested the Presidential Election in 1982. He was again forced underground, when the J.V.P. was proscribed in 1983. He led a violent campaign against the Indo-Sri Lanka Accord in 1987, and against the presence of the I.P.K.F. in Sri Lanka. In 1989 he was executed after being captured by Sri Lankan troops.

11. The following nine members of the J.V.P.'s Central Committee were present at the meeting: S.V.A. Piyatilleke, W.P. Witharana (Sanath), U.M. Jamis (Oo Mahataya), W.T. Karunarathne, Lionel Bopage, Susil Wickrama, W.M. Sunanda Deshapriya, B.A.R. Kurukulasuriya and W.D.N. Hayasinghe (Loku Athula). W.P. Vitharana (Sanath) and Susil Wickrama who was killed in the insurrection. Others left the J.V.P. during and after the trial proceedings.
12. H.F. Nyrop, et al., *Area Hand Book for Ceylon*, (Washington, Foreign Area Studies of the American Universities 1971), p. 452.
13. James Jupp, "The JVP Insurrection of 1971 and its Impact on the Marxist and Socialist Movements in Ceylon", *A Paper for Conference on Sri Lanka*, (London University, March 1974), p. 14.
14. J.M. Van Der Kroef, "The Sri Lanka Insurgency of April 1971; Its Development and Meaning", *Asia Quarterly*, Vol. 2, (1973), p. 122.
15. Robert N. Kearney and Janice Jiggins, "The Ceylon Insurrection of 1971", *Journal of Commonwealth and Comparative Politics*, Vol. 13, (1975), p. 41.
16. A.C. Alles, *Insurgency 1971*, (Colombo: The Colombo Apothecaries, 1976), Appendix 1.
17. J. Jupp, *Sri Lanka: Third World Democracy*, (London: Frank Cass 1978), p. 311.
18. Fred Halliday, *op. cit.*, p. 197.
19. The following police stations were captured by the J.V.P. in their first day of attacks: Rajanganaya, Deniyaya, Uragaha, Kataragama and Warakapola.
20. "The Statement of the Inspector-General of Police", *Judgement of the Criminal Justice Commission (Insurgency Inquiry)*, No. 1, (Colombo: Department of Government Printing, 1976), p. 410.
21. *Keesings Contemporary Archives*, (21-28 August 1971), p. 24774.
22. *Judgement of the Criminal Justice Commission (Insurgency Inquiry) op. cit.*, p. 417.

23. The Statement of the Inspector General of Police, *op. cit.*, p. 410.
24. J. Jupp, *Sri Lanka-third World Democracy*, 1978, p. 299.
25. A.C. Alles, *Insurgency-1971, op. cit.*, p. 179.
26. *Ibid.*, p. 136.
27. V.I. Lenin, "Marxism and Insurrection", in *Collected Works*, Vol. 26, (Moscow: Progress Publishers, 1964), pp. 22-27.
28. Charles Tilley, "Revolution and Collective Violence", in Fred I. Greenstein and Nelson W. Polsby, (eds), *Macropolitical Theory, Handbook of Political Science,* Vol. 3, (Reading, Mass: Addison-Wesley 1975), p. 521.
29. Ernesto Che Guevara, *Guerrilla Warfare*, translated by Brian Loveman and Thomas Davies, Jr., (Manchester: Manchester University Press 1986), p. 48.
30. A.C. Alles, *op. cit.*, p. 145.
31. Andrew C. Janow, "Unconventional Warfare: Framework and Analysis", *World Politics*, Vol. 15, (1962-63), p. 642.
32. T.H. Green, *Comparative Revolutionary Movements*, (Englewood Cliffs, N.J.: Prentice-Hall, Inc., 1974), p. 96.
33. Chalmers JHohnson, *Autopsy on People's War*, (Berkeley: University of California Press, 1973), p. 97.
34. *Ibid.*, p. 98.
35. The North Korean Embassy staff had been engaged in revolutionary propaganda, including the placing of full-page advertisements in Sri Lankan newspapers quoting from the works of Kim II Sung on revolutionary thoughts and techniques.
36. J. Jupp, "The J.V.P. Insurrection of 1971 and its impact on the Marxist and Socialist Movement in Ceylon", p. 3.
37. *Ibid.*, p. 15.
38. Ted Robert Gurr, *Why Men Rebel, op. cit.*, p. 351.
39. Judgement of the C.J.C., *op. cit.*, p. 434.
40. The government imposed a ban on the following newspapers: Janatha Vimukthi (People's Liberation); Rathu Balaya (Red Power); Rathu Lanka (Red Lanka); Gini Pupura (The Spark); Peradiga Sulanga (East Wind); Kamkaru Puwath (Workers News) and Tholilali Seydi (Worker's News).
41. Urmila Phadnis, "Insurgency in Ceylonese Politics: Problems and Prospects", *Institute for Defense Studies and Analysis Journal*, Vol. 3, (1971), p. 610.
42. *The New York Times*, (22 April 1971).

43. This information is based on reports appearing in the British newspapers in late April 1971.
44. *The New York Times*, (11 May 1971)
45. *Daily Telegraph*, (21 April 1971).
14. Ference A. Vali, *Politics of the Indian Ocean Region: The Balance of Power*, (New York: Free Press, 1976), p. 103.
14. *The Ceylon Daily Mirror*, (20 July 1971).
48. *Sunday Times*, (7 June 1971).
49. Ference A. Vali, *op. cit.*, p. 103.
50. James Manor and Gerald Segal, "Cause of Conflict, Sri Lanka and Indian Ocean Strategy", *Asian Survey*, Vol. 25, (19850, p. 1170.
51. *Ibid.*, p. 1183.
52. *International Herald Tribune*, (20 April 1971), and Statesman, [India] (20 April 1971).
53. T.H. Green, *op. cit.*, p. 96.
54. *Keesings Contemporary Archives*, (22-29 May 1971), pp. 23505-24607.
55. Swaroop Rani Dubey, *One-day Revolution in Sri Lanka: Anatomy of 1971 Insurrection*, (Jaipur: Aalekh Publishers, 1988), p. 134.
56. Ted Robert Gurr, *op. cit.*, p. 330.
57. See map in Appendix 7 for areas affected by political violence in 1971.
58. Samuel P. Huntington, *Political Order in Changing Societies*, (New Hven: Yale University Press, 1968), p. 44.
59. James E. Dougherty and Robert L. Pfattragraff, *Contending Theories of International Relations A Comprehensive Survey*, (New York: Harper and Row Publishers, 1981), p. 325.
60. Samuel P. Hungtington, *op. cit.*, pp. 291-300.
61. The Statement on Insurgency Made in Parliament on 20.7.1971 by the Honourable Prime Minister, Department of Information on Press Release, [no date] cited in Kearney and Jiggins, *op. cit.*, p. 42.
62. *The New York Times*, (25 April 1971).
63. Fred Halliday, "The Ceylon Insurrection", *New Left Review*, No. 69, (1979), p. 42.
64. Fred Halliday, "The Ceylon Insurrection" in Robin Blackburn, (ed), *Explosion in a Sub-Continent*, (Middlesex: Penguin, 1975), p. 201.

65. A.J. Wilson, "Ceylon: The People's Liberation Front and the Revolution that Failed", *Pacific Community,* Vol. 3, No. 2, (1972), p. 374.
66. R.N. Kearney, "A Note on the Fate of the 1971 Insurgents in Sri Lanka", *A Journal of Asian Studies*, Vol. 37, (1977), pp. 515-510.
67. See, Chapter 2.
68. R.N., Kearney, "A Note on the Fate of the 1971 Insurgents in Sri Lanka", *Journal of Asian Studies*, Vol. 35, No. 3, (1977), pp. 516-517.
69. Duglas Hyde, *Ceylon's Programme for the Rehaibilitation of Political Detainees*, (Colombo: Department of Government Printing Press, 1972), pp. 12-14.
70. Rs. 5.95 equals approximately one U.S. dollar. N.M. Perera, *Ceylon Daily News,* (13 September 1971).
71. Nimal Sanderatne, "Sri Lanka's New Land Reform", *South Asian Review*, Vol.6, No.1, (1972), p.8.
72. W.A.W. Warnapala, "The Marxist Parties of Sri Lanka and the 1971 Insurrection", *Asian Survey*, Vol. 15, (1975), pp. 745-757.
73. Fred Halliday, *op. cit.,* p. 218.
74. C. Johnson, *Revolutionary Change,* (Boston: Little, Brown, 1966), p. 99.
75. A.J.Wilson, *Politics of Sri Lanka, 1948-1979*, (London: Macmilan, 1979), p. 43.
76. See, Urmila Phadnis, "Tamil Bangla In Ceylon", Hindustan Times, 6th March 1972.
77. Brian Crozier, *The Rebel: A Study of Post-War Insurrections*, (London: 1960), p. 126.
78. T.P. Thornton, "Terrorism a Weapon of Political Agitation", in H. Eckstein, (ed), *Internal War: Problems and Approaches*, (New York: The Free Press, 1964), p. 91.
79. According to P. Wilkinson, political terrorism is the use of murder and destruction, and the threat of murder and destruction to terrorize individuals, groups, communities or governments into conceding to the terrorists' political demands. See.*Terrorism and the Liberal State*, (London: Macmillian, 1986), p. 51.
80. T.P. Thornton, *op. cit.,* p. 73.
81. Sinha Ranatunga, *Politics of Terrorism: The Sri Lanka Experience*, (Melbourne: Globe Press, 1988), p. 226.

82. Alfred Duraippah was a main organizer of the U.F. Government in Jaffna.
83. An ASIA Watch Report, *Cycles of Violence in Sri Lanka: Human Rights in Sri Lanka Since the Indo-Sri Lanka Agreement*, (1987), p. 37.
84. Samuel P. Huntington, "Pattern of Violence in World Politics", in S.P. Huntington, (ed), *Changing Patterns of Military Politics*, (New York: The Free Press, 1962), p. 25.
85. Sinha Ranatunga, *op. cit.*, p. 227.
86. P. Wilkinson, *Political Terrorism*, (London: Macmillian, 1974), p. 18.
87. W.I. Sireweera, "Recent Development in Sinhala-Tamil Relations", *Asian Survey*, Vol. 20, No. 9, (1980), p. 907.
88. Truth of Sri Lanka, Sri Lanka Associated Newspapers of Ceylon Ltd, (Colombo 1883), pp. 6-9.
89. For details of Ethnic Violence see, T.D.S.A. Disanayake, *The Agony of Sri Lanka*, (Colombo: Swastika Press, 1984).
90. *Parliamentary Debate* [Hansard] (19 July 1979), cited in W.I. Sirewera, *op. cit.*, pp. 907-908.
91. *Ibid.*, p. 908.
92. S.P. Huntington, *op. cit.*, p. 43.
93. Sinha Ranatunga, *op. cit.*, 1988, p. 231.
94. Government of Sri Lanka, "Tamil Terrorists: A Record of Murder and Robbery", A Ministry of State Publication, *Overseas Information Series No. 6*, (Colombo: Department of Government Printing), [pamphlet, no date].
95. T.D.S.A. Dissanayake, *The Agony of Sri Lanka, op. cit.*, (1984) pp. 53-54.
96. K.M. De Silva, *Managing Ethnic Tensions in Multi-Ethnic Societies: Sri Lanka*, 1880-1985, (New York: University Press, 1987), p. 351.
97. Sinha Ranatunga, *op. cit.*, (1988), p. 239.
98. *Asia Week*, (2 June 1985), p. 32.
99. The Asia Watch Committee, *Cycles of Violence: Human Rights in Sri Lanka Since the Indo-Sri Lanka Agreement, An Asia Watch Report*, (Washington, 1987), p. 36.
100. *Ibid.*, p. 36.
101. See, Edgar O'balance, *The Cyanide War: Tamil Insurrection in Sri Lanka 1973-1988*, (London: Brassey's Defense Publishers, 1989).

102. *India Today*, (28 February 1985), p. 25.
103. Sinha Ranatunga, *op. cit.,* p. 251.
104. *Ibid.,* p. 364.
105. R.N. Kearney, "Sri Lanka in 1984: The Politics of Communal Violence", *Asian Survey*, Vol. 25, No. 2, (1985), p. 908.
106. Penelope Tremayne, "Sri Lanka Chronology of a Conflict", in The Royal United Services Institute for Defence Studies, *Defence Year-book 1988*, (London: Brassey's Defence Publishers, 1989), p. 406.
107. Centre for Ethnic Amity, "Massacre in Madras by Eelamist Terrorists" in *the Ethnic Problem in Sri Lanka: A Collection of Articles and Essays*, [to date], pp. 128-137.
108. Anuradhapura was the capital of Sri Lanka from 4th Century B.C. to the 10th Century A.D.
109. Penelope Tremayne, *op. cit.,* p. 421.
110. Penelope Tremayn, *op. cit.,* 1988, p. 421.
111. *Far Eastern Economic Review*, (May 1987), p. 15.
112. The ASIA Watch Committee, *op. cit.,* p. 40.
113. *The Economist*, (18 May 1985), p. 49.
114. Penelope Tremayne, *op. cit.,* p. 40.
115. *Sri Lanka News*, A Weekly Digest of News, Vol. 53, No. 17, (7 May 1986), p. 1.
116. The ASIA Watch Committee, *op. cit.,* (1987), p. 39.
117. *Frontline*, (June-July 1986), p. 19.
118. Eugene Mastrangelo, "International Terrorism: A Regional and Global Overview, 1970-1986", in Yonah Alexander, (ed), *The Annual on Terrorism*,(Dordrecht: Martinus Nijhoff Publishers, 1987), p.56
119. *Frontline*, (1986), p. 19.
120. Penelope Tremayne, *op. cit.,* p. 407.
121. *Keesing's Contemporary Archives*, Vol. 30, (September 1984), p. 33099.
122. *Keesing's Contemporary Archives*, Vol. 32, (May 1986), p. 34363.
123. Eugene Mastrangelo, *op. cit.,* p. 55.
124. Sinha Ranatunga, *op. cit.,* p. 250.
125. *Penelope*, *op. cit.,* p. 413.
126. C. Manogaram, *Ethnic Conflict and Reconciliations in Sri Lanka*, (Honolulu: University of Hawaii Press, 1987), p. 175.

127. *Frontline*, (5 April 1985), p. 83.

128. Bruce Matthews, "Radical Conflict and the Rationalization of Violence in Sri Lanka", *Pacific Affairs*, Vol, 59, No. 1, (1986), p. 40.

129. Muslim and Indian Tamils are mainly supporters of the government.

130. *Tamil Information*, Vol. 1. No. 7. (15 November 1984), p. 6.

131. Bruce Matthews, *op. cit.*, p. 40.

132. S.P. Huntington, *op. cit.*, p. 27.

133. Provention of Terrorism Temporary Provisions Act 1979, No. 48, Prevention of Terrorism Temporary Provisions of 1982, No. 10, in Yonah Alexander, and Allan S. Naues, (eds), *Legislative Response to Terrorism*, (Martinus, U.S.A. Nishoff Publishers, 1986), pp. 215-228.

134. The 13th Amendment to the 1978 Constitution of Sri Lanka in November 1987 made the Tamil Language an official language along with the Sinhala Language. This language concession appears to have been too little, too late, to appease the Tamil guerrilla movement.

135. B. Matthews, "District Development Councils in Sri Lanka", *Asian Survey*, Vol. 22, (1982), pp. 1117-34, and B. Matthews, "The Situation in Jaffna", *The Round Table*, No. 290, (April 1984), p. 200.

136. *Keesing's Contemporary Archives*, Record of World Events, Vol. 30, (January 1984), p. 32632.

137. *Frontline*, (5 April 1985), p. 70.

138. See, Appendix 8.

139. S.P. Huntington, *op. cit.*, p. 44.

140. George Modelski, "The International Relation of Internal War", in James No. Rosenau, (ed), *International Aspects of Civil War*, (Princeton: Princeton University Press, 1964), p. 22.

141. *Ibid.*, p. 23.

143. P. Venkataeshwar Rao, "Foreign Involvement in Sri Lanka", *The Round Table*, Vol. 309, (1989), pp. 88-10

143. P. Venkateskwar Rao, "Ethnic Conflict in Sri Lanka; India's Role and Perception", *Asian Survey* Vol. 28, No. 4, (April 1988), p. 425.

144. A.J. Wilson, The Break-Up of *Sri Lanka: The Sinhalese-Tamil Conflict*, (London: C. Hurst and Company, 1988), p. 200.

145. P. Venkateshwar Rao, *op. cit.*, p. 425.
146. James Manor and Gerald Segal, *op. cit.*, p. 1184.
147. *Strategic Survey*, 1983-1984, IISS, (London: 1985), p. 90.
148. Rohan Gunasekera, "Sri Lankan Armed Forces Switch Focus", *International Defence Review*, Vol. 5, (1988), p. 509.
149. These forces were identified as follows: The National Armed Reserve (N.A.R.) The National Auxiliary Force (N.A.F.), Civil Defence Units, Homeguards, Towns Guards and Green Tigers.
150. Michael Brzoska and Thomas Ohlson, *Arms Transfers to the Third World, 1971-1985*, (Oxford: Oxford University Press, 1987), p. 36.
151. Marks Thomas, "People's War in Sri Lanka: Insurgency and Counterinsurgency", *Issues and Studies*, (1986), p. 84.
152. C. Manogaram. *Op. cit.*, p. 167.
153. Trincomalee, although an area of mixed population, would have been the capital of the proposed Eelam state.
154. C. Manogaram, *op. cit.*, p. 169.
155. P. Venketeshwar Rao, *op. cit.*, p. 422.
156. R.N. Kearney, "Tension and Conflict in Sri Lanka", Current History, (March 1986), p. 112.
157. The following political parties and organizations did not attend the A.P.C.: the S.L.F.P., the M.E.P., and the T.U.L.F.
158. See, Appendix 9.
159. *Keesing's Contemporary Archives*, Vol. 31, (May 1985), p. 33581.
160. K.M. De Silva, *op. cit.*, (1987), p. 348.
161. The L.T.T.E. and the P.L.O.T. did not participate in the talks but sent representatives, to Bhutan. *The Times*, (9 July 1985).
162. *Frontline*, (1985), Ministry of State (Sri Lanka) The Thimphu Talks: The Stand Taken by the Sri Lanka Government, (Colombo: Department of Information, 1985).
163. C. Manogaram, *op. cit.*, p. 167.
164. C.R. de Silva, "Ethnic Crisis", *Asian Thought and Society*, (1985), pp. 137-141.
165. C. Manogaram, *op. cit.*, p. 169.
166. *The Economist*, (28 February 1987), p. 51.
167. *Far Eastern Economic Review*, (26 February 1987), p. 19.
168. The Indian Government first attempted to send food supplies to Jaffna in a flotilla of fishing boats but it was turned back by

the Sri Lankan Navy. Within 24 hours, however, India reacted by air-dropping supplies. The main purpose of this action was to display India's disapproval of the Sri Lankan Government's military action against the Tamil guerrillas.

169. George Modelski, "International Settlement of Internal War", in James No. Rosenau, (ed), *International Aspects of Civil War*, (Princeton: Princeton University Press, 1964), p. 123.

170. For details on the Indo-Sri Lanka Accord, see, Appendix 10.

171. All these districts are Tamil majority areas.

172. V. Nithiyanandan, "An Analysis of Economic factors Behind the Origin and Development of Tamil Nationalism in Sri Lanka", in C. Abeysekera, and N. Gunesinghe, (ed), *Facets of Ethnicity in Sri Lanka*, (Colombo: Karunaratne and Sons Ltd., 1987), p. 136.

173. See, Chapter 5.

174. Bruce Matthews, *op. cit.,* p. 43.

175. Ralph R. Premdas, and S.W.R. de Samarasinghe, "Sri Lanka's Ethnic Conflict: The Indo-Lanka Peace Accord", *Asian Survey*, Vol. 28, No. 6, (1988), p. 677.

176. *Time*, (June 1986), p. 12.

177. Sinha Ratnatunga, *op. cit.,* p. 386.

178. *Armed Forces*, (June 1988), p. 280.

179. One of councils overseas the Northern and Eastern provinces which is governed by the E.P.R.L.F. The continuation of the merger of the Northern and Eastern provinces, however, will be subject to a referendum in 1992.

180. AN ASIA Watch Report, *op. cit.,* pp. 28-40.

181. Ralph R. Premdas, S.W.R. de Samarasinghe, *op. cit.,* p. 677.

182. *Ibid.,* p. 676.

8

Conclusion

The concluding chapter has four objectives. First, the author undertakes an overview of the entire study, emphasizing its main arguments. Secondly, the chapter goes on to discuss the key findings of this research study and the author's observations about them. Thirdly, it examines the implications of this study for future research. Finally, it presents a discussion of some recommendations for a solution to the problem of political violence in Sri Lanka. To accommodate all those aspects, this chapter is subdivided into the following sections: overview, findings and observations, implementations and consequences, recommendations and final summary.

8.2 Overview

Political violence in the Third World represents a new strain of inquiry in modern politics and international relations. Since the end of the Second World War, there has been a growing tendency for different manifestations of political violence within the countries of the Third World. The causes of these manifestations were complex and manifold. In its earliest appearances, political violence was concentrated either in colonial or post-colonial countries such as Vietnam, Algeria, Korea, and Malaya. The process of decolonization, however, was not the sole cause of the outbreak of political violence in the Third World. Independent countries such as Guatemala, Colombia, Ethiopia, and Nicaragua have also experienced political violence in the recent past. The indiscriminate trend toward political violence was evident in capitalist countries, e.g., Korea, the Philippines, Lebanon, and India, as well as in pro-communist countries such as Cambodia, Ethiopia and Nicaragua. One characteristic that has emerged in Third World political violence was that a majority of the governments of these countries have not been overthrown by guerrilla forces; but, nor have the governments in these regions been able to eradicate the guerrilla threat.

The basic foci of this study were the causes, patterns and consequences of political violence. This investigation empirically analysed Sri Lanka as a case study of Third World political violence, and was based on a comparative approach where the revolutionary-motivated and secessionist violence were viewed in a wider context. The left-wing insurgency waged by the J.V.P. on a recurring basis since 1971, and the Tamil guerrilla warfare pioneered and fought by the L.T.T.E., the P.L.O.T., the E.R.O.S., the T.E.L.O. and the E.P.R.L.F. since 1972, appeared interminable when compared to other political violence in the Third World. Left-wing insurrections and ethnic-insurgency were the two main manifestations of political violence evident in many Third World countries such as Burma, the Philippines, Sri Lanka and India. This study, however, was confined to political violence waged by organized groups or movements. The main focal points of this study were the socio-economic and political factors which served as preconditions for the origin of political violence movements. The author's 'modus operandi' was to apply a theoretical framework to trace the nexus between the socio-economic background of the members of the politically violent organizations and the pattern of political violence.

Given the main objectives of this study, the following hypotheses were utilized to test the main trends and features: (1) political violence in Sri Lanka was not spontaneous but pre-planned and organized; (2) the failure of the existing political system to assimilate a newly emerging social class had given rise to political violence movements; (3) political factors were more conducive for the origin and development of politically violent movements and political violence itself was a product of socio-economic and psychological factors; and (4) there was a close nexus between the socio-economic background of the members of the political violence movements and the pattern of political violence. The data gathered by the author was presented and analysed to support the above hypotheses.

The second chapter focused on the analytical framework of the study, which was comprised of a critique and review of selected literature on definitions, theories and typologies of political violence. Political violence is a concept that has diverse definitions depending on each theorist's approach.[1] The main controversy surrounding the concept was derived from the debate as to whether it embraces all forms of violent attempts to dispose or merely compromise extant states of governments. There was strong evidence to indicate that in many Third World countries, political violence was not confined to parties, groups and movements. States also resorted to violence covertly or overtly either to gain additional power or retain power. The concept of political violence eludes a precise definition due to its complexity and applicability to various situations. As a result, the present study examined political violence as pre-planned armed attacks by an organized group or groups to capture or change political power in a given political system.

By the early 1960s, the theories of political violence had been perfected to a great extent. Since then, political violence has been attributed to a variety of factors, giving rise to a large body of theoretical literature. In spite of the multiplicity of socio-economic, psychological and political literature, the author focused on the main representative theories, such as the social system theory of C. Johnson, the J-curve theory of D.C. Davies, the relative deprivation theory of Ted Robert Gurr, and the modernization theory of S.P. Huntington. The theoretical analysis led the author to conclude that the primary obstacles in studying political violence in the Third World are the diverse aspects emphasized in the theories.

The theories of political violence summarized, discussed and criticized in this study share two common features. The first is that the four theories are primarily based on empirical studies concerned with domestic forms of political violence. Secondly, these theories are mainly based on one single factor, either, socio-economic, psychological or political. Although, the theories offer important approaches in the field of political violence and emphasize significant aspects of the subject, an alarming number of methodological weaknesses have marred their effectiveness. Generally, they are unable to cope with the apparent correlation between political violence on the one hand, and socio-economic and political development on the other.

Another common weakness of the four theories is their inability to explain the frequency and intensity of political violence in the given countries.

In light of these limitations, the modernization theory presented by S.P. Huntington is an exception in its applicability to the Third World. It attempts to explain why revolutions occur predominantly in Third World countries, and argues that the process of modernization causes political instability by undermining traditional political authority and institutions. According to Huntington, revolution is most likely to occur during the transition period between traditional and modern society. It should be noted, however, that Huntington's theory of modernization has also been subject to severe and often valid criticism. There is a large body of literature which debates the utility of the term 'modernization', which is a basic tenet of Huntington's approach. Despite these criticisms, the modernization theory is the only available theory which adequately addresses political violence in the Third World. Due to the apparent correlation between political violence and the socio-economic and political development in Sri Lanka, the author has selected this theory with modification as an analytical framework. Moreover, an analysis of the literature on typologies of political violence has led to the conclusion that accurate measurement is another very complex problem to be faced in the study of political violence.

In Chapter 3, the socio-economic and political factors which were the preconditions for the origin and development of the J.V.P. as a political violence movement were examined. In this context, Huntington's modernization theory was applied with some modification. Sri Lanka is a Third World country with a long history of colonialism. The European colonial powers first conquered parts of Sri Lanka since 1505 and in 1815 conquered the entire country. In spite of the colonial occupation, the socio-economic and political fabric of the country remained largely intact until 1829. The socio-economic and political reforms initiated by the British in 1829 marked the beginning of a transition from the traditional to colonial, and finally, to a modern form of society, economy and polity. The wheels of economic modernization were set in motion with the introduction of a plantation economy. Sri-Lanka's integration into the global economy marked a decline of the traditional agricultural economy. The agrarian crisis was manifest in the acute shortage of land, in land fragmentation and rural indebtedness. This agrarian crisis was further aggravated by the expansion of social mobilization in the form of a rapid growth of population, urbanization, and educational opportunities, a high rate of literacy and the expansion of the media.

These social processes gave rise to new social classes within the semi-urban and rural sectors whose expectations and aspirations were high. The economic growth of Sri Lanka, however, did not keep abreast of these rapid social changes. The economy was beset by foreign debt, inflation, a high rate of unemployment and underemployment. The economic stagnation thwarted any fulfillment of the aspirations of the newly emerging social classes. Consequently, they were subject to a process of disillusionment and an increasing trend of politicization from the mid-1960s onwards.

The socio-economic changes during the British colonial period were accompanied by political changes as well. A traditional indigenous polity was replaced by a colonial polity and subsequently by a modern independent polity. Since independence in 1948, Sri Lanka has maintained a parliamentary structure of government akin to the British Westminster model. Furthermore, the granting of universal franchise in 1931 and the growth of a competitive political party system have expanded the level of political participation in Sri Lanka. As a result of the introduction of the competitive party system the election of 1956 marked the advent of crucial changes. From 1956 to 1977 governments were elected at six general elections and the development of a competitive party system further expanded the political participation in Sri Lanka. The availability of an alternative government in the General Election of 1956 was thus a landmark in Sri Lanka's modern political history. The election of 1956 also marked the beginning of the alienation of a section of the Sri Lankan society. The reduction in the eligible age for voting from 21 to 18 years expanded the political participation of rural youth but subsequently heightened the youth interest in politics. This could be attributed to the fact that the political parties were not sufficiently flexible to assimilate the newly emerging politicized radical youth into the existing political system.

The political parties in Sri Lanka during the 1960s were poorly organized and their power was centralized in the ruling elite. Consequently, the greater majority of the semi-urban and rural youth who were involved in politics during elections were alienated and rendered apathetic. In the context of economic underdevelopment, the democratic processes in Sri Lanka were constricted and suffocated by alternate governments. The widening gap between the election promises and the performance of elected governments, and their inability to solve the problem of unemployment created unrest among the youth.

Given the failures of the political parties, more and more educated youth were drawn toward the left-orientated parties in Sri Lanka. However, there were several factors which prevented the rural youth from being assimilated into these left-wing political parties. The disunity among the political parties was rooted mainly in ideological and personal differences, their electoral failure and the elite nature of the leadership. The failure of the major political parties, including the left-wing parties, to absorb the youth cadres into the political system generated a realization amongst a large segment of the youth population of the need for an organization committed to revolutionary changes in the socio-economic and political system of Sri Lanka.

Chapter 4 of this study examined the preconditions which gave rise to organized underground political violence movements among Sri Lanka's Tamil community. The socio-economic and political changes which occurred during the British Colonial period created a competition for limited resources between the Sinhalese majority and the Tamil minority. The political changes in Sri Lanka further exacerbated these trends. The constitutional reforms during the British period weakened the political strength of the Tamil community. The policy innovations during the post-independence period, however, had a more serious impact on the relationship between the two communities. The main issues after 1948 were the peasant resettlement schemes and the legislation of Sinhala as the official language.

Consequently, the major political parties gravitated towards an ethnic identification. The Sinhalese felt their majority position threatened by the Tamils mainly due to the Tamils' domination in the professions, trades and university education. The Tamils, on the other hand, became increasingly conscious of a separate identity. These developments led the Federal Party to demand autonomy within a federal system of government.

The Sri Lankan Government was slow, if not inert, in introducing the necessary political reforms to accommodate the demands of the Tamils. This lack of change made the Tamil youth restive. The lack of adequate access to land, employment, business enterprise and university education, together with the lack of political reform, created a discontented and frustrated Tamil youth. The Tamil youth believed that they were being discriminated against by the successive Sinhalese-majority governments as no better than second-class citizens. As a result of this added dimension, the level of political participation among the Tamils escalated, and their demands became more radical in 1972 with the formation of the Tamil United Liberation Front (T.U.L.F.). The continued inertia of the Tamil youth movement following the government's rebuff of their initially modest demand for federalism, led to the radical demand for a separate Tamil state. Peaceful demands by the Tamil community for political changes went relatively unheeded by the Sri Lankan Government due essentially to pressures from the Sinhalese-Buddhist majority. Furthermore, the political activities of the young Tamils were suppressed by the national government. Thus the failure of post-independence governments to address the deep-rooted grievances of the politically energetic Tamil youth led to the origin and development of the Tamil guerrilla organizations, which sought to achieve a separate Tamil state by means of violence.

Chapter 5 examined the organizational aspects of the J.V.P. and the Tamil guerrilla organizations, which were the key aspects of this study of political violence in Sri Lanka. The origin of the J.V.P. was closely linked to the development of the left-wing movement in Sri Lanka. The J.V.P. was a breakaway group from the Maoist-wing of the Sri Lankan Communist Party. From its inception in the mid-1960s, the J.V.P. developed as a clandestine group. The development of the J.V.P. largely depended on propaganda and indoctrination classes conducted by a small revolutionary cadre. The J.V.P., therefore, was very different from the theoretical stipulations of the foco theory of Che Guevera. According to the foco theory an outside force intervenes to instigate a military movement and then undertakes to create a political movement.[2] The J.V.P., on the other hand, first undertook to create a political movement which was transformed into a military movement. Therefore, the J.V.P. may be classified as an independent left-wing guerrilla movement.

The socio-economic background of the leaders and members of the Sri Lankan guerrilla groups was an important aspect of this study. In terms of ethnicity nearly the entire leadership and membership of the J.V.P. were members of the Sinhalese community and, by religion, were Buddhists. According to Walker Connor, it is a normal characteristic of political violence movements in multi-ethnic societies in the Third World to be identified closely with a single ethnic group.[3] Thus, the Huk guerrilla movement in the Philippines was seen as essentially Pampangan by non-Pampangan ethnicities; the Communist guerrilla movement in Malaysia was confined to the Chinese community; and the Shining Path in Peru has been confined to the Indian community. A noteworthy and curious disparity in the organizational structure of the J.V.P. was that its leaders were from the urban sector, while a majority of its members were from the rural sector. The social class of the leaders was primarily petit bourgeois rather than middle class. The representation of the peasantry was negligible. Students and unemployed rural youth swelled its party cadres. The J.V.P. was a clandestine movement until the General Election of 1970 after which it turned into an open political organization. The organizational structure of the J.V.P. was pyramidical whereby decision-making and policy-setting authority converged at the top and filtered down. Members were controlled by a tight command structure. Foreign involvement in the J.V.P. was non-existent—the movement depended entirely on domestic support.

Unlike the J.V.P., the Tamil guerrilla groups originated from the Tamil ethno-nationalist movement which was represented by the moderate Federal Party and the T.U.L.F. The Tamil guerrilla organizations were mainly represented by the following five organizations: the L.T.T.E., the E.R.O.S., the T.E.L.O., the P.L.O.T., and the E.P.R.L.F. Of these organizations, the L.T.T.E. has emerged as the most potent group. Theoretically, the origin and development of these groups fit the pattern of the foco theory in that they were challenging the concept of a 'vanguard' party, which was the basic premise of Marxist-Leninist revolutionary theory. The ethno-religious background of the leadership and general membership of these groups were, for the most part, Tamil-Hindu. The Tamil guerrilla groups, like the J.V.P., were youth-centred, organized as liberation armies, drawn from both the rural and urban sectors, and fairly well educated. Yet another shared characteristic with the J.V.P. was negligible participation of the peasantry.

Although both the J.V.P. and the Tamil groups were action-orientated, the Tamils were far better trained and equipped than were the J.V.P. All of the Tamil guerrilla groups were supported by an international network of guerrilla movements and received support from the state of Tamil Nadu in Southern India. Military bases, arms and training, unofficial political asylum and propaganda were provided by the state government and other political parties in Tamil Nadu. Most of the propaganda, however, was carried out by expatriate Tamil groups in the United Kingdom, the United States of America, West Germany, Australia and Canada.

The study has revealed that the contrasting ideologies, strategies and programmes of the J.V.P. and the Tamil guerrilla organizations were an important aspect of political violence as it occurred in Sri Lanka. The objectives of the J.V.P. were not based on any socio-economic demands, but rather were aimed at overthrowing the existing national government, capturing state power, and working towards a socialist state. Accordingly, the J.V.P.'s main objectives were the violent overthrow of the Sri Lankan Government and the bringing about of revolutionary changes in the existing socio-economic and political system. Thus, the politico-military objectives of the J.V.P. were based on the reasoning of 'justifying the means by the end result'.

The J.V.P. enlarged its membership by formulating a distinct ideology which was adapted from Marxism-Leninism to suit the indigenous socio-economic conditions in Sri Lanka. Moreover, the radical thinkers from the Third World such as Mao, Che Guevara and Regis Debray influenced the ideology of the J.V.P. This ideology was however influenced by Sinhala-Buddhist chauvinism which was manifest in the battle cry: "Mavu Bima Nathinam Maranaya" (The motherland or death).[4] The ideology of many political violence movements in the Third World, like the Mau Mau in Kenya, the Palestine Liberation Organization in Palestine, and the Sandinistas in Nicaragua, owe little to Marxism-Leninism. It was evident that the J.V.P. sought to present itself as a native challenge to the tradition of peaceful and constitutional means of socio-economic reconstruction in Sri Lanka. The ideology of the J.V.P. was, therefore, openly anti-western, anti establishment and anti-Indian.

The strategy of the J.V.P. was based on a concept of launching a one-day armed insurrection. This strategy was not derived from Mao's model of a people's war or Che Guevara's model of guerrilla warfare, but was influenced by the strategy adapted by the Zanzibar revolutionists in 1964. The tactical plan was to launch simultaneous armed attacks on all police stations and military bases at the same hour, and to capture weapons, key government personnel and the main administrative centres in Sri Lanka in one day. The J.V.P.'s military strategy thus emphasized the importance of subjective factors such as political will and dedication rather than objective socio-economic and political conditions. The strategy also sought to exploit the strength of a surprise armed attack which would alleviate the disadvantages of their military weakness and disparity in number. The weakness in the J.V.P.'s strategy was two-fold: first, their limited fighting forces were spread over too wide a line of attack; secondly, the government forces were stronger in number, training and equipment. According to the J.V.P.'s strategy there was no basis for the involvement of the masses. The J.V.P. viewed the Sri Lankan populace as mere spectators to the drama of political violence between government forces and guerrilla fighters. In essence this type of strategy has many similarities with the theory of insurrection of Louis Auguste Blanqui (1803-1881) who advocated a two-phase strategy to achieve socialism in France.[5] The post revolutionary programme of the J.V.P. was based vaguely on the socialist models in Asia such as in Communist China and North Korea. The economic policies of the J.V.P. emphasized the necessity of a self-sufficient, planned economy dependent solely on domestic resources. This was a utopian rather than a practical programme. Politically, the J.V.P. proposed a one-party government which it would lead, rather than a parliamentary democracy based on a multi-party system.

The ideology, strategy and programme of the Tamil guerrilla organizations contrasted sharply to that of the J.V.P. The long-term objective of all the major Tamil groups was to establish a separate Tamil state more popularly known as Eelam. Their main objective was not to overthrow the national government but to secede and establish an alternative seat of government encompassing the Northern and Eastern provinces in Sri Lanka.

The Tamil demand for separatism called for an ethno-nationalist ideology which was preoccupied with the survival and preservation of the Tamil ethnicity, language, culture and traditional homeland. The guerrilla groups perceived themselves to be the emancipators of the Tamil community. The ethno-nationalist ideology of the Tamil guerrillas, however, included a tendency toward leftist leanings. In contrast to the J.V.P.'s concept of a motherland, the Tamil guerrilla organizations used the concept of a 'traditional homeland'. Considering the primary objective of revolution, and in the Tamil's case, secession, both the J.V.P. and Tamil guerrilla movements were more action-orientated than theory-orientated. Both the J.V.P. and Tamil movements shared the view that they had a right to rebel against discrimination in Sri Lanka and to fight for national self-determination.

In spite of the shared ideology of the Tamil guerrilla groups, their strategies differed. The L.T.T.E. relied heavily on the classical type of terrorism-cum-guerrilla warfare. The L.T.T.E.'s strategy included the use of acts of terror and sabotage to goad the government forces into repressive countermeasures which would cause a rift between the Sri Lankan Government and the Tamil population. This plan was derived from the strategies of

Che Guevara and Carlos Marighella, the underlying logic being that an army of Tamil youth organized along those lines could emancipate the Sri Lankan Tamils from the Sinhalese rule. The T.E.L.O. and the E.R.O.S. shared a very similar strategy while the E.P.R.L.F. and the P.L.O.T. advocated a protracted people's war. All groups anticipated an Indian intervention though it proved to be a key factor only in the secessionist violence of the Tamil guerrillas. It is evident that none of the Tamil guerrilla groups had a viable socio-economic and political programme. Politically, the L.T.T.E. postulated a one-party government similar to the East European countries, and an economic programme which aimed at national self-sufficiency.

As examined in Chapter 7, political violence occurred with greater frequency during the period from 1971 to 1987. Each incident of political violence displayed its own distinct pattern and course. Class conflicts leading to revolutionary transformations, however, have yet to occur in Third World countries. The J.V.P. insurrection of April 1971 in Sri Lanka was an important instance to examine in this respect as it was the first political violence during Sri Lanka's modern period aimed at capturing state power.

Unlike many uprisings in the post-colonial period in the Third World, the insurrection was carefully devised rather than spontaneous. Furthermore, the pattern of the insurrection of 1971 was not characteristic of the general pattern of planned guerrilla warfare and insurgency in the Third World. The J.V.P. overlooked the usual first stage which was the terrorist stage, and planned insufficiently for the second stage which was the guerrilla warfare stage. Their strategy instead was to launch a sudden all-out frontal attack on the police stations and military bases under the cover of darkness. It assumed the most advanced and the most complex form of a widespread armed insurrection. At the outset of the insurrection, the J.V.P. was on the offensive and the Sri Lankan armed forces were on the defensive. This situation was soon reversed, however, when the government was able to reinforce its military strength with material received through international assistance. Strategically, the J.V.P. depended on the advantages of a surprise attack, and on the initiative and commitment of its members, thereby avoiding the need for a full-scale guerrilla campaign. When the surprise attack failed, they became involved in protracted guerrilla warfare for which they were ill-prepared. Furthermore, there was no revolutionary environment in Sri Lanka at the time of insurrection. The U.F. Government had been recently elected to office by an overwhelming majority and enjoyed the allegiance of the security forces. The Sri Lankan people did not want a revolution.[6] There were no justifiable causes which would have convinced the people of a need for an insurrection. Nor did the J.V.P. command any tangible or moral support from any inter-governmental organization (I.G.O.). Non-governmental organizations (N.G.O.), such as Amnesty International, did focus on the J.V.P. after the insurrection of 1971.

The international support extended to the Sri Lankan Government in 1971 was a significant factor. Sri Lanka was one of the few Third World countries which received assistance from both the western and the socialist blocks for their counter-insurgency policies. The Sri Lankan Government considered the insurrection to be a security threat rather than a socio-economic and political crisis. Thus, the government's counter-insurgent policies relied on military action rather than socio-economic and political reforms. The failure of the insurrection drove the J.V.P. back to underground once more. In spite of the failure of the insurrection, the surviving discontent and frustrations of the Sinhala-Buddhist rural youth over the contemporary socio-economic and political conditions were indisputable. According to C. Johnson, the case of 1971 was interesting in its illustration of a 'reverse flow' of revolutionary ideas from Latin America (i.e. Guevaraism) back to Asia.[7] It was also similar to the Communist insurrection of Hamburg in 1923.[8]

The pattern of the Tamil guerrilla warfare was without precedent in the contemporary political history of Sri Lanka. This strain of political violence differed widely from that of the insurrection of 1971. The politico-military objectives of the Tamil guerrilla warfare did not threaten to overthrow the government in power; rather it was aimed at setting up an alternative seat of government encompassing Sri Lanka's Northern and Eastern provinces. The J.V.P. insurrection of 1971 was launched by one guerrilla group whereas the Tamil guerrilla warfare was waged by five main guerrilla organizations. Moreover, the Tamil guerrilla warfare was a protracted warfare defined by three principal focuses of terrorism, guerrilla warfare and conventional warfare. Nevertheless, terrorism played the prominent role throughout the Tamil insurgency.

According to this study, the first phase of the Tamil guerrilla warfare was the organizational phase from 1972 to 1977. It was characterized mainly by urban guerrilla warfare which depended upon sabotage and terrorism, and avoided direct confrontation with the security forces. At this stage the violence was aimed against government supporters within the Tamil community, police and security personnel engaged in investigating terrorist activities, and police informers. The assassination of moderate Tamil politicians was a vital part of this violent programme. This phase conveyed a deep-rooted political dissatisfaction which assumed the character of protracted guerrilla warfare.

The second phase of the Tamil violence covers a period from 1977 to 1983 when ethnic violence broke out. The major development of this phase was the emergence of the L.T.T.E. as the dominant Tamil guerrilla organization, and the only one with clear-cut objectives and military training. The Tamil guerrilla activities were accompanied by occasional armed attacks on police stations in the Northern Province, the ambushing of army patrols and convoys, kidnappings and bank robberies. The operations were masterminded from the guerrillas' bases in Tamil Nadu in South India, from where arms were smuggled into Sri Lanka's Northern Province. The escalation of terrorist and guerrilla activities, especially attacks on Sri Lankan military personnel, triggered a spate of ethnic violence in 1977, 1981 and 1983. The most significant outbreak of ethnic violence was in 1983 when the fierce and widespread attacks by Sri Lankan Sinhalese mobs on the Tamil community in the South proved to be a vital propaganda weapon to secure sympathy for the Tamil guerrilla cause in the western countries. More importantly, this violence gained them support from India and Tamil Nadu, and helped them to recruit the Tamil youth to their cause.

The third phase of the Tamil guerrilla warfare in this study covers a period from 1983 to 1987. During this period Sinhalese civilians residing within and outside the Tamil-dominated areas became targets of terrorist activities. Another significant development during this period, but beyond the scope of this study, was infighting amongst the Tamil guerrilla groups for overall dominance. By 1985 the L.T.T.E. had emerged as the most powerful group, with control of the Jaffna peninsula. Thereafter, sporadic political violence developed into regular warfare. Unlike the J.V.P., the fundamental requirements for a successful guerrilla campaign, such as a cause to fight for, covert or overt support from the Tamil population in the Northern Province, foreign bases and armed supplies, and access to mobility, were available to the Tamil guerrillas.

At the initial stages of the Tamil campaign, the Sri Lankan Government was not prepared with a well-designed, coherent counter-insurgency programme which could subdue the Tamil guerrilla warfare. During this period the government were also engaged in quelling the J.V.P. insurgency and preoccupied with military policies. After 1977, however, the government adopted a number of conciliatory policies including amendment of the university admissions system, language concessions, and devolution of power through the District Development Council (D.D.C.) system. The objectives of these policies of appeasement were soon thwarted by the violent confrontations between the military and the Tamil guerrilla movement and by the ethnic violence in 1983.

The involvement of external parties was an important aspect of the government's counter-insurgent policies. The nature and type of involvement varied widely between that of the 1971 left-wing insurrection and the Tamil guerrilla warfare. Unlike the 1971 insurrection, the military assistance from the West, mainly the U.S.A. and the U.K., during the long period of Tamil guerrilla warfare was negligible thus indicating the non-strategic strength of Sri Lanka's position. As Marshall Singer observes, the U.S. Government took a hands-off position on the Sri Lankan issue. When the Indian Government airlifted humanitarian aid to the Tamil guerrillas in May 1987 against the Sri Lankan Government's wishes, the United States did nothing to help the Sri Lankan Government even though they had accommodated U.S. interests on some other matters.[9] The foreign states primarily involved in aiding one side or the other during the Tamil insurgency were Israel, Pakistan and India. The P.L.O.'s participation in training the Tamil guerrilla groups accounts for Israel's interest in the conflict.

India's covert involvement in the Tamil guerrilla warfare was the major reason for Pakistan extending support to the Sri Lankan Government. Thus external power struggles were reflected in the level of assistance extended to the Sri Lankan Government to counter Tamil guerrilla warfare. It was India's role as an external force which was more important here. The Indian Government's response during the prolonged Tamil insurgency differed widely from that during the short-lived insurrection of 1971. The decision of the Indian Government to intervene in the Sri Lankan Tamil conflict was guided by India's regional interests and domestic pressure. The regional factor was India's geo-political interest as a regional superpower. Domestically, over 55 million Tamils in Tamil Nadu exerted sufficient pressure to force and shape India's role in the Tamil guerrilla warfare.

Despite the intervention, India did not have a strong and unanimous policy on the conflict in Sri Lanka. At the beginning of the Tamil insurgency, the Janatha Party Government in India (1976-1980) perceived the Sri Lankan crisis as an internal problem and therefore, refrained from any involvement. This policy was reversed when the Congress Party assumed national state power under Indira Gandhi. After the ethnic violence in Sri Lanka in 1983, the Indian state government of Tamil Nadu and the more moderate Tamil politicians in Sri Lanka prevailed upon the Indian Government for positive and vigorous intervention in the Sri Lankan crisis. Under Rajive Gandhi's premiership, however, India assumed only a moderate role. He urged the Sri Lankan Government and the Tamil guerrillas to negotiate for a peaceful solution. In 1987 when the government forces came close to defeating the Tamil guerrillas in a military operation, India directly intervened by airdropping food supplies to Jaffna, thus violating Sri Lanka's sovereignty. The Indo-Sri Lanka Accord of 1987 resulted from Indian endeavours to resolve the Tamil insurgency.

Two important consequences followed from the signing of the Indo-Sri Lanka Accord. The first was the deployment of the

Indian Peace Keeping Force (I.P.K.F.) with the intention of disarming the Tamil guerrilla groups. It was an attempt by the Indian Federal Government, as a third party, to impose a settlement on the contending parties, mainly by coercion or the threat of coercion. Consequently, the deployment of the Indian troops restructured the conflict and moved it into a new phase of insurgency and counter-insurgency. The I.P.K.F. failed, however, to totally disarm the L.T.T.E., the most intransigent Tamil guerrilla group. As a result, the I.P.K.F. was engaged in combating the Sri Lankan Government's counter-insurgency until they were withdrawn from Sri Lanka in late March 1990. It was estimated that, during this period, 1,155 soldiers of the I.P.K.F. were killed and 2,984 were wounded.[10] The second consequence of the Accord was the devolution of power through the introduction of eight provincial councils. The Indo-Sri Lanka Accord was a tangible recognition of India's regional paramountancy and its role as a regional crisis manager.

The period under review therefore clearly indicates that complex social and political changes set in motion during the colonial period have had a cumulative impact on Sri Lanka's post independence polity. The youth led political violence therefore is part of the process of establishing a post independence national polity and the mediation and resolution of conflict is a vital part of the process.

8.3 Findings and Observations

The findings of this study clearly suggest that more extensive and additional research is necessary to understand the causes, nature and sequence of political violence in the Third World. The observations of this study are discussed in general terms, focusing on Sri Lanka in particular as a case study from 1971 to 1987.

The political violence waged by the J.V.P. in 1971, and the Tamil guerrilla warfare from 1972 onward, was preplanned rather than spontaneous. The origins of the Sinhalese and Tamil political violence movements were deeply rooted in the socio-economic and political developments in Sri Lanka. The violence has been largely attributed to the emergence of new social forces during the processes of socio-economic and political modernization. Of these factors, the political factors were the most important.

Politics in Sri Lanka, as in many other Third World countries, is the main avenue for upward mobility. Sri Lanka's political system was incapable, however, of absorbing the large number of politically radicalized rural Sinhalese and Tamil youth. The central cause for this lack of political viability was the steady erosion of Sri Lanka's democratic process. The contributory factors for the political violence movements in Sri Lanka were, therefore, mainly internal rather than external. The Tamil guerrilla organizations originated with the failure of the successive Sri Lankan governments to accommodate ethnic pluralism amidst perpetual economic and political under-development. These factors were basically internal but were subject to influence and pressures from external sources such as the state of Tamil Nadu in South India and the Tamil expatriates.

This study reveals that political violence in Sri Lanka is not only a mere process set in motion by the vagaries of socio-economic or political factors, but also is the outcome of organizations, leadership, ideologies and strategies. The J.V.P. and the Tamil guerrilla organizations were capable of organizing and providing leadership to the Sinhalese and Tamil youth respectively. Moreover, their ideologies formulated their group consciousness and objectives. Their respective strategies mobilized the youth toward ultimate politico-military objectives. The J.V.P. was organized as a revolutionary army while the Tamil guerrilla groups organized themselves as national liberation armies.

It is an error to assume that Sri Lankan society is a hierarchically-structured ethnic society where one ethnic group can hold the other in a subordinate position. Political violence in Sri Lanka has been an outcome not merely of ethnic factors but also of politico-economic factors. The continued political violence in Sri Lanka has been based on class exploitation and ethnic discrimination, but the ethnic aspect has proved to be the far more important factor.

The pattern and sequence of political violence as examined in this study indicates that the revolutionary insurrection in 1971 and the separatist Tamil insurgency from 1972 onward were two separate phenomenons in Sri Lanka's contemporary politics. Although there was no overt link between the insurrection of 1971 and the Tamil guerrilla warfare, it is obvious that both strains of political violence shared common characteristics. The first was the significant youth participation in and leadership of the political violence movements. It becomes evident that the youth of Sri Lanka have been increasingly exposed to a culture of political violence.

The pattern of insurrection of the J.V.P., however, differs widely in other respects from that of the Tamil guerrilla warfare. The J.V.P. violence assumes the pattern of sudden insurrections in which acts of terrorism are of minor significance. According to this pattern, the possibilities of negotiation are minimal and the only outcome is either total victory or defeat. Yet the movement has re-emerged from time to time. The Tamil guerrilla warfare, on the other hand, has been characterized by protracted warfare where terrorism and selective political assassinations have played a decisive part.

The intervention by external forces has revealed the following characteristics. The secessionist-motivated guerrilla warfare waged by the Tamil youth did not attract a great deal of intervention from the western countries, whereas during the insurrection of 1971 the western countries extended considerable support to the Sri Lankan Government. The second characteristic is that the incumbent governments in Sri Lanka tended to attract more international support than the J.V.P. and the Tamil guerrilla groups. Thirdly, India's role pertaining to the Tamil guerrilla warfare compared to the insurrection of 1971 was contradictory. India continued to maintain a strong anti-secessionist policy particularly regarding its domestic politics, yet voiced concern about or provided assistance to the secessionist movements in East Pakistan.[11] The support extended by the Indian Government to the Tamil guerrillas differed widely from India's involvement with East Pakistan.[12] India's direct involvement in the Tamil insurgency, by basing the Indian Peace Keeping Force in Sri Lanka, did not resolve or control the political violence. The involvement of external forces contributed to the escalation of political violence rather than to the control and settlement of the political conflict.

Both the political violence of 1971 and the Tamil secessionist violence were youth dominated, were mainly concerned with domestic issues, and were subject to intervention from external sources. The political violence within the Tamil community shared a dominant characteristic with that of the insurrection of 1971 in its youth domination. The former was waged by Tamil-Hindu youth whereas the latter was waged by the Sinhalese-Buddhist rural youth. The disparities, however, are much wider especially in terms of duration, intensity of violence, area of operations, number of deaths, damage to property, and the number of groups involved. The outcome of the insurrection of 1971 and the continuing Tamil guerrilla warfare point to the fact that it is impossible to eliminate political violence movements, when they are based on deep-rooted, socio-economic and political factors, by depending on military solutions. The Sri Lankan experience gives substance to the view that ethnic insurgency cannot be resolved and is harder to solve than political violence based on class conflict. The insurrection of 1971, which was class based, was controlled within three months whereas the Tamil guerrilla warfare is still on going. Consequently, this prolonged ethnic insurgency has given rise to the wide opinion that political violence and ethnic conflict cannot be solved but can only be managed. Political conflict in Sri Lanka remains unsolved due to the fact that the parties involved in it have adopted different and incompatible views as to the solutions to the problem. The obvious means of defusing the problem, such as resolution through negotiation, have already been explored and exhausted. If peaceful means of resolving the Tamil insurgency are not found soon, a full-blown civil war seems imminent.

The L.T.T.E. has succeeded in crushing the other Tamil guerrilla groups and thus has gained stature among the Tamil community. The L.T.T.E. has laid claim to the Northern and Eastern provinces which would form a separate Tamil state, and have called for the establishment of a separate Tamil national army. The central government is unable to accede to such a turn of events and therefore, the crisis, remains deadlocked despite the efforts by the parties concerned to end it. The Sri Lankan Government and the L.T.T.E. have agreed several times to call a cease-fire and negotiate a settlement, but each time the process of negotiation has resulted in a resumption of fighting because neither side has been willing to compromise and negotiate a settlement. Consequently, peaceful negotiations toward achieving the goals of each party have been accompanied by open options for renewed violent confrontations as a bargaining chip to gain concessions.

Of the theories examined in this study, S.P. Huntington's theory of modernization offers a broad analysis of the factors conducive for the origin of political violence movements. The Sri Lankan experience confirms that political violence movements originate within districts which have been exposed to the process of modernization in many crucial areas. The districts which were caught up in the process of modernization in the South gave rise to the J.V.P., while the districts which were experiencing similar changes in the North gave rise to the Tamil guerrilla movement.

The modernization theory in its empirical analysis is subject, however, to modification in this study. Hence, the political conditions and the socio-economic and psychological factors are equally important in analyzing the preconditions which were conducive to the origin of the political violence movements in Sri Lanka. All of these factors are dialectically interconnected and are equally relevant. The specific factors which are most important for an analysis of political violence are the organizational, ideological, and strategical characteristics of the guerrilla groups, and the government's response to each conflict. As in Huntington's theory, the urban middle class did not assume the leadership of the political violence in Sri Lanka. More precisely the leadership of the political violence movements there belonged to the petit-bourgeois or lower middle class. Huntington's modernization theory, however, fails to explain the actual social background of the participants in political violence in Sri Lanka. The main participants were not the peasantry as perceived in Huntington's theory, but were the youth, few of whom came from the peasant class. To grasp the role of the youth in the insurrection and the Tamil violence an additional theoretical perspective is needed.

8.4 Implications and Consequences of Political Violence

The political violence in Sri Lanka did not impact or influence the global or regional balance of power. It did however;

inflict tremendous human casualties and material losses. The large number of civilian deaths then was the major outcome of political violence in Sri Lanka. It is estimated that over 40,000 lives from 1971 to 1987 were lost during the course of the insurgencies. According to the U.S. Committee for Refugees, in 1988 an estimated 250,000 Sri Lankans were displaced, thereby placing Sri Lanka as the 13th largest 'producer' of refugees in the world.[13] Over 150,000 Tamils alone are estimated to have fled to the Southern Indian state of Tamil Nadu.

On the other hand, there is the danger that political violence could extend to other areas in Sri Lanka such as to the Muslim and the Indian Tamil communities and to other states in the region. The most important impact of the Tamil guerrilla warfare has been the resurgence of the J.V.P. as an insurgent group. The main objectives of the J.V.P.'s violence since 1987 have been to force India to withdraw the I.P.K.F. and the Sri Lankan Government to resign. After the Indo-Sri Lanka Accord was signed in 1987, the J.V.P. embarked on a strategy of assassination and occasional raids on police stations. The Sri Lankan Government was able to exert their military strength however, and control the activities of the J.V.P., thereby forcing the J.V.P. to revert to the organizational phase. As an external factor, the attempted takeover of the Maldives in November 1988 by armed invaders serves as a good example. The invasion was carried out by a group of mercenaries who are believed to have been members of the P.L.O.T.[14]

The J.V.P., as well as the Tamil guerrilla organizations, has posed a credible military threat to the incumbent Sri Lankan Government as seen by the existence of a sizeable and active guerrilla force, and the dispatch of a considerable portion of the government's security forces to suppress it. The Tamil guerrilla movement has been able to attain a considerable level of legitimacy especially by endorsing regional autonomy through the provincial councils or any other form of devolution. Political violence was the means by which this legitimacy and bargaining position has been reached.

In addition, the political violence in Sri Lanka further widened the long-standing differences between the Sinhalese majority and the Tamil minority. This weakened the pursuit of national integration and threatened the existing socio-economic and political system. The ethnic violence has further deepened the gap between the Tamil and Sinhalese communities by arousing the fears of each against living in areas dominated by the other. Consequently, there has been a trend towards geographical polarization. The long-standing multi-ethnic polity has come under threat; disintegration seems an imminent possibility. Externally, the Tamil guerrilla warfare has become the most influential factor in Indo-Sri Lankan relationships. Consequently, this political violence has the potential of developing into a regional crisis in South Asia.

The growing tendency for political violence in Sri Lanka from 1971 onward has moved the country from a relatively open democratic government to a pattern of constitutional authoritarianism, which is best illustrated by the declarations of emergency and curfew for prolonged periods. For example, a state of emergency was declared from 1971 to 1977 and again from 1983 to 1989.

As in many Third World countries, political violence has become part of the modern political process, and is now viewed by disadvantaged or disgruntled societal factions as the most expeditious means of achieving political objectives. Pre-election and post-election violence between political parties, and ethnic violence between the Sinhalese majority and the Tamil minority, have served as a means of achieving a variety of political ends in Sri Lanka. Post-election violence and ethnic violence have contributed heavily to the growing political violence in Sri Lanka. Consequently, political' violence has become institutionalized in Sri Lankan politics and society. A certainty in any occurrence of political violence is that the longer its duration, the deeper it becomes entrenched and the further it becomes institutionalized. It becomes increasingly evident that Sri Lanka is heading for widespread guerrilla war, and possibly civil war, neither of which would bring victory to any of the participants.

As a solution to this stalemate, it has been mooted that regional autonomy through provincial councils within the confines of a unified state would pave the way to resolving the quandary. The different notions on how these provincial councils should operate, however, has posed a further problem. The crux of the matter is whether or not the Northern Province and the eastern Province would merge. The Tamils prefer to merge while the Sinhalese as well as the Muslims oppose it. According to the Indo-Sri Lanka Accord, a merger should be ratified by a referendum within the two provinces. There is little doubt that the referendum would pass in the Northern Province because the Tamils are in the majority there. In the Eastern Province, however, the Tamils, the Sinhalese and the Muslims are represented in equal numbers. The Sinhalese and the Muslims would not concede to a single provincial council, especially if the union would result in domination by the Tamils. Consequently, the devolution of power under such circumstances would counter the separatist demands. Hence, the Tamil guerrilla warfare remains unresolved and a major threat to Sri Lankan geographical integrity and sovereignty. Political violence marked the redefinition of India's role from mediator to power broker. The Indo-Sri Lanka Accord was a landmark of this new development. Under the terms of the Accord, India acquired substantial control over Sri Lanka's foreign policy. The Accord excluded the involvement of outside powers in the conflict while permitting India to assert its status as a regional hegemonic state.

8.5 Recommendations

Like many Third World countries in Asia, Africa and Latin America, Sri Lanka's left-wing and ethnic insurgencies are symptomatic of a wider socio-economic and political crisis which needs careful and thorough analysis. The theories examined in this study pay little attention to the solutions for political violence. It is accepted that political violence in Sri Lanka is basically a socio-economic and political problem rather than a problem of law and order. The key to the solution does not lie in emphasizing the need to extinguish political violence, which is merely a symptom. It is more appropriate to focus on the causes of political violence movements and the violence itself. Therefore, this necessitates socio-economic and political reforms which will address the roots of the problem. Resorting to military methods will only serve to suppress the political violence movements for the short term, as proven by the resurgence of the J.V.P. Political violence is a politico-military phenomenon. Therefore, the political violence represents not only a military challenge but is a political threat as well. According to Robert Thomson, the following should be included in the counter-insurgency programme of the government: the government should have a clear political aim; it should function in accordance with the law; it should have an overall plan containing not only the military measures but also the political, social, economic, administrative, police and any other measures needed; it must give priority to defeating political subversion, not the guerrillas; and in the guerrilla phase of an insurgency it must secure its base areas first.[15]

The Sri Lankan Tamils have the advantage of a territorial base in the North where the Tamils are in the majority. They also have access to bases in South India. Considering the military advantages of the Tamil guerrillas, a totally military approach, if adopted by the Sri Lankan Government, would lead to either heavy civilian casualties in the Tamil areas or a mass migration of refugees to South India. Both developments would result in an Indian intervention and a subsequent resurgence of the J.V.P. or a similar group. These factors strongly indicate that a military approach on its own is not a viable means of defeating political violence movements in Sri Lanka. There is, of course, no immediate solution to political violence in Sri Lanka but to resolve the conflict, the following four criteria must be addressed by the Sri Lankan Government: restore legitimacy to the Sri Lankan political system; restore and maintain ethnic and political harmony; strive for a negotiated settlement with moderate Tamil parties and promote regional cooperation in addressing political violence. Using the above-mentioned criteria, the author endeavours in this section to propose the following recommendations to resolve and to manage the political violence in Sri Lanka.

In order to restore legitimacy to the national political system, democracy and rule of law should be maintained. According to P. Wilkinson, the primary objective of counter-violence strategy should be the protection and maintenance of liberal democracy and the rule of law.[16] He further maintains that any attempt to suspend parliamentary democracy, any recourse to rule by emergency decree, the abandonment of free elections, and all fundamental abridgements of a democratic constitution, must be resisted.[17] Therefore, a major effort towards the development of political democracy and its preservation should be made. Such an effort might be developed through free and fair elections, equal opportunities for political participation, mutual understanding between major political parties and the preservation of human rights.

The long-term solution to the political violence in Sri Lanka lies in the protection of human rights and the upholding of the rule of law. In controlling political violence it becomes increasingly necessary for the criminal procedure of the country to be upheld. The rule of law and the judicial system are vital institutions which in a context of crisis should be preserved. Moreover, the counter measures adopted by the Sri Lankan Government should not infringe on the norms of human rights. Another important aspect of promoting Sri Lanka's democracy is that the central government should further explore the possibilities of the policy of devolution. It appears to be the only hope in avoiding more widespread agitation by the Tamil guerrilla groups for a separate state. Whatever changes devolution introduces should address the grievances of the various communities and reflect the goals and values of the Sri Lankan society as a whole. It is also and effective mechanism to expand the system of local government in Sri Lanka and involve the people in the local decision-making process.

In order to achieve ethnic and political harmony Sri Lanka has to accommodate a national and political consensus for evolving a *modus vivendi* among the Tamil and Sinhalese communities. Therefore, the government should seriously consider the ways and means of eliminating all forms of covert and overt political and ethnic discrimination. A commitment to eradicate political and racial injustice in Sri Lanka would contribute to the improvement of the political and ethnic climate. A primary concern of the government should be to take precautions against future pre- or post- election violence and ethnic violence. The election violence is manifest in the attacks on opposition parties while ethnic violence is concentrated against the Tamil community.

Due to its geo-political reality Sri Lanka should maintain a policy of regional cooperation especially with the central government of neighbouring India. The non-alignment movement and the South Asian Regional Cooperation (S.A.R.C.) may be of in enforcing relationships with India. Considering the wider context of the Tamil guerrilla warfare and the ethnic violence, the problem calls for the intercession of a neutral third party.

8.6 Final Summary

In the introduction, which is also the first chapter of this study, it was noted that this research study is confined basically to political violence in Sri Lanka from 1971 to 1987. It represents one of the first attempts of a theoretical-cum-empirical analysis of political violence in Sri Lanka in the context of the Third World. It is an exploratory analysis rather than a comparative or conclusive examination.

In analyzing political violence over a sixteen year period, this study attempts to cover a wider canvas which includes socio-economic and political modernization and its consequences. Many new developments such as the role of the Indian Peace Keeping Force in the conflict in Sri Lanka, the resurgence of the J.V.P. violence, and the continuation of the L.T.T.E. guerrilla warfare after the Indo-Sri Lanka Accord of 1987, have been left for purposes of future research. Moreover, the author has tested and examined the basic hypothesis postulated in this study. The immediate ramifications of the main findings of this study pertaining to the causes and pattern of political violence have been discussed, and precautionary measures pertaining to future political violence have been recommended. As intended in this study the author has illustrated the need to examine the ways in which different patterns of political violence occur, change and influence one another over a period of time. The author also hopes that the data, hypotheses, results and theories discussed in this study will prove useful to other researchers who wish to examine the causes and pattern of political violence in the Third World in general and Sri Lanka in particular.

References

1. The components of the set of phenomena referred to as political violence are often identified with or include some of the same

phenomena which have been referred to as internal wars (Eckstein), domestic conflict (Tanter, Rummel), intrasocietal war (Huntington), revolution (Johnson) or civil strife (Gurr). The author's approach is limited to internal domestic forms of political conflict and thus excludes foreign wars and invasion.

2. Regis Debray, Revolution in the Revolution: Armed Struggle and Political Struggle in Latin America, (London: Penguin Books, 1969), p. 106.
3. Walker Connor, "The Politics of Ethnonationalism", Journal of International Affairs, Vol. 27, (1973), pp. 16-17.
4. Similarly, the battle cry of the Sandinistas in Nicaragua against the Samoza regime was: 'motherland free or death'.
5. In the first phase of insurrection tightly organized professional revolutionaries were to take over the key points and buildings of Paris. Then in the second phase, they were to call for a popular uprising to ward off an eventual counterattack by the military. For further detail see, Alan B. Spitzer, *The Revolutionary Theories of Louis Auguste Blanqui*, (New York: 1957), pp. 171-182.
6. The United Front won 116 seats out of 145 seats in the parliamentary election of 1970.
7. C. Johnson, *An Autopsy of People's War*, (Berkeley: University of California Press, 1973), pp. 98-99.
8. For more detail see, Andrew C. Janos, "The Seizure of Power: A Study of Force and Popular Consent", Research Monograph No. 16, (Princeton, N. J.: Centre of International Studies, Princeton University, 1964), pp.
9. Marshall Singer, "Prospects for Conflict Management in the Sri Lankan Ethnic Crisis", in Joseph V. Montville, (ed), *Conflict and Peacemaking in Multiethnic Societies*, (Lexington: D.C. Heath and Company, 1990), p. 279.
10. Kenneth Bush, "Ethnic Conflict in Sri Lanka", *Conflict Quarterly*, Vol. 10, No. 2, (1990), p. 52.
11. India faces the separatist movements within its own boarders in Kashmir, Nagaland, Dravidastan (Tamil Nadu), Khalistan (Sikhs), and Gurkhaland (Gurkhas).
12. The secession of former East Pakistan from Pakistan occurred with India's full-scale military intervention and led to the Indo-Pakistan War of 1971. Thus, Bangladesh emerged as the only

secessionist effort after World War 2 to succeed in its aim of independence. See John G. Stoessinger, *Why Nations Go to War*, (London: Macmillan, 1985), pp. 128-138.

13. Kenneth Bush, *op. cit.,* p. 42.
14. Deepak Tripathi, "India's Maldives Mission and After", *World Today*, (January 1989), pp. 3-4.
15. Robert Thompson, *Defeating Communist Insurgency*, (London: Chatto and Windus, 1966), pp. 50-57.
16. P. Wilkinson, *Terrorism and Liberal State,* (London: Macmillan, 1986), p. 125.
17. *Ibid.,* p. 127.

Appendix-1

The Tamil Guerrilla Organisations

Liberation Tigers of Tamil Eelam (LTTE)

Tamil Eelam Liberation Organisation (TELO)

People's Liberation Organisation of Tamil Eelam (PLOTE)

Eelam Popular Revolutionary Liberation Front (EPRLF)

Eelam Revolutionary Organisation of Students (EROS)

Popular Liberation Army (PLA)

Revolutionary Eelam Liberation Organisation (TELO Splinter Group)

Tamil Eelam Army (TEA)

Tamil Eelam Liberation Cobras (TELC)

Tamil Eelam Liberation Army (TELA)

Tamil Eelam Liberation Front (TELF)

Tamil Eelam Revolutionary People's Liberation Arm (TERPLA)

Tamil Eelam National Army (TENA)

Tamil Eelam Revolutionary Organisation (TERO)

National Liberation Front of Tamils (TNLF)

Liberation Communist Guerrilla Movement (LCGM)

Tamil Marxist Liberation Tigers (TMLT)

Tamil Eelam Liberation Extremists (TELE)

Appendix-2

The Theory of the J. Curve

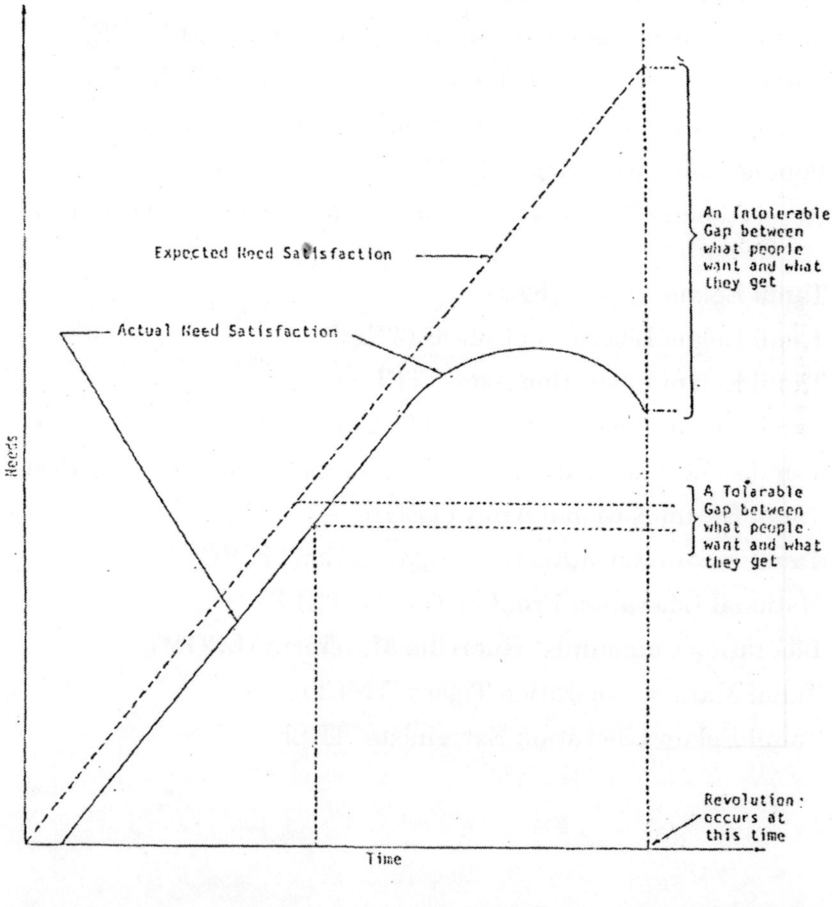

James C. Davies. "Toward a Theory of Revolution", *When Men Revolt and Why: A Reader in Political Violence and Revolution,* Editor, James C. Davies, New York: The Free Press, 1971

Appendix-3

The Theory of Tanter and Midlarsky

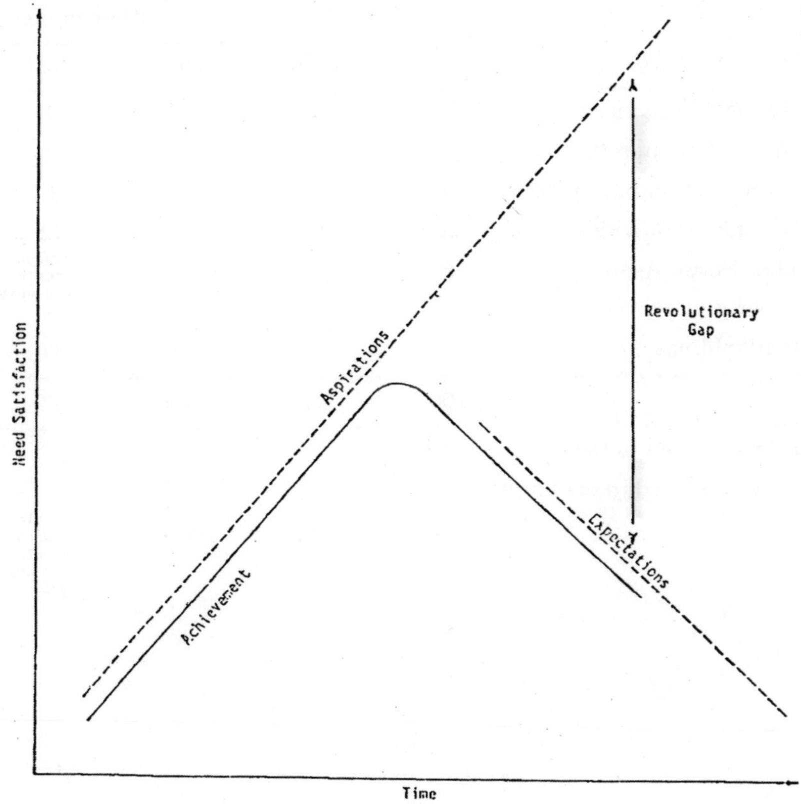

Manus Midlarsky and Raymond Tanter. "A Theory of Revolution", Revolution and Political Change. Editors Claude E. Welch, Jr. and Mavis Bunker Taintbr, Belmont: Duxbury Press. A Division of Wadsworth publishing Co., Inc., 1972, p. 6.

Appendix-4
Ownership of Land Area Under Export Crops, 1972, Prior to Land Reform

(Percentage)

For of ownership	*Tea*	*Rubber*	*Coconut*	*Total*
Sterling Companies (a)	24	11	—	9
Rupee Companies (b)	25	13	—	10
Non-Sri Lankan Individuals	2	2	—	1
Sri Lankan Individuals	26	42	49	42
Public Sector Agencies	5	1	—	1
Cooperative Farms	—	—	—	—
Smallholdings	18	31	50	37
Total	100	100	100	100

(*a*) Incoporated in the U.K.

(*b*) Incorporated in Sri Lanka.

Source: G.H. Peiris, "Land Reform and the Agrarian Change in Sri Lanka", Modern Asian Studies, Vol. 12, No. 4, 1978, and B. Moore, The State and Peasant Politics in Sri Lanka, Cambridge, Cambridge University Press, 1985, p. 67.

Appendix-5
Ethnic Population by Districts

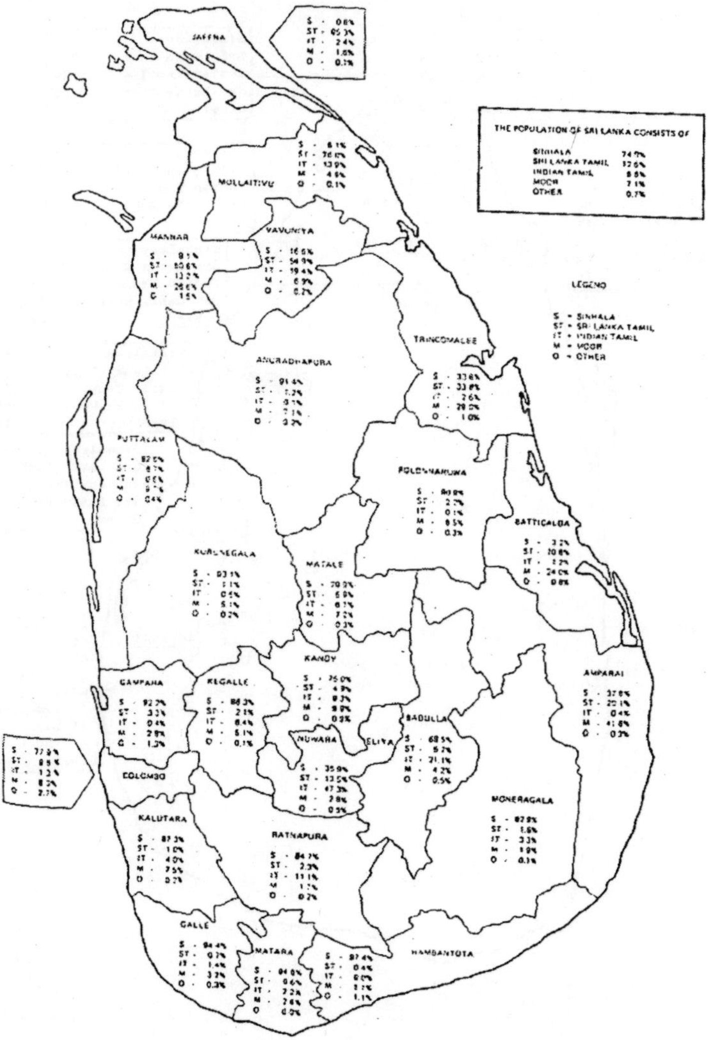

Appendix-6
Proposed Eclam State

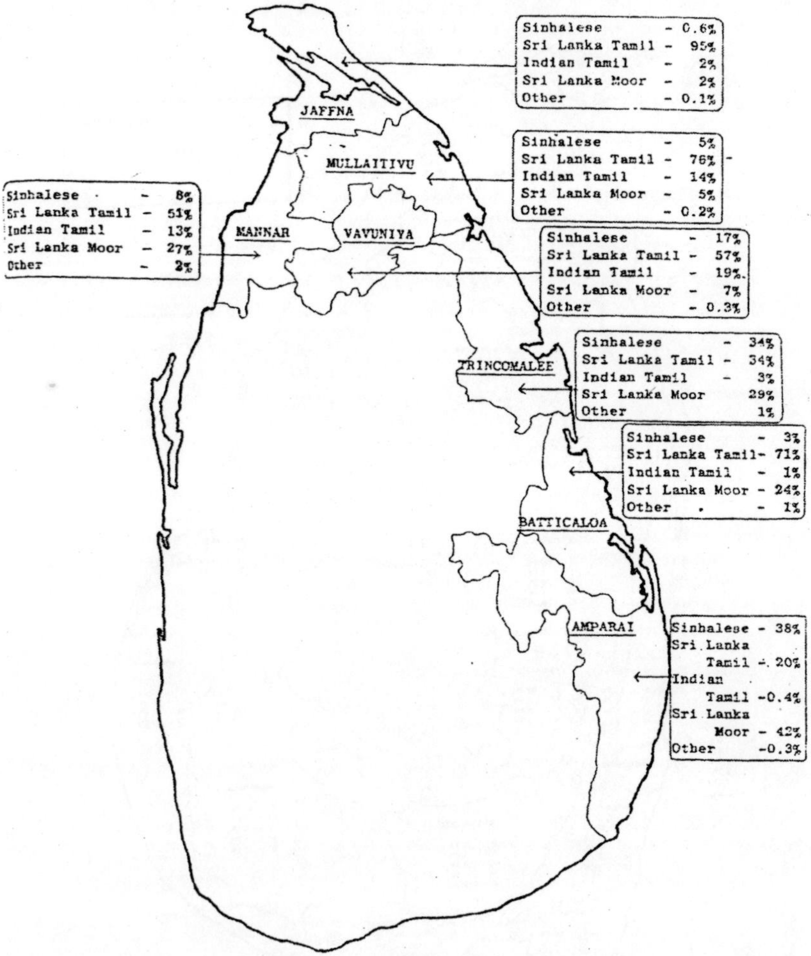

Appendix-7
Map Showing the Areas of the Insurrection of 1971

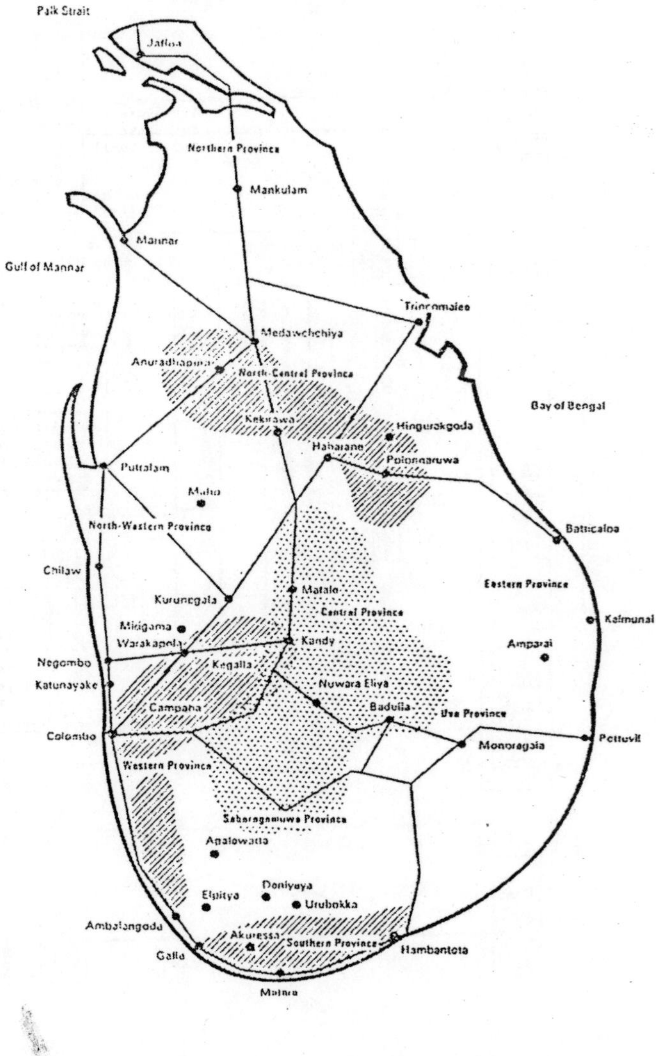

Appendix-8
Infrastructure of Counter—Insurgency

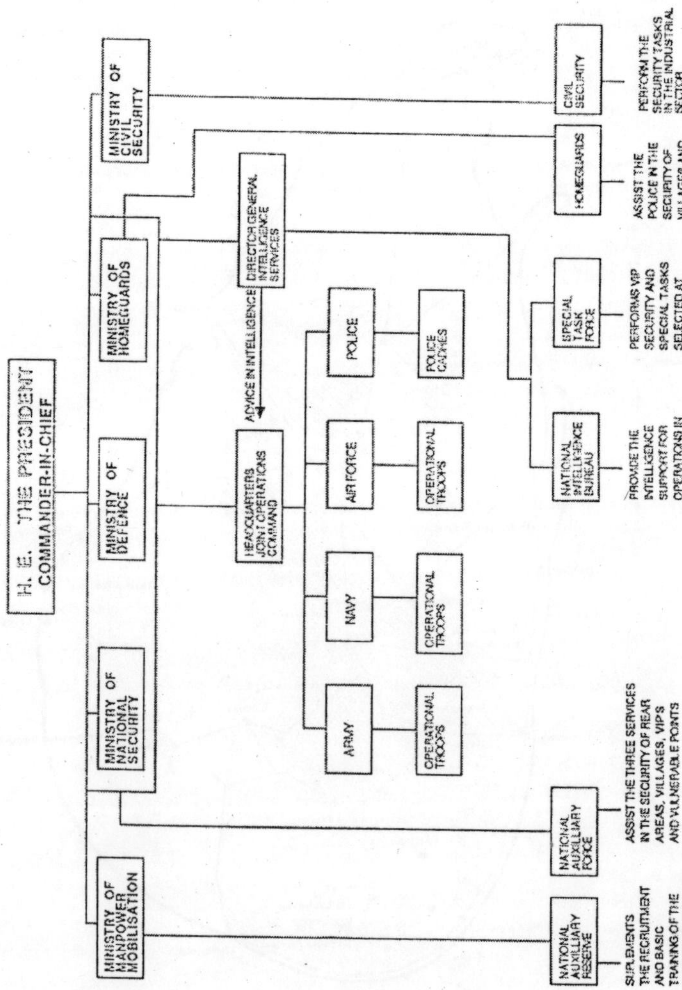

Appendix-9

Annexure C

In terms of paragraph six of President's statement of December 1st, 1983, the following proposal which have emerged as a result of discussions in Colombo and New Delhi are appended for consideration by the All-Party Conference. These proposals are in the context of unity and integrity of Sri Lanka and will form the basis for formulating the Agenda of the All-Party Conference.

1. The District Development Councils in a Province be permitted to combine into one or more Regional Councils if they agree by decisions of the Councils and approved by Referendum in that district.
2. In the case of District Councils of Northern and Eastern provinces, respectively, as they are not functioning due to the resignation of the majority of members, their union within each province to be accepted.
3. Each region will have a Regional Council if so desired. The convention will be established that the leader of the party which commands a majority in the Regional Council would be formally appointed by the President as the chief ministers of the Region. The Chief Minister will constitute a Committee of ministers of the Region.
4. The President and the Parliament will continue to have overall responsibility for all subjects not transferred to the Region and generally for all other matters relating to maintenance of sovereignty, integrity, unity, and security and progress and development of the Republic as a whole.
5. The legislative power of the region would be vested in the Regional Council is which would be empowered to enact laws and exercise executive powers in relation

thereto on certain specified listed subjects including the maintenance of Internal Law and Order in the Region, the administration of justice, social and economic development cultural matters land policy. The list of subjects to be allocated to the Regions will be worked out in detail.

6. The Regional councils will have powers to levy taxes, of fees and to mobilize resources through loans, the proceeds of which will be credited to a Consolidated Fund set up for that particular Region to which also will be credited grants, allocations or subventions made by the Republic. Financial resources will be apportioned to the Region on the recommendations of the representative Finance Commission appointed from time to time.
7. Provisions will be made to constitute High Courts in each region. The Supreme Court of Sri Lanka will exercise appellate and constitutional jurisdiction.
8. Each Region will have a Regional Service constituting (a) officers and public servants of the Region and (b) such other officers and public servants who may be seconded to the Region. Each Region will have a Regional Public Service Commission for recruitment and for exercising disciplinary powers relating to the members of the Regional Service.
9. The armed forces of Sri Lanka will reflect the national ethnic composition. In the Northern and Eastern Provinces the police force for internal security will also reflect the ethnic composition of these Regions.
10. A Port Authority under the Central Government will be set up for administering the Trincornalee Port and Harbour. The area that will come under the Port Authority as well as the powers to be assigned to it will be further discussed.
11. A national policy on land settlement and the basis on which the government will undertake land colonization will have to be worked out. All settlement schemes will be based on ethnic proportion so as not to alter the demographic balance subject to agreements being reached on major projects.

12. The Constitutions and other laws dealing with the official language Sinhala and the national language Tamil be accepted and implemented as well as similar laws dealing with the National Flag and Anthem.
13. The Conference should appoint a committee to work out constitutional and legal changes that may be necessary to implement these decisions. The Government will provide its secretariat and necessary legal offices.
14. The consensus of opinion of the All-Party Conference will itself be considered by the United National Party Executive Committee and presumably by the executive body of the other parties as well before being placed before Parliament for legislative action.

Appendix-10

Indo-Sri Lanka Agreement to Establish Peace and Normalcy in Sri Lanka

The Prime Minister of Republic of India, His Excellency Mr. Rajiv Gandhi and the President of the Democratic Socialist Republic of Sri Lanka, His Excellency Mr. J.R. Jayewardene having met at Colombo on July 29, 1987.

Attaching utmost importance to nurturing, intensifying and strengthening the traditional friendship of India and Sri Lanka and acknowledging the imperative need of resolving the ethnic problem of Sri Lanka, and the consequent violence and for the safety, well-being w1d prosperity of people belonging to all communities in Sri Lanka.

Having this day entered into the following Agreement to fulfil this objective.

1.1 desiring to preserve the unity, sovereignty and territorial. Integrity of Sri Lanka;

1.2 acknowledging that Sri Lanka is a multi-ethnic and a multi- lingual plural society consisting, inter alia, of Sinhalese, Tamils, Muslims (Moors), and Burghers;

1.3 recognising that each ethnic group has a distinct cultural and linguistic identity which has to be carefully nurtured;

1.4 also recognising that the Northern and the Eastern Provinces have been areas of historical of Sri Lankan Tamil speaking peoples, who have at all times hitherto lived together in this territory with other ethnic groups;

1.5 conscious of the necessity of strengthening the forces contributing to the unity, sovereignty and territorial integrity of Sri Lanka, and preserving its character as a multi-ethnic, multi- lingual and multi-religious plural society, in which all citizens can live in equality, safety and harmony, and prosper and fulfil their aspirations;

2. Resolve that:

2.1 Since the Government of Sri Lanka proposes to permit adjoining Provinces to join to form one administrative unit and also by a Referendum to separate as may be permitted to the Northern and Eastern Provinces as outlined below:

2.2 During the period, which shall be considered an interim period (i.e.) from the date of the elections to the provincial Council, as specified in para 2.8 to the date of the referendum as specified in para 2.3, the Northern and Eastern Provinces as now constituted, will form one administrative unit, having one elected Provincial Council. Such a unit will have one Governor, one Chief Minister and one Board of Ministers.

2.3 There will be a referendum on or 31st December, 1988 to enable the people of the Eastern Province to decide whether:

(A) The Eastern province should remain linked with the Northern province as one administrative unit, and continue to be governed together with the Northern Province as specified in para 2.2, or

(B) The Eastern province should constitute a separate administrative unit having its own distinct Provincial with a separate Governor, Chief Minister and Board of Ministers.

The President may, at his discretion decide to postpone such a referendum.

2.4 All persons who have been displaced due to ethnic violence, or other reasons, will have right to vote in such a referendum. Necessary conditions to enable them to return to areas from where they were displaced will be created.

2.5 The referendum, when held, will be monitored by a committee headed by the Chief Justice, a member appointed by the President, nominated by the Government of Sri Lanka, and a member appointed by the President, nominated by the representatives of the Tamil speaking people of the Eastern Province.

2.6 A simple majority will be sufficient to determine the result of the referendum.

2.7 Meeting and other forms of propaganda, permissible within the laws of the country, will be allowed before the referendum.

2.8 Election to Provincial Councils will be held within the next three months, in any event before December 31, 1987. Indian observers will be invited for elections to the Provincial Council of the North and East.

2.9 The emergency will be lifted *in* the Eastern and Northern provinces by August 15, 1987. A cessation of hostilities will come into effect allover the island within 48 hours of the signing of this agreement. All arms presently held by militant groups will be surrendered in accordance with an agreed procedure to authorities to be designated by the Government of Sri Lanka. Consequent to the cessation of hostilities and the surrender of arms by militant groups, the army and other security personel will be confined to barracks in camps as on May 25, 1987. The process of surrendering of arms and the confining the security personnel moving back to barracks shall be completed within 72 hours of the cessation of hostilities coming into effect.

2.10 The Government of Sri Lanka will utilise for the purpose of law enforcement and maintenance of security in the Northern and Eastern provinces the same organisations and mechanisms of Government as are used in the rest of the country.

2.11 The President of Sri Lanka will grant a general amnesty to political and other prisoners now held in custody under the Prevention of Terrorism Act and other emergency laws, and to combatants, as well as to those persons accused, charged and or convicted under these laws. The Government of Sri Lanka will make special efforts to rehabilitate militant youth with a view to bringing them back to the mainstream of national life. India will cooperate in the process.

2.12 The Government of Sri Lanka will accept and abide by the above provisions and expect all others to do likewise.

2.13 If the framework for the resolutions is accepted, the Government of Sri Lanka will implement the relevant proposals forthwith.

2.14 The Government of India will under work and guarantee the resolutions, and co-operate in the implementation of these proposals.

2.15 These proposals are conditional to an acceptance of proposals negotiated from 4.5.1986 to 19.12.1986. Residual matters not finalised during the above negotiations shall be resolved between India and Sri Lanka within a period of six weeks of sighing this agreement. These proposals are also conditional to the Government of India co-operating directly with the Government of Sri Lanka in their implementation.

2.16 These proposals are also conditional to the Government of India taking the following actions if any militant group operating in Sri Lanka do not accept tins framework of proposals for a settlement, namely:

(A) India will take all necessary steps to ensure that Indian territory is not used for activities prejudicial to the unity, integrity and security of Sri Lanka.

(B) The Indian Navy/Coast Guard will co-operate with the Sri Lankan Navy in preventing Tamil militant activities from affecting Sri Lanka.

(C) In the event that the Government of Sri Lanka request the Government of India to afford military assistance to implement these proposals the Government of India will co-operate by giving to the Government of Sri Lanka such military assistance as and when requested.

(D) The Government of India will expedite repatriation from Sri Lanka of Indian citizens to India who are resident there concurrently with the repatriation of Sri Lankan refugees from tamil Nadu.

(E) The Government of India and Sri Lanka, will co-operate in ensuring the physical security and safety of all communities inhabiting the Northern and Eastern provinces.

2.17 The Government of Sri Lanka shall be Sinhala. Tamil and English will also be official languages.

3. This agreement and the annexure there-to shall come in to force upon signature.

In witness whereof we have set our hands and seals hereunto. Done in Colombo, Sri Lanka, on this the twenty ninth day of July of the year one thousand nine hundred and eighty seven, in duplicate, both texts being equally authentic.

Rajiv Gandhi	Junius Richard Jayewardene
Prime Minister of the	President of the Democratic
Republic of India	Socialist Republic of Sri Lanka

Bibliography

1. Political Violence: Books

Alexander, Yonah, (ed). International Terrorism: National, Regional and Global Perspectives, New York: Praeger Publisher, 1976.

__________, David Carlton and Paul Wilkinson, (eds). Terrorism: Theory and Practice. Boulder: Westview Press, 1979.

__________, and Robert A. Friedlander, (eds). Self-determination: National Regional and Global Perspectives. Boulder: Westview Press, 1979.

__________, and John M. Gleason, Behavioral and Quantitative Perspective on Terrorism. New York: Pergamon Press, 1981.

Andriole, S.J. and G.W. Hopple< Revolution and Political Stability. London: Frances Pinter, 1981.

Arendt, Yonah, On Revolution. New York: Viking Press, 1963.

__________, On Violence. New York: Harcourt, Brace and World, Inc. 1970.

Bell, J.B. The Myth of the Guerrilla: Revolutionary Theory and Malpractice. New York: Alfred A. Knopf, 1971.

__________, On revolt: Strategies of National Liberation. Boston: Harvard University Press, 1976.

__________, A Time of Terror: How Democratic Societies Respond to Revolutionary Violence. New York: Basic Books, 1978.

Berman, P. Revolutionary Organization. Lexington: Lexington Books, 1974.

Black, Cyril E. (ed). Communism And Revolution: The strategic Uses of Political Violence. Princeton: N.J., Princeton University Press, 1964.

Brinton, Crane. The Anatomy of Revolution. New York: Vintage Books, 1956.

Burton, Anthony M. Revolutionary Violence: The Theories. New York: Crane, Russack and Co., 1975.

__________, Urban Terrorism: Theory, Practices and Response. New York: Free Press 1975.

Carr, E. H. Studies in Revolution. New York: Grosset and Dunlap, 1964.
Calvert, Peter, Revolution. London: Pall Mall Press, 1970.

————, A Study of Revolution. London: Oxford University Press, 1970.

Chaliand, Gerard. Revolution in the Third World: Currents and Conflicts in Asia, Africa and Latin America. New York: Penguin, 1989.

Clutterbuck, Richard. Protest and urban Guerrilla. London: Cassell, 1973.

————, The Future of Political Violence. London: Macmillan and RUSI, 1985. Cohan A.S. Theories of Revolution: An Introduction. New York: Wiley, 1975.

Crenshaw, Martha, (ed) Terrorism, Legitimacy and Power: The Consequences of Political Violence. Middletown, Conn: Wesleyan University Press, 1983.

Crozier, Brian. The Rebels: A Study of Post-War Insurrection. London: Chatto and Windus, 1960.

Davies James C. (ed). When Men Revolt and Why, A Reader in Political Violence and Revolution. New York: The Pree Press, 1971.

Dunn, John. Modern Revolutions: An Introduction to the Analysis of a Political Phenomenon. Cambridge: Cambridge University Press, 1972.

Eckstein Harry, (ed) Internal war: Problems and Approaches. New York: Free Press, 1964.

Greene, Thomas. Comparative Revolutionary Movements. Englewood Cliffs, N.J.: Prentice-Hall, 1974.

Gross, Feliks. The seizure of political power. Westport, conn: Greenwood Press Publishers, 1958.

Guevara, Che. On guerrilla Warfare. New York: Monthly Review Press, 1961. Gurr, Ted Robert. Why Men Rebel. Princeton: Princeton University Press, 1970.

————, (ed). Handbook of Political Conflict: Theory and Research, New York: Free Press, 1980.

Hagopian, Mark N. The Phenomenon of Revolution. New York: Dood, Mead and company, 1974.

Hoffer, E. The True Believer: Thoughts on the Nature of Mass Movements. New York, Harper and Row Publishers, 1951.

Huntington, Samuel P., (ed) Changing Patterns of military Politics. New York: free Press, 1962.

————, Political Order in Changing Societies. New Haven: Yale University Press, 1968.

Johnson, Chalmers. Revolution and the Social System. Standford University, Hoover Institute on war, Revolution and Peace, 1964.

————, Revolutionary Change. Boston: Little brown and Co., 1966.

————, Autopsy on People's war. Berkeley: University of California Press, 1973.

Laqueur, Walter. Guerrilla: A Historical Critical Study. Boston: Little, Brown, inc., 1976.

——————, The Guerrilla Reader: A Historical and Critical Study. London: Wilwood House, 1978.

——————, The Terrorism Reader: A Historical Anthology. Philadelphia: Temple University, 1978.

Macfarlane, Leslie. Political Disobedience. London: Macmillion, 1971.

——————, Violence and State. London: Nelson, 1974.

Marighella, Carlos. For the Liberation of Brazil. Harmondsworth: Penguin, 1972.

Nieburg, H.I. Political Violence: The Behavioral Process. New York: St. Martin's Press, 1969.

Oppenheimer, M. The Urban guerrilla. Chicago: Quadrangle Books, 1960.

Rosenau, James N., International Aspects of Civil Strife. Princeton: Princeton University Press, 1964.

Skocpol, Theda. States and Social Revolution, Cambridge: Cambridge University Press, 1979.

Tilly, Charies. From Mobilization to Revolution. New York: Random House, 1978. Wilkinson, P. Social Movement. London: Pall Mall, 1971.

——————, Political Terrorism, London: Macmillan, 1974.

——————, Political Terrorism and Liberal State, London: Macmillan, 1986.

Zimmermann, E. Political Violence, crises and Revolution: Theories and Research. Cambridge: Schenkman, 1980.

2. Political Violence: Articles

Ake, Claude, "Modernization and Political Instability: A Theoretical Exploration", World Politics 26 No. 4 (July 1974): 576-591.

Abeles, R.D., "Relative Deprivation, Rising Expectation and Black Militancy", Journal of Social Issues 32 (1976) 119-137.

Abell, P., "Why Do Men Rebel? A Discussion of Ted Roberts Gurr's Why Men Rebel, Race 13 No. 1 (July 1971) 84-89.

Amann, Peter. "Revolution: A Redefinition", Political Science Quarterly 77 No 1 (March 1962): 36-53.

Aya, Roderick., "Theories of Revolution Reconsidered: Contrasting Models of Collective Violence", Theory and Society, 8 No 1 (July 1979) 39-99.

Bell, J Bowyer, "Trends on Terror: The Analysis of Political Violence", World Politics, 29 No 3 (April 1977) 476-488.

Calvert, Peter, "Revolution: The Politics of Violence", Political Studies 15 No 1 (February 1967) 1-11.

Crosby, Faye, "Relative Deprivation Revisited: A Response to Miller, Bolce and halligan", American Political Science Review, 73 No. 1 (March 1979) 103-12.

Davies, James C., "Toward a Theory of Revolution", American Sociological Review 27 No. 5 (February 1962) 5-19.

Eckstein Harry., "On the Etiology of Internal wars", History and Theory 4 (1985) 133-63.

Goldstone, jack A., "Theories of Revolution: The Third Generation", World Politics 32 No. 3 (April 1980) 425-453.

Gurr, Ted Robert., "Psychological Factors in Civil Violence", World Politics 20 No. 2 (January 1968) 245-278.

————, "A Causal Model of Civil Strife", American Political Science Review 62 No. 4 (December 1968) 1104-24.

Huntinton, Samuel P. "Pattern of Violence in World Politics", in Changing Patterns of Military Politics, (ed) S.P. Huntington, (New York Free Press 1965): 386-430.

————, "Political Development and Political Decay", World Politics 17 No. 3 (April 1965) 386-430.

Johnson, Chalmers, "The third Generation of Guerrilla Conflict", Asian Survey 8 No. 6 (1968) 435-447.

Mass, Perry. "The Nature of Political Violence", Social and Economic Studies 24 (1975) 221-238.

Melson, Robert, and Wolpe, Howard. "Modernization and the Politics of Communalism: A Theoretical Perspective", American Political Science Review 64 (December 1970) 1112-1130.

Muller, Edward N., "A Test of a Partial Theory of Potential for Political Violence", American Political Science Review, 66 No. 3 (September 1972) 928-959.

Skocpol, Theda., "Social Revolutions and mass Military Mobilization", World Politics 40 No. 2 (January 1988) 147-168.

Stone, Lawrence. "Theories of Revolution:, World Politics 18 No 2 (January 1966) 159-76.

Tilly Charies., "Does Modernization Breed Revolution", Comparative Politics 5 No. 3 (April, 1973): 425-447.

Wilkinson, Paul., "Three Questions on Terrorism", Government and Opposition 8 No. 3 (January-October 1973) 290-312.

————, "Terrorism Versus Liberal Democracy: The Problems of Response", Conflict Studies 67 (1976) 1-19.

3. Sri Lanka 1971 Insurrection: Books

Alles, A.C., Insurgency-1971. Colombo: Apothecaries Co. Ltd., 1976. De Silva, K.M. (ed) Sri Lanka: A Survey, London: C Hurst, 1977.

————————, A History of Sri Lanka< Delhi: Oxford University Press, 1981.

Dubey, Swaroop Rani, One-day Revolution in Sri Lanka: Anatomy of 1971 Insurrection, Jaipur: Aalekh Publishers, 1988.

Gough, Kathleen and Hari P. Sharma, (eds.) Imperialism and Revolution in South Asia. New York: Monthly Review Press, 1973.

Houtart, Francois, Religion and Ideology in Sri Lanka, Colombo, Colombo: Hansa Publishers Ltd., 1974.

Jayawardene, Visakha Kumari, The Rise of the Labour Movement in Ceylon., Durham: N.C. Duke University Press, 1972.

Jennings, Ivor, Nationalism and Political Development in Ceylon, New York: Institute of Pacific Relation, 1950.

Jiggins, Janice, caste and Family in the Politics of Sinhalese 1947-1976, Cambridge: Cambridge University Press, 1979.

Jupp, James, Sri Lanka-Third World Democracy. London: Frank Cass, 1978.

Kearney, Robert N. The Politics of Ceylon (Sri Lanka). New York: Cornell University Press, 1973.

Lerske George. Origin of Trotskyism in Ceylon, California: Hoover Institute, Standford University, 1968.

Lewis, John Wilson, Peasant Rebellion and Communist Revolution in Asia. California, Calif: Standford University, 1974.

Ludowyk, E.F.C. The Modern History of Ceylon. London: Weidenfeld and Nicolson, 1966.

Mendis, G.C. Ceylon Today and Yesterday: Main Currents of Ceylon History. Colombo: Associated Newspapers of Ceylon, 1957.

————————, Ceylon under the British, Colombo, Colombo Apothecaries 1952. Ryan Bryce. Caste in Modern Ceylon. New Jersey: Rutgers University Press, 1953.

Scalapino, Robert A., (ed). The Communist Revolution in Asia, Englewood Cliffs, N.J.: Prentice-Hall, Inc., 1965.

Snodgrass, Donald R. Ceylon: An Export Economy in Transition. Homewood, 111.: Richard D. Irwin. Inc., 1966.

Sumathipala, K.H.M. history of Education in Ceylon 1796-1965. Dehiwela: Tisara Prakasakayo, 1968.

Woodward Calvin A., Growth a Party System in Ceylon, Providence, R.I.: New Brownswick University Press, 1969.

Wriggins H. Ceylon: Dilemmas of a New nation, Princeton: Princeton University Press, 1960.

4. 1971 Insurrection: Articles

Arasaratnam, S., "The Ceylon Insurrection of April 1971: Some Causes and Consequences" Pacific Affairs 45 No. 3 (Fall 1972): 356-371.

Blackton, Charles, "Sri Lanka's Marxists", Problem of Communism 22 No 1 (January-February, 1973): 28-43.

De Silva, Mervin, "Sri Lanka: The End of the Welfare Politics", South Asian Review" 6 No. 2 Oanuary 1973): 91-103.

De Silva, C,R. "Education", in Sri Lanka: A Survey, Ed, K.M. de Silva, (London: Hurst and Company, 1977):

Gough, Kathleen, "The South Asian Revolutionary Potential", in Imperialism and Revolution in South Asia, (eds) K. Gough and H.P. Sharma, (New York: Monthly Review Press, 1973): 3-42.

Haliday, Fred, "The Ceylonese Insurrection", New Left Review No. 69 (September-October, 1971): 55-91.

Jayawardene, V.K. "Origin of the Left Movement in Sri Lanka", Modern Ceylon Studies (July 1971): 195-221.

Kearney, Robert N. "The Marxist and Coalition Government in Ceylon", Asian Survey 5 No. 2 (1965): 120-124.

————————, "Sinhalese Nationalism and Social Conflict in Ceylon", Pacific Affairs 37 No. 2 (Summer 1964) 125-136.

————————, "Educational Expansion and Political Volatility in Sri Lanka: The 1971 Insurrection", Asian Survey 15 No. 9 (September 1975): 727-774.

————————, and Jiggins Janice, "The Ceylon Insurrection of 1971", The Journal of Commonwealth and Comparative Politics 13 No. 1 (1975) 40-64.

Keerawlla, G.B., "The Janatha Vimukthi Peramuna and the 1971 Uprising", Social Science Review No. 2 (1980): 1-55.

Obeysekera, Gananath, "Some Comments on the Backgrounds of the April 1971 Insurgency in Sri Lanka (Ceylon)", Journal of Asian Studies 33 No. 3 (May 1974): 367-384.

Obeysekera, Jayasumana, (pseudo.) "Revolutionary Movements in Ceylon", in Imperialism and Revolution in South Asia, (eds) Kathleen Gough and hari P. Sharma, (New York: Monthly Review Press, (1973) 368-395.

Phadnis, Urmila, "Insurgency in Ceylon Politics: Problems and Prospects", Institute for Defense Studies and Analyses Journal, 3 No. 4 (April 1971): 582-616.

Samaranayake, Gamini., "The Left Movement and Political Violence in Sri Lanka", Seminar for Asian Studies, (Peradeniya, University of Peradeniya, 1985):

Warnapala, W. A. Wiswa, "The April Revolt in Ceylon", Asian Survey 13 No. 2 (March 1972): 259-274.

————————, "The Marxist Parties of Sri Lanka and the 1971 Insurrection", Asian Survey 15 No 2 (February 1975): 745-757.

Wijeweera, Rohana, (Patabandige Don Nandasiri Wijeweera), "Speech to the Criminal Justice Commission", 2 (New Left Review, No. 84 (March-April 1974) 85-104.

Wilson, A.J., "Ceylon: The People's Liberation Front and the Revolution that Failed", Pacific Community 3 No. 2 (January 1972) 364-377.

Wriggins, W.H. and Jayawardene, C.H.S., "Youth Protest in Sri Lanka (Ceylon)", Population, Politics and the Future of Southern Asia, (eds.) W.H. Wriggins and James F. Guyot, (New York: Columbia University Press, 1973): 318-350.

5. Unpublished Thesis and Papers

Amersinghe, Y.R., Trotskyism in Ceylon-The LSSP 1935-1964, (Ph.D. Thesis, University of London, 1974).

Caspersz, Paul, "Towards a Sociological Analysis of the Youth Struggle on Sri Lanka 1971", (M.A. thesis, University of Oxford, 1973)

Fernando, L.P., Political Violence in Sri Lanka: The April 1971 Youth Insurrection, (M.A. Thesis University of New Brunswick, Canada, 1976).

Keerawella, G.B. The Origin of the New Left in Sri Lanka, (M.A. thesis, University of Windsor, Canada, 1981).

6. Tamil Ethnic Insurrection; Books

Abeysekera, Charles and Newton Gunasinghe, (eds) Facets of Ethnicity in Sri Lanka. Colombo: Social Scientists Association, 1987.

Coomarswamy, Radhika., Sri Lanka: The Crisis of the Angl-American Constitutional Traditions in a Developing Society, New Delhi: Vikas, 1984.

De Silva, K.M., Managing Ethnic Tensions in Multi-Ethnic Societies: Sri Lanka 1880-1985. Lanham N.Y. University Press of America, 1987.

Farmer, B.H. Pioneer Peacent Colonization in Ceylon. London: Oxford University Press, 1957.

————, Ceylon a Divided nation, London: Oxford University Press, 1963.

Gunarathna, Rohan., War and Peace in Sri Lanka, Kandy : Institute of Fundamental Studies, Sri Lanka, 1987.

Kearney, R.N., Communalism and Language in the Politics of Ceylon, Durham, N.C.: Duke University Press, 1967.

Manor, James, (ed.) Sri Lanka in Change and Crisis, New York: St. Martin's Press, 1984, 1984.

Manogaram, Chelvadurai., Ethnic Conflict and Reconciliation in Sri Lanka. Honolulu: University of Hawaii Press, 1987.

O'balance, Edgar., The Cyanide War: Tamil Insurrection in Sri Lanka1973-1988, London: Brassey's, 1989.

Ponnambalam, Satchi, Sri Lanka: National Conflict and the Tamil Liberation Struggle, London, Zed Books, 1983.

Ratnatunga, Sinha, Politics of Terrorism: The Sri Lanka Experience, Melbourne: Globe Press Pty. Ltd. 1988.

Spencer, Jonathan, (ed.) Sri Lanka: History and Roots of Conflict, London: Routledge, 1990.

Tambiah, S.J., Sri Lanka: Ethnic Fratricide and the Dismantling of Democracy, Chicago: University of Chicago Press, 1986.

Vadik, V.P. Ethnic Crisis in Sri Lanka: India's Options, New Delhi: National Publishing House, 1985.

Wilson A. Jayarathnam, The Break-up of Sri Lanka: The Sinhalese_Tamil Conflict, London: C. Hurst and Company, 1988.

Tamil Ethnic Conflict and Guerrilla Warfare: Articles

Arasaratnam, Sinnappah, "Nationalism in Sri Lanka and the Tamils", in Collective Identities Nationalism and Protest in Modern Sri Lanka, (ed), Micheal Robert, (Colombo: Margalnstitute, 1979) 500-519.

Balasingham, A.S., "Liberation Tigers and Tamil Eelam Freedom Struggle", Political Committee of the Liberation Tigers of Tamil Eelam, Publication No. 4. (1983).

Das Biswas, "Social Strife in Sri Lanka: Historical Background", State and Society, N4, No 4, (October- December 1983) 5-17.

De Silva, C.R., "The Sinhalese-Tamil Rift in Sri Lanka", in The States of South Asia: Problems of National Integration, (eds.) A.J. Wilson, and Dennis Dalton, (London: C. Hurst 1984) 155-174..

De Silva, K.M., "University Admission and Ethnic Tensions in Sri Lanka, 1972-82", in From Independence to Statehood: Managing Ethnic Conflict in Five African and Asian States, (eds.) Robert B. Goldman and A.J. Wilson, (London: Frances Pinter 1985) 97-110.

Gunatilleke, Godfrey, "Some Socio-Economic Aspects of Communal Problems", Logos, 16, No. 2, (1977): 17-39.

Hellmann-Rajanayagam, Dagmar, "The Tamil Tigers in Northern Sri Lanka: Origins, faction, Programmes", Internationales Asienforum, 17, Nos. 1-2 (1985): 65-85.

————, "The Tamil Militants before the Accord and After" Pacific Affairs, 61 No. 4 (Winter 1988-89): 603-619.

Hubbell, L. Kenneth, "The Devolution of Power in Sri Lanka: A Solution to the Separatist Movement", Asian Survey, 27 No. 11, (November 1987): 1176-1187.

Jayawardane, Visaka Kumari, "Class Formation and Communalism", race and Class, 26 No. 1 (1980): 173-184.

Kearney, Robert N, "Language and the Rise of Tamil Separatism in Sri Lanka", Asian Survey 18 (May 1978): 521-534.

————, "Ethnic Conflict and the Tamil Separatist Movement in Sri Lanka", Asian Survey' 25 No. 9 (September 1985): 257-263.

————, "Territorial Elements of Tamil Separatism in Sri Lanka", Pacific Affairs 60 No. 4 (1987): 561-577.

Kodikara, S.U. "The Separatist Eelam Movement in Sri Lanka: An Overview", India Quarterly 37 No. 2 (September 1980): 194-212.

————, "The Continuing Crisis in Sri Lanka: The JVP, the Indian Troops, and Tamil Politics", Asian Survey 29 No. 5 (May 1989).

Index

D

E